# The Korean Economy

To Margaret and Alan
Charles Harvie

To Myung-Hee, Suejin and Joonkyu
Hyun-Hoon Lee

To Keesun, Kowoon and Banggul
Junggun Oh

# The Korean Economy

## Post-Crisis Policies, Issues and Prospects

*Edited by*

Charles Harvie
*University of Wollongong, Australia*

Hyun-Hoon Lee
*Kangwon National University, Korea*

Junggun Oh
*Bank of Korea*

**Edward Elgar**
Cheltenham, UK • Northampton, MA, USA

Published by
Edward Elgar Publishing Limited
Glensanda House
Montpellier Parade
Cheltenham
Glos GL50 1UA
UK

Edward Elgar Publishing, Inc.
136 West Street
Suite 202
Northampton
Massachusetts 01060
USA

A catalogue record for this book
is available from the British Library

**Library of Congress Cataloguing in Publication Data**

The Korean economy : post-crisis policies, issues and prospects / edited by Charles Harvie, Hyun-Hoon Lee, Junggun Oh.
p. cm.
Includes index.
1. Korea (South)—Economic conditions—1960– 2. Korea (South)—Economic policy—1960– 3. Economic stabilization—Korea (South) I. Harvie, Charles, 1954– II. Yi, Hyon-hun, 1959– III. Oh, Junggun.

HC467.95.K6749 2004
330.95195—dc22

2004047122

ISBN 1 84376 244 7

Printed and bound in Great Britain by MPG Books Ltd, Bodmin, Cornwall

# Contents

*Editors' Biographical Notes* *vii*
*Contributors* *x*
*Acknowledgements* *xii*

PART I INTRODUCTION

1 Introduction 3
*Charles Harvie, Hyun-Hoon Lee and Junggun Oh*

2 Lessons from the Korean Financial Crisis 11
*Jong-Wha Lee*

PART II REFORM AND POLICIES

3 Financial Sector Reform 25
*Junggun Oh*

4 Corporate Restructuring in the Wake of the Financial Crisis 38
*Charles Harvie*

5 Reforming the Korean Labour Market and Social Safety Net: Key Pending Issues 78
*John P. Martin, Peter Tergeist and Raymond Torres*

6 Public Sector Reforms 120
*Junsok Yang*

7 Monetary and Exchange Rate Policies 143
*Junggun Oh*

PART III OTHER ISSUES

8 A New Economy for Korea 165
*Dong-pyo Hong, Gae-Iyong Choi and Yongkyu Kim*

9 Post-Crisis Foreign Trade and Foreign Investment in Korea: Korea's Recovery and Challenges Ahead 191
*Taekdong Yeo, Young Man Yoon and Kar-yiu Wong*

10 Korea's Embrace of Regionalism and the Economic Effects of its Bilateral FTAs with Chile and Japan 221
*Inkyo Cheong*

11 A Development Strategy for the North Korean Economy 238
*Dongho Jo*

PART IV PROSPECTS

12 A New Paradigm for the Korean Economy: Advanced State Development (ASD) Model Approach 263
*Jong Won Lee*

13 Towards a New Economic Development Model for Korea 286
*Charles Harvie and Hyun-Hoon Lee*

*Index* 319

# Editors' Biographical Notes

**Professor Charles Harvie** is presently Associate Professor of Economics at the University of Wollongong in Australia, and Director of Research at the Hunter Valley Research Foundation, Newcastle, Australia. He has published numerous journal articles, chapters and books on the economies of East Asia. He is the co-editor (with Dr Boon Chye-Lee) of a series of four books, currently in the process of completion with Edward Elgar Publishing, on the contribution of small and medium-sized enterprises to the recovery of the East Asian economies in the wake of the financial crisis. He has also authored and edited a further four books with Macmillan (Palgrave). His areas of research interest include the economies of East Asia (in particular Korea, China, Vietnam and Indonesia), the economics of transition, and SMEs and entrepreneurialism.

**Professor Hyun-Hoon Lee** was born in Korea, and graduated with a PhD in economics from the University of Oregon in 1989. He is currently Professor of Economics at Kangwon National University, Korea. He has been a visiting professor, scholar and fellow at the University of Oregon (USA), Keio University (Japan), the University of Melbourne (Australia) and the Bank of Korea. He has worked primarily on problems of intra-industry trade, international technology transfer and trade, and regional economic cooperation in East Asia and the Pacific. His research papers have been published in journals such as *Kyongjehak Yongu* (Korea), *the Korean Economic Review* (Korea), *Southern Economic Journal* (USA), *Japan and the World Economy* (USA), *Weltwirtschaftliched Archiv* (Germany), *Canadian Journal of Economics* (Canada) and *Agenda* (Australia). His books include *Korea's Economic Miracle: Fading or Reviving?* (2003, co-authored with Charles Harvie, London: Palgrave Macmillan), and *Frontiers of Research in Intra-industry Trade* (2002, co-edited with Peter Lloyd, London: Palgrave Macmillan). He is currently the managing editor of the *Journal of the Korean Economy*, an official English journal of the Association of Korean Economic Studies.

**Dr Junggun Oh** graduated with a PhD in Economics from the University of Manchester. He is a Korean economist with over 23 years of experience as a central banker. He is currently Deputy Director-General and Head of the International Finance Research Team of the Bank of Korea which he joined in 1979, and has served as Head of Monetary Studies Team and Chief Manager of Financial Studies Team. He has also served as Senior Economist of the SEACEN (South-East Asian Central Banks) in Malaysia and was a visiting fellow of the IFO Institute for Economic Research in Germany, and has been an external consultant of the ESCAP (Economic and Social Commission for Asia and the Pacific). He has taught monetary economics and financial markets at Korea University and also published numerous books and articles including *Effectiveness of Economic Policies*, *Financial Crisis and Financial and Monetary Policies*, *Financial Reform and Financial Crisis: The Korean Case*, *Inflation Targeting: A New Monetary Policy Framework in Korea*, *Exchange Rate Coordination in East Asia*, *Capital Inflows and Their Effects on Current Accounts in East Asian Countries*, *Financing for Small and Medium Scale Industries* and *Financial Disintermediation and Monetary Policy.* His main research interests are in the areas of monetary and financial policies, financial crisis and East Asian monetary cooperation.

**Other books published by Charles Harvie**

*Vietnam's Reforms and Economic Growth* (co-authored with Tran Van Hoa)
*Korea's Economic Miracle: Fading or Reviving?* (co-authored with Hyun-Hoon Lee)
*Causes and Impact of the Asian Financial Crisis* (edited with Tran Van Hoa)
*Contemporary Developments and Issues in China's Economic Transition* (editor)
*Globalisation and SMEs in East Asia, Studies of Small and Medium sized Enterprises in East Asia* (co-edited with Boon-Chye Lee)
*The Role of SMEs in National Economies in East Asia, Studies of Small and Medium sized Enterprises in East Asia* (co-edited with Boon-Chye Lee)

**Other books published by Hyun-Hoon Lee**

*Korea's economic miracle: fading or reviving?* (co-authored with Charles Harvie)
*Frontiers of Research in Intra-Industry Trade* (co-edited with Peter J. Lloyd),

**Other books published by Junggun Oh**

*Financial and Monetary Policies under Structural Changes in Korea* (co-edited with K. Kim)
*Introduction to Financial Planning* (co-authored with Y. Yeo)
*Effectiveness of Economic Policies* (co-authored with J. Kim and B. Bae)
*Financial Crisis and Financial and Monetary Policies*
*Financial Disintermediation and Monetary Policy*
*Financing for Small and Medium Scale Industries in the SEACEN Countries*
*The Structure of the Korean Economy to the Year 2000*
*Economics of Human Beings: Selected Essays on the Korean Economy*

# Contributors

**Inkyo Cheong** is Professor, Department of Economics, Inha University, Korea (Email: inkyo@inha.ac.kr).

**Gae-Iyong Choi** is Director, IT Industry Division, Korea Information Society Development Institute, Korea (Email: choigi@kisdi.re.kr).

**Charles Harvie** is Associate Professor, Department of Economics, University of Wollongong, Australia (Email: charvie@uow.edu.au).

**Dong-pyo Hong** is Research Fellow, IT Industry Division, Korea Information Society Development Institute, Korea (Email: hong@kisdi.re.kr).

**Dongho Jo** is Senior Fellow, Chief of North Korean Economy Division, Korea Development Institute, Korea (Email: dhjo@kdi.re.kr).

**Yongkyu Kim** is Associate Professor, Department of Digital Economics, Hanyang University, Korea (Email: ykkim@hanyang.ac.kr).

**Hyun-Hoon Lee** is Professor, Division of Economics and International Trade, Kangwon National University, Korea, and managing editor of the *Journal of the Korean Economy* (Email: hhlee@kangwon.ac.kr)

**Jong-Wha Lee** is Professor, Department of Economics, Korea University, Korea (jongwha@korea.ac.kr).

**Jong Won Lee** is Professor, Department of Economics, Sungkyunkwan University, Korea (Email: jwlee@skku.ac.kr).

**John P. Martin** is Director, Directorate for Employment, Labour and Social Affairs, OECD (Email: John.MARTIN@oecd.org).

**Junggun Oh** is Deputy Director-General and Head of International Finance Research Team, Bank of Korea, Korea (Email: ojunggun@bok.or.kr).

**Peter Tergeist** is Principal Economist, Directorate for Employment, Labour and Social Affairs, OECD (Email: Peter.TERGEIST@oecd.org).

**Raymond Torres** is Principal Economist, Directorate for Employment, Labour and Social Affairs, OECD (Email: raymond.torres@oecd.org).

**Junsok Yang** is Professor, Economics Department, Division of Law and Economics, the Catholic University, Korea (Email: yanjuna@catholic.ac.kr).

**Taekdong Yeo** is Associate Professor, School of International Economics and Business, Yeungnam University, Korea (Email: tdyeo@yu.ac.kr).

**Young Man Yoon** is Professor, Department of Economics, and Dean of College of Economics and Business Administration, Incheon University, Korea (Email: ymyoon@incheon.ac.kr).

**Kar-yiu Wong** is Professor, Department of Economics, and Director of the Research Center for International Economics, University of Washington (Email: karyiu@u.washington.edu).

# Acknowledgements

The Korean economy experienced a traumatic, and largely unanticipated, financial and economic crisis during 1997–98, after a prolonged period of high and sustained economic growth. In response to the crisis a number of economic reforms, aimed at putting the economy back on the fast track to economic growth and development, have been implemented. In the wake of the crisis, and in response to the reforms, the recovery of the economy has been quite remarkable. Despite this there remain ongoing concerns over the effectiveness of the reforms measures and debate over the adoption of an appropriate future development strategy that will enable Korea to face the global challenges that will intensify in the twenty-first century.

This volume consists of a number of contributions from economists who are specialists on the Korean economy, or are renowned researchers in a particular area of specialization who have applied their knowledge to interpreting and analysing developments in that area in post-crisis Korea. The range of topics and issues analysed is diverse, pertinent and thought-provoking, and provide an invaluable source of information for scholars of the contemporary Korean economy.

The editors would like to extend their appreciation and gratitude first and foremost to the contributors, without whose dedicated, timely, thought-provoking and scholarly contributions this book would not have been possible. We are indebted to Euijeong Park, Mi Hwa Shin and Inchul Shin for their skilful and efficient formatting of the final drafts of each chapter. At Edward Elgar Publishing we wish to thank Edward Elgar himself for his encouragement of, and support for, this book initiative from a very early stage, which provided the impetus for its completion. In addition, at Edward Elgar, we would like to thank Alexandra Minton for her patience and highly professional assistance. Last, but not least, we would like to thank our respective families and colleagues for their support and patience during the completion of this book.

Charles Harvie, Hyun-Hoon Lee and Junggun Oh
Wollongong, Australia and Seoul, Korea
May 2004

# PART I INTRODUCTION

# 1. Introduction

**Charles Harvie, Hyun-Hoon Lee and Junggun Oh**

## 1.1 OVERVIEW

The Korean economy and its policy-makers were taken by considerable surprise as a result of the onset of the financial and economic crisis that engulfed the country in the second half of 1997. The initial trigger for the crisis was the devaluation of the Thai baht in July 1997, which then quickly spread to other regional economies. South Korea was eventually to succumb, from October onwards. The financial crisis quickly became an economic crisis. The year 1998 was particularly painful with output declining by 6.7 per cent, and the country experienced levels of unemployment never experienced before during the years of its economic miracle from the early 1960s. It became clear that major restructuring of the economy would be required if the country was once again to return to a path of high and sustained rates of economic growth. Subsequently, economic reform has focused upon a restructuring of the country's financial and corporate sectors, labour market and public sector. During 1999 and 2000 a remarkable recovery of the economy was achieved, but during 2001 economic growth slowed and unemployment began to rise again. A number of factors contributed to this development, one of the most important being the slowdown in the global economy. This slowdown is of particular concern to Korea given its dependence upon international trade for its economic growth and development.

The financial and economic crisis of the late 1990s resulted in a reappraisal of the Asian model of economic development, with its focus upon industrialization and growth through exports. Many commentators are now suggesting that a more balanced approach to economic development, focusing upon both the domestic and external sectors, is required, and that greater focus needs to be placed upon the development of intra regional trade and the development of internationally competitive enterprises. In regard to each of these Korea has been playing an active and leading role. Specifically, in regard to the attainment of expanded regional economic cooperation and greater emphasis on intra-regional trade, Korean government officials have indicated strong support for the idea of ASEAN+3[1] consisting of the existing ASEAN members plus China, Japan and Korea. Such support is indicative of the importance of trade to countries in the region and in particular to a country such as Korea. The first meeting of ASEAN+3 took place in Brunei during 2001.

Korea has therefore played, and will increasingly play, an important role in the future development of the region. Hence a clearer understanding of this economy, its major contemporary policy and reform issues, progress made in regard to these, and how the country will develop in the future, are of particular interest from both a regional but also a global perspective.

The country is currently standing at an important crossroads in terms of its economic development and growth, and a book such as this, with its focus on contemporary policy and reform issues and analysis of the future prospects of the economy, is particularly opportune. The need to provide such an analysis, and discussion, stimulated the editors to produce such a manuscript. In addition, the participation of leading researchers of the Korean economy in this project provided a further major stimulus.

The book consists of four parts: Introduction; Reform and Policies; Other Issues; and Prospects.

## BOOK OUTLINE

In Chapter 2 Jong-Wha Lee discusses the causes of the crisis, the recovery of the economy in its aftermath, structural reform, and some key policy lessons for other developing economies. He argues that while structural vulnerabilities in the corporate and financial sectors contributed to the crisis, they were not the primary cause. Rather, this was due to large outflows of short-term capital, compounded and triggered by a shortage of foreign exchange reserves. The second IMF programme, focusing upon short-term debt restructuring, calmed investor panic and provided the basis for the recovery of the economy in 1999. This was also supported by the Korean economy's export-oriented structure, as the export sector led the recovery, and a swift adjustment of macroeconomic policies.

The author argues that while the initial tight stabilization strategy compounded the contractionary effects of the crisis, its later reversal assisted in economic recovery. While reform in the corporate and financial sectors assisted with the initial recovery, much still remains to be done in these sectors.

The author also argues that a sustained and high growth recovery of the economy will depend upon its response to two major challenges. First, its ability to move towards being a technology-driven economy. Second, its ability to change the government–business relationship by moving towards a more competitive market environment.

This chapter derives key lessons for developing economies from Korea's crisis: the need for a strong domestic financial system; a gradual and cautious approach to financial market liberalization; caution over adopting a relatively fixed exchange rate; the need for reform of the international financial architecture; the importance of a competent government-led recovery programme; and the importance of a stable macroeconomic environment.

In Chapter 3 Junggun Oh discusses financial sector reform, and key outcomes, in the wake of the financial crisis. In particular the author looks at the main contents of financial restructuring, an appraisal of financial restructuring to date and remaining issues. The author argues that the underlying cause of the crisis lay, first, in market institutions and principles that were not sufficiently developed, such as an effective corporate governance system to guide appropriate decisions, and independent financial institutions to ensure that capital was allocated efficiently; and, second, in insufficient prudential regulation. These two characteristics became less suited in the more competitive open economy and more integrated product and capital markets of the 1990s. The government-led development strategy had contributed to financially weak corporate and financial sectors, which made the economy fragile to external shocks. In addition, overall inefficiency of the economy undermined the potential for economic growth. In such an environment the rapid opening of the capital market, and the subsequent frequent inflows and outflows of foreign capital, contributed to the financial crisis.

The author argues that the main targets of financial restructuring have been the normalization of the financial intermediation function, enhancing the soundness of the financial system, and, in particular, strengthening the competitiveness of the financial industries in the wake of an almost complete opening of the financial market and industries. Despite progress in these areas the author suggests that more will need to be done to ensure that the ultimate purposes of financial restructuring have been achieved. The central aim of financial restructuring has been to raise the overall efficiency of the economy, by heightening the soundness and profitability of the corporate and financial sectors through the forced exit of ailing financial institutions and firms, improvement of the financial structure of financial institutions and companies capable of a turnaround, and the putting in place of systems relating to management transparency.

The author argues that there have been a number of promising outcomes from financial sector restructuring. For example, the bad loans of the financial sector have been considerably reduced, and the profitability of the banking industry has improved. This improvement has meant that financial institutions' function of credit intermediation, which had contracted sharply following the currency crisis as financial institutions avoided lending for fear of adding to non-performing assets, has been regained, particularly with respect to the banks, thereby providing the basis for the economic recovery.

Thanks to the pursuit of financial and corporate sector restructuring, the Korean economy has regained its dynamism after experiencing a deep downturn in the wake of the currency crisis. This is reflected in an improvement of Korea's sovereign debt rating. However, the author argues that there remain two outstanding issues in regard to reform of the financial sector. First, the privatization of government-owned financial institutions, and, second, further strengthening of the financial intermediation function.

In Chapter 4 Charles Harvie conducts an extensive review and analysis of corporate restructuring in the wake of the financial crisis. The author discusses, in particular, pre-crisis growth and performance of the sector, corporate sector restructuring in the wake of the crisis, and market liberalization measures and their impact on corporate restructuring. The author argues that, despite efforts at corporate restructuring, the sector remains highly leveraged by international standards and continues to suffer from low profitability. Although cash flows have improved and the interest coverage ratio has also improved, this improvement has not come from increased earnings, or the profitability of corporations, but rather from lower interest payments. One in four companies in the top 64 *chaebols* were unable to generate enough cash flow to meet their interest payments in 1999, and major indexes of profitability, such as ordinary income to sales, return on equity or return on assets, have all shown little improvement. The ongoing survival of financially troubled enterprises, the author argues, will constrain the growth of the economy, and also hinder the establishment of a healthy financial sector.

The author also argues that the restructuring of the Big Five, and out of court workouts of other large corporations, have had mixed results, with main creditor banks maintaining firms that should have been immediately liquidated. Further improvements in legal bankruptcy procedures will be needed. The restructuring impact of the Big Deals has also been mixed. Whether or not the excess capacity problems that plagued Korea's *chaebols* have been solved remains unclear. Evidence is also mixed as to whether the Big Four have fulfilled their commitments to improve corporate governance and slim down to a few core businesses. The effectiveness of the Big Deals therefore also remains unclear.

On a more positive note the author argues that inflows of foreign direct investment (FDI), particularly in the form of mergers and acquisitions, have increased rapidly and have exerted beneficial effects in the short run by providing desperately needed liquidity, and will contribute to an improvement in corporate governance and transparency over the longer term.

Chapter 5, by Martin, Tergeist and Torres, argues that further convergence by Korea to the living standards of the world's leading economies depends to some extent on how well the country addresses key labour market and social challenges. These include the need for an industrial relations system based on mutual trust, where basic labour standards, and in particular freedom-of-association and collective bargaining rights, are fully in line with international standards. The authors also call for a reduction in the high degree of duality that presently characterizes the Korean labour market, which not only raises job insecurity but may also hinder improved productivity performance. The authors also argue that the social safety net needs extending and strengthening. In particular, there are concerns over the coverage of the employment insurance scheme, the implementation of 'productive welfare' and the adjustment of the public pension and enterprise retirement systems to the challenges of an ageing population.

Chapter 6 by Junsok Yang focuses on public sector reforms in Korea after the financial crisis. Public sector reforms focused mainly on three areas: government structural and managerial reforms, SOE reforms including privatization and managerial reforms, and regulatory reform including deregulation. The results of these reforms are mixed, with all three areas of reform showing some improvement but none can be classified as complete successes. Government structural reforms included several missteps. There were three major government-restructuring efforts in five years, but the second and third restructuring often undid the results of the first restructuring. Privatization was more successful, as the government succeeded in forming and implementing a plan to privatize 11 SOEs including KEPCO and Korea Telecom. Korea also managed to reduce the number of workers in government and SOEs, and install more flexible management techniques that emphasize the responsibility of the individual ministries, agencies and SOEs. The government also installed a permanent mechanism to review new regulations and instituted a major deregulation programme that eliminated over 50 per cent of existing regulations in 1998. However, the reforms mostly took place in the first half of the Kim Dae Jung administration, slowing down in the second half of the administration. Thus the agencies responsible for public sector reforms, namely the Ministry of Planning and Budget and the Regulatory Reform Commission, should place renewed emphasis on further reform.

In Chapter 7 Junggun Oh reviews and assesses Korea's monetary and exchange rate policies in the wake of the financial crisis, and their contribution to economic recovery. In particular, he focuses upon foreign exchange market stabilization activities in the wake of the financial crisis, policies for economic recovery and the attainment of financial market stability, the adoption of the inflation targeting system, foreign exchange and capital market liberalization, and the remaining tasks for monetary and exchange rate policies.

The author argues that the tight monetary policy in the wake of the crisis, and the resulting high interest rates, greatly exacerbated the contraction of the economy, as well as having severely impacted upon the heavily indebted corporate sector and bad debts of the financial sector. The easing of monetary policy from the second quarter of 1998 contributed to the dramatic recovery of the economy, and the attainment of stability in financial markets thereafter.

The author argues that the Bank of Korea's monetary policy paradigm has changed greatly since the currency crisis. A new monetary policy regime of inflation targeting has been introduced to replace the previous monetary targeting. This has resulted in a lower rate of inflation, even though the system was being conducted against a background of financial and corporate restructuring. In addition, the central bank's independence in the operation of monetary policy has been greatly strengthened. In keeping with the rise in its profile as an independent institution charged with the conduct of monetary policy, the Bank of Korea's responsibility to the public has been heightened and systematic arrangements have been put in place to ensure policy transparency.

The new monetary policy environment has come about with the complete opening of financial markets and the introduction of a floating exchange rate regime. The widening of market opening, along with the recovery of confidence in Korean financial markets, resulted in substantially increased inflows of foreign portfolio investment. As a result the ratio of foreign investment outstanding to market capitalization substantially increased.

While the Bank's monetary policy has indeed advanced in terms of its system and practices, there remain new challenges and difficulties according to the author. First, it will be important to harmonize different policy objectives in spite of them operating under the inflation targeting regime. Second, there is a need to identify what kind of exchange rate system is appropriate for the inflation targeting system. Third, for inflation targeting to be successfully carried out the effectiveness of the interest rate channel of monetary transmission must be strengthened, and, accordingly, one of the key tasks of the central bank will be to encourage the development of financial markets. Finally, the Bank's economic forecasting capacity also needs to be enhanced.

Korea's growth and development was based on high capital investments and growth in labour inputs. However, this input-driven growth began to reach its limits by the early 1990s and Korea experienced its worst economic crisis at the end of 1997. Recovering from the economic crisis the IT industry has contributed significantly to sustaining economic growth, reducing inflation, increasing investment, improving the trade surplus and creating jobs. Behind these achievements have been government efforts to provide the necessary infrastructure and competitive environment through deregulation and liberalization. With its innovative entrepreneurship the private sector has also made the best use of new business opportunities by increasing investment in IT. In Chapter 8 Dong-pyo Hong, Gae-Iyong Choi and Yongkyu Kim evaluate IT policies in Korea and find that the government role calls for the interventionist policies of the past to be changed. At an early stage the Korean government actively participated in the market in order to build a firm foundation for the IT sector. However, government policy has become market friendly as the IT industry has grown into the new leading sector based on an advanced information infrastructure. Government policies are now changing to reinforce market functions, and to promote competition and entrepreneurship to facilitate innovation and the utilization of IT.

Chapter 9, by Taekdong Yeo, Young Man Yoon and Kar-yiu Wong, reviews trends in Korea's trade and FDI, as well as its policy regime during the period from the early 1990s through to recent years. This chapter analyses the development of Korean trade policy that has enabled the country to successfully transform itself into an open market-driven economy. Also, this chapter deals with Korea's trade policy under the multilateral regime of the GATT/WTO. It then discusses trade and FDI developments when Korea struggled to escape from the financial crisis. Lastly, this chapter investigates future economic agendas for the Korean government, and possible policy responses to these in the context of a rapidly changing world economy.

In Chapter 10, Inkyo Cheong evaluates Korea's Free Trade Agreement (FTA) policy. Korea has been studying the feasibility of FTAs since the 1980s. Although Korea believed FTAs were necessary for the growth of its exports, it did not join any because of the anticipated difficulties that would arise from opening its markets. However, the government began to consider the introduction of FTAs with trading countries after the Asian financial crisis. Its first FTA, with Chile, was concluded in late 2002, and since then subsequent FTAs with similar small and medium-sized countries have been pursued. The goal of Korea's new trade policy is to adapt promptly to the changing global economic environment, as well as resolving the nation's economic difficulties. Consequently, the policy aims to transform Korea into an 'open trading country', contributing to liberalizing the world trade environment.

In Chapter 11, Dongho Jo suggests a development strategy for the North Korean economy. North Korea has made bold changes in its economic policies since the latter half of 2002. As of 1 July 2002 North Korea introduced new measures to improve economic management, and in October 2002 designated Sinuiju as a Special Administrative Region. In November 2002 North Korea established economic and tourist zones in the Kaesong and Mt. Kumkang areas. All these efforts are to solve current economic difficulties and to prepare a basis for future sustainable growth. However, the author argues that it is doubtful whether such policies will be able to contribute to economic growth without succeeding in attracting foreign capital. Not only is North Korea's economic development important for the North, but it also has significant implications for the South in order to improve inter-Korean relations and to secure peace on the Korean peninsula. In the author's opinion, revitalization of the North Korean economy becomes a prerequisite for survival of the North Korean regime, improvement of inter-

Korean economic relations, and for stability in the North-East Asian region. This requires the identification of an economic strategy that will assist North Korea in escaping from its economic difficulties, and lay solid foundations for its future growth. Based on an analysis of the current economic situation and policy reactions of North Korea, this chapter proposes a set of strategies on how to develop the North Korean economy.

In Chapter 12 Jong Won Lee suggests a new development paradigm for the Korean economy. He argues that Korea's unique 'developmental state model' approach has been a root cause for both the success and the failure of the Korean economy. While government-led economic operations functioned effectively in the early stages of economic development, they created low efficiency and a high-cost economic structure during the later stages of economic development. With the outbreak of the financial and economic crisis, IMF policy recommendations advocated adoption of the neoclassical principle as a replacement for the country's traditional development approach. The author argues, however, that extreme neoclassical strategies cannot be a successful substitute for the statist model approach in Korea. The author advocates instead the adoption of the so-called 'advanced state model' as a more relevant strategy for Korea.

Finally, in Chapter 13, Charles Harvie and Hyun-Hoon Lee examine the 'old' growth and economic development model of Korea, and then construct a 'new' model emphasizing the key ingredients that will enable the Korean economy to return to its earlier strong and sustained growth path. The basis of their argument is that the financial crisis of 1997, and the subsequent economic crisis of 1998, revealed that the 'old' development model is no longer adequate in the face of a new international environment, and for the country's stage of economic development. Therefore, a new growth and development model is required. This new development model, the authors argue, needs to: be based upon market mechanisms of competitive discipline; establish the necessary institutional framework that supports competitive and open markets; place emphasis on the development of small and medium sized enterprises (SMEs); continue with an outward-looking development strategy which promotes not only exports but also imports; maintain stable macroeconomic management; place emphasis on developing an appropriate education system to produce a creative, skilled and adaptable workforce; encourage stronger cooperation with other East Asian economies in both trade and finance; and foster gradual economic integration between the two Koreas.

## NOTES

1 For example a strong advocate of ASEAN+3 is Professor Young-Ho Kim, a former Minister for Commerce.

# 2. Lessons from the Korean Financial Crisis

**Jong-Wha Lee**

The spread of the East Asian crisis to Korea in late 1997 was a surprising event that no one had anticipated. Since the 1960s, Korea's economic performance has been considered one of the most successful in the world. The growth rate surpassed 7 per cent, inflation remained at moderate levels, and domestic saving increasingly financed a rapidly rising investment rate. Korea's economic situation clearly did not fit the mould of the typical configuration of a balance-of-payments crisis.

The sudden crisis had a devastating effect on the economy. The growth rate plummeted from the pre-crisis average of 7–8 per cent to -6.7 per cent in 1998, while the inflation rate rose to 7.5 per cent. However, Korea managed an impressive recovery starting in 1999, which was faster than expected by anyone. The quick turnaround of the Korean economy was no less surprising than its sudden collapse.

The crisis is now in the past for Korea, but the startling experience of the economy presents many intellectually challenging questions as well as useful lessons for other developing countries. Many existing studies provide a wide spectrum of views about the Korean financial crisis: its causes, the desirability of IMF programmes, the progress of recovery and structural reforms, and future directions of the Korean economy. The diverse views over the Korean crisis reflect the ongoing controversy on the financial crisis in general. The sudden crisis in the East Asian economies in 1997 triggered the birth of many new analytical models of the foreign exchange crisis, and new proposals for the reform of both the domestic and international financial systems. Although we have observed some convergence among these diverse views, no consensus appears to have been achieved as yet.

This chapter summarizes these issues concerning the Korean financial crisis around three themes: causes of the crisis, progress of recovery and structural reform, and lessons from the Korean experience.

## 2.1 CAUSES OF THE CRISIS

A number of studies have pointed out that the fundamental causes of the foreign exchange crisis in Korea were the structural weaknesses in the financial system and the corporate sector. The basic macroeconomic fundamentals – such as growth, saving, price stability and budget balance – of the Korean economy were strong prior to the crisis (Table 2.1). However, the strong macroeconomic performance of the economy was disguising structural vulnerabilities. *Chaebols* pursued over-leveraged expansion, thanks to the reckless lending by financial institutions. *Chaebols* were traditionally considered to be 'too big to fail'; consequently financial institutions believed the government would protect them from any harm. Risky and unprofitable projects were financed without appropriate credit analysis. The structural vulnerabilities were further deepened with financial market liberalization, which was accelerated after 1995 in an attempt to fulfill the requirements for OECD membership. This liberalization was pursued in a hasty manner without accounting transparency and adequate prudential regulation, and contributed to the deterioration in the balance sheets of the financial sector by increasing growth of domestic credit and exposure to foreign exchange risk.

While the Korean crisis was certainly magnified by the distortions in the economy, our interpretation of the Korean crisis is rather a general one and not specific to Korea. There is no doubt that Korean banks and firms expected government support to ensure their profitability and their ability to repay their creditors. None of the *chaebols* had been allowed to fail for decades before Hanbo steel collapsed in early 1997. Financial institutions believed they would always be bailed out. There is little question that unhealthy connections among large firms, financial institutions and the government undermined the allocation of capital and weakened the financial system. Evidence shows that there was a fairly clear overinvestment in sectors such as steel and automobiles, especially among copycat *chaebols*.

But we consider it hard to argue that the crisis was primarily the result of structural problems in the Korean economy. The same problems, on at least a similar scale, had existed in Korea for decades, and yet this economy had grown very rapidly without any sign of a crisis. And similar problems prevail in almost all emerging markets. The key issue is whether these problems added up to a crisis of the magnitude that was seen in Korea in late 1997. On balance, it is difficult to make the case that these problems were so severe as to warrant complete collapse of the currency, the total breakdown of banking systems and the sharp recession. Structural problems, while they must have created some of the vulnerabilities that set the stage for the crisis, cannot alone account for the timing and severity of the Korean crisis.

The essence of the Korean crisis was a huge, sudden reversal of capital flows in 1997. An economy that had been attracting large amounts of foreign capital became subject to a sudden withdrawal of capital by foreign investors.

**Table 2.1**
**Principal Macroeconomic Indicators in Korea, 1990–2001**

(%)

| | 1990–95 average | 1996 | 1997 | 1998 | 1999 | 2000 | 2001 |
|---|---|---|---|---|---|---|---|
| GDP growth rate | 7.47 | 6.75 | 5.01 | -6.69 | 10.89 | 9.32 | 3.02 |
| Inflation rate | 6.21 | 4.92 | 4.43 | 7.52 | 0.81 | 2.26 | 4.31 |
| Current account /GDP | -1.22 | -4.42 | -1.71 | 12.60 | 6.02 | 2.65 | 2.04 |
| Budget deficit/GDP | -0.02 | 0.26 | -1.53 | -4.22 | -2.71 | 1.25 | 1.33 |
| Unemployment rate | 2.40 | 1.99 | 2.58 | 6.79 | 6.28 | 4.06 | 3.71 |

*Source*: Asian Development Bank (ADB), Asia Recovery Information Centre Indicators (http://www.aric.adb.org/pre_defined_indicators.asp) and the Bank of Korea.

Net private capital flows into Korea had increased over time from US$10.3 billion in 1994 to US$23.3 billion in 1996. But in the last three months of 1997 these inflows suddenly reversed themselves, with net private capital flows turning to an outflow of US$26.1 billion. This net outflow of US$26 billion in just three months is equivalent to about 6 per cent of the annual GDP in 1997.

Private capital flows reversed from a net inflow of 4.8 per cent of GDP in 1996 to an outflow of 3.4 per cent of GDP in 1997 (Table 2.2). Net bank lending outflows amounted to 8.3 per cent of GDP.

**Table 2.2**
**External Balance in Korea, 1990–2001**

(% of GDP)

| | 1990–95 | 1996 | 1997 | 1998 | 1999 | 2000 | 2001 |
|---|---|---|---|---|---|---|---|
| Current account | -1.22 | -4.42 | -1.71 | 12.60 | 6.02 | 2.65 | 2.04 |
| Current account (US$, billion) | -4.27 | -23.00 | -8.16 | 40.36 | 24.47 | 12.24 | 8.61 |
| Financial Flows | 2.10 | 4.80 | -3.40 | -2.20 | 3.00 | 3.10 | -0.70 |
| Direct investment | -0.20 | -0.40 | -0.60 | 0.20 | 1.20 | 1.00 | 0.10 |
| Portfolio investment | 1.60 | 3.00 | 5.40 | -0.30 | 2.10 | 2.90 | 1.50 |
| Other investment | 0.70 | 2.20 | -8.20 | -2.10 | -0.30 | -0.90 | -2.40 |
| Changes in reserves | -0.60 | -0.20 | 4.40 | -8.30 | -5.40 | -5.80 | -1.80 |
| Use of IMF fund credit | 0.00 | 0.00 | 4.10 | 1.30 | -2.40 | 0.00 | 0.00 |

*Source*: International Monetary Fund, *International Financial Statistics,* March 2002 and the Bank of Korea.

One reason that such a large amount of capital was able to leave so quickly was that a substantial portion had a short-term maturity. In 1997 the ratio of short-term foreign exchange liabilities to official foreign exchange reserves reached nearly 326 per cent, leaving the economy vulnerable to liquidity problems in the event of a sudden withdrawal of foreign capital (see Table 2.3).

**Table 2.3**
**External, Financial and Corporate Sector Indicators in Korea, 1994–2000**

(%)

| | 1994 | 1995 | 1996 | 1997 | 1998 | 1999 | 2000 |
|---|---|---|---|---|---|---|---|
| **External Sector** | | | | | | | |
| Usable gross reserves (billion $) | 21.5 | 28.5 | 29.4 | 9.1 | 48.5 | 74.1 | 96.1 |
| Total debt/GDP | 20.8 | 22.1 | 27.6 | 33.5 | 45.4 | 32.1 | 26.8 |
| Short-term debt/total debt | 52.7 | 55.4 | 52.3 | 41.4 | 29.3 | 34.2 | 34.8 |
| Short-term debt/foreign reserves | 172.0 | 184.0 | 219.0 | 326.0 | 80.0 | 60.0 | 44.0 |
| **Financial Sector** | | | | | | | |
| ROE in Banking Sector | -- | 4.6 | 4.2 | -21.6 | -78.4 | -27.7 | -12.9 |
| Gross foreign liabilities/gross foreign assets | 1.0 | 1.1 | 1.3 | 0.9 | 0.9 | 0.8 | 0.7 |
| Share of NPLs, including those transferred to AMCs | -- | -- | -- | -- | -- | 19.7 | 20.3 |
| Capital adequacy ratios of Commercial Banks | -- | -- | -- | -- | 8.23 | 10.83 | 10.52 |
| **Corporate Sector** | | | | | | | |
| Debt-equity ratio | -- | 470.0 | 470.0 | 600.0 | 470.0 | 280.0 | 210.0 |
| Return on equity | -- | 11.4 | 2.6 | -1.6 | -1.0 | 7.3 | 5.5 |
| Percentage of companies with negative returns | -- | 7.1 | 23.2 | 30.0 | 27.6 | 11.0 | 20.5 |

*Source*: Asian Development Bank, Asia Recovery Information Centre Indicators (http://www.aric.adb.org/pre_defined_indicators.asp).

The key question is: why did all this capital suddenly leave Korea? A self-fulfilling panic of foreign investors must have played a critical role. It occurred when each investor came to expect that the other investors would suddenly pull their funds. When the investors knew Korea had a high level of short-term foreign liabilities relative to short-term foreign assets, they had to flee Korea ahead of other creditors. It was when this exodus happened that a severe economic crisis unfolded in an otherwise healthy country (Radelet and Sachs 1998).

Although Korea's economic fundamentals and macroeconomic policies in the pre-crisis period were regarded as sound and credible, many foreign investors fled the Korean financial market when they feared that Korea would suffer similar macroeconomic and structural problems as those that were driving Thailand and Indonesia to the brink of default on their debts. With the withdrawal of foreign lending, Korea experienced a sharp liquidity crisis and balance sheet problems, and severe currency depreciation (Park and Lee 2002). The balance sheets of financial institutions were very vulnerable to the withdrawal of foreign credit. Korean banks suffered from currency mismatch and maturity mismatch. Table 2.4 shows that by mid-June of 1997 the foreign liabilities of the banking sector exceeded its foreign assets, and short-term foreign liabilities were more than twice as large as short-term foreign assets.

In summary, the Korean economy clearly exhibited several growing weaknesses in the mid-1990s, including rapidly expanding and undersupervised financial systems, large short-term capital inflows financing increasingly weak investments, and over-leveraged *chaebols*. But the crisis cannot be easily explained by these fundamentals alone. No one had anticipated the crisis in Korea prior to 1997, and the consequences of the crisis were too severe to be justified without the investors' complete panic.

**Table 2.4**
**Foreign Assets and Liabilities Outstanding at Financial Institutions in Korea**

(Billion US$, %)

| | 1996.12 | 1997.3 | 1997.6 | 1997.9 | 1997.12 | 1998.3 | 1998.6 | 1998.9 | 1998.12 |
|---|---|---|---|---|---|---|---|---|---|
| **Assets** | | | | | | | | | |
| Total | 67.2 | 70.4 | 72.1 | 72.0 | 72.0 | 70.5 | 71.2 | 68.1 | 63.9 |
| Long-term | 30.6 | 33.2 | 33.2 | 32.5 | 27.3 | 25.9 | 27.1 | 26.0 | 24.7 |
| | (46)[1] | (47) | (46) | (45) | (38) | (37) | (38) | (38) | (39) |
| Short-term | 36.6 | 37.2 | 38.9 | 39.5 | 44.7 | 44.6 | 44.1 | 42.1 | 39.2 |
| | (54) | (53) | (54) | (55) | (62) | (63) | (62) | (62) | (61) |
| **Liabilities** | | | | | | | | | |
| Total | 116.5 | 126.2 | 129.4 | 127.1 | 89.9 | 83.8 | 79.8 | 74.0 | 70.9 |
| Long-term | 43.5 | 46.0 | 48.1 | 51.7 | 47.5 | 45.0 | 58.6 | 55.6 | 52.0 |
| | (37)[2] | (36) | (37) | (41) | (53) | (54) | (73) | (75) | (73) |
| Short-term | 73.0 | 80.2 | 81.3 | 75.4 | 42.4 | 38.8 | 21.2 | 18.4 | 18.9 |
| | (63) | (64) | (63) | (59) | (47) | (46) | (27) | (25) | (27) |
| **Net Liabilities** | | | | | | | | | |
| Total | 49.3 | 55.8 | 57.3 | 55.1 | 17.9 | 13.3 | 8.6 | 5.9 | 7.0 |
| Long-term | 12.9 | 12.8 | 14.9 | 19.2 | 20.2 | 19.1 | 31.5 | 29.6 | 27.3 |
| Short-term | 36.4 | 43.0 | 42.4 | 35.9 | -2.3 | -5.8 | -22.9 | -23.7 | -20.3 |
| Long-term Asset /Liabilities(%) | 70.3 | 72.1 | 69 | 62.8 | 57.4 | 57.5 | 46.2 | 46.7 | 47.5 |
| Short-term Asset /Liabilities(%) | 50.1 | 46.3 | 47.8 | 52.3 | 105.4 | 114.9 | 208 | 228.8 | 207.4 |

*Note*: 1 Percentage of total assets
2 Percentage of total liabilities

*Source*: Bank of Korea.

## 2.2 THE RECOVERY AND STRUCTURAL REFORM

The easing of the Korean crisis reflects the end of the creditors' panic. The first IMF programme, signed on 3 December 1997, like its predecessors in Thailand and Indonesia relied heavily on fiscal and monetary austerity. Within weeks, nonetheless, the financial panic had only intensified and it was clear the initial approach did not help to restore foreign investor's confidence. A more effective approach that calmed down the panic came with the second IMF programme, signed on 24 December 1997.[1] The second programme eased off on the monetary and fiscal targets, and had as its centrepiece a restructuring of Korean bank loans owed to international banks. US$24 billion in short-term debt falling due in the first quarter of 1998 was rescheduled to 1~3 year bonds. The debt restructuring lessened the pressure on the won, and almost immediately the exchange rate began to appreciate and the panic subsided.

Korea managed an impressive recovery starting in 1999. It was steeper and more robust than anyone could have expected. The growth rate rebounded from –6.7 per cent in 1998 to 10.9 per cent in 1999 and 9.3 per cent in 2000. The V-shaped recovery in real GDP growth in Korea is similar to the stylized pattern that we observe from previous crisis episodes (Lee and Rhee 2002, Park and Lee 2002). However, the adjustment is in marked contrast to the stylized pattern of adjustment in GDP growth, in that the degree of initial contraction was much greater and the subsequent recovery was much stronger than what could have been predicted from previous episodes of crisis elsewhere. The deeper contraction in the 1997 Korean crisis is attributable to the severe liquidity crisis caused by investors' panic, and the problem of weak balance sheets in the corporate and financial sectors.

It is clear that the speedy recovery of the Korean economy was thanks to the early resolution of creditors' panic. In addition, the Korean economy's export-oriented structure and the swift adjustment of macroeconomic policies contributed to speedy post-crisis adjustment to the financial crisis. It is one of the stylized facts from previous crisis episodes that the external sector has led the recovery, and contributed to the sharp turnaround in GDP growth (Park and Lee 2002). A large real exchange rate depreciation following a currency crisis has a strong impact on post-crisis export growth. As the Korean economy is more export oriented, they benefited more from their increasing export competitiveness following the substantial real exchange rate depreciation after the crisis.

The quick improvement in the Korean economy was also supported by the swift adjustment of macroeconomic policies. After the onset of the crisis, implementation of tight stabilization policies, as well as financial restructuring supported by the IMF, reinforced the contractionary effects of the crisis. Although a tight macroeconomic policy might be unavoidable in order to stem capital outflows and to prevent depreciation–inflation spirals, its contractionary impact was much larger than had been expected by anyone including the IMF. Starting in the middle of 1998, Korea began to change its monetary and fiscal policy stance toward expansion. Evidence shows that easing of monetary and fiscal policy quickened the pace of recovery in the Korean economy (see Park and Lee 2002).

The financial and corporate sector restructuring programme has progressed well in Korea.[2] The government-led financial restructuring must have helped the quick recovery of the economy. Expansionary monetary policy would not have been effective without successful financial restructuring, since domestic credit was being constrained by the weak balance sheets of the banking sector. Without the strong initiative in the restructuring of the financial sector, it would have taken much longer to completely resolve the credit crunch problem.

The initial financial and corporate restructuring, led by the Financial Supervisory Commission, was based on the agreement between the IMF and the Korean government. The reforms have contributed to a strengthening of the supervisory and regulatory framework, increasing the transparency of financial sector information, improving the mechanisms to deal with troubled institutions and managing troubled loans, and facilitating the entry of foreigners into the system. Most commercial banks have now improved their capital adequacy ratio to well above 10 per cent. Restructuring of the corporate sector has also progressed well in many areas. There have been various regulatory changes aimed at improvement in management transparency and corporate governance structure. There were also substantial improvements in debt reduction. The debt–equity ratio of the corporate sector declined to about 210 per cent as of end-2000, from an average of about 600 per cent as of end-1997 (Table 2.3).

Despite all this progress, we find that the economy still has many remaining problems. In the financial sector, despite the progress in financial structural reform, whether real practices in banking management and supervision of the financial sector have improved is still questionable. There are certain human capital constraints in rebuilding the banking system. Bank managers are inexperienced and are not accustomed to commercial practices. Fundamental change of the behaviour in credit appraisal and loan allocation requires substantial practice over a long period. One way to improve the efficiency of the banking institutions is to expedite the introduction of foreign ownership and placement of foreign expertise at the highest management level. In Korea, financial institutions still remain under the heavy influence of the government. As a result of the recapitalization process some large banks are effectively nationalized, thus increasing government involvement in the banking system. Strengthening the autonomy of the financial institutions and insulating them from government intervention must be a longer-term agenda.

The assessments of the basic objectives and progress of corporate reform are still far from having achieved a consensus. While recognizing that overdiversification of business activities and duplicate investment in key sectors have incurred low profitability and highly leveraged large conglomerates, the government has also urged the top five *chaebols* to focus on core business as well as exit nonviable business. In September 1998 the government and the top five *chaebol* leaders announced a framework for mergers and business swaps – referred to as 'Big Deals'. The 'Big Deals' mergers were intended to help the economy by resolving two major problems in the corporate sector, that is excess capacity and overleveraging. However, the top *chaebols* agreed on the deals only reluctantly, and the swaps have not been particularly successful. The deals seem to be very hastily driven by the government initiative without sufficient consideration of commercial factors.

An important question still remains for the future direction of the Korean economy. What is the appropriate development paradigm for Korea after the crisis? We believe that there was little in Korea's fundamental growth strategy that inevitably led to the crisis.[3] The depth of the crisis was, rather, due to financial mismanagement and global financial instabilities. The 'fundamental growth factors' of Korea's growth were high saving, good human resources, more openness to international trade and relatively high-quality institutions. Thus, with a return to core fundamentals, the Korean economy can again return to sustained growth.

Nevertheless, it is unavoidable that Korea's growth rate will be lower than the previous pre-crisis average of 7 per cent. Korea now faces a much smaller gap in reproducible (physical and human) capital and technical efficiency from their long-run potential levels than they had in the past decades. Hence, the Korean economy will encounter a smaller chance for rapid 'catching up' through high rates of capital accumulation as well as the diffusion of technology from more technically advanced economies, and will inevitably become adjusted to a lower growth path (Radelet et al. 2001).

Thus, how the economy can switch itself to a new technology-driven economy is a challenge. The US patents ownership data, which is often used for international comparisons of innovative activities, shows that Korea has substantially improved her share in US patents from 0.6 per cent during the 1988–95 period to 1.9 per cent during the period 1996–2002 (see Table 2.5). Korea ranked seventh in the number of US patents granted. However, she is still lagging significantly behind the leading innovators - such as the US, Japan and Germany.

The new business–government relationship, which has yet to be built, is a tough question as well. The structure of the economy, in particular exports, is heavily concentrated on a few products, which are mainly produced by big *chaebols*. Despite the *chaebol* reform, which may have decreased the political power of the big *chaebols*, their sheer economic power has changed little. The government has continued to pursue more reform in the corporate sector. Ensuring a competitive environment will be good for the economy, such that the reduction of the size in the big conglomerates will necessarily improve economic performance.

## 2.3 POLICY LESSONS

The Korean experience suggests many policy lessons that can be useful for other developing countries. We summarize them in six lessons.

First, and foremost, the Korean crisis shows that in order to enhance an economies' ability to confront a creditor's panic, developing countries must strengthen their financial systems. Lack of prudential regulation and supervision of the financial sector can lead to large-scale capital inflows, imprudent lending, and a consumption boom and asset bubbles, which make the economy vulnerable to adverse developments. Establishing transparent accounting standards and practices, increasing the public disclosure of information, and strengthening bank's profitability and capitalization are important in improving the financial infrastructure. The entry of foreign banks should be relaxed.

Second, the Korean crisis is a cautionary tale about rapid financial liberalization in emerging markets. It demonstrates that the downside costs of globalization were magnified in the economy where the financial system had structural weaknesses. Financial markets are far from being perfect even in industrialized countries. Hence, developing countries must proceed more slowly and carefully in liberalizing domestic bank transactions and portfolio markets until necessary regulatory frameworks are in place.

Third, the financial crisis in Korea, as well as in other emerging markets, makes clear the dangers of fixed, or nearly fixed, exchange rates. While flexible markets may be more prone to regular volatility, fixed rates are more susceptible to huge shifts when they can no longer be defended (Radelet and Sachs 2000). Attempts by the Korean government to defend the exchange rate in the face of speculative attacks simply led to the exhaustion of usable foreign exchange reserves, and ultimately a huge depreciation of the won. The flexibility of exchange rates will also provide most developing countries, especially export-oriented commodity-based economies, with an easier means of adapting to foreign shocks, such as from a sharp decline in export prices.

Fourth, the Korean crisis, and the financial crises in general, has painfully revealed that there are few effective mechanisms in place to stop international financial panics in emerging markets. We need to develop the institutions needed to provide a more solid foundation for well-functioning international capital markets. The IMF did not play the role of an effective lender of last resort.[4] There is a need for a more formal mechanism for international private debt workouts for emerging markets, that ultimately relies more on private funds than IMF bailouts.

**Table 2.5**
**Trends in Ownership of US Patents, 1977–2001**

| | Patents granted during | | | | | |
|---|---|---|---|---|---|---|
| | 1977–87 | | 1988–95 | | 1996–2001 | |
| | Number | Share (%) | Number | Share (%) | Number | Share (%) |
| US | 456 779 | 59.20 | 459 121 | 54.80 | 519 809 | 55.40 |
| Japan | 109 346 | 14.20 | 174 203 | 20.80 | 180 695 | 19.30 |
| Germany | 68 384 | 8.90 | 60 659 | 7.20 | 56 610 | 6.00 |
| France | 24 869 | 3.20 | 24 865 | 3.00 | 22 935 | 2.40 |
| U.K. | 27 722 | 3.60 | 22 401 | 2.70 | 21 650 | 2.30 |
| Canada | 14 321 | 1.90 | 17 434 | 2.10 | 20 658 | 2.20 |
| Taiwan | 1 450 | 0.20 | 9 845 | 1.20 | 25 698 | 2.70 |
| Switzerland | 13 845 | 1.80 | 10 437 | 1.20 | 8 150 | 0.90 |
| Italia | 9 713 | 1.30 | 10 986 | 1.30 | 10 254 | 1.10 |
| Sweden | 9 639 | 1.20 | 6 716 | 0.80 | 8 502 | 0.90 |
| Netherlands | 8 012 | 1.00 | 7 993 | 1.00 | 7 463 | 0.80 |
| Korea | 341 | 0.00 | 4 712 | 0.60 | 17 808 | 1.90 |
| Australia | 3 817 | 0.50 | 4 239 | 0.50 | 4 686 | 0.50 |
| Israel | 1 559 | 0.20 | 2 748 | 0.30 | 4 581 | 0.50 |
| Finland | 1 817 | 0.20 | 2 568 | 0.30 | 3 663 | 0.40 |
| Denmark | 1 909 | 0.20 | 2 121 | 0.30 | 2 919 | 0.30 |
| Hong Kong | 668 | 0.09 | 1 407 | 0.20 | 2 462 | 0.30 |
| Ireland | 271 | 0.04 | 471 | 0.06 | 656 | 0.10 |
| Singapore | 52 | 0.01 | 270 | 0.03 | 1 031 | 0.10 |
| Mexico | 447 | 0.06 | 354 | 0.04 | 461 | 0.05 |
| Brazil | 280 | 0.04 | 420 | 0.05 | 560 | 0.06 |
| China | 48 | 0.01 | 405 | 0.05 | 730 | 0.08 |
| India | 123 | 0.02 | 196 | 0.02 | 603 | 0.06 |
| Others | 10 788 | 1.40 | 7 706 | 0.92 | 8 893 | 0.95 |
| World | 772 237 | 100.00 | 838 251 | 100.00 | 938 441 | 100.00 |

*Source*: US Patents and Trademarks Office. 2001, *TAF Special Report: All Patents, All Types, January 1977–December 2001.*

Fifth, the quick recovery of the Korean economy shows the importance of appropriate post-crisis management policies by a competent government. The V-shaped recovery in real GDP growth in Korea is similar in general to the stylized pattern we can observe from previous crisis episodes. But Korea showed much faster recovery of real output, in addition to improvement of the structural weaknesses of the financial and corporate sectors. The Korean experience demonstrates that the government-led financial restructuring programmes and macroeconomic adjustment policies played an important role in alleviating the cost of the financial crisis.

Sixth, it is clear that although a crisis brings economic growth to an abrupt halt, the crisis-hit economy can again return to a sustained growth path by maintaining its fundamental growth factors. However, the long-term sustained growth must warrant that the economy will not be susceptible to a severe crisis again. Maintaining a stable macroeconomic environment and sound financial system should be a prerequisite for long-term sustained growth.

## NOTES

1 See Radelet and Sachs (1998) and Blustein (2001) for a detailed description.
2 See World Bank (2000), Borensztein and Lee (2002) and Park (2001) for a detailed discussion of the process of corporate and financial restructuring in the 1997 East Asian crisis.
3 See Radelet et al. (2001) for a detailed discussion.
4 See Barro et al. (2002) for a discussion of the effectiveness of IMF programmes.

## REFERENCES

Barro, Robert. J. and Jong-Wha Lee (2002), 'IMF Programs: Who is Chosen and What are the Effects?', *NBER Working Paper*, No. 8951.

Blustein, Paul (2001), *The Chastening: Inside the Crisis that Rocked the Global Financial System and Humbled the IMF*, New York: Public Affairs.

Borensztein, E. and J. Lee (2002), 'Financial Crisis and Credit Crunch: Evidence from the Korean Firm Level Data', *Journal of Monetary Economics*, **49**(4), 853-75.

Lane, Timothy D., Atish R. Ghosh, Javier Hamann, Steven Philips, Marianne Schulze-Ghattas and T. Tsikata (1999), 'IMF-Supported Programmes In Indonesia, Korea and Thailand: A Preliminary Assessments', *IMF Occasional Paper*, No. 178, IMF.

Lee, Jong-Wha and Changyong Rhee (2002), 'Macroeconomic Impacts of the Korean Financial Crisis: Comparison with the Cross-country Patterns', *World Economy*, **25**(4), 539-62.

Park, Y.C. and Jong-Wha Lee (2002), 'Recovery and Sustainability in East Asia', in M. Dooley and J. Frankel (eds), *Managing Currency Crises in Emerging Markets*, Chicago: University of Chicago Press.

Radelet, Steven and Jeffrey D. Sachs (1998), 'The East Asian Financial Crisis: Diagnosis, Remedies, Prospects', *Brookings Papers on Economic Activity I*, 1–74.

Radelet, Steven and Jeffrey Sachs (2000), 'What Have We Learned, So Far, From the Asian Financial Crisis', manuscript.

Radelet, Steven, Jeffrey Sachs and Jong-Wha Lee (2001), 'Determinants and Prospects of Economic Growth in Asia', *International Economic Journal*, **15**(3), 1–30.

World Bank (2000), *East Asia: Recovery and Beyond*, Washington, DC, May.

# PART II REFORM AND POLICIES

# 3. Financial Sector Reform

**Junggun Oh**

## 3.1 INTRODUCTION

Since the 1997 financial crisis, numerous studies and discussions on its causes have been conducted from various perspectives. However, the underlying cause of the crisis lay in certain characteristics of the Korean economic system, which had promoted rapid growth in the past but became less suited to face the more competitive open economy and more integrated product and capital markets of the 1990s. These characteristics mainly reflected two factors. First, market institutions and principles were not sufficiently developed. For example, Korea lacked an effective corporate governance system to guide appropriate decisions, as well as independent financial institutions to ensure that capital was allocated efficiently. Second, there was insufficient prudential regulation. Instead, a 'too big to fail' mentality in the corporate sector and a 'never fail' attitude created serious moral hazard for both the financial and corporate sectors, while at the same time corporate investment decisions seemed to aim more at growing in size than assuring adequate profitability.

One can define the Korean economic development model as a government-led *chaebol*-centred export-oriented growth model. *Chaebol* means the family-controlled Korean-style big business conglomerate. Since the first five-year Economic Development Plan, introduced in 1962, the Korean government mobilized and allocated scarce financial resources to strategically selected sectors and firms, mainly the light export-oriented industries in the 1960s and the heavy and chemical industries (HCIs) in the 1970s. To allocate financial resources strategically the government controlled the financial sector, in particular the banking sector, and through the procedures to support the strategically selected sectors and firms the government–business relationship became very tight. Such a government–business relationship is defined as a quasi-internal organization (Lee 1992). Consequently, a unique tripartite government–banking–corporate relationship was established. The government was in all aspects a leader, or principal player, while banks and business corporations were its agents or followers

(Yoo 1999), and such a relationship contributed to the remarkable achievement of the miracle of high economic growth in an environment where the market system was not institutionalized at an early stage of economic development.

However, the usefulness of the tripartite relationship began to diminish as the Korean economy developed. As the economy developed financial resources should have been more efficiently intermediated, and consequently a new role for the government should have been identified. The long-established tripartite relationship of the government, financial and corporate sectors, which had once contributed to remarkable economic growth, should have been changed perhaps around the beginning of the 1980s, when the overall inefficiency problem of the economy arose as an important issue (Oh 2001a).

In addition, an interlocking close tripartite relationship resulted in problems of agency, moral hazard and even corruption. The inertia of the government having become accustomed to high growth, its intervention into the financial sector, and the *chaebols*' quest for large investment funds to fulfill their ever-lasting expansionary drive, resulted in the weakening of the financial intermediation function in the financial sector and highly indebted and destabilized the financial structure in the corporate sector.

The domestic financial sector had not been fully liberalized in spite of the government's attempt at financial liberalization since the 1980s, and thus its competitiveness had not been sufficiently strengthened (Oh 1998a and 1998b). Such intertwined structural problems of the government, financial and corporate sectors internally made the economy fragile to external shocks. Overall inefficiency of the economy undermined the potentials of economic growth. In such an environment the rapid opening of the capital market, and the subsequent frequent inflows and outflows of foreign capital, contributed to the financial crisis (Oh 1999, 2000, 2001a and 2001b).

Accordingly, the main targets of financial restructuring must be (1) the normalization of the financial intermediation function: it is crucial not only to the reform in the financial sector but also to the normalization of the national economy as a whole, that is to searching for the new paradigm of the economy; (2) enhancing the soundness of the financial system and (3) strengthening the competitiveness of the financial industries, in particular, in the wake of an almost complete opening of the financial market and industries (Oh and Park 1999).

Currently, considerable restructuring in the financial sector has been carried out, and huge financial resources have been injected into it since the crisis. First, for the normalization of the financial intermediation function, non-viable financial institutions have exited the market; ailing financial institutions have been merged, acquired and sold; public funds were injected into financial institutions for recapitalization and purchasing non-performing assets; and the structure of governance and ownership have been changed.

Second, to enhance the soundness of the financial system, prudential regulations and supervisory systems have been introduced, and the power of main creditor banks in corporate restructuring has been strengthened. That is a new relationship between banks and corporations has been introduced.

Finally, a financial holding company system has been introduced to strengthen financial institutions' competitiveness through enlargement of their scale and universal banking.

Nevertheless, some doubts still remain as to whether the ultimate purposes of financial restructuring have been achieved. In the following section the main contents of financial restructuring after the crisis are reviewed, and then an assessment of this financial restructuring is conducted in section 3.

## 3.2 MAIN CONTENTS OF FINANCIAL RESTRUCTURING

### 3.2.1 Exit of Non-viable Financial Institutions and the Disposal of Ailing Financial Institutions

Since the financial crisis five commercial banks have exited the market, and 14 banks have been merged to form five successor banks as of the end of March 2003 (see Table 3.1). As a result the total number of banks has been reduced from thirty-three in 1997 to 19 by 2003. Meanwhile, 28 merchant banking corporations, 8 securities companies, 7 investment trust (management) companies and 13 insurance companies have exited the market or merged.

The number of employees of financial institutions has declined 31.1 per cent, from 317 623 at the end of 1997 to 214 747 at the end of 2002. In particular, staff numbers at commercial banks have reduced 39.4 per cent from 145 530 to 88 262. The number of commercial banks' branches dropped 18.7 per cent from 6 177 to 5 021 during the same period.

Ailing financial institutions such as Korea First Bank, Seoul Bank, Korea Life Insurance and Daeshin Life Insurance Companies and Kukje Fire & Marine Insurance Company have been merged, acquired and sold in the domestic or foreign markets. Korea First Bank was sold to Newbridge Capital in December 1999. Hanvit, Peace, Kwangju and Kyongnam Banks were brought together under Woori Holdings Company in March 2001. Seoul Bank was sold to Hana Bank in September 2002. H&S, Korea, Yongnam and Central Merchant Banking Corporations were brought together into Woori Merchant Banking Corporation in November 2000. Kukje Fire & Marine Insurance Company was sold to the Kunwha Pharmaceutical Company in January 2002. The Korea Life Insurance Company was sold to the consortium led by the Hanwha Group in October 2002. The Daeshin Life Insurance Company was sold to the Green Cross Corporation in October

2002. The Regent Securities Company merged with the Ileun Securities Company in January 2002, the name of which was changed to Bridge Securities Company. Good Morning Securities Company merged with the Shinhan Securities Company in July 2002, the name of which was changed to Good Morning Shinhan Securities Company. It is worth emphasizing that many of these examples of financial restructuring involved prolonged and convoluted negotiations, especially where they involved foreign companies buying into or taking over ailing Korean financial companies.

**Table 3.1**
**Changes in the Number of Financial Institutions (January 1998–March 2003)**

| | No. of institutions as of the end of 1997 (A) | Exit | Merger | Total (B) | No. of institutions newly established (C) | No. of institutions operating (A-B+C) |
|---|---|---|---|---|---|---|
| Banks | 33 | 5 | 9 | 14 | - | 19 |
| Commercial banks | 26 | 5 | 7 | 12 | - | 14 |
| Nationwide banks | 16 | 3 | 5 | 8 | - | 8 |
| Local banks | 10 | 2 | 2 | 4 | - | 6 |
| Specialized Banks | 7 | - | 2 | 2 | - | 5 |
| Merchant banking corporations | 30 | 22 | 6 | 28 | 1 | 3 |
| Securities companies | 36 | 6 | 3 | 9 | 17 | 44 |
| Investment trust (management) companies | 31 | 6 | 1 | 7 | 8 | 32 |
| Insurance companies | 45 | 8 | 6 | 13 | 3 | 34 |

*Notes*: 1 Excluding bridge financial institutions and branches of foreign financial institutions.
2 Including revocation of license, bankruptcy and liquidation.
3 The number of financial institutions that ceased to exist following a merger.

*Source*: Financial Supervisory Service.

### 3.2.2 Public Funds Support for Purchasing Non-performing Assets and Recapitalization

A total of 160 trillion won of public funds was injected into financial institutions for recapitalization, purchasing non-performing assets, and repayment of deposits during the period from November 1997 to April 2003 (see Table 3.2). These public funds were raised mainly by issuing Insurance Deposit Fund Bonds (81.6 trillion won) and Non-performing Loans Management Fund Bonds (20.5 trillion won), and government fiscal sources (20.9 trillion won).

### 3.2.3 Improving the Transparency of Financial Institutions' Management

A new governance structure for financial institutions has been introduced. For a financial institution whose assets are above a certain level,[1] outside directors (January 2000), of whom there should be at least three, should make up at least half of the total membership of the board of directors and an audit committee (January 2000) must be set up. A system for a compliance officer[2] (April 2000) has also been introduced.

Standards for accounting and public disclosure have been strengthened: (1) banks (June 1998) and merchant banking corporations (March 1999) are now obliged to set aside full provisions against loan losses; (2) the accounting treatment of financial institutions' holdings of marketable securities has been changed to a mark–to–market system[3] (June 1998–March 2000); (3) a quarterly disclosure system for banks has been introduced (September 1999) – detailed matters for disclosure include organization and personnel, finance and net losses/profits, sources and uses of funds, soundness, profitability and productivity indicators, management guidelines and risk management.

**Table 3.2**
**Public Funds Injected**

(billion won)

| Source | Support type | Injected fund |
|---|---|---|
| KDIC | Recapitalization | 47 551 |
| | Compensation for losses | 17 525 |
| | Purchase of assets | 8 063 |
| | Repayment of deposits | 29 188 |
| | Subtotal | 102 327 |
| KAMCO | Purchase of NPLs | 39 073 |
| Fiscal sources | Recapitalization | 11 757 |
| | Purchase of subordinated debentures | 6 335 |
| | Subtotal | 18 092 |
| Bank of Korea | Recapitalization | 900 |
| Total | | 160 392 |

*Note*: November 1997 – April 2003.

*Source*: Public Fund Management Committee.

### 3.2.4 Introduction of Financial Holding Companies and Deregulation of Ownership of Commercial banks

Legislative provision for financial holding companies has been introduced to strengthen financial institutions' competitiveness through enlargement of their scale and universal banking (November 2000). Woori Finance Holdings Company (March 2001), Shinhan Financial Group (September 2001) and Dongwon Financial Group (May 2003) were established.

For the purpose of inducing sound financial capital and promoting responsible management the Banking Act was revised to lighten restrictions on bank ownership (April 2002). The upper limit on single holdings of a bank's equities has been revised from 4 per cent to 10 per cent, but the voting rights of shares held by industrial capital in excess of 4 per cent is limited.

### 3.2.5 Strengthening Prudential Regulation and Supervision

The Financial Supervisory Commission (FSC) was newly introduced on 1 April 1998 and then the Financial Supervisory Service (FSS) was officially established on 2 January 1999. The FSS was created by integrating the four previously existing supervisory bodies – the Banking Supervisory Authority, Securities Supervisory Board, Insurance Supervisory Board and Non-bank Supervisory Authority – into a single consolidated organization. Therefore the main functions of the FSS are the supervision and examination of the whole financial industries including the banking, non-banking, security and insurance industries.

A prompt corrective action system was introduced for commercial banks and merchant banking corporations (1 April 1998), and it was expanded to securities companies (26 April 1998), insurance companies (26 April 1998) and mutual savings and finance companies (31 December 1999).

Asset soundness classification standards have been strengthened. First, the criterion for classification of an asset as 'substandard' for commercial banks and merchant banking corporations has changed, from those non-performing for six months to those non-performing for three months (September 1998). The criterion for classification as 'precautionary' has also changed from those non-performing for three months to those non-performing for one month (September 1998). The standard was also applied to security companies and insurance companies (March 1999). Second, forward-looking criteria (FLC) standards for classifying asset soundness based on the future payment ability of borrowers, were introduced sequentially for banks (January 2000), merchant-banking corporations (June 2000) and insurance companies (September 2000).

To reduce the risk resulting from large credit exposures to a single entity, ceilings on credits to a single individual or juridical person, as well as to a single large business group, and ceilings on large credits were lowered to commercial banks (April 1999) and merchant banking corporations (June 1999). Specifically, the ceiling on credits to a single individual or juridical person and that on credits to a single business group have been reduced to 20 per cent and 25 per cent of a bank's equity capital respectively. The ceiling on large credits (more than 10 per cent of a bank's equity capital) to a single individual or juridical person has been reduced to five times a bank's equity capital.

### 3.2.6 Strengthening the Power of Main Creditor Banks for Corporate Restructuring

After the currency crisis main creditor banks assessed the viability of their client corporations and had them merge, find a buyer, or exit if they were found non-viable, and put them on a workout programme if they were thought capable of a turnaround. In particular, it was decided to arrange a workout for the Daewoo Group, the second-largest conglomerate at that time, by rescheduling debts and providing additional finance (August 1998). Creditor banks rescheduled debt and swapped debt for equity in the Hyundai Group, the largest conglomerate at that time, which was suffering from liquidity problems, on the condition that it spin-off Hyundai Motors and Hyundai Heavy Industries and withdraw from its position as the majority stockholder (mid-2000).

Creditor banks sought to secure the sale of ailing companies such as Samsung Motors, Daewoo Motors, Hanbo Steel and Hynix Semiconductor. Samsung Motors was sold to Renault Motors Corporation. General Motors and the Korea Development Bank, the main creditor financial institution of Daewoo Motors, signed the final contract for the sale of Daewoo Motors on 30 April 2002.

Major creditor banks reached agreement with their business groups to lower their debt–equity ratios below the 200 per cent ceiling as part of their capital structure improvement by the end of 2000, among them four top-five business groups by the end of 1999. Starting from April 1998 payment guarantees among a business group's affiliated companies was prohibited and all outstanding guarantees had to be withdrawn by March 2000.

A 'Continuous Assessment System of Corporate Credit Risk' was introduced in February 2001. The main creditor bank semi-annually selects companies that should be subject to assessment of their credit risk such as those that display symptoms of insolvency and those under court receivership or court mediation. After evaluating the possibility of their turnaround, it decides on the way they should be handled.

To facilitate companies' prompt rehabilitation the Corporate Restructuring Promotion Act was enacted in July 2001. The Act calls for creditor banks to regularly appraise the credit risk of companies that have obtained credits from financial institutions of a total 50 billion won or more. In particular, where, after appraisal of the business plan of a company considered to exhibit symptoms of insolvency on evaluation of its credit risk, the main creditor bank considers that its turnaround is feasible, it may have that company adopt joint management by creditor financial institutions on the determination of a committee set up by creditor financial institutions. Ssangyong Cement

Industrial Co., Hyundai Petrochemical Co., Hynix Semiconductor Inc. Hyundai Engineering & Construction Co. and Ssangyong Corp. are in the process of turnaround under the Corporate Restructuring Promotion Act.

## 3.3 APPRAISAL OF FINANCIAL RESTRUCTURING

### 3.3.1 Outcome

The central aim of financial restructuring has been to raise the overall efficiency of the economy. That has been done by heightening the soundness and profitability of the corporate and financial sectors through the forced exit of ailing financial institutions and firms, improvement of the financial structure of financial institutions and companies capable of a turnaround, the putting in place of systems relating to management transparency, and so forth.

Let us see how the financial restructuring pursued from the outbreak of the currency crisis until quite recently measures up in the light of its declared objectives. Dealing with financial sector restructuring, the fruits have been quite promising. A considerable degree of success has been attained. A number of troubled financial institutions have exited the market, and through the injection of public funds other financial institutions have been recapitalized and purged of their bad loans. Through these and other measures to improve financial structures, the financial system has been rehabilitated so as to provide the foundation for the recovery of business activity generally. As can be seen from Table 3.3 the total bad loans of the financial sector were greatly reduced from a total of 103 trillion won, as of the end of 1998, to 32 trillion won as of the end of 2002.

**Table 3.3**
**Trend of Non-performing Loans of Financial Institutions**

(trillion won)

| 1997 | 1998 | 1999 | 2000 | 2001 | 2002 |
|---|---|---|---|---|---|
| 86.4 | 102.7 | 88.0 | 64.6 | 35.1 | 31.8 |

*Note*: As of the end of period, based on FLC standard.

*Source*: Financial Supervisory Service.

The weight of the financial sector's bad loans has also been cut by a large amount, from 17.8 per cent as of the end of 1998 to 3.9 per cent as of the end of 2002. Commercial banks' ratio of non-performing loans fell substantially from 13.6 per cent as of the end of 1999 to 2.4 per cent as of the end of 2002 (see Table 3.4).

**Table 3.4**
**Trend of Non-performing Loan Ratios of Banks**

(%)

| | 1999 | 2000 | 2001 | 2002 |
|---|---|---|---|---|
| Commercial banks | 13.6 | 8.8 | 3.3 | 2.4 |
| (Including specialized banks) | (12.9) | (8.0) | (3.4) | (2.3) |

*Note*: As of the end of period.

*Source*: Financial Supervisory Service.

The financial structure and profitability of the banking industry have been improved, through a focus on banks in the provision of support from public funds for financial institutions' recapitalization and the disposal of their bad loans. The average capital adequacy of commercial banks, in terms of the Basel Accord ratio, rose from 7.0 per cent at the end of 1997 to 10.5 per cent at the end of 2002 (see Table 3.5). Commercial banks had continued to pile up large losses from 1997 onwards, but in 2002 they recorded a total net profit for the period of 3 875 billion won.

**Table 3.5**
**Trend of BIS Ratios and Net Profit of Commercial Banks**

(%, billion won)

| | 1997 | 1998 | 1999 | 2000 | 2001 | 2002 |
|---|---|---|---|---|---|---|
| BIS ratio | 7.04 | 8.23 | 10.83 | 10.53 | 10.81 | 10.50 |
| Net profit | -3 919 | -12 511 | -5 996 | -2 841 | 4 167 | 3 875 |

*Source*: Financial Supervisory Service.

This improvement has meant that financial institutions' function of credit intermediation – which had contracted sharply following the currency crisis as financial institutions avoided lending for fear of further non-performing assets – has been regained, particularly with respect to the banks, thereby providing the backing for the economic recovery (see Table 3.6).

**Table 3.6**
**Loans and Net Issue of Corporate Bonds and CPs of Financial Institutions**

(trillion won)

| | 1998 | 1999 | 2000 | 2001 | 2002 |
|---|---|---|---|---|---|
| Bank Loans to | -14.7 | 42.3 | 57.7 | 49.0 | 98.6 |
| (Enterprises) | (-3.6) | (18.0) | (23.5) | (13.0) | (37.0) |
| (Households) | (-9.5) | (19.3) | (26.4) | (44.8) | (61.6) |
| Non-bank financial institution Loans to | -16.4 | 0.0 | 5.5 | 4.8 | 12.4 |
| (Mutual Credit Facilities) | (-0.2) | (1.4) | (5.1) | (4.3) | (6.8) |
| (Others) | (-16.2) | (-1.4) | (0.4) | (0.5) | (5.6) |
| Total | -31.1 | 42.3 | 63.2 | 53.8 | 111.0 |
| Net issue of CPs | 16.6 | -29.7 | -0.6 | 8.1 | 10.9 |
| Net issue of Corporate Bonds | 32.6 | -3.0 | -8.5 | 8.3 | -7.9 |

*Note*: Since the data is flow data, they represent additions during the respective years.

*Source*: Bank of Korea.

Thanks to the pursuit of financial and corporate sector restructuring the Korean economy has regained its dynamism after experiencing a deep downturn in the wake of the currency crisis. Just after the outbreak of the currency crisis Korea's sovereign rating was reduced to below investment grade (speculative), but at the beginning of 1999 it regained its investment grade status and in 2002 it was upgraded to 'A' level by Moody's, Fitch, IBCA and S&P (see Table 3.7).

**Table 3.7**
**Korea's Sovereign Credit Rating from International Credit Rating Agencies**

| | | | | | | | | | | | |
|---|---|---|---|---|---|---|---|---|---|---|---|
| S&P | Previous<br>AA - | 97.<br>Oct.24<br>A + | Nov.25<br>A - | Dec.11<br>BBB - | Dec.23[1]<br>B + | 98.<br>Feb.17<br>BB + | 99.<br>Jan.25[2]<br>BBB - | Nov.11<br>BBB | | 01.<br>Nov.13<br>BBB+ | 02.<br>Jul.24<br>A- |
| Moody's | Previous<br>A1 | | 97.<br>Nov.28<br>A3 | Dec.11<br>Baa2 | Dec.21<br>Ba1 | | 99.<br>Feb.12<br>Baa3 | Dec.16<br>Baa2 | | | 02.<br>Mar.28<br>A3 |
| Fitch IBCA | Previous<br>AA - | 97.<br>Nov.18<br>A + | Nov.26<br>A | Dec.11<br>BBB - | Dec.23<br>B - | 98.<br>Feb.2<br>BB + | 99.<br>Jan.19<br>BBB - | Jun.24<br>BBB | 00.<br>Mar.30<br>BBB+ | | 02.<br>Jun.27<br>A |

*Notes*: 1 This was the lowest grade during Dec. 1997.
2 BBB - rated by S&P and Fitch IBCA, and Baa3 rated by Moody's are the lowest investment grades.

*Source*: Financial Supervisory Service.

### 3.3.2 Remaining Issues

**Privatization of government-owned financial institutions**

The government intended to move ahead with the disposal of the equity of the nationalized banks in 2002, through sale to strategic investors, block-sale (a method of collective sale of some portion of equity at a pre-set price through securities companies), public subscription and issue of DR and OPERA bonds (January 2002).

Seoul Bank was sold to Hana Bank in September 2002. In connection with the privatization of Chohung Bank, Shinhan Financial Group has been selected as the preferred negotiating partner (January 2003) and talks are now proceeding on the details of the sale. Korea Exchange Bank also recently announced the selection of Lone Star Fund as the preferred negotiating partner for the sale of government-owned shares (July 2003). Korea Life Insurance was sold to the consortium led by Hanwha Group in October 2002 and Daeshin Life Insurance to the Green Cross Corporation in April 2003.

Due to the continuation of the liquidity problems of Hynix Semi-conductor, its creditor financial institutions, which had extended financial assistance in May 2001 including the provision of 1 trillion won in fresh loans and the extension of the maturity of existing credits, decided on a rescue plan in October that year. This included 660 billion won in fresh loans, a 3 trillion won debt-for-equity swap, and the deferment of interest payments.

Creditor financial institutions that declined to extend new loans were required to convert a certain percentage of their credits into equity, equivalent to its liquidation value, and to write off the remainder. Following the breakdown of negotiations with Micron Technology for the sale of Hynix Semiconductor, creditor financial institutions planned to split the company into separate units for sale with a view to attracting foreign investment (May 2002).

Since early 2002 the government has been involved in negotiations with Prudential Financial Co. for the sale of Hyundai Investment & Securities Company and Hyundai Investment Trust Management Company, and signed a Memorandum of Understanding (MOU) with the Prudential Financial Co. for the sale of the Hyundai companies to the Prudential Financial Co. (March 2003).

**Strengthening the financial intermediation function**

With the help of financial restructuring the financial intermediation function has been much improved. However, so far it does not seem to have been completely normalized. In order to strengthen it, internally the structures of governance and ownership of financial institutions need to be further improved. The financial institutions' function of information production through *ex ante* screening and *ex post* monitoring, and their risk management system, should be enhanced to efficiently intermediate financial resources to the profitable sectors and thus to sustain the ratio of non-performing loans at a low level. Externally, the financial supervisory authorities should not intervene in financial institutions' self-management systems, while prudential regulation and supervision should be enhanced. The financial supervisory system itself also needs to be improved to enhance its independence. It is also important that market discipline should be established in the financial sector.

## NOTES

1 Banks and merchant banking corporations, securities companies and insurance companies and credit card companies whose total assets are more than 2 trillion won, investment trust management companies whose trust assets are more than 6 trillion won, and mutual savings banks whose total assets are more than 300 billion won.

2 A compliance officer is an officer with authority to check whether employees of financial institutions fulfill internal regulations of the financial institutions. This was newly introduced after the crisis.

3 A mark-to-market system is an accounting system to evaluate the value of marketable securities held by financial institutions based on the market price, not on the book price.

## REFERENCES

Oh, Junggun (1998a), 'Financial Reform Liberalization and Management in the Republic of Korea', in ESCAP (ed.), *Financial Sector Reform, Liberalization and Management for Growth and Stability in the Asian and the Pacific Region: Issues and Experiences*, Bangkok, Thailand: UN.

Oh, Junggun (1998b), Policies for the Development of the Financial Industry after the Crisis, *Staff Paper* 98-2, Economic Research Institute, Bank of Korea (in Korean).

Oh, Junggun (1999), 'Bank Privatization and Performance: The Korean Experience', *Working Paper* No. 98, Economic Research Office, Bank of Korea (in Korean).

Oh, Junggun (2000), *The Financial Crisis and Financial and Monetary Policies* Dasanbooks Seoul 2000 (in Korean).

Oh, Junggun (2001a), 'Governance Reinvented: The Progress Constraints and Remaining Agenda in Bank and Corporate Restructuring in Korea', in ESCAP (ed.), *Governance Reinvented: The Progress Constraints and Remaining Agenda in Bank and Corporate Restructuring in East and South East Asia* Bangkok, Thailand: UN

Oh, Junggun (2001b), 'Financial Crisis Management in Korea: Its Processes and Consequences', (with Hyun-Hoon Lee and Charles Harvie) in Tran Van Hoa (ed.), *Economic Crisis Management: Theory, Practice, Outcomes and Prospects*, Cheltenham: Edward Elgar Publishing.

Oh, Junggun and Donghyun Park (1999), 'Financial Reforms and Financial Crisis: The Korean Case', *Review of Pacific Basin Financial Market and Policies*, **2**(3), 265–84.

Lee, Chung H. (1992), 'The Government, Financial System and Large Private Enterprises in the Economic Development of South Korea', *World Development*, **20**(2), 187–97.

Yoo, Seoung Min (1999) 'Corporate Restructuring in Korea: Policy Issues before and during the Crisis', *Working Paper*, No 9903, Korea Development Institute.

# 4. Corporate Restructuring in the Wake of the Financial Crisis

**Charles Harvie**

## 4.1 INTRODUCTION

The outbreak of the financial crisis in Korea in 1997, and the resulting economic crisis in 1998, revealed severe structural weaknesses in the country's economy. While superficially, at least, the crisis appeared to be one of a short-run liquidity shortage, arising from low foreign exchange reserves and excessive short-term foreign debts,[1] at the core of the problem were structural problems relating to a heavily indebted corporate sector and chronically weak and underdeveloped financial sector. However, the adverse short-term effects from the liquidity crisis, and the contagion effects from the Asian financial crisis, magnified the impact of these long-term structural problems. The corporate debt problem and the weak financial sector were the culmination of a prolonged period of accumulated inefficiency, dating back to the beginnings of Korea's development and covering the country's period of rapid economic growth and development, centred around the country's close and collusive government–business–banking sector relationship (Sohn 2002b). The government-led development strategy, that included the provision of loans, corporate bailouts and other assistance to selected companies, ultimately resulted in an inefficient allocation of financial resources in the corporate sector, the creation of moral hazard problems in the financial sector, and the accumulation of substantial non-performing loans. This was compounded by an inefficient corporate governance and ownership structure that contributed to underlying low firm valuation (Sohn 2002b).

As a consequence, corporate sector restructuring and reform is of paramount importance for the sustained recovery of the economy. The success of this will fundamentally depend upon: resolving the substantial debts of the corporate sector, particularly that of the *chaebols*,[2] by implementing measures to recover non-performing loans and the liquidation of corporate debts; optimizing the role of foreign capital in Korea's post-crisis corporate restructuring, involving the liberalization of foreign capital flows in the form of cross-border mergers and acquisitions (M&As) and in the privatization process; and corporate governance and ownership reform.

The primary aims of this chapter are to review the performance of the corporate sector before and after the financial and economic crisis of 1997–98, identify the various corporate restructuring and reform programmes that have been carried out in the private and the public sector, and assess the success of these measures to date. Progress in regard to corporate governance and ownership reform is also addressed. In doing so the chapter proceeds as follows. Section 2 reviews the pre-crisis development of the corporate sector, identifying the reasons for its weaknesses and its contribution to the financial crisis. Section 3 focuses upon the restructuring initiatives and measures in the wake of the financial and economic crisis of 1997–98, in particular corporate debt restructuring and corporate governance reform. Section 4 considers the contribution of market liberalization measures to the corporate restructuring efforts, especially that affecting cross border M&As and privatization. Finally, section 5 provides a summary of the major conclusions from this chapter.

## 4.2 PRE-CRISIS GROWTH AND PERFORMANCE OF THE CORPORATE SECTOR

The government-led economic development strategy, dating back to the early 1960s, provided the basis for the growth of the *chaebols*. During this period the government allowed a few selected corporations to enter protected, or targeted, growth industries, that were to provide the basis for export expansion. Since these were usually heavy and chemical industries (HCIs) that were subject to strong economies of scale, it was inevitable that the corporations operating in them would significantly increase in scale. The government continued to make use of, and rely upon, the experience and managerial skills of these successful corporations in subsequent economic development. However, the evolution of *chaebols* into massive business conglomerates primarily occurred during the period of the government initiated Heavy and Chemical Industry Promotion Plan (HCIP) from 1973 to 1979 (see Harvie and Lee 2003). The following HCIs were classified as 'strategic': steel, heavy machinery, automobiles, industrial electronics, shipbuilding, non-ferrous metals and petrochemicals and were to be subject to generous government assistance. Selected corporations were given preferential access to these targeted industries, and were also offered financial and tax inducements. The main tool of targeted industry promotion, however, was preferential access to bank credit. Since the government exerted considerable control over the banking system, a disproportionate amount of financial resources were channelled towards the expansion of successful big businesses, in line with government policy, particularly during the period of the HCI drive of the 1970s, or to bail out less successful large businesses. Hence the rapid growth of the *chaebols* during this period was made possible by financing through the financial system, which was heavily skewed toward indirect financing through banks in comparison to direct financing through the stock market. Consequently, the *chaebols* ended up having disproportionately high debt and high debt–equity ratios, which provided the seeds for their ultimate weakness during the crisis period of the late 1990s.

In seeking entrepreneurs and businesses to lead the HCI drive the government inevitably turned to the successful exporters of the 1960s and early 1970s, having already developed close relationships with them and being familiar with their business potential. The successful exporters in turn wanted to expand their businesses, and the involvement of the government greatly reduced the risks of investing in these new business areas. The reduced risk also allowed these businessmen to exercise considerable power in managing their businesses, since they were not accountable to private lenders, investors or stockholders. Thus the ties between the government, businesses and the financial sector became even stronger during the period of the 1970s. The successful large corporations had every incentive to diversify their operations according to the government's industry-targeting policy, and consequently they became larger and larger. This increasingly collusive behaviour hindered competition in domestic markets and protected these large firms from external competition in targeted sectors.

Other factors contributed to *chaebol* growth. In disposing of insolvent firms, and to avoid job losses, the government transferred their ownership to other more successful big business groups, thereby further reinforcing the growth of the *chaebols*. In addition, and in order to minimize the huge potential social cost of *chaebol* bankruptcies, the government resuscitated insolvent *chaebols* or their subsidiaries through preferential measures. Hence the period of the 1970s and early 1980s established the precedent for government bailouts, which created expectations for further bailouts and moral hazard on the part of the corporate and financial sectors. An important implication of these policies was that the big business groups had little chance to restructure themselves according to market discipline, because of a 'too big to fail' mentality.

Korea's macroeconomic and trade policies also reflected the change in industrial policy during the period of the 1970s, with macroeconomic policies designed to channel funds to the targeted HCI industries. The expansionary policies raised inflation and increased real labour costs. Further, while those businesses favoured by the government were showered with cheap credit and profits, light manufacturing industries and new start-up firms had difficulty in finding credit. It was widely thought that only 'insiders' with close connections to the government could gain access to various preferential treatments. Such policies explain Korea's high dependency on the large *chaebols* and the relative weakness of small and medium-sized enterprises (SMEs), as well as the development of 'crony-capitalism'. While the growth of the *chaebols* during the period of the 1960s and 1970s had provided the basis for rapid growth of the country, the excesses of the HCI drive during the 1970s resulted in their growth and dominance of the domestic economy becoming an increasing burden and restriction on the implementation of economic policy.

The HCI drive led to a weakening of the independence and competitiveness of the financial sector. By allocating credits to the *chaebols* the government was doing the job that would normally have been done by banks. Instead of using market forces and credit ratings as guides to lending, as in the 1960s, the government's criteria for guaranteeing loans in the 1970s became its policy goals, which increased government intervention in the market and weakened the banks' ability to assess the creditworthiness of its borrowers. *Chaebols* were encouraged to engage in risky businesses with high growth potential, and they did so on the basis that implicitly the government would bail them out if they got into difficulty. While it cannot be denied that this development strategy contributed greatly to the country's economic 'miracle', the legacies of this strategy such as 'implicit guarantees' for *chaebol*s by the government, the growth of *chaebol*s to such a size that they were 'too big to fail', as well as the weak financial sector with little capacity for credit evaluation, arose in large part from this development strategy. These legacies resulted in moral hazard problems on the part of the Korean financial and corporate sectors.

Many of these problems were recognized in the late 1970s and 1980s (see for example Sohn 2002b, Harvie and Lee 2003), and the government did much, subsequently, to try and eliminate its formal ties with the private sector. By the early 1980s, for example, preferential credits for exporters, as well as the policies promoting the HCIs, were formally eliminated. However, there remained substantial informal ties that made the complete separation between the public and the private sector difficult. While the government recognized the need for an expanded role of the market mechanism in private decision-making, there also remained the strong belief that the government should actively lead the development process and intervene in the marketplace. In addition, because the policies of the 1960s and 1970s had not concentrated on strengthening the financial foundations of both the Korean financial and corporate sectors, the government found it difficult to disengage itself from the economy completely. Thus, the government decided upon a strategy of gradual withdrawal from the marketplace.

By the early 1980s the *chaebols* had become leading companies in major export-oriented industries such as petrochemicals, automobiles and semiconductors. Concerns over their increasing influence over the economy resulted in the introduction of an anti-monopolistic policy focusing upon the regulation of economic concentration. The Regulation on Monopoly and Fair

Trade Act was enacted in 1980 and regulations on M&As by big business groups were introduced in 1986. Regulations on market concentration and cross-debt guarantees among *chaebol*-affiliated firms were later introduced in 1990 and 1992, respectively. The distorted structure of the corporate sector, with its emphasis on large enterprises and lack of competition in domestic markets, resulted in an increased recognition during the 1980s of the need to encourage the growth of SMEs (see Gregory et al. 2002). The growth of SMEs had long been inhibited because of difficulties in gaining access to the necessary finance to enable their development.

By the 1990s the Fair Trade Commission began to select on an annual basis the top 30 *chaebols*, based on the size of their assets, as its main target for regulation. The government then attempted to introduce various regulations, such as restrictions on loans to the *chaebols*, to prevent further lending concentration, and the introduction of a business specialization policy that required the *chaebols* to limit diversification to two or three specialized business lines. Despite this the working ties between the government, the financial sector and the corporate sector remained strong, and persisted in the 1990s even after the banks were privatized, from the early 1980s, and the government officially stopped interfering with banks' lending practices.

These regulatory measures were, however, not effective. Both the net assets and cross-holdings of the *chaebols* approximately doubled during 1993 to 1997. Market concentration remained high (see Table 4.1) – the top 30 *chaebols* accounted for 41.5 per cent and 45.5 per cent of total sales in 1990 and 1997, respectively. The top 30 *chaebols* accounted for 40.3 and 44.8 per cent of total assets in 1990 and 1997, respectively. However the top 30 *chaebols* accounted for only 4.2 per cent and 4.1 per cent of total employment in 1990 and 1997, respectively. Consequently, it can be seen that they were very heavily involved in capital-intensive areas of business activity. The top 30 *chaebols* accounted for 24.2 and 21.5 per cent of total financial loans in 1990 and 1995, respectively.

**Table 4.1**
**Economic Concentration of the *Chaebols***

(%)

| | | 1985–89 (average) | 1990 | 1991 | 1992 | 1993 | 1994 | 1995 | 1996 | 1997 |
|---|---|---|---|---|---|---|---|---|---|---|
| Assets | 5th | 30.7 | 23.4 | 24.0 | 24.5 | 24.0 | 23.5 | 25.4 | 27.2 | 28.7 |
| | 30th | 48.0 | 40.3 | 43.5 | 44.4 | 43.2 | 41.7 | 44.6 | 46.7 | 44.8 |
| Sales | 5th | 24.4 | 27.0 | 27.2 | 28.6 | 27.6 | 28.2 | 30.7 | 32.8 | 32.4 |
| | 30th | 44.3 | 41.5 | 41.3 | 43.8 | 41.7 | 42.4 | 45.8 | 48.5 | 45.5 |
| Employment | 5th | 2.6 | 2.5 | 2.6 | 2.4 | 2.4 | 2.5 | 2.6 | 2.7 | 2.7 |
| | 30th | 4.4 | 4.2 | 4.3 | 4.2 | 4.1 | 4.2 | 4.4 | 4.6 | 4.1 |

*Source*: Hwang (2000).

Several reasons explain the failure of regulation to contain economic concentration in Korea. First, restrictions on competition, including entry barriers and price regulations, were still in effect. Second, the government was not prepared to accept the demise of uncompetitive *chaebols*, because of the potential social cost of their financial problems and bankruptcy. As a result, the government sustained inefficient *chaebol* subsidiaries with public money or merged them with other *chaebol* subsidiaries. Furthermore, the M&A market remained inactive and bankruptcy laws, including reorganization processes, were inadequate and usually ignored. Third, the financial industry was too immature to exercise its role as a check on the *chaebols*' overexpansion. Korean banks did not perform their duty of loan screening thoroughly because, as previously explained, they were only used as tools to support the government's industrial policies. Local banks were therefore reduced to nothing more than an instrument of government intervention in the banking sector. As banks and other financial institutions became accustomed to government guidance and coordination, they hardly needed, and so lacked, the requisite ability to conduct credit and project analyses. Since their ability to function as banks deteriorated, for every loan they provided, even for credit loans, they tended to prefer debt guarantees by a third party or collateral to reduce risks. So the *chaebols* satisfied the banks with cross-debt guarantees among subsidiaries, enabling them to obtain the finance for their further expansion.

### 4.2.1 Legacies of the Government's Interventionist Industrial Policies[3]

The government's interventionist industrial policy strategy contributed, by the 1990s, to a number of structural problems. First, industry and firm targeting of industrial policies greatly distorted resource allocation. They frequently tended to substitute for the price mechanism and resulted in severe overinvestment in industrial sectors, particularly during the HCI drive of the 1970s, subsequently recognised and reversed from the early 1980s. Preferential industrial policies: worsened economic concentration, resulted in a structural imbalance between large firms and SMEs, and produced a monopolistic domestic economic structure. Second, government control of the financial sector to support its industrial policy undermined the ability of financial institutions to discriminate between competent and incompetent firms and projects, and to monitor the performance of borrowing firms. Third, persistent government intervention destroyed private sector incentives for creative economic ventures. State support of selected industries and firms, and government control of the financial sector, resulted in private sector dependence on government guidance and coordination. In addition, government assistance to large enterprises during periods of financial difficulties resulted in a 'too big to fail' legacy and moral hazard ensued. Lastly, the government's ability to select and support strategic industries, and to enforce restructuring programmes, generated room for corporate rent seeking.

### 4.2.2 Corporate Sector Weakness and the Onset of the Crisis – a Profile

Table 4.2 identifies some key statistics for the overall corporate sector in the pre-crisis period, which was marked by high debt ratios, usually over 300 per cent,[4] very high borrowings versus total assets, usually over 45 per cent, and very low return on assets, usually below 2 per cent. Some analysts point out that firms in developing countries often have high debt ratios because they do not have a fully developed capital market, and thus must finance their investment through debt rather than stock issues. However, at some stage of development, in order to foster better management techniques as well as to create a functioning capital market, firms should lower their debt ratios. For Korea, given the level of its development and that some local companies were already globalized, the debt ratios were much too high.

**Table 4.2**
**Corporate Statistics before 1998**

(%)

| | 1992 | 1993 | 1994 | 1995 | 1996 | 1997 |
|---|---|---|---|---|---|---|
| Equity to total assets | 23.9 | 25.3 | 24.8 | 25.9 | 24.0 | 20.2 |
| Debt ratio | 318.7 | 294.9 | 302.5 | 286.8 | 317.1 | 397.3 |
| Total borrowings/Total assets | 47.2 | 46.8 | 44.5 | 44.8 | 47.7 | 54.2 |
| Return on equity | 3.7 | 4.2 | 7.6 | 11.0 | 2.0 | -4.2 |
| Return on assets | 0.9 | 1.0 | 1.9 | 2.8 | 0.5 | -0.9 |

*Source*: Bank of Korea (1999).

The debt ratios for the top 30 *chaebols*, and their number of subsidiaries, is shown in Table 4.3. The high number of subsidiaries and the very high debt ratios indicate that the *chaebols* relied heavily on debt financing in order to expand. The profitable subsidiaries of *chaebols* often guaranteed loans to the less profitable subsidiaries or for expansion of the *chaebol* group. Table 4.4 shows the debt guarantee levels for major conglomerates. As a result of these guarantees the profitable subsidiaries were also made vulnerable to the weaknesses of their affiliates, further weakening the foundations of the corporate sector. These weaknesses had their roots in the government-led industrial development policies discussed previously. These management habits persisted, however, even after formal government aid was eliminated.

These weaknesses in the corporate sector finally surfaced in the form of a series of large-scale bankruptcies. The number of bankruptcies, including those of the *chaebols*, jumped by about 50 per cent during the outbreak of the crisis, from 11 589 in 1996 to 17 168 in 1997 (see Table 4.5). These bankruptcies included some of Korea's largest *chaebols*. Seven of the 30 largest *chaebols*, accounting for 4 per cent of the assets of non-farm and non-financial businesses, failed in 1997. These included Hanbo Steel in early 1997, Sammi, Jinro and Kia Motors in the summer of 1997. These corporate problems raised the level of non-performing loans (NPLs) of the financial sector.

**Table 4.3**
**Debt Ratio and the Number of Affiliated Companies of the 30 Major *Chaebols* up to 1998**

| | 1995 | 1996 | 1997 | 1998 |
|---|---|---|---|---|
| Debt ratio (%) | 355.7 | 373.5 | 386.5 | 518.9 |
| Number of affiliated companies | 623 | 669 | 819 | 804 |

*Source*: Bank of Korea (1999).

**Table 4.4**
**Debt Guarantees of Major Conglomerates**

(trillion won, %)

| | Capital (A) | Debt guarantees | | | Capital ratios (%) | |
|---|---|---|---|---|---|---|
| | | Total (B) | Limited (C ) | Excluded | B/A | C/A |
| 1 Apr. 1993 | 35.2 | 165.5 | 120.6 | 44.9 | 469.8 | 342.4 |
| 1 Apr. 1995 | 50.7 | 82.1 | 48.3 | 33.8 | 161.9 | 95.2 |
| 1 Apr. 1997 | 70.5 | 64.4 | 33.1 | 31.2 | 91.3 | 47.0 |

*Source*: Zang and Wang (1998).

**Table 4.5**
**Number of Bankruptcies**

| **Number of bankrupted firms** | **1994** | **1995** | **1996** | **1997** | **1998** | **1999** | **2000** | **2001** |
|---|---|---|---|---|---|---|---|---|
| Total | 11 255 | 13 922 | 11 589 | 17 168 | 22 828 | 6 718 | 6 693 | 5 277 |
| Incorporated firms | 4 503 | 6 031 | 5 157 | 8 226 | 10 536 | 3 371 | 3 840 | 3 220 |
| % | 40.0 | 43.3 | 44.5 | 47.9 | 46.2 | 50.2 | 57.4 | 61.0 |
| Large firms | 5 | 5 | 7 | 58 | 39 | 7 | 33 | 11 |

*Source*: Bank of Korea.

Three factors contributed to this. First, excessive and inefficient investment and diversified business activities that were funded by debt, by the increasingly highly leveraged *chaebols*, contributed to, low profitability, and a cash flow shortage that made the sector structurally vulnerable to external shocks. The crucial element for the viability and soundness of the sector is cash flow. In the wake of the crisis, measures aimed at improving the cash flow of the cash-strapped corporate sector, by attracting foreign capital in particular,[5] became increasingly necessary.

Indicators of corporate profitability plummeted in 1996: return on assets, 0.5 per cent; return on equity, 2 per cent; year-to-year operating income rate, -14.4 per cent. In 1997, the first two rates even turned negative, to -0.9 per cent and -4.2 per cent respectively. Equity prices, a sign of growing problems in the financial and corporate sectors, plummeted when the overall stock market index (KOSPI) fell by over 40 per cent by the end of 1996 from its peak in November 1994 (Chopra et al. 2001).

Second, the collusive relationship between the government and business groups led to inefficient allocation of capital in the financial system. Through its strong control of the financial sector the government implicitly guaranteed loans to selected companies, in particular *chaebols*, without prudential regulations. This often resulted in a situation where some companies could not repay their debts. The inability of the corporate sector to service its debt is equivalent to an increase in the NPLs of financial institutions. Consequently, the demise of the corporate and financial sectors was intertwined: the increasing number of bankruptcies in the corporate sector burdened the financial sector with NPLs.

Third, the traditional and inefficient corporate governance continued. The owners, who were often the controlling shareholders and usually non-professional managers, were deeply involved in corporate governance. The headquarters of *chaebols* controlled affiliates with a relatively small share of their equity through a centralized hierarchy system known as the 'control pyramid system'.[6] In fact, the average number of affiliates of the top 30 *chaebols* increased from 16 in 1983 to 27 in 1997, while the mean percentage of shareholders decreased from 15.8 per cent to 8.5 per cent during the same period. This type of corporate governance contributed to inefficiency, poor performance and low firm value. In addition, the absence of mechanisms that checked and disciplined management, for example M&As, prudential supervision in the financial market, and competition through entry and withdrawal, did not exist.

The very high leverage and overinvestment of Korean firms played a crucial role in causing the financial crisis. In particular, the *chaebols* tended to borrow excessively through cross-payment guarantees among interlinked subsidiaries. By the end of 1997 the top 30 *chaebols* had debt–equity ratios of 519 per cent, in sharp contrast to the 154 per cent in the United States and 186 per cent in Japan. Poor corporate practices and governance also contributed to the 1997 crisis in the form of inaccurate company financial information, non-transparent corporate decision-making, no credible exit threat, insufficient financial institution monitoring, and few legal rights and forms of protection for minority shareholders. Hence, the priority in corporate sector reform has been to focus on achieving a major reduction in corporate indebtedness, bringing corporate governance practices into line with international standards, and in attaining corporate international competitiveness.

## 4.3 CORPORATE SECTOR RESTRUCTURING IN THE WAKE OF THE CRISIS

The Korean government called upon emergency support from the IMF in November 1997. On 3 December a US$57 billion IMF stand-by arrangement was signed, the central focus of which was to speed up and reinforce efforts on restructuring the financial and corporate sectors. On 13 January 1998, in an effort to reform the Korean economy, five tasks for the corporate sector were established:

- Enhance transparency
- Eliminate mutual debt guarantees
- Improve the financial structure of corporations
- Focus the conglomerates on core activities
- Strengthen the responsibility of controlling shareholders and management.

As a result of changed conditions and new problems, three further tasks were added on 15 August 1999:

- Improve the managerial governance of the non-bank financial institutions
- Eliminate cross-financing and illegal intra-transactions
- Prevent irregular inheritances and donations.[7]

Corporate restructuring can be divided into two pillar measures - corporate restructuring and debt resolution, and corporate governance reform. Each of these is now discussed in turn.

### 4.3.1 Corporate Restructuring and Debt Resolution

**The system for corporate restructuring**

To deal with corporate insolvency the government sought to improve and expedite the existing court-based procedures as well as to introduce a new out-of-court settlement mechanism (a workout programme). Insolvent companies were to be liquidated or rehabilitated through these two main mechanisms. Figure 4.1 illustrates the system for corporate restructuring. A viable insolvent corporation follows either the court-based procedure or the out-of-court procedure. All these procedures lead to the same goal of normalizing the functions of corporations. An insolvent corporation that was not viable followed the bankruptcy procedure leading to liquidation.

The court-based insolvency system in Korea is composed of three procedures: bankruptcy, composition, and reorganization. Bankruptcy is a procedure that liquidates debtors' assets by a court-appointed liquidator. Composition is a settlement procedure between the debtor and creditors and is available to enterprises that owe less than 250 billion won, but it offers very few guarantees to the creditors. In the reorganisation procedure the court directs the creditors to handle the debtor, and the latter's estate is administered by an external administrator under the influence of the debtor. Creditors and debtors can start any of the procedures if there is evidence of cash flow insolvency (OECD 1998). Before the crisis, such a court-based insolvency system was inefficient and hardly functional.

**Approaches to restructuring: first stage programme and reform efforts**
In the aftermath of the crisis the Korean government adopted a three-pronged approach to reforming the corporate sector. Companies were divided into three groups according to their restructuring capacities, and different approaches were adopted for each of them: the big five *chaebols*, sixth- to sixty-fourth-largest *chaebols* plus Daewoo and SMEs. The top five *chaebols* had the capacity to absorb the resulting losses from restructuring and were allowed to pursue 'self-directed restructuring'. The Daewoo Group and the medium-sized *chaebols*, the sixth- to sixty-fourth-largest conglomerates, which could not restructure successfully on their own, entered into 'workouts' with financial institutions. The SMEs, financially too small and weak to bear the costs of restructuring, were supported by their creditor financial institutions. Each of these approaches is now discussed in turn.

*Big five chaebols* The five largest *chaebols*, known as the Big Five, were to be reformed and restructured through specific plans to improve their capital structure. The parameters within which corporate reform of the Big Five proceeded was contained in an agreement on five major principles made in January 1998, between the then President-elect Kim Dae Jung and the leaders of the five largest *chaebols*.

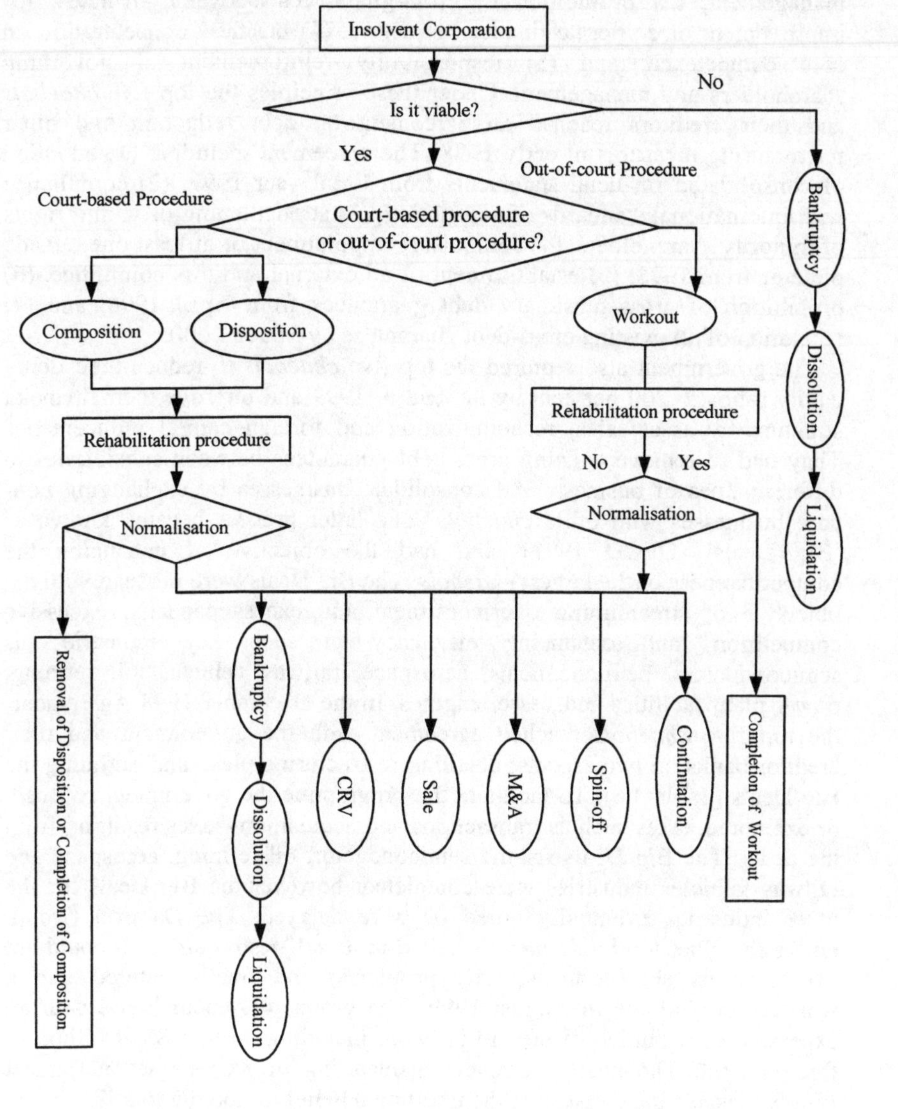


*Source*: Yook et al. (2001).

*Figure 4.1 The System for Corporate Restructuring*

The five principles are: (1) heightening the transparency of corporate management, (2) prohibition of cross-guarantees between affiliates, (3) improvement of corporate financial structure, (4) business concentration on core competence, and (5) responsibility reinforcement of governing shareholders and management. Under these principles the top five *chaebols* and their creditors reached an agreement on debt reduction and other restructuring measures in early 1998. The agreement included: (1) adoption of consolidated financial statements from fiscal year 1999, (2) compliance with international standards of accounting, (3) strengthening of voting rights of minority shareholders, (4) compulsory appointment of at least one outside director from 1998, (5) establishment of an external auditors committee, (6) prohibition of cross-subsidiary debt guarantees from April 1998, and (7) resolution of all existing cross-debt guarantees by March 2000.

The government also required the top five *chaebols* to reduce their debt–equity ratios to 200 per cent by the end of 1999 and improve their financial structure by asset sales, recapitalization and foreign capital inducement.[8] They had to remove existing cross-debt guarantees between subsidiaries in different lines of business, and consolidate businesses by exchanging non-core businesses with other *chaebols*. The latter process became known as 'Big Deals' (OECD 1999), and had the objective of enhancing the competitiveness of the largest *chaebols*. The Big Deals were pursued with the objective of streamlining overinvestment and excess capacity, excessive competition, and enhancing efficiency in such key industries as semiconductors, petrochemicals, aerospace, railway vehicles, oil refining, power plant facilities and vessel engines. In the December 1998 Agreement[9] the top five *chaebols* reached agreement with the government and their creditor banks on two aspects: detailing restructuring plans and outlining the Big Deals (Table 4.6). To facilitate the programme the government reduced, or exempted, taxes such as transactions and acquisitions taxes resulting from the deals. The Big Deals for the semiconductor, oil refining, aerospace and railway vehicles industries were completed; however the Big Deals for the other industries eventually failed or were delayed. The Daewoo Group, unlike the other top four *chaebols*, failed in its self-restructuring. It could not overcome its short-term liquidity problems, and finally entered into a workout programme in August 1999. The group was encumbered with an excessive debt burden of 60 trillion won, including up to US$10 billion in foreign debt. The nearly complete dismantling of Korea's second-largest *chaebol* caused the collapse of the traditional belief in 'too big to fail'.

*Daewoo Group and medium-sized chaebols* The mid-ranking *chaebols* and other large corporations, the sixth- to sixty-fourth-largest *chaebols*, and subsequently the Daewoo Group, were subject to restructuring through out of court debt workout programmes with their designated lead creditor bank based on the London Approach.[10] This is an out-of-court settlement process

**Table 4.6**
**Big Deals**

| Industry | Plan | Controlling body |
|---|---|---|
| Semiconductors | Samsung Electronic Co. →<br>Hyundai Electronics Ind. } Combine →<br>LG Semiconductor Co. | Samsung Electronics Co.<br>Hyundai Electronics Ind.<br>(Agreement reached in January 1999) |
| Power-generating equipment | Hyundai Heavy Industries Co.<br>Korea Heavy Industries & Construction Co. } Combine<br>Samsung Heavy Industries Co. | Korea Heavy Industries & Construction Co. |
| Petrochemicals | SK, LG, Daelim, Lotte, Hanwha →<br>Hyundai Petro-chemical Co. } Combine →<br>Samsung General Chemical Co. | SK, LG, Daelim, Lotte, Hanwha, New entity |
| Aircraft manufacturing | Samsung Aerospace Industries Co.<br>Daewoo Heavy Industries Co. } Combine →<br>Hyundai Space & Aircraft Co. | New entity |
| Railroad vehicles | Hyundai Precision & Ind. Co.<br>Daewoo Heavy Industries Co. } Combine →<br>Hanjin Heavy Industries Co. | Third-party professional manager |
| Ship engines | Hyundai Heavy Industries Co. →<br>Korea Heavy Industries & Construction Co. } Combine<br>Samsung Heavy Industries Co. | Hyundai Heavy Industries Co.<br>Korea Heavy Industries & Construction Co. |
| Oil refining | SK, LG, Ssangyong →<br>Hyundai Oil Co. } Combine →<br>Hanwha Energy Co. | SK, LG, Ssangyong<br>Hyundai Oil Co. |
| Cars[1] | Hyundai Motors[2] →<br>Daewoo Motors[3] } Combine →<br>Samsung Motors | Hyundai Motors[2]<br>Daewoo Motors |

*Notes*: 1 Added in December 1998.
2 Hyundai Motors acquired Kia Motors earlier in 1997.
3 Daewoo Motors acquired Ssangyong Motors in 1997.

*Source*: OECD (1999).

for creditors and debtors based on the principle of burden-sharing with financial institutions, through the firm's own efforts for rehabilitation as well as debt adjustments. A Corporate Restructuring Accord (CRA) was signed in June 1998 in which 200 banks and non-bank financial institutions committed themselves to following the agreed workout procedure, which provided informal debt workout as an alternative to the formal procedures of the insolvency law regime. These bank-led workout plans included various tools for adjusting debts, through the analysis of mid- and long-term cash flows, which contained debt–equity swaps, term extensions, deferred payment of principal or interest, interest rate cuts, waiver of indebtedness, cancellation of existing guarantee regulations, sale of non-core businesses, and provision of new credits. For some cases, favourable tax treatments were available: a bank acquiring shares was exempt from the acquisition tax in a debt–equity swap; taxes were not imposed on firms selling real estate holdings to reduce their debts. In addition, to accelerate the workout process, a three-month time limit was imposed, with a one-month extension. Creditor banks were also required to oversee the management of workout firms. But many of these creditor banks lacked management expertise and their role was limited to external supervision, leaving management responsibilities in the hands of company officials.

In the process of corporate restructuring the Korea Asset Management Corporation (KAMCO) also played a fundamentally important role, by managing the bailout fund and purchasing non-performing loans from commercial banks. The loans purchased by KAMCO, by the end of September 1997, amounted to 37 trillion won at a cost of 17.2 trillion won (Ahn 2001). To promote more efficient management of insolvent firms under workout programmes, the government recently established Corporate Restructuring Vehicles (CRVs). A CRV is an independent agency specialized in corporate restructuring. In place of creditor banks, it assumes the authority to manage debt workout firms. Problems between financial institutions and a debtor were resolved through the Corporate Restructuring Co-ordination Committee (CRCC), an arbitration committee.

*Small and medium-sized enterprises* SMEs were severely affected by the 1998 recession, especially by the credit crunch, as banks reduced loans to them resulting in an increase in their bankruptcy rate. Prior to 2000 they were supported from several measures. First, loans to SMEs were rolled over. SMEs were first classified into three groups: priority support (38.9 per cent), conditional support (55.6 per cent), and other support (5.5 per cent). For firms in the first two categories, accounting for almost 95 per cent of SMEs, banks were instructed to roll over loans maturing by December 1998.[11] In addition, the government provided 33 trillion won of guarantees for loans to small firms and additional budgetary support of 2.2 trillion won through a variety of programmes – the Guarantee Fund and the Enterprise Promotion Fund for Software. Twenty-five financial institutions also established the Corporate Restructuring Fund and raised 1.6 trillion won to assist small companies. The central bank changed its criteria for setting credit ceilings to encourage banks to support small firms. Lastly, small firms were granted tax benefits: income tax or corporate tax was reduced by half for newly established SMEs during their first five years; tax benefits associated with facility investments were made more generous.

However, support for SMEs was reduced from full to partial guarantee in 2000. Namely, the rate on bank loans to the SMEs was 7.8 per cent at the end of 2000, compared to financing from government programmes with rates of 5.5–8.25 per cent (OECD 2000). The support for technology development and venture businesses increased instead. The number of business lines reserved for SMEs, which totalled 237 in 1989, was reduced to 88 in 2000 and further lowered to 45 in 2001. In addition, the number of designated goods for government procurement decreased from 258 items in 1998 to 154 in 2000.

In addition to the previous measures by size of enterprise, various measures for enhancing the corporate governance structure were also introduced: the legal rights of minority shareholders were strengthened, by lowering the holding threshold of certain rights,[12] the role of boards of directors was further strengthened; corporations had to appoint outside directors to form one-quarter of the total board membership; and an audit committee had to be established with outside directors forming at least two-thirds of its membership. In addition, owners who played an active role in the management of corporations should be registered as their directors. These have the objective of making corporate decision-making more transparent. Transparency was further enhanced by upgrading accounting standards and requiring *chaebols* to prepare combined financial statements. Bankruptcy procedures were improved by introducing time limits, and giving greater weight to economic criteria.

Further significant reforms in the area of corporate governance implemented in 2000 included: the new corporate governance framework was expanded to include firms listed on the KOSDAQ,[13] the shadow voting requirement for mutual funds was removed,[14] and the use of cumulative voting was facilitated. In addition to these changes in the corporate governance framework, a number of other reforms were introduced: activating M&As,[15] and easing requirements on holding companies.

**Outcomes from the first stage reforms**

The initial corporate reforms achieved mixed results regarding the success in restructuring the Big Five, the top 30 *chaebols*, and in the-out-of court workouts of other large corporations.

First, in terms of the Big Five, by the end of 1999 they had succeeded in keeping their plans as agreed to in the restructuring Memorandum of Understanding (MOU) with the government. In accordance with their 1998 plan the average debt–equity ratio of the top four *chaebols*, excluding the dismantled Daewoo Group,[16] fell to 173.9 per cent by the end of 1999, down from 352 per cent in 1998 and from over 500 per cent in 1997 (see Table 4.7).[17] They also successfully implemented other restructuring plans they had announced, with an implementation rate of all over 100 per cent (see Table 4.8).

**Table 4.7**
**Improvement of the Financial Structure of the Big Four *Chaebols***

| | End-1998 | June 1999 | Implementation | | | |
|---|---|---|---|---|---|---|
| | (A) | (B) | End-1999 | | Changes | |
| | | | Plans(C) | Achievement (D) | (D-A) | (D-B) |
| Debt/equity ratio | 352.0 | 254.6 | 197.7 | 173.9 | 178.1 | 180.7 |
| Debt | 165.1 | 160.9 | 128.3 | 139.6 | 25.5 | 21.3 |
| Equity | 46.9 | 63.2 | 64.9 | 80.3 | 33.4 | 17.1 |

*Source*: Ahn (2001).

**Table 4.8**
**Implementation of the Restructuring Plans of the Top Four *Chaebols***

| | Plan | Accomplishment | Implementation rate |
|---|---|---|---|
| | 1998 (A) | 1999 (B) | (B/A, %) |
| Self-restructuring effort (trillion won) | 33.0 | 37.7 | 114.4 |
| Asset sales | 13.7 | 15.0 | 109.6 |
| Raising capital | 19.3 | 22.7 | 117.8 |
| Inducement of foreign capital (billion won) | 71.9 | 84.3 | 117.2 |
| Prohibition of cross-debt guarantee (trillion won) | 2.7 | 3.1 | 116.7 |
| Spin-offs | 173.0 | 442.0 | 255.5 |
| Improvement of corporate governance | 136.0 | 143.0 | 105.1 |
| Reduction of affiliates | 84.0 | 94.0 | 111.9 |

*Source*: Ahn (2001).

Second, broadening this to include developments in the top 30 *chaebols*, since the crisis they have experienced a number of important changes. Of the top 30 groups in 1997, 18 remained on the list in 2001 (see Table 4.9). Five of the new groups were previously part of Hyundai, the largest *chaebol* in 2000. As before the crisis the (new) top five *chaebols* still dominate, accounting for one-third of affiliated companies and almost two-thirds of assets of the top 30 groups.

**Table 4.9**
**The Top 30 *Chaebols* in 2001**

(trillion won)

| Group | Number of affiliates | | Total assets | Rank in 1997 |
|---|---|---|---|---|
| | 2000 | 2001 | | |
| 1. Samsung | 45 | 64 | 69.9 | 2 |
| 2. Hyundai | 35 | 26 | 53.6 | 1 |
| 3. LG | 43 | 43 | 52.0 | 3 |
| 4. SK | 39 | 54 | 47.4 | 5 |
| 5. Hyundai Motors | -- | 16 | 36.1 | Not on list |
| 6. Hanjin | 18 | 19 | 21.3 | 7 |
| 7. POSCO | -- | 15 | 21.2 | Not on list |
| 8. Lotte | 28 | 31 | 16.7 | 10 |
| 9. Kumho | 20 | 17 | 11.6 | 11 |
| 10. Hanwha | 23 | 25 | 11.5 | 9 |
| 11. Doosan | 16 | 18 | 11.2 | 14 |
| 12. Ssangyong | 22 | 20 | 9.0 | 6 |
| 13. Hyundai Petrochemicals | 3 | 2 | 7.2 | Not on list |
| 14. Hansol | 19 | 19 | 7.0 | 16 |
| 15. Dongbu | 19 | 19 | 5.8 | 22 |
| 16. Daelim | 18 | 17 | 5.4 | 15 |
| 17. Tongyang | 25 | 30 | 5.1 | 23 |
| 18. Hyosung | 13 | 15 | 4.9 | 17 |
| 19. Cheil Chedang | 18 | 30 | 4.8 | Not on list |
| 20. Kolon | 17 | 25 | 4.6 | 20 |
| 21. Dongkuk | 14 | 8 | 4.3 | 18 |
| 22. Hyundai Industrial Dev. | 7 | 9 | 4.1 | Not on list |
| 23. Hanaro Communications | -- | 7 | 3.4 | Not on list |
| 24. Shin Sehgye | 10 | 9 | 3.2 | Not on list |
| 25. Yeongpoong | 21 | 24 | 2.9 | Not on list |
| 26. Hyundai Department Store | -- | 15 | 2.9 | Not on list |
| 27. Dongyang Hwahak | -- | 22 | 2.8 | Not on list |
| 28. Daewoo Motors | 3 | 4 | 2.7 | Not on list |
| 29. Taekwang Sanob | -- | 15 | 2.6 | Not on list |
| 30. Kohap | 6 | 6 | 2.5 | 21 |
| Total of top 30* | 544 | 624 | 437.9 | |
| Total of top 5 | 180 | 212 | 259 | |

*Note*: *The 2000 totals are based on the rankings in 2000.

*Source*: Korea Fair Trade Commission.

The financial crisis has brought about a turning point in the behaviour of the *chaebols* in a number of ways. First, the average number of affiliates of the top 30 groups fell by a third between 1997 and 2000, as the *chaebols* sold assets to reduce their debt. The average number of affiliates, however, increased in 2001, largely as a result of an increased number of information technology-related firms. However, the new *chaebol*-affiliated companies appear to be relatively small, with the average amount of assets per firm falling by 10 per cent in 2001. In addition, the average number of business lines declined from 19 to 15 over the same period. Total assets declined between 1999 and 2001, reversing the large increases that occurred in the wake of the crisis. Second, the average debt–equity ratio of the top 30 *chaebols* has fallen significantly. The debt to equity ratio was 519 per cent in 1997, falling to just below 380 per cent in 1998, to 219 per cent at the end of 1999 and to 171 per cent at the end of 2000 for the top 30 groups, excluding their financial affiliates (see Table 4.10). To achieve the 200 per cent debt-to-equity target imposed by the government the *chaebol* issued large amounts of new equity, which rose by 125 per cent between 1997 and 2000. A 26 per cent decline in debt over the same period also contributed. Third, all of the cross-debt guarantees were resolved by March 2000, as planned, and *chaebols* were required to publish consolidated financial statements. Legal proceedings for corporate rehabilitation and bankruptcy filing have been simplified to facilitate market exit for non-viable firms, and to ensure better representation of creditor banks in the resolution process.

Additional beneficial developments included the following. Reductions in financial costs, at least relative to 1998, were accompanied by lower labour costs. The number of workers at listed firms affiliated with the *chaebols* declined by 30 per cent between 1996 and 1999, compared to a 6 per cent fall within independent companies. Consequently, labour costs fell from 12 to 8 per cent for total costs over the same period. Such cost reductions also improved profitability. The percentage of firms with interest coverage ratios[18] of less than one fell to 44 per cent for the *chaebol*-affiliated companies and to 29 per cent of independent companies. Finally, the increase in equity in 1998 and 1999 boosted the proportion of the top 30 *chaebol* that were owned by their affiliated companies in 1999. Consequently, the 'inside ownership ratio' surpassed 50 per cent in 1999, despite the continued decline in the share of the principal owner and family. The reimposition of the rule in April 2000 prohibiting *chaebol*-affiliated firms from owning more than 25 per cent of another firm, reversed the rise in shareholding by sister companies. That share declined further as firms tried to meet the 25 per cent limit by the March 2002 deadline for compliance.

As of the end of 2000, 104 firms, including Daewoo Group affiliates, had been nominated for the workout process. Of the 104 companies nominated, 36 firms had graduated while 34 remained in the programme (Table 4.11). Of the remaining 34, 19 had either been dropped out or been rejected from the programme, while 15 merged with other companies. Of the agreements reached in early 2003 20 have had to be renegotiated, as firms have been unable to meet their restructuring commitments. Ten of the remaining companies were affiliated with the Daewoo Group, which collapsed in 1999. The companies still in the programme had received a total of 71.5 trillion won of concessions as of December 2000. Of the total, 60 trillion won consisted of interest rate cuts or exemptions, while debt–equity swaps and the conversion of bonds to equity accounted for less than 6 trillion won (OECD 2001).

**Table 4.10**
**The Debt to Equity Ratio for the Top 30 *Chaebol***

| | 1997 | 1998 | 1999 | 2000 |
|---|---|---|---|---|
| A. In trillion won | | | | |
| Equity | 68.9 | 96.9 | 129.6 | 154.8 |
| Liabilities | 357.4 | 367.0 | 283.4 | 265.1 |
| Ratio (%) | 518.9 | 378.8 | 218.7 | 171.2 |
| B. Percentage change | | | | |
| Equity | | 40.7 | 33.8 | 19.5 |
| Liabilities | | 2.7 | -22.8 | -6.5 |

*Source*: Ministry of Finance and Economy.

**Table 4.11**
**Firms under the Workout Programme and Their Progress (as of end 2000)**

(number of companies)

| | Nominated (A) | Excluded: Total (B) | Dropped out | Merged | Ejected | Present: Graduated (C) | Remaining (A-B-C) |
|---|---|---|---|---|---|---|---|
| Daewoo companies | 12 | 1 | 0 | 0 | 1 | 1 | 10 |
| Affiliates of 6–64 *chaebols* | 49 | 22 | 5 | 12 | 5 | 12 | 15 |
| Medium-sized firms | 43 | 11 | 3 | 3 | 5 | 23 | 9 |
| Total | 104 | 34 | 8 | 15 | 11 | 36 | 34 |

*Source*: Shin et al. (2000).

Despite these *chaebol* advances a number of shortcomings associated with corporate restructuring remained. For example, the concentration of economic power in the hands of the top five *chaebols* deepened. According to the Fair Trade Commission the total amount of the top five *chaebols*' assets increased by 13.8 per cent in 1998. Furthermore, the total debts of the top five *chaebols* increased to 234 trillion won in 1998, up from 221 trillion won in 1997. Nonetheless the debt–equity ratios of the top five *chaebols* decreased due to the fact that the *chaebols*' mode of financing changed drastically in favour of direct financing through the stock market. Some *chaebols* attracted liquidity through trusts and mutual funds. The Big Deals for the semiconductor, oil refining, aerospace and railway vehicles industries were completed, however the Big Deals for the other industries eventually failed or were delayed.

The government repeatedly announced that the structural reforms had been, and would continue to be, driven by market forces. However, the government deeply intervened in the pace and methods of the restructuring process. For example, the government supported the Big Deals for the *chaebol* subsidiaries, informally selected the bankrupt firms for workout programmes, set a uniform reduction of the debt–equity ratio regardless of the characteristics of the business, and implicitly placed a limit on *chaebols*' entry into new business. Thus, the government needed to reduce its level of corporate intervention and institutionalize a basic corporate governance system, and the direction of corporate sector reforms needed to concentrate on profit maximization, or cost minimization, rather than just fitting the standard itself.

**The second stage programme: from government-initiated to market-driven restructuring**

As the pace of reform and growth slowed, and the financial sector was being threatened by high credit risk in mid-2000, a more market-based second round of reforms was initiated to address the outstanding problems and restore confidence in the economy. Despite the recovery in profitability, and progress in reducing debt–equity ratios and streamlining operations, a substantial portion of the corporate sector still remained financially troubled. More than a quarter of externally audited firms failed to earn enough profits to cover the interest payments on their debt in 1999, let alone repayment of principal, and this situation continued in 2000 despite buoyant growth. The situation seemed even more severe among *chaebol*-affiliated companies. The high degree of credit risk was clearly undermining confidence in the Korean economy during the course of 2000. As the impact of the injections of public funds in the first stage financial restructuring programme faded, financial institutions became increasingly cautious about lending. The tightening of loan classification standards also made banks more reluctant to lend. The resulting credit crunch conditions, combined with slower growth, exacerbated balance sheet difficulties and made it clear that the strong post-crisis expansion would not resolve all problems.

In this context the authorities launched a second round of restructuring that consisted of forcing the exit of non-viable companies, and the introduction of bond recycling schemes to allow the survival of firms judged as viable. In October 2000 the government instructed the banks to evaluate the prospects of financially distressed firms in an effort to identify which ones they should continue to support. This approach had been used previously in May 1998, resulting in the examination of 313 companies of which 55 were designated as non-viable. Firms were singled out for the second evaluation process based on three criteria: their loans were classified as precautionary or worse under the forward-looking loan classification scheme; their interest coverage ratio had been less than one for three consecutive years; or they were already being monitored by banks for default risks. A total of 287 firms were identified under at least one of these criteria for evaluation. However, this total was considerably below the number of externally audited firms found to have interest coverage ratios of below one for three consecutive years. Of the enterprises that were evaluated, 52 were classified as non-viable, of which 18 were to be liquidated, 11 were put under court receivership and 23 were to be disposed of through mergers and acquisitions. In addition, almost half of the companies (136) were judged to be normal. The remainder were classified as having 'temporary' (28) or 'structural' (69) liquidity problems. The small number of firms judged as non-viable raised doubts about the government's commitment to ensure the exit of non-viable firms.

For companies that were classified as viable and could provide normal operations, the major credit banks assumed full responsibility in providing them with financial support. Companies experiencing a temporary liquidity problem received short-term loans after they signed an agreement promising to carry out necessary self-restructuring. Companies facing structural liquidity problems, but which were able to recover, gained loan adjustments if they agreed to improve their management and business structures. Companies classified as non-viable were liquidated through transparent exit procedures. The Financial Supervisory Commission regularly monitored financial institutions and investigated whether their mechanisms were working properly.

### 4.3.2 Reforming the Corporate Governance, Control and Ownership Structure

Approaches to dealing with the issue of corporate governance and reform of the control and ownership structure are of fundamental importance to an improvement of the performance of the corporate sector. The various reforms to change corporate governance and ownership structure in Korea are now discussed, and progress made to date identified and outcomes assessed.

**Corporate governance structure**

Deficiencies in the corporate governance structure are recognized as having played a major role in the Korean financial crisis. Consequently, various reform measures have been implemented with the objective of improving corporate performance in this area. Reforms have focused upon four major areas: improving the transparency of corporate management; strengthening the rights of minority shareholders; strengthening the responsibility of controlling shareholders and management; and improving intra-group relationships.

*Improving the transparency of corporate management*

Transparency is at the core of good governance since it allows shareholders and creditors to monitor management effectively, and to prevent managers and controlling shareholders from taking actions in their own interest at the expense of that of the company (OECD 1999). Good transparency is the basis for good governance. It is especially important in Korea where the 'arbitrary imperial rule' of the *chaebol* owners has persisted. Key to better transparency, and improving and internationalizing corporate accounting standards, include, improving account auditing, the introduction of combined financial statements, and corporate public disclosure.

*Improving corporate account auditing* Korea has long been noted as a country having low comparability with international standards. Although the country's Generally-Accepted Accounting Practices (GAAP) are generally consistent with international accounting standards, important loopholes remain in terms of accuracy, timeliness, and depth and veracity of the reported information (OECD 1998). The introduction of international accounting standards is expected to enhance the credibility of accounting information and further encourage foreign investment and acquisitions. Major changes include, the elimination of deferred assets and liabilities, the introduction of new rules for the accounting of derivatives, the adoption of limits on asset revaluation; and reduction in the scope for shifting between different accounting standards in corporate accounts (OECD 1999).

The government also improved the credibility of auditing procedures by guaranteeing the independence of certified public accountants. In addition, the Law Concerning External Auditing of Joint Stock Corporations, passed in February 1998 and effective since April 1998, required corporations to establish an Auditor Selection Committee including outside directors and major creditors and shareholders. The law was aimed at increasing public confidence in the external auditing of the listed companies and affiliates within conglomerates, and at increasing penalties on external audits and company accounts, so that trustworthiness of the financial statements and transparency of the business management would be enhanced. Furthermore, listed companies with assets of more than 1 trillion won had to appoint a full-time statutory auditor. In addition, the government extended the minimum contract for an auditor to three years and restricted shareholders with more than 3 per cent of common stock from executing their voting power above that level in the appointment of auditors.

*Combined financial statements* The second effort to enhance transparency was the introduction of the mandatory combined financial statement.[19] The Korean government agreed with the IMF to set the standards for combined financial statements by October 1998, introduce them in 1999, and require quarterly reporting in 2000. In the absence of combined financial statements, the extremely complicated web of intra-group loans, guarantees and other transactions remained opaque to most investors (OECD 1998). Thus, the new combined financial statements system would make it easier to control management by unifying the *chaebols*' financial statements, which used to be under the control of the powerful owners, and clarifying intra-group transactions, shares held among affiliates, cross–debt guarantees and credit trading.

A unique aspect of Korea's approach is the broad definition given to the concepts of joint control or common management by the Fair Trade Commission in the combined statements (OECD 1998). At the same time the combined statements are to include disclosure of intra-group transactions and individual affiliate information in the footnotes, as well as segmented reporting (also known as business-line accounting) (OECD 1998).

*Improving corporate public disclosure* The purpose of corporate public disclosure is to enable investors to apply reasonable judgement and to conduct fair business in the securities market, by giving fast and accurate information on corporations, such as past, current and future management, financial affairs and business plans. Thus, corporate public disclosure activates the monitoring of management and the establishment of an efficient corporate governance structure, by making public important information on matters related to corporations.

In the sixth Letter of Intent the government agreed with the IMF to publish biannual financial statements, prepared and reviewed by external auditors in accordance with international standards, by the end of August 1998; and to publish quarterly the non-audited financial statements as from 1 January 2000. In the case of Korean business conglomerates, publication of the combined financial statements for their affiliate companies is also required.

### *Strengthening minority shareholder rights*

The government strengthened the rights of minority shareholders, and relaxed the conditions for exercising these rights, through a revision of the Commercial Code in December 1998, protecting them from expropriation by dominant shareholders and managers (OECD 1999). A summary of these is contained in Table 4.12. In particular, the government lowered various kinds of minimum shareholding requirements. The requirements for the judicial removal of a director were reduced from 5 per cent to 3 per cent, and the right to injunction from 5 per cent to 1 per cent. The requirement to launch derivative suits was lowered from 5 per cent to 1 per cent and the requirement for the inspection of a company's account books, affairs and company property reduced from 5 per cent to 3 per cent. A new article on shareholder proposals in statements was added to the new Commercial Code, requiring 3 per cent of total shares.

**Strengthening the responsibility of controlling shareholders and management**
An important measure to strengthen the responsibility of controlling shareholders and management was the introduction of outsider directors. The introduction of outside directors normalized the role of the board of directors, by breaking from former practice of the board merely serving as a 'rubber stamp' for management decisions. The controlling shareholders exercised enormous power over the appointment of directors, making it very difficult for directors to secure their independence from, and to monitor, management.

**Table 4.12**
**Minimum Ownership to Exercise Rights**

(share of common stock in %)

| | Former Commercial code | New code | For listed companies[1] | |
|---|---|---|---|---|
| | | | Small | Big |
| Judicial removal of a director | 5 | 3 | 0.5 | 0.25 |
| Right to an injunction | 5 | 1 | 0.5 | 0.25 |
| Right to file a derivative suit | 5 | 1 | 0.01 | 0.01 |
| Shareholder's proposal in statements | – | 3 | 1 | 0.5 |
| Right to inspect account books | 5 | 3 | 1 | 0.5 |
| Right to inspect affairs and company property | 5 | 3 | 3 | 1.5 |
| Removal of liquidator | 5 | 3 | 0.5 | 0.25 |

*Note*: Small companies are those with paid–in capital of less than 100 billion won.

*Source*: KERI.

From February 1998 the government required listed companies to appoint and authorize outside directors. Thereafter, all listed companies were required to have at least one outside director on their boards. Furthermore, since 1999 most listed companies have been required to appoint outside directors to fill one-quarter of their board seats. In order for outside directors fully to fulfill their function, individual companies need to formulate and make public the operational guidelines for their executive boards to demonstrate their commitment to transparent management.

Another measure to strengthen the responsibility of controlling shareholders and management was the systemizing of the voting rights of institutional investors with the new Securities Investment Trust Law. Before the crisis the role of institutional investors in supervising the controlling shareholders and management was severely curtailed because of the severe restrictions on their voting rights. Institutionalizing the voting rights of institutional investors would force management to make their business decisions on the basis of profitability.

*Prohibition of inappropriate intra-group transactions and debt guarantees*

*Inappropriate intra-group transactions* The Korea Fair Trade Commission has investigated inappropriate intra-group transactions[20] since 1997, and has the authority to demand the submission of financial statements from the 30 largest conglomerates.

The rate of intra-group transactions of the listed companies of the top 30 groups in 1997 was 27.74 per cent, with the bigger groups showing a higher rate of such transactions (see Table 4.13). Also, the rate of these types of transactions had been on an upward swing since 1987. A provision added to the Fair Trade Act in 1996 made the 'undue provision of money', illegal, with 'undue' defined as 'a substantial deviation from the expected result of an arm's length relationship in the market' (OECD 2000). The Korea Fair Trade Commission can impose fines of up to 2 per cent of the amount of inappropriate intra-group transactions.

**Table 4.13**
**The Rate of Intra-group Transactions among the Top Thirty Groups before 1998**

| Group | 1986 | 1987 | 1988 | 1989 | 1996 | 1997 |
|---|---|---|---|---|---|---|
| Top 5th | 28.25 | 25.52 | 27.71 | 29.62 | 29.80 | 35.77 |
| Top 10th | 26.27 | 24.36 | 25.55 | 26.37 | 29.16 | 32.77 |
| Top 20th | 24.17 | 22.61 | 24.14 | 24.42 | 27.14 | 29.85 |
| Top 30th | 23.14 | 21.98 | 23.39 | 23.73 | 26.94 | 27.74 |

*Source*: KERI.

The FTC launched three rounds of investigations between 1998 and 1999 on intra-group transactions among the top five *chaebols*. Eighty companies had provided a total of 4 trillion won of support to 35 affiliates and were fined 72.2 billion won as a result of the first round of investigations. The second round of investigations found that 33 companies had provided 1.4 trillion won of support to 21 affiliates and were fined 20.9 billion won for inappropriate intra-transactions. In the third round of investigations, 53 companies were fined 78.9 billion won for a total of 12.3 trillion won of support to 21 affiliates. These results appeared to confirm suspicions that the owners of the conglomerates were trying to support their weak firms by cross-subsidizing them with funds from affiliated companies (OECD 1999).

*Abolishing mutual debt guarantees* The Korean government had begun regulating mutual debt guarantees with the amendment of the Fair Trade Act in 1993. As a result the ratio of debt guarantees substantially decreased from 342 per cent in 1993 to 47.7 per cent in 1997 (see Table 4.14). However, bankruptcies caused by excessive borrowing and affiliate expansion using debt, as in the cases of Hanbo, Jinro and Kia, raised questions about the effectiveness of the regulations. Consequently, the government strengthened the limits on debt guarantees between affiliates of the top 30 groups to 100 per cent from April 1998. New debt guarantees among *chaebol* affiliates were prohibited, and existing guarantees eliminated by March 2000. Debt guarantees scheduled to expire in 2001 or beyond were to be negotiated with banks for extensions.

**Table 4.14**
**Debt Guarantees, Trend of the Top 30 Groups**

(trillion won, %)

| Date | Equity (A) | Debt guarantee | | | Net worth to total assets | |
|---|---|---|---|---|---|---|
| | | Total (B) | Restricted companies(C) | Excluded companies (D) | B/A | C/A |
| April 1993 | 35.2 | 165.5 | 120.6 | 44.9 | 469.8 | 342.4 |
| April 1994 | 42.8 | 110.7 | 72.5 | 38.2 | 258.1 | 169.3 |
| April 1995 | 50.7 | 82.1 | 48.3 | 33.8 | 161.9 | 95.2 |
| April 1996 | 62.9 | 67.5 | 35.2 | 32.3 | 107.3 | 55.9 |
| April 1997 | 70.4 | 64.9 | 33.6 | 31.3 | 92.2 | 47.7 |
| April 1998 | 68.1 | 63.5 | 26.9 | 36.6 | 93.1 | 39.5 |
| April 1999 | 100.1 | 22.4 | 9.8 | 12.6 | 22.3 | 9.7 |

*Source*: Fair Trade Commission (2000).

## Corporate control and ownership structure

A crucial characteristic of the *chaebols* is their ownership concentration. The founding families of a *chaebol* group normally owned a large share of the firms. The common practice in management of the *chaebol* is that the owners, who are often non-professional managers, have greater voting power than other shareholders and thus can exercise exclusive control of the firm. In addition, in these *chaebols*, controlling shareholders exercise control in excess of their holdings through a hierarchical chain of ownership (Chang

2002). This is an example of the non-separation of ownership and management of the *chaebol*. It is apparent that the two concepts – the concentration of ownership and non-separation of ownership and management – are a related issue.

Agency theories suggest two different predictions. According to the convergence-of-interest hypothesis the non-separation of ownership and management is beneficial to the performance of firms, since there is a smaller degree of conflict of interest between the two groups. The other prediction, based on the entrenchment hypothesis, is that firm value decreases as managerial ownership increases, because managers – be they professional or the owners – with substantial shares of the firm can provide them with sufficient voting power to guarantee their employment with high compensation.[21]

These different hypotheses, however, converge to an agreed conventional wisdom that the ownership structure affects firm performance or value. Morck et al. (1988), based on empirical investigation of American firms, found that there is a non-linear relationship between ownership structure and firm value and that ownership structure indeed affects firm value. However, recent research on Korean firms gives a different result. Chang (2002) shows that it is performance that determines ownership, rather than the other way around. Cho and Chae (2002) argue that while individual ownership does not affect corporate value, vertical relationships among the affiliates of *chaebols* through equity holdings is an important factor that positively affects corporate value.

## 4.4 MARKET LIBERALIZATION MEASURES AND CORPORATE RESTRUCTURING

While the reforms identified previously were aimed directly at the corporate sector, indirect market liberalizing reforms were also implemented to enhance its performance. Market liberalization measures were aimed at solving the structural problems of the corporate sector, inherited from development strategies in the past, and, most importantly, to inject liquidity into the credit-stricken economy. Hence, market liberalization reforms were seen as indirect measures, reinforcing explicit corporate debt restructuring measures and corporate governance reforms.

Three market liberalization measures affecting the performance of the corporate sector were those focusing upon investment, capital and foreign exchange markets, and trade. Emphasis is given here to the first two only. These, it was hoped, would result in an inflow of foreign capital, which would help in solving two major problems. First, foreign capital inflows could assist in overcoming deep-rooted structural inefficiency inherent in the corporate sector by introducing competition, a more market-oriented and less government-led corporate environment, and the application of more advanced management techniques. Second, foreign capital inflows would inject badly needed liquidity into the corporate sector. The financial crisis led to a credit crunch in the economy, further worsening the illiquid corporate sector. Liquidity was desperately needed from abroad, and the three major channels through which it could enter the economy were FDI, capital and foreign exchange markets, and trade. A brief assessment of the contribution of FDI and foreign capital flows more generally to corporate sector restructuring, as well as to the overall recovery of the economy after the crisis, is now conducted.

**Investment and foreign capital liberalization**

Korea was remarkably successful in attracting foreign capital after the financial crisis. While foreign direct investment (FDI) inflows had been increasing steadily from the early 1990s they increased noticeably after 1997, increasing nearly fivefold in three years from US$3.2 billion in 1996 to US$15.5 billion in 1999 (see Table 4.15). FDI inflows during the four-year period from 1998 to 2001 amounted to about 68 per cent of total FDI inflows in Korean history. This increased foreign investment, especially in the period directly after the financial crisis, helped improve the liquidity and cash flow of the cash-strapped, highly leveraged and indebted corporate sector. However, and perhaps more importantly in the long run, it also promoted and funded the market-oriented corporate restructuring, and it also brought other non-financial and non-tangible benefits such as foreign participation in management and financial market discipline.

Investment liberalization contributed to corporate restructuring in five key areas: foreign capital, foreign currency, domestic production, exports, and non-financial and non-tangible benefits. First, FDI liberalization attracted foreign capital which promoted, and funded, more market-oriented corporate restructuring. Foreign capital inflow was the only source of liquidity that helped the cash flow of highly leveraged and indebted Korean corporations. Second, by bringing in foreign currency it also increased the country's foreign reserves and stabilized the won. Third, domestic production and employment increased due to increased FDI, offsetting to some extent domestic shocks from the financial crisis. In addition, FDI restrained the fall in employment in the manufacturing sector. Fourth, FDI increased exports and improved the balance of payments. Finally, there are non-financial and non-tangible benefits from increased FDI. They include more modern management techniques introduced by the new foreign owners, and more advanced technologies transferred through the intensive technological consultation of the foreign companies with the Korean subcontractors. These enhanced the competitiveness of Korean firms.

Prior to the financial crisis, foreign investors faced direct or indirect restrictions on investment activities such as restrictions on investment in certain businesses, limits on the amount of shares held in a company, or restrictions in relation to land ownership. But many of these were significantly

**Table 4.15**
**FDI Inflows into Korea**

(US$ million)

| Year | FDI Inflows [1] |
|---|---|
| 1962–81[2] | 93.3 |
| 1982–86[2] | 353.5 |
| 1987–88[2] | 1 173.5 |
| 1989 | 1 090.3 |
| 1990 | 802.6 |
| 1991 | 1 396.0 |
| 1992 | 894.5 |
| 1993 | 1 044.3 |
| 1994 | 1 316.5 |
| 1995 | 1 947.2 |
| 1996 | 3 020.6 |
| 1997 | 6 970.9 |
| 1998 | 8 852.5 |
| 1999 | 15 541.5 |
| 2000 | 15 696.7 |
| 2001 | 17 870.0[3] |
| 2002. 1–8 | 9 718.0[3] |
| Cumulated | 83 324.0[3] |

*Note*: 1 Equity investment of more than 10 per cent of equity capital by a single person or firm, and intra-company loans with maturities of five years or more are considered foreign direct investment. FDI inflows are on a notification basis.
2 Figures are the annual average for 1962–81, 1982–86, and 1987–88.
3 Only available as whole figures.

*Source*: Ministry of Commerce, Industry and Energy (MOCIE).

removed, or at least eased, through the enactment of the Foreign Investment Promotion Act in 1998, that led to the liberalization of the capital market and the removal of restrictions on hostile takeovers of local companies by foreign ones (KPMG 2001).

A number of investment liberalization measures were adopted. First, by 2002, 99.8 per cent of all business sectors were opened to foreign investment (Kim and Choo 2002), a level on a par with other OECD economies. Two areas, however, remain entirely closed to foreign investment: radio and television broadcasting. Second, all types of FDI are now permitted, including the establishment of a new business, acquisition of shares from capital increases arising from existing companies, acquisition of existing shares in a business, M&As, and long-term loan investment such as investment in privately owned companies. Third, cross-border M&As were liberalized. The requirement for foreign investors to obtain approval from the Minister of Finance and Economy when acquiring shares of a Korean company with an asset size of more than 2 trillion won, was abolished. Also, restrictions on hostile M&As of Korean companies by foreign companies were freed. The requirement that foreign investors wishing to purchase more than 25 per cent of the shares of a listed company had to publicly acquire more than 50 per cent of the company's shares, was also abolished. Fourth, land acquisition by foreigners was liberalized. The real estate market was fully opened to foreign purchasers in June 1998, with very few exceptions for cultural landmarks and military purposes. Various strict controls of foreign ownership of land had previously limited foreign business activities in Korea. But now, regardless of their purposes or the size of the land, they are on equal terms with Korean nationals. Foreign purchases of land amounted to US$880 million dollars in 1998, and the area of land held by foreigners increased fourfold in 1998. Finally, restrictions on fund transfers by foreigners were eased. The Foreign Investment Promotion Act now legally and unconditionally guarantees international remittances by foreign investors.

This series of liberalization and reform measures, as indicated previously, sharply increased FDI inflows. The two major channels through which FDI flowed into Korea were cross-border M&As and privatization. These are now examined briefly.

**Cross-border M&As**

The liberalization of M&As had two purposes. First, to bring in foreign exchange. Second, and more importantly, to introduce more modern management techniques and to intensify competition in Korea, with the objective of making the economy more efficient. Cross-border mergers increased significantly after they were first allowed in 1997. In 1998, sales of newly issued and outstanding corporate stocks and corporate assets bought by foreign investors reached US$1.8 billion and US$2.9 billion respectively. Together they accounted for 60.9 per cent of total foreign investment in that year. In the case of acquisition of outstanding stocks, foreign companies acquired the shares of troubled domestic joint venture partner companies and subsequently became the sole owner. In the case of acquisition of newly issued stocks the investments were in the formation of joint ventures through additional capital infusion in already existing businesses, and in the establishment of new companies through asset acquisition.

M&As by foreign firms increased after the financial crisis in response not only to deregulation of laws restricting hostile M&As, but also due to lower domestic asset prices and the depreciation of the won. In addition there were abundant acquisition opportunities, as many distressed firms were selling off parts of their business lines in the process of restructuring. In many cases, rescue funds flowed in from existing foreign partners to ease liquidity constraints. Common forms of M&As have included buying out joint venture partners, existing investors expanding through acquisition and the creation of new establishments in collaboration with Korean partners to acquire existing business units.

As Table 4.16 shows, a large part of FDI was made through M&As rather than greenfield investment. A large part of corporate restructuring was conducted through the acquisition of outstanding stocks by foreigners. In 1998, for example, M&As accounted for 47.8 per cent of all FDI inflows and, in particular, the acquisition of assets accounted for 37.4 per cent.

**Table 4.16**
**Pattern of Inward FDI in 1998**

(US$ million, %)

| **Classification** | Acquisition of newly issued **Stocks** | | | **M&A** | | | **Long-term Loan** | **Total** |
|---|---|---|---|---|---|---|---|---|
| | New | Added | Sub-total | AOS | AA | Sub-total | | |
| Invested amount US$m | 1020 | 2049 | 3069 | 820 | 2930 | 3750 | 1019 | 7838 |
| (%) | (13.0) | (26.1) | (39.2) | (10.5) | (37.4) | (47.8) | (13.0) | (100.0) |
| Investment size per case | 46.4 | 42.7 | 43.8 | 27.3 | 154.2 | 76.5 | 113.2 | 61.2 |

*Note*: Investment exceeding US$10 million.
AOS (Acquisition of outstanding stocks).
AA (Acquisition of Asset).

*Source*: MOCIE, and Rhee (1999).

Table 4.17 shows that the level of M&As increased dramatically from US$192 million in 1995 to US$3.65 billion in 2001. Of particular note is the sudden jump of inward M&As from US$836 million in 1997 to US$3.97 billion in 1998. FDI inflows also increased from US$1.78 billion in 1995 to US$9.28 billion in 2000. The low figures in 2001 can be accounted for by the global economic recession.

This massive scale of foreign purchases of the shares and assets of Korean companies enlarged their scope and scale of business. Increased cross-border M&As by foreign companies increased their market shares in Korea. In addition, cross-border M&As have brought global management practices such as good capital structure, profit orientation, efficient management processes and a merit-based personnel system (Rhee 1999). Market competition has also been affected, with domestic companies facing fiercer competition both domestically and in global markets.

**Table 4.17**
**Trends of FDI and Cross-border M&As**

(US$ million, %)

| | 1995 | 1996 | 1997 | 1998 | 1999 | 2000 | 2001 |
|---|---|---|---|---|---|---|---|
| FDI inflow (A) | 1 776 | 2 325 | 2 844 | 5 412 | 9 333 | 9 283 | 3 198 |
| Cross-border M&A sales (B) | 192 | 564 | 836 | 3 973 | 10 062 | 6 448 | 3 648 |
| Ratio (B/A) | 10.8 | 24.3 | 29.4 | 73.4 | 100.0* | 69.5 | 100.0* |
| FDI outflow (C) | 3 552 | 4 670 | 4 449 | 4 740 | 4 198 | 4 999 | 2 600 |
| Cross-border M&A purchase (D) | 1 392 | 1 659 | 2 379 | 187 | 1 097 | 1 712 | 175 |
| Ratio (D/C) | 39.2 | 35.5 | 53.5 | 3.9 | 26.1 | 34.2 | 6.7 |

*Note*: FDI includes cross-border M&As and greenfield investment. Thus, theoretically the Ratio (B/A) cannot exceed 100 per cent. But calculation from the data yields figures greater than 100 per cent because the figure for FDI has been measured on the arrival basis while cross-border M&As have been measured on the notification basis. All calculated figures exceeding 100 per cent are thus adjusted to 100 per cent.

*Source*: UNCTAD (2002).

**Privatization**

A second, and new, channel for FDI is privatization. On 3 July 1998 the first privatization plans for public enterprises were announced. This included 32 public enterprises – 11 public investment and financing institutions and their 21 subsidiaries – out of 108.[22] There were two stages of privatization: immediate and phased privatization. As a general rule more market-oriented public enterprises were privatized, and, when early privatization was not feasible in the first instance, privatization followed structural reforms of the enterprises with yearly check-up programmes.

The former case included five public enterprises and the latter case included six others. The number of public enterprises subject to privatization accounted for only 30 per cent of the total 108 public enterprises, but in terms of the number of employees and sales revenue they accounted for 70 per cent (Cho 2001).

Foreign investors could acquire shares of a Korean company without being restricted by foreign investment ceilings except in POSCO (Pohang Steel and Iron Corporation), KEPCO (Korea Electric Power Corporation), Korea Telecom, Korea Gas Corporation and Korea Tobacco and Ginseng Corporation, although the specified ceilings varied for different state-owned enterprises. However, in the process of privatization, the government gradually reduced the level of regulation: POSCO's 30 per cent ceiling on acquisition of shares by foreigners and 3 per cent ceiling by a single foreign investor were lifted in 2001; the restriction on acquisition of Korean Tobacco and Ginseng Corporation by a single person was eliminated in 2000 (Yun and Park 1999).

## 4.5 SUMMARY AND CONCLUSIONS

Despite the restructuring of the corporate sector it still remains highly leveraged by international standards, and continues to suffer from low profitability. Although cash flows have improved and the interest coverage ratio (ICR) has also improved greatly, to 132.6 per cent in 2001 from 68.3 per cent in 1998, this improvement, however, did not come from increased earnings or the profitability of corporations, but rather came from the reductions of interest payments due to the lower interest rate in 2000 and 2001. One in four companies in the top 64 *chaebols* were unable to generate enough cash flow to meet their interest payments in 1999 (Richards et al. 2002). Major indexes of profitability, such as ordinary income to sales, return on equity or return on assets, have all shown little improvement.

The survival of such financially troubled firms can impose a drag on the economy. In 1999, 5 per cent of firms had been unable to even meet their interest payments for three consecutive years.[23] Non-viable companies absorbed resources that could be allocated to more productive enterprises. In addition, being protected from creditors, they are able to dump products, thereby eroding the profit margins of viable companies and distorting competition both domestically and abroad. They also hinder the establishment of a healthy financial sector.

The restructuring of the Big Five, and out of court workouts of other large corporations, have had mixed results, and lead banks have been accused of including firms that should have been immediately liquidated. Further improvements in legal bankruptcy procedures are needed. Given their financial fragility the banks were reluctant to absorb losses, and tried to keep many troubled firms on their balance sheets that were in fact unlikely to survive. The lead banks were also unable to devise a comprehensive set of workout criteria involving debt–equity swaps, debt write–downs and debt rescheduling. The absence of comprehensive criteria raised concerns about the fairness and effectiveness of using differential measures to support different firms in various industries. Disagreements over loan loss provisioning, disputes over asset valuation, and managers' resistance to losing control all further complicated the process. Consequently, many firms failed to meet their obligations to their lead banks. Some critics also argued that preferential financial treatment for the indebted firms might unnecessarily prolong the lives of failing firms, eat away at banks' assets and exacerbate the credit crunch on other firms.

The restructuring impact of the Big Deals has also been mixed. Whether or not the excess capacity problems that plagued Korea's *chaebols* have been solved remains unclear. Evidence is also mixed as to whether the Big Four have fulfilled their commitments to improve corporate governance and slimming down to a few core businesses. The effectiveness of the Big Deals remains unclear. The new firms created by the Big Deals remain in financial distress due to weak finances because no debt reduction or injection of new capital had taken place. Without lay-offs and plant closures excess capacity problems will remain, while reducing the number of firms reduces competition and facilitates collusive behaviour. However, inflows of FDI, particularly in the form of M&As, have increased rapidly and this has exerted beneficial effects in the short run, in terms of providing desperately needed liquidity, and will also do so over the long term.

Finally, many aspects of corporate governance, in particular transparency and auditing, have shown significant improvement after the reforms.

## NOTES

1 Indeed, the level of Korea's short-term foreign debt was more than six time higher than its foreign exchange reserves (Lim 2001b).

2 Korea's large industrial conglomerates.

3 See Jwa (2001), p. 31.

4 In 1997 the debt to equity ratio of Korean firms was 397.3 per cent, much higher than that of other countries such as the US and Japan whose ratios were 153.8 per cent and 186.4 per cent respectively (OECD 1998). In addition, this debt was becoming increasing short term in nature and owed to foreign institutions. In 1997, short-term debts accounted for two-thirds of total corporate debt, of which a quarter was from foreign institutions.

5 Discussed in more detail in section 4.4.

6 The 'control pyramid system' means that a certain shareholder has control over the management of the main business, which becomes the dominant shareholder of other business lines by controlling the assets of other businesses with its small amount of assets.

7 In addition to the above eight tasks, three accompanying principles were added to reinforce them. First, financial institutions, which had provided loans to corporations, were to take a leading role in promoting corporate restructuring. Second, the principle of burden sharing was to be applied in the process of corporate restructuring. Third, the workout programme was to be used as the main tool for corporate restructuring (Zang and Wang 1998).

8 The Capital Structure Improvement Plans (CSIPs), established

through an agreement between the top 64 Korean business groups and their lead creditor banks in early 1998, required the *chaebols* to reduce their debt-to-equity ratios to less than 200 per cent, sell off non-viable affiliates and reduce intra-group debt guarantees (Zang and Wang 1998). They also had to consult with their lead banks on these material developments and report to them on their CSIP implementation twice a year.

9 The agreement also emphasized the reduction of debt-to-equity ratios. Other points included the exit of non-viable firms, independent management of *chaebol* affiliates, the elimination of intra-group debt guarantees and the transparency of corporate management (OECD 1999).

10 There are three approaches to corporate restructuring: the centralized approach, the decentralized approach and the London approach. The London approach is a mixture of the first two, where corporate debt restructuring is overseen by an arbitrator mediating between the companies and financial institutions (Shin et al. 2000).

11 Firms in the category of conditional support were required to reduce their debt-to-equity ratios and to improve their capital structure by disposing of real-estate holdings (OECD 1999).

12 Initiating derivative suits: from 1 per cent to 0.01 per cent of total issued shares. Requesting dismissal of directors for misconduct: from 3.0 per cent to 0.5 per cent of total issued shares, reduced further to 0.05 per cent in 2000. Right to inspect the books and records: from 3.0 per cent to 1.0 per cent of total issued shares, reduced further to 0.1 per cent in 2000. Shareholders' right to make a proposal: from 3 per cent to 1 per cent of total issued shares.

13 Such firms had to have at least two outside directors in 2001 and 2002, and outside directors must account for a quarter of the number of directors. Companies listed on KOSDAQ that have more than 2 trillion won of capital have to comply with the same corporate governance practices required of firms listed on the Korea Stock Exchange.

14 Allowing them to exercise their voting rights, and to become a new monitor of corporate performance.

15 Purchasers no longer had to report to the Financial Supervisory Commission prior to the announcement of a takeover bid. In addition, they could acquire shares three days after the announcement rather than seven.

16 The Daewoo Group was dissolved in 1999.

17 Sakong (2000) suggests that the debt to equity ratio of the top five *chaebols* fell to 150 per cent in 2000, although the absolute amount of the *chaebols*' debt remained about the same as in 1997.

18 The ratio of operating profits to interest expenses.

19 Combined financial statements are similar to consolidated financial statements, as their main purpose is to net out intra-group transactions (OECD 1999).

20 Intra-group transactions mean business transactions between affiliates of one *chaebol*. Not all intra-group transactions can be regarded as illegal, because there are likely to be necessary transactions between affiliates. There are four types of illegal intra-group transactions: to give an advantage in terms of prices and conditions for manufactured goods to business affiliates; to put pressure on executives and employees to buy or sell the manufactured goods of affiliates; to force suppliers to buy the manufactured goods of affiliates; and to avoid business transactions with non-affiliates without a good reason.

21 See Cho and Chae (2002).

22 Public enterprises include 13 public investment institutions and their 30 subsidiaries, and 13 public financing institutions and their 52 subsidiaries.

23 In 1999 and 2000 a quarter of externally audited companies did not earn enough profits to pay even the interest cost on their debt, let alone repay the principle (OECD 2001, p. 9).

## REFERENCES

Ahn, C.Y. (2001), 'Financial and Corporate Sector Restructuring in South Korea: Accomplishments and Unfinished Agenda', *Japanese Economic Review*, **52**(4), 452–70.

Ahn, C.Y. (2002), 'Restructuring the Financial and Corporate Sector: The South Korean Experience', prepared for the MDT Workshop, University of Tokyo, 22–24 July.

Bank of Korea (1999), *Financial Statement Analysis,* Seoul.

Chang, S.J. (2002), 'Ownership Structure, Expropriation, and Performance of Group-Affiliated Companies in Korea', paper presented at the Second Asian Corporate Governance Conference, hosted by Asian Institute of Corporate Governance, 16 May.

Cho, M.H. and H.B. Chae (2002), 'Ownership Structure and the Value of the Firm in Korean Chaebols: An Empirical Analysis', in R. Hooley and J. Yoo (eds), *The Post-Financial Crisis Challenges for Asian Industrialization*, Amsterdam: Elsevier Science.

Cho, S.H. (2001), 'The Policy of Privatization through Capital Market', *Issue Paper* 01-03, Korea Stock Exchange (in Korean).

Chopra, A., K.H. Kang, M. Karasulu, H. Liang, H.P. Ma, and A.J. Richards (2001), 'From Crisis to Recovery in Korea: Strategy, Achievements, and Lessons', *IMF Working Paper*, WP/01/154.

Gregory, G., C. Harvie and H.H. Lee (2002), 'Korean SMEs in the Twenty First Century: Strategies, Constraints and Performance in a Global Economy', *Economic Papers*, **21**(3), 64–79.

Haggard, S., W.H. Lim and E.S. Kim (eds) (2003), *Economic Crisis and Corporate Restructuring in Korea*, Cambridge: Cambridge University Press.

Haley, U.C.V. (2000), 'Corporate Governance and Restructuring in East Asia: An Overview', *Seoul Journal of Economics*, **13**(3), 225–51.

Harvie, C. and H.H. Lee (2003), 'Export Led Industrialisation and Growth – Korea's Economic Miracle 1962-89, *Australian Economic History Journal*, **43**(4), 256–86.

Hwang, I. (1999), 'The Ownership and Control of Chaebols', in S. Lee, S.H. Jwa, K.S. Jung, and K.T. Kim (eds), *Present and Future of Corporate Governance Stucture in Korea*, Seoul: Korea Institute for Management Development.

Hwang, I. (2000), 'Aggregate Concentration, Market Concentration and Diversification: The Korean Case', *Korean Journal of Industrial Organization*, **8**(1), 49–74.

IMF (1998) 'Corporate Debt Restructuring in East Asia: Some Lessons from national Experience', *IMF Paper on Policy Analysis and Assessment*, 98/13.

Jwa, S.H. (2001), *A New Paradigm for Korea's Economic Development*: *from Government Control to Market Economy*, Basingstoke: Palgrave Macmillan.

Jwa, S.H. (2002), *The Evolution of Large Corporations in Korea: A New Institutional Economics Perspective of the Chaebol*, Cheltenham: Edward Elgar Publishing.

Kim, W.S. and M.J. Choo (2002), *Managing the Road to Globalization: the Korean Experience*, KOTRA.

Korea Institute for Industrial Economics and Trade (2001), 'Five Economic Effects of FDI', Monograph, Seoul.

Korea National Statistical Office (2002) Statistical Database KOSIS, available at http://www. nso.go.kr:7001/main.cfm.

KPMG Consulting (2001), 'Foreign Direct Investment in Korea', *Summary Report.*

La Porta, R., F. Lopez-de-Silanes, A. Shleifer and R.W. Vishny (1999), 'Investor Protection: Origins, Consequences, and Reform', NBER.

Lim, W.H. (2001a), 'The Evolution of Korea's Development Paradigm: Old Legacies and Emerging Trends in the Post-Crisis Era', *ADB Institute Working Paper Series*, No. 21.

Lim, W.H. (2002), 'Korea: Corporate Vulnerabilities and Restructuring', mimeo, Sep. Korea Development Institute.

MOCIE ~ Ministry of Commerce, Industry and Energy (2001), *Trends of Foreign Investment*, Seoul, Korea.

Morck, R., A. Shleifer and W. Vishney (1988), 'Market Ownership and Market Valuation: an Empirical Analysis', *Journal of Financial Economics*, 20, 293–315.

Nam, I.C., J.K. Kim, Y.J. Kang, S.W. Joh and J.I. Kim (1999), 'Corporate Governance in Korea', *KDI Working Paper*, 9915, Korea Development Institute.

OECD – Organization for Economic Corporation and Development (1998, 1999, 2000, 2001), *OECD Economic Surveys,* Paris.

Park, Y.C. (2001), 'The East Asian Dilemma: Restructuring Out or Growing out?' *Essays in International Economics*, No. 223, August, Princeton: Princeton University.

Rhee, D.K. (1999), 'The Entry of Foreign Multinationals and Its Impact on Korean Market', paper presented at the International Seminar on the Entry of Foreign M&A and the Globalization of the Korean Economy, hosted by Korean Institute for International Economic Policy, 30 November

Richards, A., K. Kang, H. Liang, S. Kalra, A.T. Win, C. Christofides, M. Karasulu and Q. Kong (2002, 2001), 'Republic of Korea: Selected Issues', *IMF Country Report*, No. 02/20.

Sakang, I. (2000), 'Korean Economic Restructuring: Current Status and Prospects', Keynote address at the conference entitled 'Has Economic Reform in Korea Stalled? Assessing Progress in Restructuring the Korean Economy, Korean Society', New York, 11 December.

Shin, I., D.Y. Yang, Y. Wang and S.B Lee (2000), *Korea's 3-Year IMF Program*, Korean Institute for International Economic Policy (KIEP) (in Korean).

Sohn, C.H. (2002a), 'Debt Resolution, Cross-Border M&As, Governance and Control in Korea's Post-Crisis Corporate Restructuring', *Discussion Paper*, 02-10, KIEP.

Sohn, C.H. (2002b), 'Korea's Corporate Restructuring since the Financial Crisis', *Discussion Paper*, 02-12, KIEP.

Sohn, C.H. and J.S. Yang (1998), 'Korea's Economic Reform Measures under the IMF Program', *Policy Paper*, 98-01, KIEP.

Sohn, C.H., Yang, J.S., and Kim, S.B. (2002), 'Liberalization Measures in the process of Korea's Corporate Restructuring: Trade, Investment and Capital Account Market Openings', *Discussion Paper*, 02-11, KIEP.

Stiglitz, J. (1999), 'The Korean Miracle: Growth, Crisis, and Recovery Accomplishment of the Past, Challenges of the Future', a keynote speech at the International Conference on Economic Crisis and Restructuring in Korea hosted by Korea Development Institute, 3 December.

UNCTAD (2002), *World Investment Report 5: Transnational Corporations and Export Competitiveness.*

World Bank (1999), *Asian Corporate Recovery: Corporate Governance,*

*Government Policy,* Washington, DC.

Yoo, Y.J. (2000), 'Foreign Capital and the Korean Economy', *CEO Information*, No. 24, Samsung Economic Research Institute (in Korean).

Yook, S.H., B.I. Choi, and E.K. Lee (2001), 'Conditions for a Successful Workout', *Research Paper*, Bank of Korea (in Korean).

Yun, M. and Y.H. Park (1999), 'The Role of Foreign Investment in Korean Privatization', *Journal of International Economic Studies*, **3**(2).

Zang, H. and Wang, Y. (1998), *Adjustment Reforms in Korea since the Financial Crisis I: A Comprehensive Report I*, Korea Institute for International Economic Policy (in Korean).

# 5. Reforming the Korean Labour Market and Social Safety Net: Key Pending Issues

**John P. Martin, Peter Tergeist and Raymond Torres**

## 5.1 INTRODUCTION

Korean economic performance has been truly remarkable since 1960. During the past four decades, GDP growth averaged more than 9 per cent on an annual basis, permitting current per capita income (measured in purchasing power parities) to reach about three-quarters of the OECD average.

The financial crisis at the end of 1997 brought the growth process to a sudden halt. The crisis forced the government to agree to a rescue package with the IMF. Unemployment rocketed from 2.5 per cent to a peak of 8.5 per cent in early 1999, labour force participation declined substantially, and more than 1 million Koreans were thrown into poverty. However, the authorities reacted quickly to the difficult economic and social situation provoked by the crisis and implemented a wide range of macroeconomic and structural reforms. As a result, the economy quickly turned the corner and recovered strongly from 1999 onwards. In fact, no other country in South-East Asia has mastered the 1997 crisis as successfully as Korea. Despite temporary slowdowns in 2001 and 2003, real GDP growth between 1999 and 2003 was over 6 per cent on average, and the latest OECD projections show continuing growth in the 5 per cent range for 2004 (OECD 2003). The unemployment rate has stabilized at around 3½ per cent, which is slightly above pre-crisis rates. Korea is now the tenth-largest economy in the OECD area, soon to rival with Spain and Canada.

Despite these exceptional achievements, Korea's living standards are still well below the OECD average: per capita GDP is only twenty-third out of 30 OECD countries. Further convergence to the living standards of the leading world economies depends partly on how well Korea will address key labour market and social challenges. The latter include: (1) the need for a system of industrial relations based on trust; (2) reducing the high degree of duality that presently characterizes Korean labour markets – which may hamper economic efficiency while also raising job precariousness; and (3) the establishment of a social safety net that responds to the requirements of a modern economy and adapts to population ageing. The purpose of this chapter is to discuss the significance of these challenges and present possible reform avenues. It updates and extends the analysis presented in OECD (2000) and Martin and Torres (2000), based on a cross-country comparative approach, but bearing in mind the limitations inherent in any international comparison of labour market institutions and social protection systems.

The following sections of the chapter discuss these three labour market and social challenges facing the Korean economy: industrial relations and labour law reform (section 5.2), labour market duality and employment challenges of ageing (section 5.3) and social safety nets (section 5.4).

## 5.2 ADDRESSING PENDING ISSUES IN INDUSTRIAL RELATIONS AND IMPROVING TRUST AMONG SOCIAL PARTNERS

### 5.2.1 Labour Law and Labour Standards

When Korea joined the OECD in 1996 the Korean authorities made a commitment to the Organization that they would reform existing laws on industrial relations in line with internationally accepted standards, including those concerning basic worker rights such as freedom of association and collective bargaining. The OECD's Employment, Labour and Social Affairs (ELSA) Committee has since been monitoring closely progress on labour law reforms in Korea in the light of that commitment. Simultaneously, the ILO's Freedom of Association Committee has been monitoring Korean regulations and practice on freedom-of-association and the right to bargain collectively.

The Korean authorities have taken a number of important steps since 1997 to meet their commitment, steps which have been welcomed by both the OECD and the ILO. There is no doubt that the two reform packages passed by the National Assembly in March 1997 and February 1998, as well as further measures since, have moved Korean labour law closer to internationally - accepted standards.[1] However, as documented in OECD (2000), in several unpublished reports by the ELSA Committee to the OECD Council, as well as in recurring reports of the ILO Freedom-of-Association Committee (for example ILO 2002), there remain a number of outstanding problems, where the Korean government has not responded satisfactorily to concerns expressed by both international organizations. The most important outstanding issues are:

- the prohibition of multiple unions at the enterprise level;
- the prohibition of employers' payment of full-time union officials (scheduled to enter into force at the end of 2006);
- the denial of civil servants' right to organize;
- the broad definition of 'essential public services', where strike action is prohibited or severely restricted;
- the prohibition for dismissed or unemployed workers to become or remain trade union members.

Further, the arrest and imprisonment of trade unionists as a result of their trade union activities, often on the basis of the provision on 'obstruction of business' in the Penal Code, remains a persistent problem in Korea, which is not conducive to the peaceful resolution of labour disputes or to the much-needed improvement of the overall industrial relations climate.

**Multiple trade unions at the enterprise level**

The revized 1997 Trade Union and Labour Relations Adjustment Act makes it legally possible to form multiple trade unions at industrial and national levels. By contrast, at the enterprise level multiple unions competing to organize their company's workforce remain prohibited. While initially trade union pluralism at the enterprise level was to be allowed from January 2002 onwards, the Tripartite Commission in 2001 took the decision to provide an additional five-year grace period (up to 31 December 2006) before lifting this ban; this decision was linked to the postponement of the prohibition of employers paying full-time trade union officials (see below). This provision makes it virtually impossible for new trade unions to challenge the position of established unions as bargaining units in a particular enterprise. Based on Conventions 87 on Freedom of Association and 98 on the Right to Organize and Bargain Collectively, the ILO has held that this prohibition of multiple trade union representation in Korea does not conform to international norms and practices.

Ever since the end of the monopoly position of the FKTU (Federation of Korean Trade Unions) in the early 1990s, the Korean government has been concerned about possible inter-union rivalry and recognition disputes between FKTU- and KCTU-affiliated trade unions at the firm level. Employers are particularly concerned about the costs and time-loss involved in bargaining separately with several unions in an enterprise. This latter problem was supposed to be prevented by the introduction of separate legislation regulating 'single-channel' bargaining at the enterprise level. However, a half-hearted attempt to legislate on the issue failed in the

National Assembly. The renewed moratorium was justified by the Korean government on the grounds that:

- it was based on an agreement between labour (as represented by the FKTU) and management at the Tripartite Commission;
- it had proved impossible to find a consensus for the set-up of a 'single bargaining channel';
- permitting multiple unions operating at the enterprise level at this stage would hamper the recovery from the economic crisis of the late 1990s.

The KCTU did not participate in the decision on the moratorium, as it has been absent from the Tripartite Commission since 1999. It subsequently submitted a complaint against the Government of Korea to the ILO's Freedom of Association Committee for violation of freedom-of-association principles. The ILO Committee, which had repeatedly urged Korea to recognize trade union pluralism before the initial grace period ended in 2002, regretted in its March 2001 session 'that the situation is now worse with the lengthy additional postponement for such recognition' (ILO 2001).

**Payment of full-time union officials**

The 1997 Trade Union Act prohibited in principle the remuneration of full-time trade union officers by the employer, as well as any financial payment for regular trade union operations. This clause was supposed to take effect by 2002, at the same time that multiple trade unions were to be allowed at company level. The law thus tried to incorporate employer concerns that they would, at that time, be forced to support large numbers of full-time union officials.[2] Together with its decision to postpone the recognition of multiple trade unions at the enterprise level, the Tripartite Commission in 2001 decided to provide an additional five-year grace period (up to 31 December 2006) before prohibiting the payment of full-time trade union officials by their employers. This implies that previous practice will continue unchanged: trade union officials in unionized enterprises – around 6600 according to a government count in 2000 – are likely to remain on their enterprises' payroll until the end of 2006.

The ILO's Freedom-of-Association Committee has argued that payment for union officials by employers is a matter which 'should not be subject to legislative interference', and it is indeed not at all clear why the law should have to regulate this matter rather than leaving it to be decided by collective bargaining. A survey of practices in other OECD countries shows that paid working time off for trade union (and works council) representatives is a common feature of their industrial relations systems (Japan being the only other OECD country that has outlawed this practice). In French enterprises, for example, separate hours credits (laid down in the labour code) for trade union officials, so-called personnel delegates and works council members can be cumulated, which implies that many union officials devote their full time to union matters while being on the company payroll. In Germany, while there are no paid union officials *per se*, thousands of works council members, who are usually affiliated to the branch-level trade union, get time off for representing employee interests. In fact, a recent law lowered the company size threshold, beyond which firms need to give full-time off to at least one works council member, from 300 to 200 employees.[3] It is therefore something of a myth that the apparently high ratio of full-time officials to staff in Korea is unique among industrialized countries.[4]

Importantly, the Tripartite Commission moratorium deals jointly with both issues outlined above (multiple unions and pay for union officials). The employer associations and the FKTU apparently agreed on a *quid-pro-quo*, whereby employers received a five-year grace period before being confronted with possibly several rival unions in their enterprise (with the disruptive potential this might entail for collective bargaining), and the FKTU received the assurance that unions can still get the necessary resources to function effectively at company level. In fact, for the FKTU the issue of financial resources for its enterprise unions seemed to be a more important concern than the issue of trade union pluralism (albeit a 'fundamental' labour standard, as defined by the ILO).

**Union status of dismissed workers**

According to the 1997 Trade Union Act, an organization will not be regarded as a trade union when persons who are not workers are allowed to join it. In particular, dismissed workers are not allowed to retain their membership in a trade union. In addition, non-members are ineligible for union office.

As the long-drawn-out saga over the official recognition of the KCTU has shown, the fact that some trade union officials are dismissed or unemployed workers can lead to difficulties in securing legal recognition of a trade union by the authorities. If the law remains unchanged, this problem may reappear as new unions are formed and seek to register with government authorities. This particular provision of Korean labour law has no counterpart in other OECD countries, which consider qualifications for membership as a matter for the union itself to decide and not to be set down in legislation.[5] As noted by Choi (2002) the provision rather reflects traditional security-sensitive government attitudes towards industrial relations, in particular the fear of 'outside agitators'.[6]

**Union rights of civil servants**

Civil servants are not allowed to join trade unions. Following agreement in the Tripartite Commission public officials in 1999 were given the right to organize workplace associations, mainly to consult with management over working conditions and grievance handling. About two-thirds of the 680 000 civil servants in Korea (apart from teachers who can already form trade unions) are eligible to join the workplace associations, the exceptions being police, firemen, supervisors, and officials involved in personnel administration, budgeting and accounting.

Although associations have formed at hundreds of administrative units and reportedly have over 80 000 civil servants as members (already a higher membership rate than unions in the private sector), national umbrella groups or federations of the workplace associations are still considered illegal under the State Public Officials Act (Article 66) which prohibits 'any collective act for any labour movement'. The original 1998 Tripartite Agreement envisaged that, after some stock-taking of the experience with workplace associations, trade unions endowed with bargaining rights would be allowed to form at national, provincial and local levels. After long-drawn-out discussions within the Tripartite Commission, and a series of public hearings organized by the government, the Ministry of Government and Home Affairs prepared a bill on 'Public Servants Association' (avoiding the term 'trade union'), which was introduced to the National Assembly in October 2002.

This bill would allow trade unions in the public service (under a different designation), with membership restricted to the lower four out of nine grades of public officials and with no right to sign collective agreements. The current government under President Roh has prepared an alternative bill that would grant such representative organizations the liberty to carry the title of 'trade union' and to join trade union confederations. This bill strengthens the right to conclude collective agreements that, however, would still be subject to parliamentary approval. It recognizes trade union pluralism, but does not allow payment for full-time union officials. Apart from the restrictions to potential membership an Act based on these principles would make the Korean situation not all that different from other OECD countries, where agreements reached through collective bargaining in the public service often need the approval of parliament.[7]

**The right to strike in the public sector**

Strikes by workers in central and local government are prohibited in Korea, which is not unusual in OECD countries. However, the 1997 trade union legislation also restricted the right to strike in the more broadly defined public sector delivering 'essential services', including railways and inner-city buses; gas, electricity and water; oil refineries and oil supply; hospitals and other medical services; banks; and telecommunications services. In these sectors, industrial conflict is subject to compulsory arbitration.

The ILO has repeatedly asked the Korean government to ensure that restrictions on the right to strike only apply to essential services in the 'strict sense of the term', under conditions of an 'imminent threat to the life, personal safety or health of the whole or part of the population' (ILO 1996, 1998). This would seem to exclude at least banking, transportation and oil supply and refining. Korea has indeed dropped inner-city bus services and banking (with the exception of the Bank of Korea) from the list in 2001, but no further cuts have been proposed either by the government or the Tripartite Commission. The government tends to invoke national security concerns and important potential losses for the national economy as reasons for keeping the current restrictions. The divergence of views is illustrated by the fact that in 2001 union representatives in the Tripartite Commission proposed to drop oil refineries from the list of essential services, whereas employers proposed to add airlines. Following a public discussion about the inclusion of airlines in 2001, a group of parliamentarians even proposed a bill to that effect to the National Assembly.

While Korea is not unique in restricting the right to strike in some public services its labour law provisions seem to go further than in other OECD countries in that they set out an unusually broad definition of 'essential services' where a strike ban covering entire sectors is maintained, instead of pursuing alternative solutions such as a minimum service obligation. However, one positive indication that things may be handled more flexibly in the longer run is that over the past few years a declining share of disputes in essential services has been referred to the National Labour Relations Commission for compulsory arbitration. The Commission therefore argues that it is no longer possible to speak of a comprehensive strike ban in essential services.

**Possible reform avenues**

As noted above, there is no doubt that since 1996 legislative reforms have shifted Korean labour laws significantly in the desired direction. However, this section has also highlighted the persistence of several important outstanding issues. On all of these issues the government, in consultation with social partners, should explore avenues for amending the relevant provisions of the law. Concerning the formation of trade unions for civil servants, for example, solutions should be found both for expanding potential membership and for shortening the grace period before the law takes effect. Likewise, after the consensus in principle achieved in the 1998 Tripartite Agreement, it should be easy to remove the restrictions on trade union membership; neither should it be too difficult to resolve the issue – of concern to business – as to whether dismissed trade union members, by being able to remain union members, can have free access to company premises.

Of all the contentious issues the prohibition of trade union pluralism at the enterprise level is arguably the most flagrant violation of internationally - recognised labour standards. Importantly, the Tripartite Commission moratorium outlined above has once again clarified that in Korea this issue is inextricably linked with that of the payment for full-time union - officials. One issue is not likely to be solved without the other, so that arguably the payment issue is holding hostage the full realization of freedom-of-association principles. There needs to be a strong political will to cut through this Gordian knot. In order to avoid yet another moratorium after the end of 2006, a full-fledged effort needs to be undertaken way before the expiration of the current moratorium. The government should now intensify its effort to reach simultaneous solutions ensuring (1) the possibility for paid time-off for union officials and, more broadly, worker representatives; and (2) a single bargaining channel at the enterprise level which would avoid the need for employers to bargain separately with several unions in their enterprise. The result must be the simultaneous lifting of the prohibition on payment of union officials (a violation of ILO Convention 135 and Recommendation 143) and the prohibition of multiple enterprise unions (a violation of ILO Convention 87).

Some new elements have emerged that may enable Korea to solve the payment issue, thus opening up the way for introducing multiple firm-level unions. First, after the wave of mergers and acquisitions since the 1997 crisis, a situation has developed *de facto* where two or more unions can and do exist side by side within one particular enterprise (where, for example, the unions of the former independent firms remain the bargaining representatives in the various establishments), and this should exert some pressure towards finding an early solution to the 'single-bargaining channel' issue.[8] Second, there seems to be a current trend for enterprise unions to establish themselves as local chapters of an industrial or sectoral union organization. The establishment of sectoral unions has developed furthest among banking and finance employees (FKTU), and among hospital workers, construction workers and teachers (KCTU), although in most cases employers still refuse to bargain at the sectoral level (Lee and Lee 2001, Lee 2002). Importantly, in 2003 sectoral bargaining is also being held in the metal industry, for the first time in many decades.

Of importance in this context the establishment of stronger sectoral-type union bodies tends to imply a different flow of membership fees. If the sectoral-level body fulfills more functions, employs more staff, intervenes in enterprise or sectoral bargaining and so on, it will also need to receive a larger share of membership fees. This, in turn, will enable the sectoral body to transfer some funds from larger to smaller enterprise unions and thus ensure the continuous operation of union officials based, at least in part, on an auto-financing model. Since the most likely solution to the stalemate will be a legislative ceiling on the ratio of paid officials to union members, or to the workforce, within an enterprise (a ratio of 1 to 300 has already been proposed in a draft bill that did not manage to pass the Assembly), trade unions will need to devise a way, based on their own resources, to channel money to their smaller chapters (for example SMEs with less than 300 members). In principle, union dues of 1 per cent of salary from each of the 1.4 million Korean union members should suffice to finance the activities, salaries and overhead costs of 6000–7000 trade union representatives, once the SME problem is solved – although it is true that, in the past, many unions have demanded much smaller membership fees.

In sum, trade unions will need to substantially improve their self-sufficiency over the next few years. The gradual shift from enterprise to industrial unions may be of help in this regard, as it might imply a more equitable distribution of membership fees. However, trade unions should also be prepared to compromise and accept partial, instead of full, time off for their representatives in smaller enterprises (there already exists a large number of part-time officials, see Lee and Cho 2002), and the French example of credit hours varying by company size could be one inspiration for a future time-off system. As noted above, a situation where the full-time activities of even national union leaders are financed by their (former) enterprises seems quite untenable in the long run.

### 5.2.2 Overcoming the Lack of Trust Among the Social Partners

The labour regulations and practices referred to above not only violate internationally recognized labour standards, they also continue, to varying degrees, to poison the labour relations atmosphere in Korea. It is more necessary than ever to create a less confrontational and more consensual labour relations system if the Korean economy and society is to modernize and prosper. Trust and cooperation among the social partners can play an important role in fostering a dynamic, knowledge-based economy. However, it seems that after agreeing on a successful compromise agenda in early 1998, in order to help the country out of the recession, past confrontational attitudes between management and labour have resurfaced with the recovery. As a result, consensus on necessary reforms of employment conditions and workforce practices is increasingly difficult to achieve. Not only is management reluctant to allow more employee participation, but also the trade unions seem unwilling to negotiate constructive compromises on the necessary economic restructuring. Moreover, satisfactory tripartite solutions to outstanding issues in the Tripartite Commission seem more and more elusive.

The industrial relations climate is bound to remain depressed when Korea, as the only OECD country, continues to arrest and sometimes imprison dozens, even hundreds, of trade unionists every year. This particular feature of industrial disputes in Korea is a matter of considerable concern to the OECD and the ILO. Successive waves of arrests of trade unionists not only represent a threat to fundamental workers' rights, but they also damage trust among the social partners. During the economic crisis and its aftermath, many union members reacted strongly to the announcement of business restructuring and collective dismissals. This included takeovers of plants and equipment, and strike action in some essential services where, as noted above, Korean law regulates conflict resolution through arbitration. These events gave rise to a sharp upsurge in arrests of workers and union officials. While arrests are in part explained by the often-violent nature of industrial disputes, they also reflect an unusually heavy reliance on the Penal Code in combating strike activity and trade union demonstrations that, in other OECD countries, would be considered legitimate trade union activities. The use of the Penal Code contrasts with developments in most other industrialized countries, where criminal sanctions are on the wane in favour of civil litigation (Jacobs 1998).

During 2001, for example, the number of arrests and imprisonments of trade unionists (altogether over 200) was higher than in any year since 1992. The ILO's Committee on Freedom of Association has repeatedly urged the Korean government to take appropriate measures so that the persons detained or on trial as a result of their trade union activities are released or that the charges against them are dropped. It has objected, in particular, to the use of the clause in the Penal Code relating to 'obstruction of business' (Article 314) as a basis for the arrest of union demonstrators and strike participants. According to a KCTU count, about two-thirds of the trade unionists detained at the end of 2001 were being charged with 'obstruction of business'.

The Korean authorities, for their part, argue that the concerned trade unionists have been arrested on such grounds as violence during strikes, unlawful occupation of premises or serious damage to company facilities. However, in 2001 they also arrested airline pilots and bank and hospital union representatives who did not commit violent acts but, as noted by the Ministry of Labour, 'brought pain and discomfort to the people and economic loss to their companies and had negative effects on the national economy and international confidence'. True, the Korean authorities have also announced a plan to 'minimize' the number of arrests through focusing mainly on strike leaders and through applying fines, but not detaining other participants. However, as the arrest figures show, this 'minimization plan' has been far from effective to date.

The OECD's ELSA Commission, while condemning violent acts in connection with industrial disputes, has repeatedly argued that the definition of 'unlawful acts' in Korea is very broad and appears to cover many union activities that would be regarded as lawful (or at least borderline) in many other OECD countries. In other words, police action in Korea seems to be triggered by a lower level of disruptive action than in many other countries – for example, the blocking of intersections or the parading of pickets in front of factory gates – or simply by lack of respect for procedural requirements, such as giving sufficient advance notice for strike action or observing cooling-off or mediation periods. Also, the wide definition of 'essential services' (noted above) where strike action is severely restricted has triggered numerous police interventions.

In sum, the use of criminal law to arrest trade union members and officials continues to undermine labour–management relations in Korea. Addressing this issue as a matter of urgency will tend to contribute to a better climate of trust between the social partners. It will thus be particularly important for the Korean authorities to take all the necessary steps to avoid large-scale arrests and detentions of trade unionists and to use their police and judicial powers with the utmost restraint.[9] Not only would this benefit Korean workers and firms but it would also increase the attractiveness of Korea as a location for foreign direct investment.

In view of the confrontational stance in Korean industrial relations, which resurfaces time and again, it is important to strengthen the institutional framework for social dialogue. The Tripartite Commission, which was set up by incoming President Kim Dae-Jung in early 1998, has to some extent embodied that institutional framework. It has reached agreement on implementing most of the 90 items originally contained in the Tripartite Agreement of February 1998. It has also contributed to much of the progress on social and labour rights since then, in particular the extension of the social safety net, the legalization of teachers' unions, the establishment of workplace councils for civil servants and the recognition of the KCTU. Newly elected President Roh has come out strongly in favour of improving the operation of the Tripartite Commission; however, its functioning remains hampered by the continuing absence of the KCTU, which left the body in 1999. Social consensus will continue to remain elusive to achieve in a tripartite or multipartite body, where one of the main constituent parties – the trade unions – have only limited representation. Consequently, the KCTU should consider ending its 'empty chair' policy and make its influence felt inside this important policy body.

At the same time the new Korean government should continue to make every effort to implement the social agreements struck inside the Commission, as required by the 1999 Act on the Establishment and Operation of the Tripartite Commission. However, the actors also need to reconsider the relationship between the legislative branch of government and the Tripartite Commission, which is not part of government as such but fulfills an advisory role. Absence of consensus within the Commission, for example on freedom-of-association rights of civil servants, trade union pluralism and the scope of essential services, should not prevent the government from making proposals to the National Assembly to break the logjam. At the same time the social partners need to recognize the futility of 'empty chair' attitudes, and come forward themselves with constructive proposals rather than always looking to the government to solve deadlocks. Perhaps, more importantly, from the point of view of Korean productivity performance, tripartite agreements at the national level need to be supplemented by active labour–management consultation and effective cooperation at the enterprise level.

## 5.3 REDUCING LABOUR–MARKET DUALITY AND ADDRESSING THE EMPLOYMENT CHALLENGES OF POPULATION AGEING

Despite the sharp fall in the open unemployment rate after 1999, and the corresponding climb of the employment–to–population ratio, there remains room for increasing the number of jobs. Indeed, the employment–population ratio in Korea is still relatively low by international comparison. In 2001 the overall employment–population ratio was around 62 per cent – up from 59.5 per cent in the recession year 1998, but still over 3 percentage points below the OECD average (Table 5.1).

But one of the most striking features of the Korean labour market is the high incidence of so-called non-regular forms of employment, including temporary and daily work, unpaid family work and other non-permanent arrangements. The result is a marked duality, with a relatively small proportion of workers (regular workers) enjoying a degree of employment protection, while non-regular workers face more precarious conditions. Looking further ahead, Korea will have to face the challenge of population ageing. This means that the current practice of "mandatory retirement" around age 55 for regular workers will have to be adapted. More generally, there will be pressure to change wage, employment and training practices.

### 5.3.1 An Extremely High Degree of Labour Market Duality

The prospect for continuing convergence in Korean living standards towards the OECD average depends crucially on continuing rapid economic growth. Economic growth, in turn, is mainly determined by (1) the investment effort, (2) the extent to which unused labour supply can be mobilized in the economy, and (3) multi-factor productivity growth, which is a measure of the underlying efficiency gains recorded by firms. As is well known the fast growth recorded until 1997 was mainly based on the first factor, namely a spectacular investment effort. Thus over the period 1990–96, Korea devoted 37 per cent of its yearly national income to real fixed capital accumulation. On the other hand over the 1990s multi-factor productivity practically stagnated, whereas it grew in nearly all other OECD countries.[10] This is all the more surprising because multi-factor productivity is generally expected to grow faster in countries such as Korea which are catching up on the most advanced OECD countries.

It is therefore essential that future policy strategies focus on improvements in productivity, as well as a greater mobilization of individuals who are presently on the margins of the labour market. The experience of other OECD countries suggests that effective labour and social policies, which are reviewed in section 5.4, are vital ingredients in such a strategy. However,

**Table 5.1**
**Employment–population Ratios[1] 2001**

| | Total | | | | Men | Women |
|---|---|---|---|---|---|---|
| | All ages[1] | 15–24 | 25–54 | 55–64 | All age[2] | All ages[2] |
| Australia | 68.9 | 60.6 | 76.4 | 46.3 | 76.0 | 61.7 |
| Austria[3] | 68.2 | 53.1 | 82.2 | 28.1 | 76.8 | 59.4 |
| Belgium | 59.7 | 28.5 | 76.6 | 25.2 | 68.5 | 50.7 |
| Canada | 70.9 | 56.4 | 79.8 | 48.3 | 75.9 | 66.0 |
| Czech Republic | 65.3 | 36.1 | 82.1 | 37.1 | 73.6 | 57.0 |
| Denmark | 75.9 | 61.7 | 84.5 | 56.6 | 80.2 | 71.4 |
| Finland | 67.7 | 40.3 | 81.5 | 45.9 | 70.0 | 65.4 |
| France | 62.0 | 24.3 | 79.3 | 36.5 | 69.0 | 55.2 |
| Germany | 65.9 | 47.8 | 80.0 | 36.8 | 73.0 | 58.6 |
| Greece | 55.6 | 26.0 | 70.4 | 38.0 | 70.9 | 41.2 |
| Hungary | 56.6 | 32.4 | 73.1 | 24.1 | 63.5 | 49.8 |
| Iceland[4] | 84.6 | 66.8 | 90.7 | 85.6 | 88.0 | 81.1 |
| Ireland | 65.0 | 47.0 | 76.4 | 46.6 | 76.0 | 54.0 |
| Italy | 54.9 | 27.4 | 69.2 | 28.0 | 68.7 | 41.1 |
| Japan | 68.8 | 42.0 | 78.6 | 62.0 | 80.5 | 57.0 |
| **Korea, 1995** | **63.7** | **34.2** | **74.4** | **63.5** | **77.2** | **50.6** |
| **Korea, 1998** | **59.5** | **26.3** | **70.3** | **59.0** | **71.7** | **47.4** |
| **Korea, 2001** | **62.1** | **29.1** | **72.7** | **58.0** | **73.4** | **50.9** |
| Luxembourg | 63.0 | 32.3 | 78.7 | 24.8 | 74.9 | 50.8 |
| Mexico | 60.1 | 47.7 | 67.8 | 52.1 | 83.4 | 39.4 |
| Netherlands | 72.8 | 67.0 | 81.9 | 38.8 | 81.6 | 63.9 |
| New Zealand | 71.8 | 56.0 | 79.3 | 60.7 | 78.9 | 64.8 |
| Norway[4] | 77.5 | 56.5 | 85.1 | 67.4 | 81.0 | 73.8 |
| Poland | 53.5 | 22.1 | 69.3 | 29.0 | 59.2 | 47.8 |
| Portugal | 68.7 | 43.5 | 82.4 | 50.3 | 76.7 | 61.1 |
| Slovak Republic | 56.9 | 27.9 | 74.8 | 22.3 | 62.1 | 51.8 |
| Spain[4] | 58.8 | 37.1 | 69.5 | 39.2 | 73.8 | 43.8 |
| Sweden[4] | 75.3 | 47.9 | 84.6 | 67.0 | 77.0 | 73.5 |
| Switzerland | 79.0 | 62.8 | 86.0 | 68.1 | 87.6 | 70.4 |
| Turkey | 45.1 | 32.0 | 53.3 | 32.9 | 66.0 | 24.1 |
| United Kingdom[4] | 72.8 | 61.1 | 80.7 | 52.2 | 79.3 | 66.1 |
| United States[4] | 73.1 | 57.8 | 80.6 | 58.4 | 79.3 | 67.1 |
| Total OECD | 65.3 | 44.6 | 75.8 | 48.3 | 75.6 | 55.3 |

*Notes*: 1 Employment–population ratios refer to persons in employment divided by the working-age population for the relevant groups.
2 'All ages' refers to 15–64.
3 Data refer to 2000.
4 Age group 15–24 refers to 16–24, and 'All ages' refers to 16–64.

*Source*: OECD, Labour Force Statistics database.

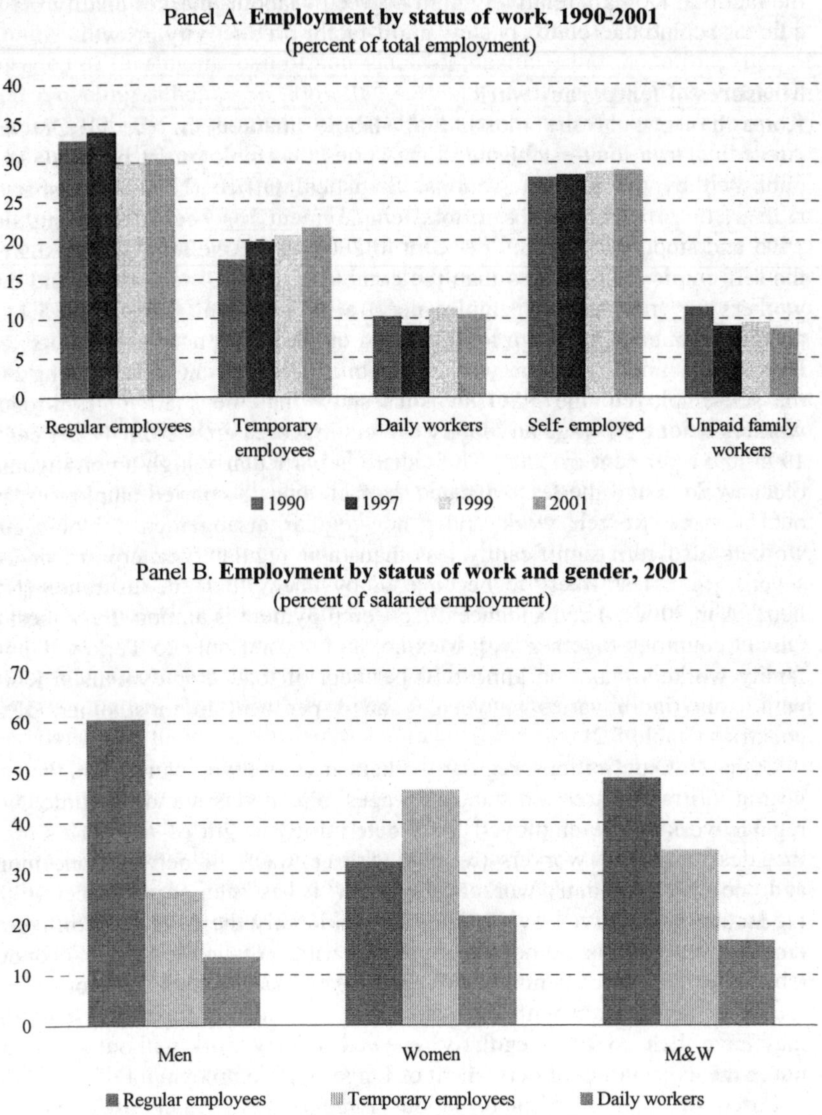


*Source*: National Statistical Office, *Annual Report on the Economically Active Population* Survey, various issues.

*Figure 5.1 Composition of Employment by Status of Work*

before examining these policy issues in some depth, it is essential to stress the fact that Korea's relatively high degree of labour–market duality may be a factor behind the relatively slow multi-factor productivity growth.

**Measures of temporary work**

Korea has one of the most 'dual' labour markets in the OECD area. According to a long-established time series on employment by work status published by the Korean National Statistical Office (NSO), the share of regular, or permanent, jobs in total employment has been decreasing since 1995 and stood at only 28.9 per cent in 2001, the same level as the share of the self-employed, and less than the combined share of temporary and daily workers (or 'non-regular' employment) at 32 per cent (see Figure 5.1). In absolute numbers, although total salaried employment now exceeds its 1997 level, the number of regular workers is almost 10 per cent less. Leaving aside the self-employed, the NSO statistics show that the share of non-regular workers among all wage and salary earners in Korea grew from 47 per cent in 1995 to 51 per cent in 2001. Their share is particularly high among women, older workers and the less educated. In fact, among salaried employees, two out of three women work under non-regular arrangements. Non-regular workers also earn significantly less than their regular counterparts, and are several times less likely to be covered by unemployment insurance (NSO 2001, Ahn 2002). The incidence of self-employment is among the highest for OECD countries together with Mexico, and second only to Turkey. Unpaid family workers make up almost 10 per cent of total employment in Korea, while this figure varies between 0 and 3 per cent in most other OECD countries (Table 5.2).

Under NSO definitions, regular workers are those who work more than one year at a firm and are paid standard wages, plus bonuses and overtime. Non-regular workers are employed for a determined length of time. This group includes temporary workers (usually with contracts of between one month and one year) and daily workers. However, it has been argued recently that the labour force survey overestimates considerably the extent of non-regular employment - that is the degree of job precariousness in the Korean economy - because a significant number of employees classified as 'temporary' and 'daily' in fact remain with their employer on a semi-permanent basis; they may have their contract regularly renewed or may work without a contract, but in the expectation of permanent or longer-term employment.

Based on a supplementary labour force survey, which asks expressly whether respondents expect to continue their current employment relationship, the Korean Ministry of Labour has tried to arrive at a new estimate of the size of the non-regular workforce. Using the concepts of 'contingent' employment on the one hand and 'alternative' or 'non-standard' employment arrangements on the other (roughly identical to the approach

**Table 5.2**
**International Comparison of Employment by Status of Workers, 2000**

(% of total employment)

| | Employees | | | Unpaid family workers[1] | Self-employment |
|---|---|---|---|---|---|
| | Total | Permanent/Regular[2] | Non-permanent/ Non-regular[2] | | |
| Australia[3] | 84 | 79 (94) | 5 (6) | 1 | 15 |
| Austria | 87 | 80 (92) | 7 (8) | 3 | 11 |
| Belgium[4] | 83 | 74 (90) | 9 (10) | 3 | 14 |
| Canada | 89 | 78 (87) | 11 (13) | 0 | 11 |
| Czech Republic | 85 | 77 (91) | 8 (9) | 1 | 14 |
| Denmark | 91 | 82 (90) | 9 (10) | 1 | 8 |
| Finland | 86 | 72 (84) | 14 (16) | 1 | 13 |
| France | 90 | 76 (84) | 14 (16) | 0 | 10 |
| Germany | 89 | 78 (87) | 11 (13) | 1 | 10 |
| Greece | 58 | 51 (87) | 8 (13) | 9 | 32 |
| Hungary | 85 | 78 (92) | 7 (8) | 1 | 14 |
| Iceland | 82 | 45 (55) | 37 (45) | 0 | 18 |
| Ireland | 80 | 76 (95) | 4 (5) | 1 | 19 |
| Italy | 72 | 64 (90) | 7 (10) | 4 | 24 |
| Japan | 83 | 73 (87) | 11 (13) | 5 | 11 |
| **Korea[5,6]** | **62** | **30 (49)** | **32 (51)** | **9** | **29** |
| **Korea[5,7]** | **62** | **52 (83)** | **11 (17)** | **9** | **29** |
| Luxembourg | 91 | 88 (97) | 3 (3) | 0 | 9 |
| Mexico | 64 | 51 (79) | 13 (21) | 8 | 29 |
| Netherlands | 88 | 76 (86) | 12 (14) | 1 | 11 |
| New Zealand | 79 | .. | .. | 1 | 20 |
| Norway | 93 | 84 (91) | 9 (9) | 0 | 7 |
| Poland | 73 | 68 (94) | 4 (6) | 5 | 22 |
| Portugal | 74 | 59 (80) | 15 (20) | 2 | 24 |
| Spain | 79 | 54 (68) | 25 (32) | 2 | 19 |
| Sweden | 90 | 76 (85) | 14 (15) | 0 | 10 |
| Switzerland | 87 | 77 (88) | 10 (12) | 2 | 11 |
| Turkey | 50 | 40 (80) | 10 (20) | 21 | 30 |
| United Kingdom | 88 | 82 (93) | 6 (7) | 1 | 11 |
| United States | 93 | .. | .. | 0 | 7 |

*Notes*: .. Data not available.

1 Figures less than 0.5 appear in the column as zeros in italics.

2 Figures in brackets show the shares of permanent and non-permanent employees in dependent employment.

3 Data refer to 1997.

4 Data refer to 1999.

5 Data refer to 2001.

6 Using the 'regular/non-regular worker' categories from the Economically Active Population Survey.

7 Using the 'temporary worker' categories from the Supplementary Survey to the Economically Active Population Survey.

*Sources*: OECD, Labour Force Statistics database (unpaid family workers and self-employed), OECD Temporary Work database (permanent and non-permanent work). Korea: Supplementary Survey to the Economically Active Population Survey, 2001. Australia: Forms of Employment Survey, 1998.

originally used by the US Bureau of Labour Statistics) [11], the Ministry arrived at a share of 13.9 per cent for contingent workers in mid-2001 and an additional 13.6 per cent for non-standard employment arrangements.

The former are defined as workers with a fixed-term contract and other workers who do not expect their employment to continue. The non-standard category comprises, *inter alia*, temporary agency workers, contractors, home workers and on-call workers. Most of the discrepancy between the Ministry's figures and the 51 per cent share from the labour force survey can be explained by the fact that large numbers of employees in Korea either have no written work contract or are not entitled to certain allowances and hence are classified as non-regular workers, whereas in the supplementary survey many of them respond that they expect their employment relationship to last.

There continues to be controversy about the exact size of the precarious workforce in Korea (see for example Ahn 2002, Ahn et al. 2001). Meanwhile, the NSO continues to publish every month its long-established time series on permanent and non-regular workers. Table 5.3 presents the authors' own calculations based on the 2001 supplementary survey, which attempt to conform as much as possible to the concept of temporary employment applicable to the majority of countries in the OECD's 'temporary employment' database (see OECD 2002). It does so by eliminating those categories (such as contractors) that would normally be classified as self-employed and by adding temporary agency workers and on-call workers to the 'contingent' workforce, as defined in the Korean supplementary survey. Taking this approach, the share of temporary workers among all wage and salary earners would be about 17 per cent.[12]

Whatever the 'true' figure for the extent of non-regular employment, the following conclusions can be drawn from the data analysis:

- The estimate of 13.9 per cent 'contingent workers' given by the Ministry of Labour and the 51 per cent figure for 'temporary and daily workers' from the labour force survey are the two extreme estimates of the extent of non-regular employment.
- Although the data from the supplementary survey suggest that the problem of labour market dualism may be less serious in Korea than was previously thought to be the case, the available NSO time series also indicate that non-regular employment has been on the increase since the economic crisis of 1997. One reason why Korean policy-makers need to strengthen the social safety net for workers in small firms and with short employment durations.[13]
- While under the traditional approach of classifying 'non-regular' workers Korea would have the highest share of temporary workers in total dependent employment among OECD countries, even the alternative type of calculation proposed by the Korean authorities would put Korea in the top quintile of OECD countries in terms of the share of

temporary workers among dependent employees, after Spain, Mexico, Portugal and Turkey (see Table 5.2).[14]

**Table 5.3**
**Temporary Workers in Korea, 2001**

| | | Number of workers (000s) | As % of dependent employment |
|---|---|---|---|
| Workers with a fixed-term contract | Less than or equal to 1 month | 763 | 5.7 |
| | More than 1 month to less than 1 year | 370 | 2.8 |
| | Exactly 1 year | 187 | 1.4 |
| | More than 1 year to less than 3 years | 73 | 0.5 |
| | 3 years or more | 59 | 0.4 |
| | ***Subtotal*** | ***1 452*** | ***10.9*** |
| Workers without a fixed-term contract, where employment is not expected to continue | For involuntary reasons | 387 | 2.9 |
| Temporary agency workers | | 130 | 1.0 |
| On-call workers | | 305 | 2.3 |
| **Total** | | **2 274** | **17.0**[1] |
| ***Memorandum item:*** **Total dependent employment** | | **13 339** | |

*Note*: 1 The overall total is likely to be higher, as two employee categories which were classified separately in the Supplementary Survey (home workers and workers provided by contract firms) contain an unspecified number of persons with a fixed-term contract, or other short-term employment arrangements.

*Source*: Supplementary Survey of Economically Active Population Survey, August 2001.

### Job tenure

Reflecting the high incidence of non-regular employment, average job tenure (that is the length of stay with the same employer) is low by international comparison. In 2000 the average Korean worker (in firms with five or more employees) stayed less than six years with the same employer – in comparison, the figure was almost ten years in the case of the European Union and 12 years in Japan (Table 5.4). Average tenure is even lower in Korea than in the United States. It is especially low for Korean female workers: while average job tenure for men was over six years in 2000, average job tenure for women was only four years – by contrast, the unweighted average for EU countries was over ten years for men and around nine years for women. It also appears that workers with a college degree enjoy longer job tenures than lower-educated ones.

However, tenure is higher for the lower educated (those with educational attainment of middle school and below) than for those with high school education or junior college – signalling problems in the school-to-work transition.

**Table 5.4**
**Job tenure in Korea and Selected OECD Countries**

| | Korea | | | European Union [1,2] | Japan [1] | United States [1] |
|---|---|---|---|---|---|---|
| | 1996 | 1998 | 2000 | 2000 | 2000 | 2000 |
| Total employees | **5.4** | **6.1** | **5.6** | **9.7** | **12.0** | **6.7** |
| Men | 6.1 | 6.8 | 6.4 | 10.4 | 13.3 | 7.1 |
| Women | 3.7 | 4.3 | 4.0 | 8.9 | 8.8 | 6.2 |
| Middle school and below | 5.7 | 6.4 | 6.3 | 9.9 | 15.7 | 4.5 |
| High school | 5.1 | 5.8 | 5.3 | 9.6 | 11.7 | 6.8 |
| Junior college | 4.5 | 5.1 | 4.4 | | | |
| College and university and over | 6.2 | 7.0 | 6.5 | 9.8 | 8.7 | 7.4 |

*Notes*: 1 The two highest educational levels are not shown separately, and correspond to some or completed tertiary education.
2 Unweighted average of the European Union member states.

*Sources*: Korea: *Wage Structure Survey*, various editions; Japan: *Basic Survey on Wage Structure*, 2000; European Union: *European Union Labour Force Survey*, 2001; United States: "Job tenure" *Supplement to the Current Population Survey*.

### The importance of firm size

Regular workers tend to work in large firms, often enjoy lifetime employment and are covered by a seniority-based wage system. Indeed, among the wage differentials shown in Figure 5.2, the wage gap between large and small firms is the only one that has grown since the mid-1980s. Working in a large firm entails other benefits to workers: (1) the unionization rate in firms with more than 300 workers is high (over three-quarters), whereas it is almost nil in small businesses; (2) workers in large firms are covered by both the Employment Insurance System and the National Pension System which, despite government efforts to expand coverage, is far from being the case in small firms; and (3) a much larger share of workers in large firms, compared with those in SMEs, receive continuous vocational training.

### Underlying factors

While there are probably many factors that account for the pronounced degree

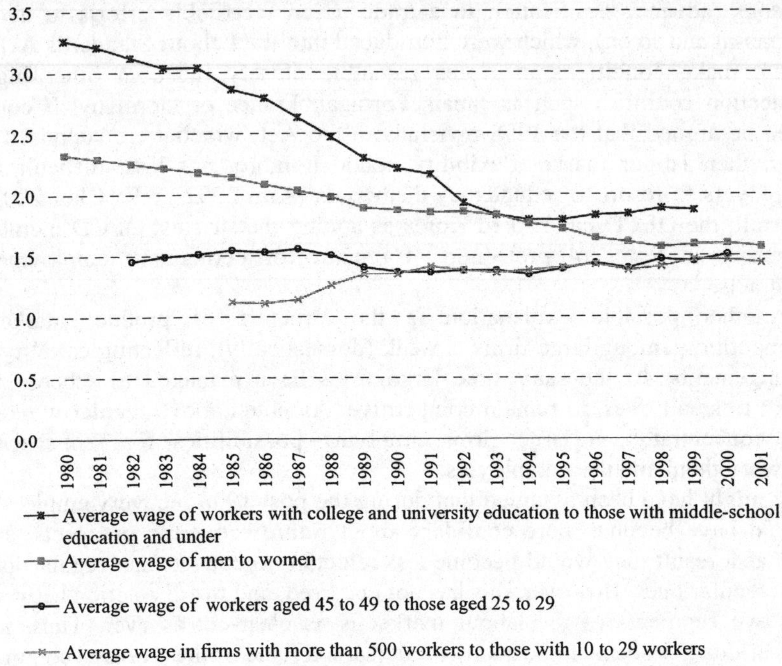


*Notes*: Including all wage components (regular pay, overtime pay and bonuses).

*Source*: Ministry of Labour, Survey Report on Wage Structure, various issues, for data by gender (up to 1995), age group and educational attainment; Monthly Labour Survey, various issues, for data by firm size and gender (1996 and after).

*Figure 5.2 Wage Differentials*

of duality in the Korean labour market, strong employment protection for permanent workers is an important part of the story. It is less costly for employers to hire non-regular workers as, according to the Labour Standards Act, temporary and daily workers with less than one year of tenure are not entitled to certain benefits such as severance pay (the 'retirement allowance') and childcare and maternity leave. In addition, daily workers have so far been totally excluded from the EIS.

By contrast, regular workers enjoy a relatively high level of employment protection. For instance, severance pay amounts to one monthly wage per year of seniority (with no maximum) and dismissal procedures remain complex and cumbersome despite recent reforms. In addition, the preconditions and procedural requirements for dismissals based on economic reasons (advance notification to a trade union, verifiable efforts to avoid dismissal and so on), which were introduced into the Labour Standards Act in 1998, make conditions in Korea resemble closely those in other high-protection countries such as Japan, Portugal, France or Germany. It could even be argued that the 1998 revisions to the Act, which were supposed to strengthen labour market flexibility, made it more, not less, difficult for employers to resort to redundancy dismissals (Kim 2002, Y.K. Choi 2002). Overall, the OECD has ranked Korea as among the strictest OECD member countries in terms of protection of regular (or permanent) employment contracts.[15]

Another possible explanation is the structure of product markets. Competition among large firms is weak (domestically), reflecting cartel-type arrangements. At the same time large firms have managed to subcontract work to small ones, to remain competitive. As noted above regular workers are concentrated in large firms, implying possibilities for rent-sharing between them and their employers.

It might have been assumed that during the post-1998 recovery employers would have become more confident about future economic prospects, and that as a result they would become less reluctant to convert non-regular jobs into regular ones. However, this has not occurred, and the distinction between the two segments of the labour market is as clear-cut as ever. Thus, job precariousness seems to be a structural characteristic of the Korean economy, which is problematic not only from the social point of view but also for reasons of economic efficiency. Indeed, as noted earlier, job precariousness seems to be associated with a relatively low incidence of vocational training (in particular in small businesses), in turn inhibiting productivity growth.

**Policy requirements**

In sum, despite the amendment to the Labour Standards Act adopted in 1998, which made it possible to dismiss workers for 'urgent managerial needs', regular workers still enjoy a relatively high degree of employment protection compared with their counterparts in other OECD countries. There would, therefore, seem to be room for easing the legal severance pay requirements for regular workers. This reform, however, should take place gradually, and be dependent on (1) the EIS becoming more firmly established in coming years (see below); and (2) the public pension system being adequately funded (which is far from being the case at present), and pension benefits providing sufficient income support.

Relaxing relatively strict employment protection for regular workers, under the above conditions, could also help ease job instability for temporary and daily workers (who form the core of 'outsiders' in Korea). This would, hopefully, encourage employers to convert more non-regular contracts into regular ones, thereby reducing the degree of labour market segmentation and laying the ground for greater investment by both workers and firms in on-the-job training.

At the same time, it would be highly desirable to undertake more research on the causes and implications of the marked duality that presently exists in the Korean labour market. For instance, it would be useful to examine workers' perceptions of the non-regular forms of employment – certain workers may prefer temporary jobs rather than permanent ones. In addition, labour market duality has gone hand-in-hand with a stagnant multi-factor productivity performance – itself one of the symptoms of the 1997 crisis – and more attention should be devoted to the possible causality at work. Analysing transitions between non-regular and regular jobs would help to determine which groups are at greatest risk of getting trapped in non-regular jobs. Finally, the possible links between the stringency of employment protection legislation and the lack of competition in product markets on the one hand and the incidence of non-regular forms of employment on the other should be investigated.

### 5.3.2 Addressing the Employment Challenges of Population Ageing

The Korean population is ageing rapidly, under the combined effect of improving longevity and falling fertility rates. The result is that the growth in the working-age population will slow considerably in coming decades – from 2020 or so, the working-age population is projected to decline in absolute terms. In other words, there will be less and less labour resources available. In addition, the average age of the available workforce will rise dramatically. As shown in Figure 5.3 the share of the population between 50 and 64 years of age among the total working-age population will practically double over the next 50 years, from 22 per cent to 41 per cent in 2050. Clearly, demographic changes of such a size will require a major adjustment of Korean labour markets.

**The challenge ahead**

In many OECD countries, population ageing means that public pension systems are already under pressure to adjust to the new demographic realities. However, in the case of Korea, the public pension system and other social safety nets are relatively new and have not matured as yet. Therefore, the current financial situation of the public pension system is less of a problem than in other OECD countries. Moreover, social benefits are not very generous and have relatively little impact on work incentives.

However, the main problem lies in the fact that job contracts often include mandatory retirement provisions – at an age as early as 45–50.[16] Once they have retired from their regular job, many workers are then forced to accept a job of much lower quality, entailing lower pay and considerable job insecurity, as well as a waste of resources. Indeed, the abrupt retirement pattern that currently characterizes Korean firms raises an efficiency issue: some older workers may have performed more productively had they stayed in their 'regular' job. Of course, as discussed below, such career paths may reflect a rational decision if wages are too disconnected from productivity after a certain age.

Other factors (sometimes closely interrelated with the mandatory retirement system) may explain why regular workers tend to leave their job so early. First, the age – profile of earnings is very steep in Korean firms. This reflects the fact that seniority (and not individual performance or competence development) is the main determinant of wage progression within firms. Available data show that wages of male workers of age 45–49 (the age when wages tend to peak) are, on average, 70 per cent higher than wages of male workers of age 25–29. This gap is larger than in other OECD countries for which data are available – higher even than in the case of Japan, where there is also a well-established practice of seniority-based earnings. However, it is interesting to note that the age–earnings profile for female workers is much less pronounced than is the case for their male counterparts.[17]

Second, given the strict employment protection rules, it is very difficult (and quite costly) to dismiss regular workers in Korea. The combination of steep age–earnings profiles and strict employment protection rules is one reason why job contracts include mandatory early retirement provisions – such provisions mean that workers have to leave the firm at a certain age, without being dismissed. It also explains the relatively high incidence of non-regular employment among older workers. Moreover, according to C. Lee (quoted in KLI 2002), there is a strong sectoral component in the employment of older workers. For instance, more than half of people working after age 65 are employed in agriculture.

Third, unusually long working hours make it difficult for older workers to perform some jobs after a certain age.

However, the Korean training system is not as developed as is the case in other OECD countries. In 2000, only 16 per cent of prime-age workers participated in some form of job-related training (which is lower than in any other OECD country for which data are available). The incidence of training among older workers is less than 10 per cent.

**Policy requirements**

Despite the fact that the current financial burden of public pensions is relatively small, there are strong grounds to believe that the current system is not sustainable. First, available estimates suggest that the system is not adequately funded. Second, pension benefits are calculated in a way that, some time in the future, may discourage work. So far this has not had any labour market impact, given that the pension system was created in 1988 and that few workers receive pension benefits as yet.

Ratio of 50-64-year-olds to 20-64-year-olds, 2000–2050

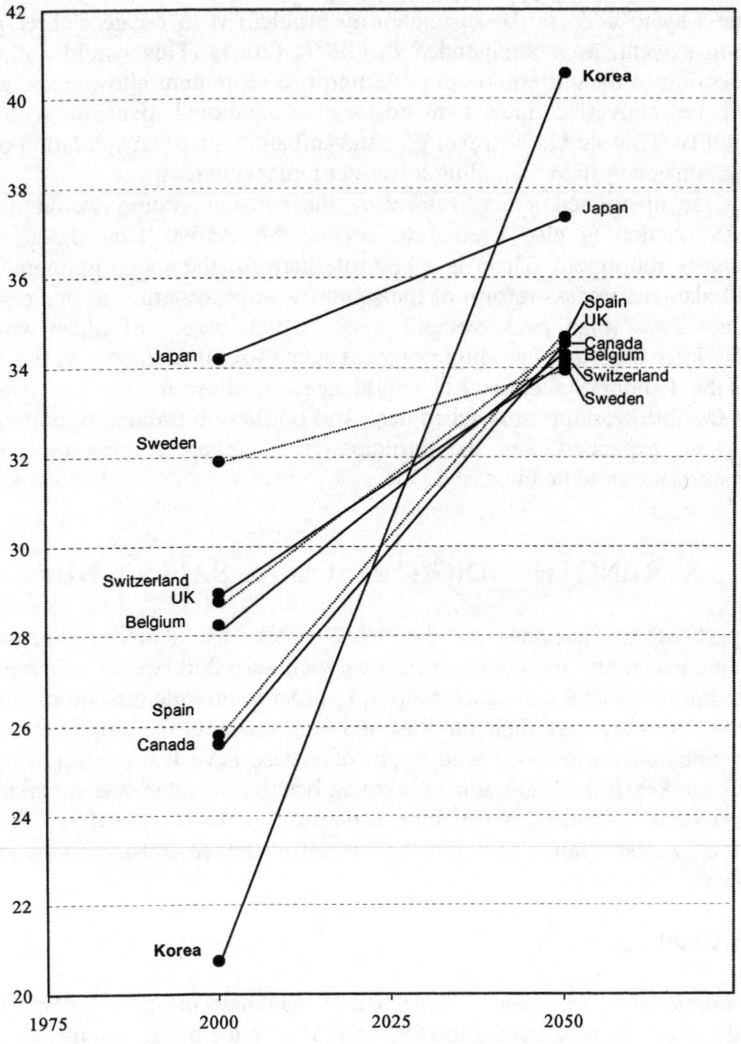


*Sources*: Population projections by national statistical offices.

*Figure 5.3 A Rapidly Greying Workforce*

However, the net replacement rates are likely to be high, once the pension system has matured. In the future, there is a risk that many older low-paid workers will prefer to exit the labour market and receive a pension rather than work in low-wage, poor-quality occupations.

One way to address the sustainability problem is to create a three-pillar pension system, as recommended in OECD (2001). This would include a suppression of the current system of enterprise retirement allowances, which would be converted into a mandatory occupational pension with full portability. This should however go hand-in-hand with a consolidation of the public pension system, including lower net replacement rates.

But, as mentioned above, reforming the pension system would not be enough. Action is also needed to review the current firm practices of mandatory retirement. There is a key role here for the social partners. This would also encompass reform of the seniority wage system – in this respect, the Japanese 'wage peak system' under which wages of older workers decline after a certain age might provide some useful pointers. At the same time, the Labour Standards Act would need to allow for the provision of more flexible working time schedules. And on-the-job training opportunities should be expanded, and the participation of other workers in training programmes should be increased.

## 5.4 STRENGTHENING THE SOCIAL SAFETY NET

As part of its response to the 1997 crisis, the Korean government implemented many temporary measures such as public works programmes and temporary social assistance support in order to provide income support to displaced workers and their families and help maintain the employability of many unemployed persons who might otherwise have lost contact with the labour market. In addition, unemployment benefit coverage was expanded in several steps. Despite this welcome expansion of the social safety net, it is still too modest relative to equity and social insurance considerations in the following dimensions.

### Main Challenges

The *Employment Insurance System* (EIS), which is the main pillar of the social safety net, was created in 1995 and, despite the recent extensions of its coverage to include all firms with at least one employee, still does not cover all eligible workers. According to the latest available data for October 2002, only about 70 per cent of wage and salary earners are eligible for the EIS[18] and only 73 per cent of these are actually insured (Table 5.5).[19]

All in all, as of October 2002, there were only about 7.1 million insured workers out of a dependent workforce of 13.9 million, a proportion of no more than 51 per cent. Reflecting these problems in coverage and eligibility, the proportion of unemployed workers who actually receive a benefit has always been very low and is still less than one in five. In all other OECD countries for which data are available the share of the unemployed that receive benefits is significantly larger – in certain countries almost all unemployed workers are granted an unemployment benefit, once they fulfill the preconditions of active job search and a sufficient work record.

**Table 5.5**
**Coverage of the Employment Insurance System (EIS)[1]**

| | Jul. 1995 | Jan. 1998 | Jul. 1999 | Dec. 2000 | Sept. 2001 | Oct. 2002 |
|---|---|---|---|---|---|---|
| Wage and salary earners | 12 824 | 12 500 | 12 603 | 13 142 | 13 265 | 13 932 |
| Eligible for EIS | 4 280 | 5 190 | 8 342 | 8 700 | 9 269 | 9 700[3] |
| Actually insured | 4 204 | 4 309 | 5 876 | 6 747 | 6 884 | 7 102 |
| Eligible as % of wage and salary earners | 33.4 | 41.5 | 66.2 | 66.2 | 69.9 | 70[3] |
| Insured as % of eligible workers | 98.2 | 83.0 | 70.4 | 77.6 | 74.3 | 73[3] |
| Insured as % of wage and salary earners | 32.8 | 34.5 | 46.6 | 51.3 | 51.9 | 51.0 |
| Proportion of unemployed receiving benefits | .. | .. | 13.5[2] | .. | 17[2] | |

*Notes*: 1 Number of workers are expressed in thousands.
2 Annual averages.
3 Estimates.

*Source*: Information supplied by the Korean authorities.

Most changes to the EIS were introduced between 1998 and early 2000 (expansion of coverage by size of enterprise; relaxation of length of previous employment period required for benefit receipt; prolongation of benefit duration; increase in minimum benefit amounts; increase in contribution rates), after which only relatively minor modifications have been introduced (for example, financial compensation for outplacement services provided by employers).

However, several important changes are planned for the near future. First, the waiting period before receipt of unemployment benefit will be reduced from 14 to 7 days. Second, it is planned to incorporate in the EIS daily workers, whose employment period is less than one month, and part-time workers who work at least 15 hours weekly (previously 18 hours). Most importantly, a new law will tackle the under-reporting of temporary and daily workers by their employers (see the discussion in Hur 2001).

Not only is EIS coverage limited by comparison with other OECD countries but, in addition, benefits are rather modest for the limited number of unemployed workers who receive them. The (daily) job-seeking allowance amounts to 50 per cent of the so-called 'basic daily wage' at the time of separation.[20] The maximum duration of payment of unemployment benefits ranges between three and eight months, depending on the recipient's age at the time of job loss and the period of contribution to the EIS. OECD (2000) shows that, in most respects, benefits provided by the EIS are less generous relative to expected earnings than is the case in the majority of other OECD countries.

*Training programmes* for the unemployed were expanded considerably during the crisis: for example, the number of participants rose eightfold from 1997 to 1998.[21] In both 1998 and 1999 more than 350 000 unemployed attended a training course, accounting for roughly one-fifth of the unemployed in the period considered. Since then the number has fallen sharply again, to around 200 000 in 2001 and 100 000 in 2003.

However, most training programmes for the unemployed appear to be insufficiently targeted at disadvantaged labour market groups. First, there has been an age bias in participation: in 1999, for example, most participants were under 29, while those over 40 were a small minority (OECD 2000, Table 3.9). Second, unemployed workers covered by the EIS are more likely to receive training than other unemployed individuals, and they also receive a higher training allowance than other trainees. Moreover, training programmes for the unemployed tend to suffer from relatively high drop-out rates, while re-employment probabilities of those who complete the courses are relatively low – for example, the Korean authorities estimated that the drop-out rate for 2000 was 52 per cent. This suggests some mismatch between the contents of the courses and labour market requirements.[22]

The limited evidence on the effectiveness of these programmes is mixed. Two 'matched pairs' evaluation studies of training programme participants and non-participants resulted in contradictory findings: while Lee (2000) found that the re-employment rate was higher for training participants, Kang and Lee (2001) found that it was slightly lower than that for non-participants. Korea should consistently evaluate its training programmes rigorously in order to determine which works best, for what participants and in what circumstances.

*Public Works* emerged as a crucial programme to combat rising unemployment; they also fulfilled an important social function as complementary income support in view of the immaturity of the EIS (Lee 2001, Phang and Kim 2001). Figure 5.4 gives an idea of the significance of public works in the Korean arsenal of unemployment measures. For example, their proportion in all spending on active labour market programmes exceeded 70 per cent in both 1999 and 2000, and was still at 55 per cent in 2001.

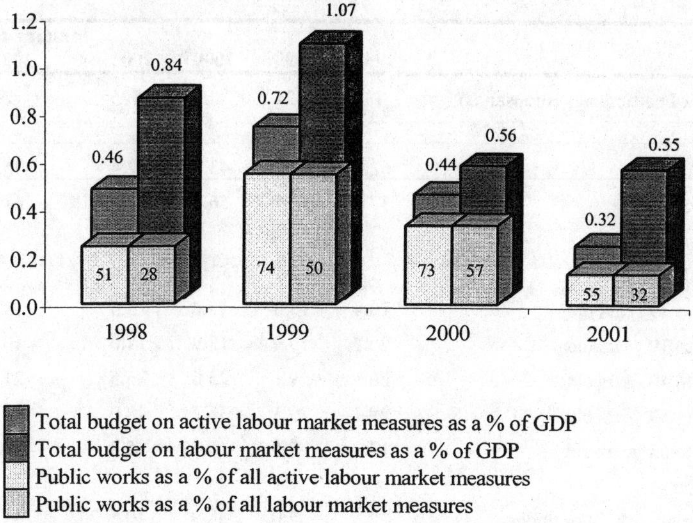


*Source*: Ministry of Labour.

*Figure 5.4 Share of Public Works in Expenditure on Labour Market Measures*

Available data suggest a certain success of public works in terms of holding down the number of unemployed during the financial crisis. For example, in the peak year 1999, over 1.5 million workers participated in public works projects.[23]

However, the implementation of the programmes has been criticized on various grounds. First, selection criteria for participation seem to have been applied with some laxity. In contrast with the official targets, the incidence among participants of well-educated individuals and prime-age workers has been relatively high. Table 5.6 shows the composition of participants on public works by age, gender and educational attainment. Shifts over time in the target population are particularly apparent by gender, where women now represent the majority of participants, reversing the initial dominance of males. Also, the share of 50–59-year-olds has increased considerably between 1998 and 2001, while the largest declines were recorded for 30–39 and 60–65-year-olds. These shifts may reflect a more strict application of the selection criteria, with a focus on the truly needy and disadvantaged.

**Table 5.6**
**Participants on Public Works by Sex, Age and Educational Attainment, 1998–2002**

(%)

<table>
<tr><th></th><th>1998</th><th>1999</th><th>2000</th><th>2001</th><th>January-October 2002</th></tr>
<tr><td>Number of participants (thousands)</td><td>438</td><td>1524</td><td>886</td><td>575</td><td>535</td></tr>
<tr><td>Gender</td><td></td><td></td><td></td><td></td><td></td></tr>
<tr><td>Men</td><td>62.4</td><td>49.7</td><td>43.1</td><td>42.4</td><td>38.1</td></tr>
<tr><td>Women</td><td>37.7</td><td>50.3</td><td>56.9</td><td>57.6</td><td>61.9</td></tr>
<tr><td>Age</td><td></td><td></td><td></td><td></td><td></td></tr>
<tr><td>Under 20 years old</td><td>1.0</td><td>1.1</td><td>1.5</td><td>1.4</td><td>1.6</td></tr>
<tr><td>20 to 29 years old</td><td>10.4</td><td>13.5</td><td>15.0</td><td>13.3</td><td>13.4</td></tr>
<tr><td>30 to 39 years old</td><td>20.2</td><td>19.9</td><td>15.9</td><td>14.0</td><td>10.6</td></tr>
<tr><td>40 to 49 years old</td><td>26.5</td><td>29.1</td><td>25.6</td><td>25.5</td><td>21.5</td></tr>
<tr><td>50 to 59 years old</td><td>29.1</td><td>29.1</td><td>36.2</td><td>40.0</td><td>43.6</td></tr>
<tr><td>60 to 65 years old</td><td>12.9</td><td>7.5</td><td>5.7</td><td>5.8</td><td>9.3</td></tr>
<tr><td>Education</td><td></td><td></td><td></td><td></td><td></td></tr>
<tr><td>Primary school or under</td><td>..</td><td>37.0</td><td>38.9</td><td>40.5</td><td>45.8</td></tr>
<tr><td>Middle school or dropouts</td><td>..</td><td>22.3</td><td>20.5</td><td>20.4</td><td>18.5</td></tr>
<tr><td>High school or dropouts</td><td>..</td><td>26.4</td><td>24.3</td><td>24.0</td><td>22.3</td></tr>
<tr><td>2-year college or dropouts</td><td>..</td><td>5.3</td><td rowspan="2">16.3</td><td rowspan="2">15.1</td><td rowspan="2">13.4</td></tr>
<tr><td>University or higher</td><td></td><td>8.9</td></tr>
</table>

*Sources*: Lee (2001) for 1998–99; and information supplied by the Ministry of Labour for 2000–02.

Second, the rapid expansion of public works ran the risk of crowding out private sector jobs. Indeed, wages paid to participants on public works programmes initially were higher than market wages for certain occupations in agriculture and low-quality (or '3-D') jobs. In response the government cut the wages paid on public works in two stages for most skill levels, so that they are now closer to the legal minimum wage and at a larger discount from local market wages. This is supposed to exert pressure on participants to keep searching for jobs in the market sector. However, there is no evaluation evidence as to whether the reduction in hourly wages has speeded up exit rates from public works into paid employment.

The Ministry of Labour intends to further cut spending on public works, thus decreasing its share in total active measures which, at 55 per cent in 2001, was still much higher than the OECD average of around 15 per cent.

There is an attempt to target programme participation more consistently on the over-40s (already more than 70 per cent of current participants) and to strengthen the outplacement function of the programme.[24]

*Social assistance* in Korea continues to be characterized by strict eligibility criteria, low coverage rates, low benefit levels and certain administrative deficiencies. The 1997 financial crisis threw large numbers of Korean families into poverty and increased the need for social assistance. According to estimates based on the official poverty line, the share of households in poverty rose abruptly from about 5.5 per cent in 1997 to 11 per cent during the financial crisis. While it is the case that the extended family has long provided an effective source of income support in Korea, the supportive role of the extended family has weakened in recent years and the public social safety net has not expanded sufficiently to take up all the slack. In response to this situation the Korean authorities enacted a new social assistance system, the National Basic Livelihood Security Law (NBLS).

The NBLS, which has been in force since October 2000, guarantees year-round cash benefits for everyone earning less than the minimum cost of living and regardless of age and ability to work.[25] It was introduced against the background of the 'productive welfare' concept, which requires reciprocity in benefit receipts for those who are able to work and envisages promoting clients' employability through their referral to active labour market programmes. The Korean productive welfare or 'welfare through work' concept comes close to the recent social welfare reforms in North America, which aim at keeping social assistance clients closely attached to the labour market (see the presentation of the concept in MHW 2001).

Budgetary allocations for social welfare spending in Korea have been increasing rapidly since 1997. Welfare-related spending increased from 1400 to 3675 billion won between 1997 and 2001, almost 4 per cent of the total government budget in 2001 compared to 2 per cent just four years previously. In recent years social assistance benefits accounted for between one-third and one-half of welfare-related spending, with the remainder going into medical aid and other social welfare services.

As the government, during the financial crisis, added to its traditional assistance programme (Livelihood Protection) an additional category for able-bodied unemployed individuals of working age (Temporary Livelihood Protection), the number of recipients increased temporarily to over 1.9 million before falling back with declining unemployment (and the abolition of the latter programme) to about 1.5 million in fiscal year 2001.[26] This figure corresponds to 3.3 percent of the population.[27] Thus, contrary to some expectations, neither the number of beneficiaries nor the proportion of beneficiaries among the total poverty population has risen to any significant extent, the latter still not exceeding more than about half. To some extent, the relatively low coverage rate can be explained by the fact that some potential beneficiaries do not apply for benefits either because they are not aware of their existence or because receiving benefits entails a certain stigma. Other factors have also played a role, notably the relatively strict eligibility criteria and the low level of assistance benefits:

- Strict eligibility criteria: benefits under the NBLS are subject to a means-test based on the capacity (to earn) of extended-family members.[28] Among OECD countries, this is an unusually strict interpretation of family support criteria. The usual practice is that actual income is taken into account – as for example in Switzerland (OECD 1999b).
- The relatively low level of benefits: under the previous social assistance schemes, maximum payments were equivalent to 60 per cent of the official poverty line (Martin and Torres 2000, Table 6). Under the NBLS the official poverty line which, together with household size, serves as the basis for the calculation of benefits, has been raised significantly. The cash benefit levels as a proportion of the minimum cost of living (MCL) have increased by an even greater amount. Table 5.7 shows that households with negligible income of their own (0 to 40 000 Won) get between 80 and 90 per cent of the MCL, whereas they previously received only 50 to 60 per cent (OECD 2000, Table 4.6). Taking into account additional in-kind benefits, this means that Korea has indeed followed OECD recommendations to raise social assistance up to the level of the poverty line. Nevertheless, Table 5.7 also implies that a couple with four children and no earnings of their own receive benefits of just over half of average wages, while in many other OECD countries the assistance benefit to large families would be closer to the national average wage.

**Policy requirements**

Labour market programmes have to be evaluated in the light of their twin objectives, namely (1) to provide income support to the unemployed; and (2) to foster the future employment and earnings prospects of unemployed workers, while minimizing the deadweight, substitution and displacement effects often associated with such policies. Regarding the first objective, the portfolio of labour market programmes in Korea has been expanded considerably since 1997. However, as noted above, only a small minority of the unemployed actually receive unemployment benefits, while the remainder are potential clients for social assistance benefits unless they quickly find re-employment or, alternatively, are offered temporary public works or training slots.

While EIS coverage has greatly expanded and its scope will be further expanded to daily workers and a larger share of part-timers, there remain serious implementation problems in particular among small firms which often

**Table 5.7**
**Monthly Benefit Levels per Household, under the National Basic Livelihood Security Law in 2001**

(% of the monthly minimum cost of living (MCL))

| | Household size persons | | | | | |
|---|---|---|---|---|---|---|
| | 1 | 2 | 3 | 4 | 5 | 6 |
| Household income, in won[1] | | | | | | |
| 0 to 20 000 | 86 | 87 | 88 | 88 | 88 | 88 |
| 20 000 to 40 000 | 80 | 84 | 85 | 86 | 86 | 87 |
| 100 000 to 120 000 | 56 | 69 | 75 | 78 | 79 | 80 |
| 200 000 to 220 000 | 26 | 51 | 61 | 67 | 70 | 72 |
| 300 000 to 320 000 | 7 | 33 | 48 | 57 | 61 | 64 |
| 400 000 to 420 000 | - | 15 | 35 | 46 | 51 | 56 |
| 600 000 to 620 000 | - | - | 10 | 25 | 33 | 39 |
| 800 000 to 820 000 | - | - | - | 8 | 15 | 23 |
| 1 000 000 to 1 020 000 | - | - | - | - | 7 | 9 |
| *Memorandum items* | | | | | | |
| Average monthly wage, won (000s) | | | 1752 | | | |
| MCL, in won (000s) | 333 | 552 | 760 | 956 | 1087 | 1226 |
| MCL, in US$[2] | 278 | 461 | 634 | 797 | 906 | 1022 |
| MCL as % of average monthly wage | 19 | 32 | 43 | 55 | 62 | 70 |

*Notes*: No benefits are paid.
1 For reasons of space, the table shows only a limited number of income categories out of 61 income categories.
2 Assuming an exchange rate of 1 US$ = 1200 won.

*Source*: Information by Ministry of Health and Welfare; and *Monthly Labour Survey* for average wages.

evade altogether the payment of social contributions. The current situation is still not satisfactory and the government should assign a high priority to including most categories of workers in the insurance system, and ensuring that vulnerable groups are not left unprotected. With the incorporation of daily workers and an improved reporting framework, it should be easier to establish a system where, in principle, all employees are affiliated to the EIS as soon as they start to work (apart from public officials and some employees below a certain hours threshold).[29]

As to the effects of active labour market programmes (ALMPs), it is not possible to draw clear-cut conclusions in the relative absence of systematic evaluation studies. However, based on the examination of specific design features of the programmes, the following observations can be made:

- There has been a general lack of targeting in many of the programmes. As a result it is unclear whether they really reach disadvantaged groups, such as unemployed workers not covered by the EIS and young unemployed workers. Targeting is especially important in the case of subsidies to SMEs, given that this programme is the largest in terms of government spending on ALMPs.

- Now that unemployment has fallen back to pre-crisis levels, there is a strong case for keeping public works programmes at a modest level. International evidence (see Martin and Grubb 2001) suggests that these programmes, unless they are well targeted on hard-to-place groups, are particularly ineffective.
- Training institutions have had difficulties in coping with the rapid and massive expansion of training programmes. In addition, the type of training provided by some of them may not be closely tied to the requirements of a complex, modern economy such as Korea's. Apart from careful targeting and keeping programmes relatively small in scale, there is a need to ensure that (1) the programme results in a qualification or certificate that is recognized and valued by the market; and (2) there is a strong on-the-job component in the programme, necessitating strong links with local employers (Martin and Grubb 2001). There is also a good case for a greater involvement of the social partners at the local level in programme design.
- Korea should monitor and evaluate the outcomes of its active labour market programmes rigorously.

The role of the public employment service (PES) in the design and implementation of ALMPs, also needs to be strengthened. Table 5.8 shows the expansion of public, as well as private, placement offices since the mid-1990s. The Ministry of Labour, which ran a very small office network before the financial crisis, has tripled its chain of offices since then. The offices also employ many more job counsellors than before. The parallel chain of local offices run by municipalities and other local governments employs today a much larger number of job counsellors than in the period before 1997. Taken together the 4300 staff in public employment offices are still less than the staff working for the over 5000 private placement agencies, which specialize in temporary and lower-skilled workers and which have also become much more numerous since the financial crisis.

The concept of the 'one-stop office' pursued by the Korean Labour Ministry is a good one, and should be generalized. While it may have been useful in the period of rising unemployment to operate another chain of placement offices under the authority of municipalities and other local governments, the rationale behind the coexistence of two types of 'public employment services', one operating under the Labour Ministry and the other under local government, that are involved in the same tasks (apart from benefit payment), should be reviewed.

**Table 5.8**
**Public and Private Employment Offices**

| | Ministry of Labour offices | | | Local government offices | | | Private employment offices | | |
|---|---|---|---|---|---|---|---|---|---|
| | 1995 | 2001 | October 2002 | 1995 | 2001 | October 2002 | 1995 | 2001 | October 2002 |
| Offices | 52 | 191 | 166 | 285 | 269 | 253 | 1271 | 4361 | 5265 |
| Staff | 1000 | 2497 | 2354 | 360 | 1370 | 1975 | 3500 | .. | .. |

*Note*: .. Data not available.

*Source*: Information by Ministry of Labour.

As mass unemployment declines, PES officers will need to devote more efforts to in-depth counselling and monitoring of those job - seekers who are at high risk of long-term unemployment and benefit dependency – at present there is little 'profiling' of the unemployed. Improved contacts with employers are also required to ensure that the PES receives a sufficient flow of new vacancies for its clientele. Needless to say the efficiency of the PES crucially depends on the quality of its staff, and the high turnover of counsellors, almost all of whom work under one-year temporary contracts (apart from the few civil servants hired before 1997), is problematic in this respect. Additional recruitment is desirable to improve officer-to-client ratios, but improving training and job prospects for existing PES staff is equally important. The return to low unemployment levels should provide the necessary breathing space for the PES to concentrate on improving staff quality, and to shift more personnel from the benefit payment function to job-search assistance.

In addition, Korea should seek to take advantage of the extensive network of private employment agencies that presently exist. Even after the recent expansion of the PES, private employment agencies outnumber PES offices by a factor of 12 to one. These agencies have an excellent intermediation record in the unskilled labour market and the PES could seek complementarities with them, for example by contracting out the placement of low-educated unemployed. Many OECD countries are beginning to rethink the role of the PES and expanding the opportunities for market forces to improve its effectiveness. Given that Korea already has a large infrastructure of private employment agencies in place, the authorities should seek to exploit this potential to the maximum.

As to social assistance programmes, although the new NBLS system now grants cash benefits as a matter of right, many low-income individuals still remain unprotected. This partly reflects the fact that benefit entitlement, as noted above, is subject to unusually strict income criteria, based on the income capacity (and not the actual income) of the extended family. This particular provision of the law may have to be revised if the official target of providing benefits of last resort to all those in need is to be reached. Also, despite their increase, benefits have remained modest. The authorities need to ensure that they are at least equivalent to the official poverty line.

In addition, making productive welfare a reality depends on a certain number of institutional preconditions being met. In 1998/99 there were only 3000 local social welfare officers for a caseload of 850 000 households, representing a very high caseload-to-staff ratio in comparison with other OECD countries. Their number increased to about 5500 in 2001, and local authorities planned to hire 1700 more social workers during 2002 so that the caseload-to-staff ratio would decline considerably and approach the international benchmark of 100 – to - 1. Much lower caseloads are important if social workers are to take on a more active role in reintegrating their clients into the labour market. It will also be necessary to train social workers in their new role as case managers and to equip them with the necessary information technology to manage their recipient database in the newly-created Welfare-Net, as well as link up with the vacancy information contained in the PES Work-Net.

Local frontline officers are now required to conduct intensive screening interviews, establish a personalized follow-up plan on the basis of the client's work ability and family circumstances, and refer the employable clients either to the local PES job centres or to public works projects. The extent to which this transition to a type of Korean 'workfare' system has been successful, cannot be fully assessed yet. Experts in the field have argued that the new system will probably take several years to implement to any satisfactory degree. They consider it difficult to provide private sector jobs for social assistance recipients and report instead an increasing reliance on public works. More generally, policy coherence between the Ministries for Labour and for Health and Welfare is considered difficult to achieve both at national and at local levels:

- For example, while it is a welcome feature of the 'productive welfare' paradigm that able-bodied social assistance clients are, in principle, referred to PES offices, it is not evident where the principal responsibility lies for reintegrating these clients into the labour market (that is with municipalities or with the PES). Also, there seem to be no new incentives for PES offices to deal with this client group (which tends not to have paid EIS contributions). However, Korea is certainly not alone among OECD countries in facing such difficulties of better synchronizing social assistance and employment-related policies.[30]
- A final concern is whether the NBLS enhances financial incentives to work or rather implies benefit traps by denying any financial advantages to clients, who seek to top up their social assistance benefits by earnings

from some gainful employment. Any encouragement to take up work would require a system of earnings disregards. However, the benefit amounts underlying Table 5.7 contain no such earnings disregard for most types of assistance recipients. The Ministry of Health and Welfare has pointed out to the authors the existence of a 10 to 15 per cent earnings disregard for students and the disabled, and its plan to extend this scheme to all NBLS - beneficiaries.

## 5.5 CONCLUDING REMARKS

In sum, despite the return to a high-growth path, Korea should not reduce the momentum of labour market and social policy reforms. It has managed to catch up rapidly *vis-à-vis* other OECD countries, but further progress may be more difficult to achieve than is often thought. Indeed, future improvements in living standards may have to rest on using resources more efficiently, rather than more intensively as was the case before the 1997 crisis. A more qualitative approach to the development strategy may be called for, encompassing an increased emphasis on enterprise training, a reduced labour–market duality and the establishment of a well-functioning social safety net that covers all individuals.

More analytical work is needed to understand how policy reforms may improve the long-term socio-economic performance – and, in the absence of this work, policy options have to be discussed with due caution. With this caveat in mind, this chapter has suggested that it is particularly important to (1) improve the quality of education and foster enterprise training; (2) expand effectively the coverage of both the EIS and social assistance benefits, while scaling back some ALMPs adopted as a temporary response to the crisis; (3) ensure that employers pay their contributions to the employment security and public pension systems and, provided that is the case, gradually reduce enterprise retirement allowances for regular workers, thereby helping to reduce the marked duality that presently exists and laying the ground for higher productivity gains; (4) adapt the retirement system and employment practices to the challenges of ageing; (5) better target ALMPs, enhance the quality of the PES staff and undertake rigorous evaluations of the programmes; and (6) make sure that work continues to pay in Korea.

Obviously, these measures need to be adopted in a context of full respect for basic workers' rights and, in this sense, resolving remaining industrial relations issues should rank high on the policy agenda. In a modern, productive economy, it is important that all social actors be involved in the reform process in a climate of mutual respect and trust.

## NOTES

1 These reforms include: (1) the recognition of the principle of trade union pluralism, and the subsequent recognition of the KCTU (Korean Confederation of Trade Unions) as the second trade union centre in Korea; (2) the granting of the right to organize teachers' unions; (3) the lifting of the ban on political activities of trade unions; (4) the establishment of the Tripartite Commission as a consultative framework for intensive discussions and compromise agreements on labour issues; and (5) the adoption of a government plan to limit arrests of trade union members and leaders.

2 Already under current conditions, employer associations complain that their members are forced to pay an overly large number of union officers in relation to the workforce members they represent, compared with the situation in other OECD countries.

3 According to a recent survey by the German Trade Union Confederation, there are over 220 000 works council members representing 10.5 million salaried employees (the majority of German firms, particularly SMEs, do not have works council representation). Of these, about 20 000 works council members are full-time officials, while most of the others get time off only for special occasions (EIRO 2002, Ratayczak 1999).

4 What is indeed unique in Korea, is that even officials working in FKTU and KCTU national or sectoral headquarters often maintain a formal employment relationship with their previous enterprise and remain on its payroll.

5 Most trade unions in OECD countries have varying proportions of students, self-employed, unemployed and retired workers among their ranks (OECD 1991, Chapter 4).

6 Although the February 1998 Tripartite Commission Agreement did recognize unemployed workers' rights to join a trade union or remain a union member (although not at the enterprise level), a corresponding bill, subsequently submitted by the government, was rejected by the National Assembly. Despite repeated statements of intent by the government, no further bill has been submitted to resolve this problem.

7 In some other countries as well (Germany and Japan, for example), the representative associations of civil servants do not carry the designation 'trade union'. These countries' experiences also show that to allow bargaining rights without the formal recognition of a right to conclude collective agreements does not necessarily 'render collective bargaining rights meaningless', as suggested for example by Moon (2002).

8 According to government estimates, there were up to 40 cases of

multiple unions at the firm level in 2002, resulting mainly from mergers and acquisitions, or based on occupational demarcation. In the former case management can insist on a single-bargaining channel, that is refuse separate bargaining with individual unions, without this being considered an unfair labour practice.

9 In this context it is interesting to consult a summary of comments by ILO Committees on strike sanctions, focusing on the aspect of proportionality and their impact on labour relations stability: 'restrictions on strike pickets and workplace occupations should be limited to cases where the action ceases to be peaceful … Sanctions for strike action should be possible only where the prohibitions in question are in conformity with the principles of freedom of association. Even in such cases, both excessive recourse to the courts in labour relations and the existence of heavy sanctions for strike action may well create more problems than they resolve. Since the application of disproportionate penal sanctions does not favour the development of harmonious and stable industrial relations, if measures of imprisonment are to be imposed at all, they should be justified by the seriousness of the offences committed' (ILO 1994, p. 76f).

10 See Martin and Torres (2000) and Pilat (1993).

11 See Hipple (2001) for a recent presentation of the US concept and data.

12 With about 24%, this share was even higher in the 2003 supplementary survey.

13 Longitudinal data also show that the share of non-regular workers among the newly employed is much higher than the non-regular share among all employed – it was over 70 per cent in September and October 2001, for example (KLI 2001).

14 It should be added that if other countries (apart from the United States) eliminated those workers from the temporary employment category that have either a limited contract or no contract at all, but expect their current employment to last, the share of temporary workers would fall in these countries as well.

15 For details, see OECD (1999a, Chapter 2).

16 Some evidence is quoted in KLI (2002) that, on average, regular workers leave their firm in their mid-50s.

17 One reason may be that relatively few women have a regular job in Korea. Seniority-based wage increases mainly apply to regular jobs.

18 Major exceptions are: public officials; private and public school teachers; daily workers employed for less than one month; workers over age 65 and new employees over age 60; part-time workers working less than 18 hours a week or 80 hours a month; construction workers in very small enterprises; and household workers.

19 There are several reasons for this: (1) there is a general lack of awareness of the need for unemployment insurance among both labour and management; (2) many small businesses avoid paying social security contributions to save non-wage labour costs and avoid administrative red tape (this applies particularly to temporary workers); and (3) labour inspectors have difficulties in surveying EIS coverage in the large number of very small businesses.

20 The job-seeking allowance is subject to a ceiling and it cannot fall below a minimum level. The ceiling for the job-seeking allowance is currently set at 35 000 won per day, that is approximately US$30 per day, or a little over half the average daily wage. The minimum job-seeking allowance is 90 per cent of the minimum wage, that is currently around 16 000 won or US$13 per day.

21 The main training programmes available to the unemployed are: (1) re-employment training of the unemployed, a programme targeted to workers dismissed from enterprises covered by the EIS, independently of whether these workers are entitled to unemployment benefits or not; (2) training for employment promotion, which focuses on dismissed workers not previously insured under the EIS, that is mostly temporary, daily and part-time workers; (3) training for unemployed new entrants into the labour market (but most young unemployed have been granted internships under public works programmes, as discussed below); (4) training for business start-ups, targeted at elderly unemployed, disabled individuals and school drop-outs; and (5) manpower development training, which comprises initial training for craftsmen and training for '3-D' jobs. Of these, only the first programme is set up under the EIS and therefore funded by the Employment Insurance Fund. The others are financed out of the general government budget.

22 Lee et al. (2001) have argued: 'diverse training programmes that were loosely regulated and lacked appropriate monitoring and inspection led to moral hazard of some training institutions and trainees. Some unqualified training institutions took advantage of the training programmes and provided time-killing courses in order to receive reimbursement from the government, thus limiting the[ir] effectiveness … Little consideration was given either to changing demands in the labour market or to the needs of the potential participants. Training institutions tended to routinely provide the same training programmes as were conducted in the past.'

23 In 2001, the number of participants fell to 575 000.

24 One difficulty in cutting back spending on public works is that central government spending is tied in with expenditure by regional governments.

25 Previously, certain groups of social assistance clients (particularly

those able to work) received their benefits mainly in-kind, and/or over the winter months only.

26 A quarter of these (360 000) were classified as 'employable', and the remainder as non-employable.

27 The share of the population reached by public assistance increases to over 5 per cent, if other programmes are taken into account in addition to the NBLS.

28 Thus, under present rules, a person with an income barely above subsistence level may not be entitled to social assistance benefits if the combined earnings' capacity of the individual and his or her family exceeds a certain threshold.

29 An improved coordination of administrative records relating to unemployment insurance, taxes and pensions would also help in this regard.

30 For example, a recent analysis of the cooperation between social assistance and public employment offices in European countries came to the conclusion that 'the PES currently lacks strong institutional incentives to cooperate with local authorities in serving the social assistance clientele of local authorities' (de Koning and Mosley 2001).

## REFERENCES

Ahn, J. (2002), 'What have we learned about Alternative Employment Arrangements in Korea?' *e-labor news* No. 3, Korea Labor Institute, January, www.kli.re.kr/english/labornews/03/subpaper.html.

Ahn, J., J. Cho and J. Nam (2001), *Non-standard Employment and Policy Suggestions*, Seoul: Korea Labor Institute (in Korean).

Choi, Y.K. (2002), 'Labor Reforms during Restructuring', *Korea Journal*, Spring, 100–28.

EIRO (2002), 'Provisional results of 2002 works council elections', http://www.eiro.eurofound.ie/2002/12

Hipple, S. (2001), 'Contingent Work in the Late 1990s', *Monthly Labor Review*, March.

Hur, J.-J. (2001), 'Expanding the Coverage of Korea's Unemployment Insurance', in F. Park, Y.-B. Park G. Betcherman and A. Dar (*eds*) (2001), *Labor Market Reforms in Korea: Policy Options for the Future*, World Bank and Korea Labor Institute.

ILO (International Labour Office) (1994), *Freedom of Association and Collective Bargaining*, Geneva.

ILO (1996), Freedom of Association. Digest of Decisions and Principles of the Freedom of Association Committee of the Governing Body of the ILO, 4th edn, Geneva.

ILO (1998), 309th Report of the Committee on Freedom of Association, Geneva.

ILO (2001), *Complaints against the Government of the Republic of Korea*, 324th Report of the Committee on Freedom of Association, Geneva.

ILO (2002), 327th Report of the Committee on Freedom of Association, Geneva.

Jacobs, A.J.M. (1998), 'The Law of Strikes and Lockouts', in R. Blanpain and C. Engels (eds), *Comparative Labour Law and Industrial Relations in Industrialised Market Economies*, 6th edn, Hague: Kluwer Law International.

Kang, S.-H. and B.H. Lee (2001), 'Evaluating the Training for the Unemployed in Korea', in F. Park, Y.-B. Park G. Betcherman and A. Dar (*eds*), *Labor Market Reforms in Korea: Policy Options for the Future*, World Bank and Korea Labor Institute.

Kim, D.I. (2002), 'The Korean Labor Market: The Crisis and After', in David T. Coe and Le-Jik Kim (eds), *Korean Crisis and Recovery*, IMF and Korea Institute for International Economic Policy.

KLI (Korea Labor Institute) (2001), *e-Labor News No. 2*, December, www.kli. re.kr/english/labornews/02/subtrends.html.

KLI (Korea Labor Institute) (2002), proceedings from a seminar on Labor Market Policies in an Aging Era, mimeo, June.

de Koning, J. and M. Mosley (2001), 'Conclusions', in Jaap de Koning and Hugh Mosley (eds), *Labour Market Policy and Unemployment: Impact and Process Evaluations in Selected European Countries,* Cheltenham: Edward Elgar Publishing.

Kwack, S.Y (2000), 'Total Factor Productivity Growth and the Source of Growth in Korean Manufacturing Industries, 1971~1993', *Journal of the Korean Economy*, **1**(2), Autumn, 229–65.

Lee, B.-H. (2000), 'Quasi-Experimental Evaluation of the Impact of Training for the Unemployed', *Korean Journal of Labor Economics*, **23**(2).

Lee, C.S. and J. Cho (2002), 'Facts and Policy Issues regarding Full-Time Labor Union Officials', paper presented at international conference on International Labor Standards and Industrial Relations in Korea, Seoul, November.

Lee, W.D. and J. Lee (2001), 'Will the Model of Uncoordinated Decentralisation Persist? Changes in Korean Industrial Relations after the Financial Crisis', manuscript, Korea Labor Institute, March.

Lee, J. (2001), 'Income Assistance and Employment Creation through Public Works in Korea', in F. Park, Y.-B. Park G. Betcherman and A. Dar (*eds*), *Labor Market Reforms in Korea: Policy Options for the Future*, World Bank and Korea Labor Institute.

Lee, J. (2002), 'Pressure Towards Centralisation and Changes in Collective Bargaining Structure', paper presented at an international conference on International Labor Standards and Industrial Relations in Korea, Seoul, November.

Lee, W.-D., J.J. Hur and H. Kim (2001), 'Assessing the Role of Korean Employment Insurance and Work Injury Insurance as a Social Safety Net', paper presented at the International Symposium for Sharing Productive Welfare Experience, Korea Labor Institute, September.

Martin, J.P. and Grubb, D. (2001), 'What Works and for Whom: A Review of OECD Countries' Experience with Active Labour Market Policies', *Swedish Economic Policy Review*, **8**, 9-56.

Martin, J.P. and Torres, R. (2000), 'Korean Labour Market and Social Safety-Net Reforms: Challenges and Policy Requirements', *Journal of the Korean Economy*, **1**(2), Autumn, 267–300.

MHW (Ministry of Health and Welfare) (2001), *Health and Welfare Services*, Seoul.

Moon, M.G. (2002), 'Protection of Fundamental Labor Rights of Civil Servants', paper presented at an international conference on International Labor Standards and Industrial Relations in Korea, Seoul, November.

NSO (2001), *Annual Report on the Economically Active Population Survey*, Korea National Statistical Office.

OECD (1991), *Employment Outlook*, Paris.

OECD (1999a), *Employment Outlook*, Paris, July.

OECD (1999b), *The Battle Against Exclusion*, 3, Social Assistance in Canada and Switzerland, Paris.

OECD (2000), *Pushing Ahead with Reform in Korea*, Paris.

OECD (2001), *OECD Economic Surveys: Korea*, Paris, September.

OECD (2002), *Employment Outlook*, Paris.

OECD (2003), *Economic Outlook*, Paris.

Park, F., Y.-B. Park G. Betcherman and A. Dar (*eds*) (2001), *Labor Market Reforms in Korea: Policy Options for the Future*, World Bank and Korea Labor Institute.

Phang, H. and D.-H. Kim (2001), 'Policy Options for Income Support and Active Labor Market Programs: A Synthesis of the Korean Experience', paper prepared for the World Bank Conference on Labour Market Policies: Implications to East and Southeast Asia, Korea Labor Institute.

Pilat, D. (1993), 'The Economics of Catch Up: The Experience of Japan and Korea', Groningen Growth and Development Centre, Monograph Series, No. 2.

Ratayczak, J. (1999), 'Novellierungsvorschläge des DGB zum Betriebsverfassungsgesetz', *WSI-Mitteilungen*, No. 11.

# 6. Public Sector Reforms

**Junsok Yang**

## 6.1 INTRODUCTION

Due to the Asian financial crisis and the recession that followed, 1998 was the first year Korea recorded a negative growth rate in real GDP since 1980. While the crisis and the recession were triggered by the contagion effect from South-East Asia, Korea suffered a much harsher effect than many other Asian countries due to its various structural problems. In order to overcome the financial crisis and strengthen the underlying structure of the economy, Korea instituted various reform measures. While no area of the Korean economy was completely untouched by these, most of the reform measures related to the financial crisis can be classified into one of four categories: financial sector reforms, corporate sector reforms, labour market reforms and public sector reforms. There were, of course, other major reform measures that do not quite fit into these four categories, such as measures to facilitate and increase foreign investment and various measures to reduce trade barriers. However, the four categories are often referred to collectively as the 'four major reform areas' to emphasize their importance.

This chapter focuses on public sector reforms. Public sector reforms perhaps differ from the other three areas of major reforms in that many of the reforms began before the financial crisis, but they were accelerated and intensified following the financial crisis.

Public sector reforms focused mainly on three areas. The first was the streamlining of government structure, and making government administration and management more efficient. The second was privatizing various state-owned enterprises (SOEs) and improving the management of the remaining state-owned or state-controlled enterprises. The final area was deregulation and regulatory reform. This chapter looks at each of these three areas in detail.

## 6.2 GOVERNMENT STRUCTURAL AND MANAGERIAL REFORMS

### 6.2.1 Government Structural Reforms

From the beginning of the financial crisis, it was obvious that the structure of the government would be changed.[1] The financial crisis hit Korea just weeks before a presidential election, and incoming presidents typically change the structure of the government to fit their policy emphasis. The previous president, Kim Young-Sam, had initiated four government-restructuring efforts, and had combined many individual ministries to obtain synergies and reduce overhead costs. For example, the Ministry of Finance and the Economic Planning Bureau were combined as the Ministry of Finance and Economy (MOFE), and the Ministry of Transportation and the Ministry of Construction were combined into the Ministry of Construction and Transportation. Whether these changes actually improved government efficiency is still under debate.

Thus, most political observers had believed that the new president would change the structure of the government even before the financial crisis. However, when the crisis hit, many observers argued that the crisis showed that there was an urgent need for government structural reform. They argued that a major reason why the government did not foresee and deflect the crisis, and could not effectively combat it, was the cumbersome size of the government ministries and inefficient organization. Further, due to the massive economic shock, the government budget would have to be decreased substantially, with reduction and even elimination of some ministries and agencies.

When President Kim Dae Jung was elected, he assigned a study committee to examine how the government structure should be changed. The committee consisted of fourteen civilians and nine public officials, and it met for 50 days between January and February of 1998. The discussions were open to the public for the most part, but there was reportedly heavy behind-the-scenes political pressure by various interest groups[2]. There was also strong pressure to reduce the role and influence of the Ministry of Finance and Economy (MOFE), which had been acting as 'first among equals' among economic ministries because its minister was also the deputy prime minister for economic affairs. Many critics accused MOFE of being negligent, and bearing the primary responsibility for not being able to deal with the financial crisis.

President Kim Dae Jung took office on 25 February 1998. Shortly before the inauguration on 17 February 1998, legislation was passed to change the structure of the government. This was the first of the three government restructurings during the Kim Dae Jung administration. The underlying principles behind the first restructuring included downsizing the government, strengthening the authority of the president and the prime minister, eliminating redundancies within the government, and improving the quality of government.

Perhaps the biggest change in the first restructuring was the establishment of the Office of Budget, which later became the Ministry of Planning and Budget (MPB), and a reduction in the power of MOFE. Responding to calls for reduction of the power of MOFE the position of deputy prime minister for economic affairs was eliminated, and its minister would now be an ordinary minister. The budget and economic planning functions of MOFE were transferred to an independent office and a committee: the Office of Budget, and the Planning and Budget Committee. The Korean title for MOFE was changed to reflect the reduction of power. It was presumed that the prime minister would take the responsibilities of the deputy prime minister,[3] while the Minister of MOFE would have no overarching role in economic policy-making. The financial supervisory role of MOFE was also transferred to new agencies, the Financial Supervisory Commission and the Financial Supervisory Service.[4]

A Planning and Budget Committee, along with a Special Committee for Gender Affairs, and a Special Committee for Small and Medium Enterprises were established directly under the president. In order to strengthen the role of the Prime Minister, the role of the Administrative Coordination Office was expanded and strengthened, and became the Office of the Prime Minister. The Prime Minister also took strong roles in the newly established Financial Supervisory Commission and the Regulatory Reform Commission (RRC). The Ministry of Information, the ministry responsible for the government's public relations work, was eliminated. That ministry was substantially downsized and became the National Information Office, placed under the control of the Prime Minister. Korea had formerly maintained two deputy Prime Ministers, one in charge of reunification, and one in charge of economic affairs, but both of these positions were eliminated, and its responsibilities were given to the Prime Minister. As a result, the Korean titles for the Ministry of Reunification and MOFE were changed to reflect the reduction in status.

Another major change in government structure was the shift of responsibility for trade negotiations. Previously, the responsibility for trade negotiations was under the individual ministries, with the Ministry of Trade and Industry (MTI) responsible for coordinating various ministries. However, some critics argued that the responsibility for trade negotiations should be more centralized so that negotiation strategies could be more unified. Some critics also argued that MTI was not appropriate as the coordinating agency because it had a conflict of interest. They claimed that since MTI had the responsibility for promoting and regulating domestic industries it had a bias toward protecting domestic industries, and it did not give due attention to trade issues. Thus, the primary responsibility for trade negotiations was given to the Ministry of Foreign Affairs. As a result, the Ministry of Foreign Affairs became the Ministry of Foreign Affairs and Trade (MOFAT), and MTI became the Ministry of Commerce, Industry and Energy (MOCIE). Personnel were transferred from MTI to MOFAT to create the Office of the Korea Trade Representative, which deals with trade negotiations. The Korea trade representative is considered a vice-minister in MOFAT domestically, but considered a full minister abroad when he is negotiating overseas.

Other changes included a merger of the Ministry of Government Administration and the Ministry of Home Affairs, which became the Ministry of Government Administration and Home Affairs (MOGAHA), and the establishment of the Korea Food and Drug Safety Administration. Overall, as a result of the first restructuring, the number of central government ministries and agencies fell from two (large) ministries, 14 ministries, two offices, and 14 agencies to 17 ministries, two offices, and 16 agencies. The number of minister-level positions was reduced from 21 to 17.

The public reaction to the restructuring was at best lukewarm. From November 1998 to February 1999, 19 private agencies examined the results of the first restructuring and suggested further restructuring. Their reports and recommendations were completed and submitted in February 1999. The government and the National Assembly finalized the second reorganization plan in May 1999 but, in many ways, the political expediencies won out over efficiency goals.

First, the government de-emphasized their previously stated goal of downsizing government and emphasized increased efficiency and quality of service. Unlike the first restructuring, the number of ministries and offices rose as a result of the second restructuring. Two relatively small offices, which had been created in the first restructuring, the Office of Budget, and the Planning and Budget Committee, were combined to form the Ministry of Planning and Budget. The downsized National Information Office was combined with public relations offices in the Ministry of Culture and Tourism to form an independent agency, the Government Information Agency, in effect undoing the elimination of the Ministry of Information. The Civil Service Commission was founded to reinforce transparency and fairness in personnel decisions.

Meanwhile, the report by the 19 private agencies had recommended that the Ministry of Information and Communication, the Ministry of Science and Technology, and the Ministry of Commerce, Industry and Energy be merged; the Ministry of Labour and Ministry of Health and Welfare be merged; and the Ministry of Maritime Affairs be eliminated. None of these recommendations were taken, reportedly because of heavy lobbying by interest groups and the ministries themselves.[5]

The third restructuring took place in January 2001. The intended goal of this round of restructuring was to reinforce certain social and economic policies that were expected to be important in the future. First, the position of deputy prime minister for economic affairs was revived. While the separation of budgetary and financial supervisory functions from MOFE was successful in reducing its power, there had been numerous critics who argued that, with the elimination of the position of deputy prime minister, there was no longer a central figure who was fully in charge of economic policy, and the lack of leadership and coordination was making economic policy-making difficult. These critics argued that the deputy prime minister was necessary to act as a coordinator and a final decision-maker in charge of economic policy. Thus, the Minister of Finance and Economy would again serve as the deputy prime minister for economic affairs.

Education had always been a sensitive political issue in Korea and, since the financial crisis, re-education of displaced workers and the development of human capital had emerged as politically sensitive issues. To reinforce the role of government in these issues, the position of the Minister of Education and Human Resources was raised to that of a deputy prime minister in charge of human resource development.

The final major development was the establishment of the Ministry of Gender Affairs. In the first restructuring, a Special Committee for Gender Affairs had been created to examine gender inequality issues and, when necessary, take steps to correct them. However, critics had complained that the Special Committee was not strong enough to overcome the institutional and cultural biases against women in Korea. Thus, the Special Committee was expanded into a full ministry.

By this time, the goal of government restructuring lay strongly on the side of 'efficiency and quality of service' rather than downsizing of the government. While the number of government employees fell between 1998 and 2002, the number of ministries rose. At the end of the third restructuring, there were 18 ministries, four offices and 16 agencies, more than the number at the end of 1997.

### 6.2.2 Government Managerial Reforms

During the post-crisis period, along with the structural reforms, managerial reforms were taken as well. Most notably, there had been major changes in the personnel system. First, the number of government employees fell significantly during the post-crisis era. The total number of government employees at the end of 1997 were estimated to be 936 000, including employees in the judicial and legislative branch, employees in provincial and local governments, as well as educators and police. This number was reduced to 868 000 by the end of 2001. If the judicial and legislative employees are excluded, the number of employees was reduced from 919 000 to 850 000.[6] The number of departments, bureaus and offices in the central government fell as well.

The cuts were not limited to the central government. Two major waves of restructuring took place in the provincial and local governments, the first in June 1998 and the second in February 1999. The number of offices, bureaus and departments within the provincial and local governments were cut, and the number of government employees was reduced by more than 56 000. A reduction of more than 19 per cent. At the end of 2002 the number of employees in provincial and local governments stood at 245 735 workers, similar to the levels of 1991.[7]

Methods of hiring government employees changed significantly. In the Korean government, there are nine grades of employees. Previously, new entrants had to take civil service examinations to become grade 5, 7 or 9, and rise through the ranks. Hiring new government employees without having them go through the examination process was difficult at best. However, after the financial crisis, leeway had been given to hire civilians, bypassing the civil service examinations. Early in the Kim Dae Jung administration MOFAT began hiring civilian trade negotiation experts for the Office of the Korea Trade Representative, and the Financial Supervisory Service hired civilian financial experts to serve along with government employees. However, the experts for MOFAT were hired on a contract basis and were considered temporary consultants,[8] while the Financial Supervisory Service, a special judicial entity, is sometimes considered a government–civilian partnership rather than a full government agency so the leeway to hire employees without taking the civil service examination was effectively very limited.

However, the government positions were further opened to civilians. In the past promotions to grades 1 to 3 had been available only to current government employees, but, currently, private sector applicants can be employed in these categories. The Civil Service Commission established an Open Employment System where 130 positions were designated for open employment to attract more talented people from outside the government.[9]

The pay scale for government employees was adjusted as well to bring pay more in line with civilian pay, and also introduce various pay incentives for government employees. In 1998 MOGAHA introduced a performance-related pay programme for government employees, and in 1999 the government introduced a 'yearly stipend system' for government employees of grades 1 to 3 who are mostly assistant ministers and bureau directors in the central government. The new system moved away from the fixed salary system based on seniority and rank, and toward a system where pay is differentiated within each pay grade band depending on performance. In 1998 MOGAHA estimated that the income for government employees was approximately 87 per cent that of civilian employees, and this incentive system was a part of a five-year plan to bring government pay more closely in line with civilian pay.[10] However, some newspaper reports have claimed that because there are as yet no clear criteria for giving out these incentives the incentive system does not truly reward superior work, but, rather, is used as a mere pay increase for government workers.[11]

The Korean government also began using the concept of an 'executive agency'. Executive agencies are semi-autonomous agencies responsible for their own operational management. These agencies are kept at a distance from the central department so that they have more freedom to manage, and provide better customer-oriented service, as well as foster a performance-oriented culture. These agencies have clearly stated missions and standards of performance that are the responsibility of the agency head. The agency head is selected through open recruitment, and he is contracted for three years. If he succeeds in delivering performance standards and business plans as stated in the contract, the contract will be renewed. Initially, the executive agency concept was applied to ten agencies such as national medical centres and automobile license testing stations. By the end of 2002, 23 agencies were operating under the executive agency concept.[12]

Other management reforms included the increased use of outsourcing and contracting out for services previously provided or carried out by government employees, such as janitorial work for government buildings and development of computer networks. Also, the government began a major effort toward establishing an 'e-government'. Measures included establishing a 'G4C' network where the Internet would be used for routine paperwork or applications, providing information about government policy, and receiving comments from the public; establishing information-sharing networks among regional governments; and establishing an electronic network for government procurement.[13]

These management measures typically concerned efficiency, transparency and improvement in the delivery of government services. There has also been an attempt to change the culture of bureaucracy – to reinforce the idea that the government is a service provider that must serve the public, rather than the traditional idea of 'top-down' government where government forces the public to obey. It is not yet clear whether the cultural change has been successful.

### 6.2.3 Evaluation

For government restructuring the post-crisis reforms have been a series of missteps. Government took several reforms, such as the elimination of the deputy prime minister for economic affairs, that it had to undo later on. The first restructuring was a result of the public demand for retribution and change as a result of the financial crisis, as seen by the downsizing of MOFE; and political compromise, as seen in the elimination of the position of deputy prime ministers and the strengthening of the prime minister to accommodate the ruling party's coalition partner. The second and third restructuring may be considered a victory for bureaucracy and political expediency. In the second restructuring, even though major studies were carried out on government restructuring, the final result ignored many of the major recommendations of these studies. Also, while it is debatable whether the government's stated goal of downsizing the government was actually desirable, it is notable that the government began to ignore this goal outright from the second restructuring effort onwards.

These changes may have had adverse effects on Korean businesses. In the 2001–2002 Global Competitiveness Report by the World Economic Forum (WEF), Korea ranked twenty-fourth highest out of 75 countries surveyed in terms of the costs of institutional change over the last five years. However, the reforms may have had a positive effect overall, as the 2002 World Competitiveness Report by the IMD show that Korea's ranking in the government efficiency category rose from thirty-eighth place out of 45 countries surveyed in 1997 to thirty-first place out of 49 in 2001.[14]

As seen, government restructuring in the post-crisis period seems to have been driven more by politics than by a considered examination and review, since many of the efforts made in the first restructuring had to be undone in the second and third restructurings. However, there have been some positive developments as well. Kim (2002) argues that the newly created Budget and Planning Committee served as an agency within government whose purpose was to drive the reforms, and thus played a key role in government reform. The committee played an important part in SOE reforms as well. However, Kim (2002) also notes that when the Budget and Planning Committee became a full ministry its ability to push for reforms may have weakened since the committee had been directly answerable to the president and had his full support, but when it became the MPB it became just another ministry headed by an appointed minister.[15]

## 6.3 PRIVATIZATION AND REFORM OF STATE OWNED ENTERPRISES

### 6.3.1 Privatization

Korea began privatizing many of its SOEs long before the financial crisis. The first wave of privatization began in 1968 during the Park Chung Hee administration, as the Park regime transferred ownership of several state-owned enterprises (SOEs) to solve the endemic government budget deficit problem. One of the problems from this first wave of privatization was that many of these businesses were sold to *chaebols*, increasing their strength over the Korean economy.[16]

During the 1980s, the Chun Doo-Hwan administration and the Roh Tae Woo administration carried out privatization and managerial improvement policies for SOEs. The second wave of privatization took place between 1980 and 1986, where many government-owned banks such as Korea First,

Seoulbank and Choheung Bank were privatized via open competitive bidding. However, there had been criticism that the new ownership of these banks was too dispersed to allow effective management.

The third wave of privatization took place between 1987 and 1992, when the Roh Tae Woo administration sold off substantial portions of stock in some SOEs such as Pohang Iron and Steel and Korean Electric and Power (KEPCO) as part of the Citizen Share Ownership (CSO) programme. Under the CSO programme the shares were sold to over 6 million citizens at reduced and preferentially fixed rates, with the condition that no free trade of stocks occur during the first three years of the sale. The stocks issued under the CSO programme were mostly assigned to lower-ncome families, or the middle-and lower-echelon employees of the SOEs.[17] There were again critics who argued that because the sales took place mostly in small lots there were no major stockholders and the ownership of the SOEs was dispersed, not allowing responsible management.

In 1993, the Kim Young-Sam administration abandoned the CSO programme and restored *chaebol*-centred privatization. One of the goals of privatization under the Kim Young-Sam administration was that privatization should result in major stockholders who can take the former SOE and install responsible management, increasing the efficiency of the company.[18] Since foreign participation in the privatization process was limited by laws and regulations, and only the *chaebols* were typically large enough to procure funds needed to buy up large chunks of the SOEs for privatization, this policy meant that only the *chaebols* could effectively take part in the privatization efforts. However, typically, there were also ownership limits so that no single *chaebol* could take complete control over a privatized SOE.[19] Fifty-five companies, including Korea Gas, Korea Tobacco, National Textbook Publishing, several banks and the subsidiaries of the larger SOEs were targeted for privatization, but, due to intense lobbying by various interest groups along with worries about disruption in the stock market and the possible concentration of market power, major SOEs such as KEPCO and Korea Telecom were later exempted from privatization and only 22 smaller SOEs were subject to privatization.

There was a lukewarm attempt to restart the privatization process in 1996 and 1997, but the efforts focused more on managerial improvement rather than privatization.

After the financial crisis hit, as part of a comprehensive reform of the public sector, the privatization of key SOEs was emphasized, both as a means to increase efficiency and as a means to bring in foreign exchange. In April 1998 the Planning and Budget Committee began formulating a plan for SOE reform, and the government consulted IBRD as well as the public sector labour unions in drafting its SOE privatization and reform plans. The first plan concentrated more on privatization, and was approved by the Cabinet in July 1998. The more comprehensive second plan, which also included managerial reforms and plans concerning subsidiaries of SOEs, was approved in August 1998. At that time the Planning and Budget Committee stated that there were a total of 108 SOEs, which included 13 government-invested enterprises, 13 government-funded enterprises and 82 subsidiaries. A total of 214 000 workers were employed by these SOEs and subsidiaries.[20] Privatization of government-owned banks, especially the banks where government bought stock as part of the bailout process after the financial crisis, are typically not included in the discussions on privatization, and this chapter will follow that example.

In the first privatization plan the government targeted 11 SOEs as targets for complete privatization, including KEPCO, Korea Telecom, Korea Tobacco and Ginseng, Pohang Iron and Steel, and Korea Heavy Industries. Five of these SOEs, including Pohang Iron and Steel and Korea Heavy Industries, were targeted for immediate privatization between 1998 and 1999. Much of the government shares in these SOEs had already been sold off during the previous rounds of privatization. Six SOEs, including KEPCO, Korea Tobacco and Ginseng, Korea Telecom and Korea Gas were targeted for privatization in the medium to long term. Ownership limits and limits on foreign investment were either removed, or substantially weakened.[21] While many of these plans were carried out during the Kim Dae Jung Administration, the Roh Moo Hyun Administration, which followed, delayed or weakened many of these privatization plans. This chapter looks at the privatization plans as the Kim Dae Jung Administration formulated them, and examines how the Kim Administration carried out the plans in the aftermath of the financial crisis.

KEPCO had been perhaps the most complex case of privatization under the plans of the Kim Administration, since its privatization had been a part of a comprehensive reorganisation of the Korean electricity market. According to the plans and legislation during the Kim Administration, KEPCO, which handles power generation, network delivery of electricity and commercial retailing of electric power, would have ultimately been responsible only for the network delivery of electricity, which is widely considered a natural monopoly. In the first stage of the restructuring process the non-nuclear power generation component of KEPCO was split into five independent subsidiaries within KEPCO. Under the privatization plan, one of the generation subsidiaries, Namdong, would have been sold off in 2003. The nuclear generation component would have become a wholly owned subsidiary of KEPCO. In the second stage the other non-nuclear generation subsidiaries would have been privatized. In the third stage the distribution component of KEPCO would have been divided up into several wholly owned subsidiaries, and some of them would have been privatized as competition is introduced in the wholesale electricity market. In the fourth stage, competition at the retail stage would have been introduced.

The electricity restructuring plan had been long-range in nature. Initially the plan called for the first and second phase to be completed by 2002, and the fourth phase to begin in 2009.[22] However, the plan has been changed significantly by the new Roh Moo Hyun Administration.[23]

It is notable that the Korean National Railroad, which runs at a loss, was not selected for privatization. The Korean National Railroad is currently a government agency under the Ministry of Construction and Transportation, and not an SOE. Attempts have been made to privatize the Korean National Railroad since 1980 but have met with strong resistance from labour unions and political interest groups, and 1998 proved no exception.[24]

At the end of 2002 privatization of eight of the eleven SOEs was completed, as seen in Table 6.1.[25] While the Kim Administration continued the privatization plans for the three remaining SOEs – KEPCO, Korea Gas Corporation and the Regional Heating Corporation, the incoming Roh Moo Hyun administration has placed a hold on further privatization of these companies stating that privatization for these companies must proceed slowly and carefully because they deal with "network". Some commentators have accused that the reluctance for further privatization by the Roh Administration reflects intense opposition and lobbying by labour groups, the SOEs themselves, and other interest groups.[26]

**Table 6.1**
**Completed Privatization (1998–2002)**

| Enterprise | Date completed | Notes |
|---|---|---|
| National Textbook Publishing | Nov. 1998 | |
| General Technology Finance Corp. | Jan. 1999 | |
| Korea Pipeline Corp. | April 2000 | |
| Pohang Iron and Steel | Oct. 2000 | |
| Korea General Chemical Corp. | Nov. 2000 | The company was liquidated when no buyer could be found after three auction attempts. |
| Korea Heavy Manufacturing Corp. | Dec. 2000 | |
| Korea Telecom | May 2002 | |
| Korea Tobacco and Ginseng Corp. | Oct. 2002 | |

*Source*: MPB (2002b) p. 94, Graph 2-22.

At the beginning of 1998 there were 24 major SOEs. By November 2002 eight were privatized but five, including the Incheon Airport Authority, were created, so there are currently 19 major SOEs.

Labour unions with members in SOEs have typically been vocal in resisting privatization, and sometimes have staged violent strikes and demonstrations. In January 2003 a suicide by a former union leader at Doosan Heavy Industry Corporation, formerly Korea Heavy Industry Corporation and one of the first SOEs to be privatized, became major news. According to one major newspaper the workers of Doosan Heavy Industry Corporation were having a difficult time adjusting to the new work environment after privatization, due to differences in management culture. When Korea Heavy Industry Corporation was an SOE, management emphasized the concept of 'workers as owners and stewards of the company'. Thus, even when there were massive and violent strikes against the company the management and the labour unions would arrive at a mutually satisfactory agreement, and no charges would be filed against the union and the workers. However, when Korea Heavy Industry was sold the new owners emphasized that 'stockholders are owners of the company', and took harsh measures against the union leaders after a strike. The union leader who committed suicide had been convicted by the court of instigating the strike, and had been fined heavy personal penalties.[27] The incident served as a reminder of how difficult privatization can be, and it may strengthen labour unions' efforts against further privatization.

### 6.3.2 SOE Management Reforms

Along with the privatization efforts the government carried out various measures to improve the management of the other SOEs and government affiliated organizations, including the Korean National Railroad, SOEs not targeted for privatization, 82 subsidiaries of major SOEs, and 133 government-affiliated organizations such as the Consumer Protection Board, and government-funded research organizations such as the Korea Development Institute (KDI) and the Korea Institute for International Economic Policy (KIEP). Additional reform plans for SOE subsidiaries were announced in March 2001.

Of the 82 subsidiaries, the subsidiaries of SOEs targeted for privatization were sold along with their parent SOEs. Additional subsidiaries were targeted for individual privatization. In all, as of the end of 2002, 50 subsidiaries were privatized. A further 16 subsidiaries were closed down or merged with their parents or with other subsidiaries. Eleven subsidiaries are currently undergoing the privatization process, though the effort is sometimes being delayed because the price offered for these subsidiaries are considered too low. Only 16 subsidiaries,[28] such as Korea Nuclear Fuel, will remain.[29]

There has also been a significant reduction in the manpower of SOEs. Initial plans in 1998 called for a reduction in manpower of 24 per cent, or 41 200 employees between 1998 and 2000. The actual reduction exceeded the target by about 500 employees. Since 2000, the results of further employee reductions have been mixed. Downsizing programmes by individual SOEs resulted in further reductions of about 3600 employees by November 2002, but this reduction was overcome by an increase of 5100 public employees mostly in the social infrastructure area.[30] In all, through privatization and downsizing efforts, the number of employees in SOEs fell from 212 000 in March 1998 to 81 000 in November 2002.[31]

Reforms in the area of management and hiring include increased independence of each SOE for personnel, organizational and budgetary decisions, as well as the elimination of the practice of assigning government designated directors who sometimes had extraordinary powers on the board of directors. The selection criteria and the responsibility of the chief of the SOEs were reformed as well. Instead of the minister of the relevant ministry appointing the chief officer, the candidate is now selected by a panel consisting of the board of the SOE and civilians. Then, the president appoints the chief officer on the basis of the recommendation of the minister. The contract for the chief officer must include various performance indicators and requirements. The minister of MPB can recommend the firing of the chief officer and members of the board if their performance is unsatisfactory.

In addition, the incentive pay range for SOE officers was widened, from 125–425 per cent of base pay to 0~500 per cent of base pay. Some aspects of retirement pay and severance pay, which had seemed excessive compared to the private sector, were adjusted.

As with the government reforms the SOE reforms attempted to create a new culture of transparency, efficiency and customer-oriented service delivery. There are some encouraging early signs, but it seems too early at this time to see whether a true cultural change has taken place in the SOEs.

### 6.3.3 Evaluation

Privatization had been one of the more successful public sector reform efforts in the post-crisis era. Despite strong opposition from interest groups, especially the labour unions, the government formed a viable plan for beginning, or completing, the privatization process of 11 SOEs, including major SOEs such as Korea Telecom, KEPCO, Pohang Iron & Steel, and Korea Tobacco & Ginseng. In addition, it implemented these policies relatively on schedule. As with the government reforms, MPB played an important role in the SOE reforms. It was instrumental in creating the initial plans in 1998, and implementing them. The government's strong commitment toward privatization, as well as allowing active foreign participation in the privatization process despite strong opposition from the labour unions as well as critics who claimed that the government was selling off 'national wealth' to foreigners, contributed greatly to increasing foreign investor confidence in Korea in the post-crisis era. However, in recent months, the government's desire for further privatization seems to have died down.

It may be too soon to judge the results of the management reforms of the remaining SOEs. The reduction in manpower of SOEs is a sizable achievement and, according to surveys sponsored by MPB, public satisfaction in services provided by the SOEs has risen since 1998,[32] but it remains to be seen whether the SOEs will truly be more efficient in the long run.

## 6.4 REGULATORY REFORM AND DEREGULATION

### 6.4.1 Regulatory Reform

The financial crisis showed that the regulatory structure in Korea was woefully inadequate. In the financial sector the regulatory regime could not adequately monitor the transactions of financial institutions, or guarantee their soundness. For foreign direct investment there were not only explicit investment barriers, but also excessive regulations and an inefficient regulatory structure that made direct investment by foreigners difficult and unattractive. Thus the government, in cooperation with the IMF, began to reform the regulations in these two areas from the very earliest days of the financial crisis. With foreign investment the reforms concentrated on deregulation, while in the financial sector the reforms concentrated on building a regulatory structure to improve the prudential supervision of the industry.

The results from the regulatory reforms in these two areas proved very encouraging, and President Kim Dae Jung decided to expand regulatory reform and deregulation efforts to all sectors of the government.

However, the process of regulatory reform had begun much earlier, in the preceding administrations. Korean businesses had long complained of inefficiencies arising from Korea's complex and opaque regulatory regime, and there had been various attempts at regulatory reform since the early 1980s.[33] While the Kim Young-Sam administration did succeed in establishing laws which allowed for permanent institutions which engage in regulatory reform, it failed in raising the quality of the regulatory regime as many of its deregulatory and reform measures were not very effective. A crucial problem seems to have been the lack of expertise, and a failure to allocate appropriate personnel.[34]

In 1997, during the last days of the Kim Young-Sam administration, the Basic Act on Administrative Regulation was passed. The law contained provisions on the basic direction of regulatory policy, research and development of the regulatory system, reviews of new and amended (or strengthened) regulations, reviews of existing regulations, drawing up plans for comprehensive regulatory clearance, registration and publication of regulations, obtaining and responding to public opinions on regulatory improvement, as well as monitoring and evaluation of regulatory improvement efforts in each ministry. On April 1998, following the provisions of the new law, the Kim Dae Jung administration established the Regulatory Reform Committee (RRC), which examines new and existing regulations. Provisions for regulatory impact analysis[35] (RIA), sunset clauses,[36] and registration of regulations were also put in place. RRC was to consist of 15 to 20 members, the majority of whom had to be civilians. As of December 2002 there were 20 members, 13 of whom were civilians. The civilian members consisted of academics, industry leaders and a representative from a consumer group. The seven government members were the prime minister and ministers of various relevant ministries. The RRC is co-chaired by the prime minister and a civilian co-chairman.

All new regulations, or regulations which are to be strengthened, must be approved by the RRC. Under the RRC, there are three committees responsible for examining the technical details of the regulations submitted for approval. Two committees examine economic regulations, and one examines administrative regulations.[37] Ministries seeking to install new regulations or strengthen existing regulations must file an RIA. However, currently, the government and the RRC do not release these RIAs to the public. Also, under the current provisions, all regulations have five-year sunset clauses, so that unless the regulation is explicitly renewed the regulations will lapse in five years.

The RRC also maintains a registry of regulations, which is accessible through the Internet. Technically, a regulation is only valid and enforceable if the regulation has been registered in the registry.

Regulatory reform was also encouraged in the provincial and local governments, though their reforms were not as extensive as those for the central government.

### 6.4.2 Deregulation

From the beginning of the Kim Dae Jung administration the president had expressed the desire to carry out a comprehensive regulatory reform, and ordered each ministry to submit reform plans. Reportedly, the president was not impressed with the submitted plans, and ordered the ministries to review and eliminate 50 per cent of their regulations across the board.[38] The reviews were carried out under the following principles: all regulations must be examined on a 'zero-basis', that is without preconceptions or predisposition; regulations which hinder competition and the market are to be eliminated, but for those regulations which are required for the preservation of the environment, public safety or health, the regulation should be modified to achieve the goals as efficiently as possible. In addition, all regulations without legal basis would lose their status by the beginning of 1999. Thus if the regulation does not have a legal basis it must either be eliminated, or appropriate legislation must be introduced to establish a legal basis.

As a result of the presidential order, by the end of 1998, of the 11 125 regulations in place before the presidential order, 5430 (48.8 per cent) were eliminated and 2411 (21.7 per cent) were revised. Table 6.2 lists the number of regulations in place, eliminated and modified in 1998 and 1999 by the central government as a whole, and for the ministries which had more than 500 regulations before the reform effort began.

The number of regulations perhaps understates the effects of regulations on the Korean economy. Compared to the United States, which reportedly has hundreds of thousands of regulations, the number of Korean regulations in 1998 – 11 125 – does not seem excessive. However, various international reports pointed out excessive regulations as a crucial problem in Korea.[39] These reports typically point out the lack of transparency in how the regulations are created, imposed and implemented, and make the accusation that the front line government workers often interpret the regulations arbitrarily. In the 1997 Global Competitiveness Report, compiled by the World Economic Forum (WEF), Korea had ranked forty-eighth-highest out of 53 countries in terms of burden from administrative regulations. However, the reforms of 1998–99 seem to have had a positive effect. In the 2002 report, Korea ranked twenty-sixth-highest out of 75 countries in terms of the general burden from regulations.[40]

**Table 6.2**
**Number of Regulations 1998–2002**

| | All Govt | MoW | MoCT | MoMA | MoA | MoCIE | FSC | MoE | MoFE |
|---|---|---|---|---|---|---|---|---|---|
| 1998 (initial figures) | 11125 | 1,703 | 917 | 778 | 701 | 667 | 630 | 643 | 509 |
| Eliminated in 1998 | 5430 | 857 | 467 | 422 | 362 | 345 | 315 | 224 | 255 |
| Modified in 1998 | 2411 | 256 | 232 | 169 | 165 | 174 | 131 | 170 | 137 |
| End of 1998* | 6820 | 883 | 606 | 535 | 423 | 355 | 407 | 536 | 336 |
| Eliminated in 1999 | 503 | 90 | 23 | 53 | 23 | 16 | 35 | 25 | 12 |
| Modified in 1999 | 570 | 36 | 33 | 38 | 15 | 25 | 64 | 67 | 28 |
| End of 1999* | 6308 | 793 | 583 | 482 | 400 | 339 | 372 | 511 | 324 |
| End of 2002* | 7435 | 765 | 754 | 567 | 491 | 410 | 541 | 576 | 434 |

*Notes*: MoW = Ministry of Welfare, MoCT = Ministry of Construction and Transportation, MoMA = Ministry of Maritime Affairs, MoA = Ministry of Agriculture, MoCIE = Ministry of Commerce, Industry and Energy, FSC = Financial Supervisory Committee, MoE= Ministry of Environment, MoFE = Ministry of Finance and Environment
* = includes previously omitted, newly established or newly found regulations.

*Source*: Regulatory Reform Commission website, www.rrc.go.kr.

### 6.4.3 Evaluation

The Kim Dae Jung administration took significant first steps toward reducing the regulatory burdens on the Korean economy. It went beyond the previous administrations in two crucial ways. First, the Kim Dae Jung administration put in place permanent regulatory reform institutions and mechanisms such as the RRC, RIA and the sunset clause. These institutions and mechanisms could be very effective tools in reducing the future regulatory burden. Second, President Kim set a numerical target for deregulation which acted as a concrete goal that the ministries had to accomplish. The setting of numerical targets had mixed effects, but it did serve as a signal that the government was serious about regulatory reform.

While several national and international observers lauded the reform measures of the Korean government in 1998 and 1999, these observers also warned that the measures were only first steps in the long road toward regulatory reform. The initial deregulation was perhaps less effective than it could have been because it set a numerical goal rather than an efficiency goal. A more focused effort on a sector-by-sector basis was recommended by most observers.[41] While there has been some effort toward that goal, it has not moved very quickly.

Furthermore, while a mechanism for regulatory reviews were established, it is questionable whether they are being used effectively. The RIAs are not revealed to the public, and, while the RRC regularly examines new regulations, the reviews of existing regulations have been slow. Furthermore, some of the first decisions by the RRC were culturally controversial, and these decisions may have weakened public support for the RRC.

There has been a long list of critics who point out that despite a 50 per cent reduction in the number of regulations, a typical citizen or business does not feel that the regulatory burden has been lifted. This was one of the key shortcomings of the number-based deregulation, where the lesser regulations were given priority for elimination[42] and overlapping regulations were not fully eliminated.

In many ways Korea seems to have successfully installed the appropriate means, tools and mechanisms to carry out true reforms, but has not been willing to actually utilize these tools. For example, according to an OECD review of Korean regulatory reform, Korea's mechanism for maintaining transparency and public participation lies above the OECD average. In addition, Korea's policies toward regulatory reform and regulatory review is also above the OECD average.[43] However, the lack of transparency and the level of regulatory burden are still pointed out as major problems, indicating that the Korean government and the RRC has not been able to effectively use the tools and policies at their disposal to actually reduce the regulatory burden and reduce the problems in Korea's regulatory structure.

Shin (2002) points out that interested parties can bypass the regulatory review process and increase the regulatory burden by enacting new laws. Since the RRC and the regulatory review mechanism are not empowered to reject laws passed by the National Assembly, new laws allow interest groups to increase regulations de - facto.[44]

In all, regulatory reform in Korea was carried out mostly in terms of quantity rather than quality. There have been numerous articles from within and outside Korea urging the Korean government to raise the quality of the regulatory reform process, by increasing transparency and reducing the regulatory burden in such a way that a typical citizen or business can clearly feel the change. Most of these critics argue that Korea has the necessary mechanism in place, but perhaps is unwilling to use it.[45]

There have been some indications that the regulatory burdens have eased somewhat since 1998. However, the business sector, both Korean and foreign, consider regulation one of the biggest problems in Korea, and businesses have requested the incoming Roh Moo Hyun administration to place serious emphasis on further reducing the regulatory burden.

## 6.5 CONCLUSION

While the public sector reforms did not originate with the financial crisis, the crisis did give public sector reforms an added sense of urgency and forced the government to commit to a stronger set of reform measures. Korea's public sector reforms after the financial crisis had three major components: government structural and managerial reforms, SOE reforms which included privatization as well as managerial reforms, and regulatory reform. The results of these reforms are mixed, with all components showing some signs of improvement but none being an outright success.

For reforms dealing with government structure, the Kim Dae Jung administration changed the structure of the executive branch three times. While this is less than the previous administration the number of restructurings seems excessive considering that the presidential term in Korea is only five years, and the later restructuring measures sometimes undid the previous restructuring measures. It is also questionable whether the restructuring resulted in a more efficient government. A more prudent and thoughtful process is needed to make sure that government restructuring does what it is intended to do, and limit the number of restructurings that can disrupt the smooth functioning of government.

The Korean government did succeed in reducing the number of government employees, and the process of integrating the Internet and methods of electronic commerce into the administrative process seems to be proceeding well and shows great potential.

In the area of SOE reforms, the privatization effort should be considered a success. Despite opposition, the government managed to carry out most of its commitments despite some minor delays. However, the incoming Roh Moo Hyun administration does not seem to be as enthusiastic about privatization as the Kim Dae Jung administration. Citing domestic political pressures as well as missteps in privatization in other countries, the Roh administration has signalled that it will re-examine government policies on privatization, especially its effect on the governance structure of the firm, and perhaps slow down the process. However, the Roh administration has also signalled that it will keep its commitment to privatize the Namdong electric power generation subsidiary as scheduled, and it is generally committed to the principles of privatization. In many ways the privatization of Namdong will serve as a guide to future privatization, for both the Roh administration and outside observers.

The government also succeeded in reducing the manpower in SOEs, and there are promising initial signs that service delivery has improved although it is much too early to make a final judgement. Overall, the government's effort to reform the state-owned enterprises should be considered a moderate success.

Finally, in the area of regulatory reform, the initial measures by the Kim Dae Jung administration should be considered a success. The forced deregulation gave a much-needed push to regulatory reform, and the establishment of the RRC allows Korea to examine and reduce the number of new and excessive regulations in the future. Also, the RIA requirement and the sunset requirement can be good tools for reducing the regulatory burden in the future, to maintain checks on the government's ability to impose new regulatory burdens.

However, it also seems that in the latter half of the Kim Dae Jung administration, much of the initial drive toward regulatory reform has weakened. While the RRC still examines new regulations, there has not been a strong effort to reduce the existing regulatory burden or increase regulatory compliance.

A common thread in these public sector reforms is the establishment of agencies that can oversee and lead the reform process: MPB for government and SOE reforms, and RRC for regulatory reform. These agencies have taken strong actions initially after the financial crisis, but their willingness for undertaking major reforms seem to have weakened considerably in the second half of the Kim Dae Jung administration. Whether the weakening is due to the weakening in the political strength of the Kim administration, or whether it is due to reform fatigue, or whether it is due to a combination of these and other factors is unclear. However, there is a need for further public sector reforms, as evidenced by various domestic and international surveys on government efficiency and regulatory burden. A disturbing possibility is that many Koreans mistake the establishment of an organizational structure with actual reforms; that is they establish the mechanism for reforms without realizing that mere establishment of a mechanism is not enough, and that a continually active reform effort is also required.

These agencies should take an active role again, but perhaps in a more measured way, especially in the case of government restructuring, to continue public sector reforms.

## NOTES

1 A detailed explanation of the changes in government structure from 1998 to 2001 from the government's point of view is available in Ministry of Planning and Budget (2002a) and Ministry of Planning and Budget (2002b).

2 See Kim (1999).

3 The prime minister at the time was Kim Jong Pil, who led the United Liberal Democrats Party, and was a coalition partner of Kim Dae Jung. Giving the responsibilities and powers of economic coordination to the new prime minister was also seen as a way to share power amongst Kim Dae Jung's Millennium Democratic Party and its coalition partner.

4 The relationship between the Financial Supervisory Commission (FSC: which had sometimes been called the Financial Supervisory Board) and the Financial Supervisory Agency (FSA: which had been at one time called the Financial Supervisory Service) as first announced by the government, is available in Sohn and Yang (1998) pp. 71–77. Simplifying considerably, the FSC sets the policies, and FSA implements them.

5 Kim (2002), p. 26, as well as numerous newspaper reports such as Chosun Ilbo 7 January, 2003, p. 5

6 MPB (2002a), pp. 56–57.

7 MPB (2002b), pp. 48–50.

8 Reportedly, the retention rate for these civilian consultants is very low.

9 Kim (2002), pp. 27–28.

10 Kim (2002), pp. 28–29.

11 Yonhap News Agency, "Up to 95 per cent of Government Employees Receive Incentive Pay" (in Korean, April 1, 2002) and "Government Employees Incentive Pay Divides Up Taxes" (in Korean, Jan. 15, 2003).

12 Kim (2002), pp. 26–27, MPB (2002b), p. 39.

13 MPB (2002b), pp. 256–276.

14 WEF (1998), WEF (2002), IMD (1997) and IMD (2002).

15 Kim (2002), pp. 33–34.

16 Ahn and Kim (2002), pp. 86–88.

17 Ahn and Kim (2002), pp. 89–91.

18 MPB (2002b), p. 85.

19 Ahn and Kim (2002), p. 94.
20 MPB (2002b), p. 89
21 In the areas relevant to privatization, foreign direct investment is limited in the electric power, gas and telecommunications areas.
22 OECD (2000), pp. 261–5.
23 The Roh Moo Hyun Administration, citing possible adverse effects from privatization on the public and the workers of KEPCO, as well as concerns over negative effects of electricity privatization and deregulation in the United States, most notably in California, has drastically slowed down and weakened the pace of privatization for KEPCO. Plans to sell off the Namdong subsidiary to a private investor were scrapped. By some accounts, potential buyers were driven off by intense labour opposition (Chosun Ilbo June 3, 2003 p. A-2). In late 2003 and early 2004, efforts were made to sell 10~20% of Namdong's stock in lieu of full privatization, but both efforts effectively failed. In April 2004, the new president of KEPCO was quoted as saying he was against privatization for privatization's sake (Chosun Ilbo April 3, 2004, A-19). Separation of the retail delivery network was also delayed to 2005, and they may remain public corporations. In effect, privatization of KEPCO has been delayed considerably. Meanwhile, KEPCO ranked first in the corruption ranking compiled by the President's Independent Commission Against Corruption.
24 MPB (2002b), p. 77.
25 While the government has sold most, or all, of its shares in these companies, government-owned banks and government-affiliated organizations sometimes hold minority shares in these companies.
26 Interview with the Minister of MPB, Seoul Economic Daily, March 8, 2004, p.7. Meanwhile, some critics have pointed out that KEPCO and Korea Gas Corporation rank consistently highly using measures of corruption and mismanagement, and, in 2003, the President of Korea Gas Corporation was arrested for receiving bribes from a supplier. (*Chosun Ilbo*, May 19, 2003, p.A7.)
27 *Chosun Ilbo*, January 20, 2003, p.A8.
28 Not including the newly formed generation subsidiaries for KEPCO.
29 MPB (2002b), p. 118–119.
30 MPB (2002b), p. 121.
31 MPB (2002b), p. 140.
32 MPB (2002a), p. 88–89.
33 Choi (2002), pp. 58–60.
34 Lee and Han (1999), pp. 225–33.
35 Regulatory Impact Analysis examines the costs and benefits of a regulation, and examines whether there are more efficient and less market-disruptive ways to accomplish the goals of the regulation in

question.
36 Sunset clauses limit the duration of a regulation to a certain fixed period.
37 OECD (2000), pp. 139–40 and Regulatory Reform Committee (1999), pp. 34–46.
38 Summaries of presidential orders are included in Regulatory Reform Committee (1999) Appendix Chapter 1.
39 For example OECD (2000), as well as various IMD and WEF reports.
40 Yang and Kim (2001), p.130. Note that the categories used by WEF changed between 1997 and 2002.
41 For example, OECD (2000) and Kim (1999).
42 Kim (1999), pp. 457–458.
43 OECD (2000), p. 139 Box 2, p. 157 Box 5, and p. 233 Box 5.
44 Shin (2002), pp. 46–8.
45 OECD (2002), Kim (1999), Yang and Kim (2000), Choi (2002) and others.

## REFERENCES

Ahn, Byong-man and In Chul Kim (2002), 'Reforming Public Enterprises in South Korea', in Byong-man Ahn, John Halligan and Stephen Wilks (eds), *Reforming Public and Corporate Governance*, Cheltenham: Edward Elgar Publishing.

Choi, Byung-sun (2002), 'Gyujaegaehyuk Chujin Chaejae' ('Mechanism for Regulatory Reform'), in Byung-sun Choi and Chong-Ik Shin (eds), *Sijangkyungjaewa Gyeujaegaehyuk* (*Market Economy and Regulatory Reform*), Seoul: FKI Media (in Korean).

IMD (1997), *The World Competitiveness Yearbook*, IMD International.

IMD (2002), *The World Competitiveness Yearbook*, IMD International.

Kim, Jong Suk (1999), 'Gyujae Gaehyukui Gwajaewa Bhanghyang' ('Regulatory Reform: Tasks and Direction') in *Journal of Regulation Studies*, Seoul: Korea Economic Research Institute (in Korean).

Kim, Pan Suk (2002), 'Administrative Reform in the Korean Central Government: A Case Study of the Dae Jung Kim Administration', in Byong-man Ahn, John Halligan and Stephen Wilks (eds), *Reforming Public and Corporate Governance*, Cheltenham: Edward Elgar Publishing.

Lee, Joosun and Sunok Han (1999), *Kim Young Sam Haengjungbuui Gyujaewanhwasiljuk Pyeongga* (*Evaluation of Deregulation Results of the Kim Young Sam Administration*), Seoul: Korea Economic Research Institute (in Korean).

MPB – Ministry of Planning and Budget (2002a), *Gaehyukgwa Doyakui Gil (The Way of Reform and Challenges)*, Ministry of Planning and

Budget, Seoul (in Korean).

MPB – Ministry of Planning and Budget (2002b), *Gonggong Gaehyuk Baeksuh* (*Public Sector Reform White Paper*), Ministry of Planning and Budget, Seoul (in Korean). Also available for download from the Ministry website http://www.mpb.go.kr.

OECD (2000), *Regulatory Reform in Korea*, Paris.

Regulatory Reform Committee (Gyujae Gaehyuk Uiwonhwae) (1999), *1998 Nyundo Gyujae Gaehyuk Baeksuh* (*1998 Regulatory Reform White Paper*), Seoul (in Korean).

Shin, Jong Ik (2002), 'Gyeujae Gaehyuk Wae Jal Andwenah?' ('Regulatory Reform: Why It Doesn't Work Well') in Byung-sun Choi and Chong-Ik Shin (eds), *Sijangkyungjaewa Gyeujaegaehyuk* (*Market Economy and Regulatory Reform*), FKI Media, Seoul (in Korean).

Sohn, Chan-Hyun and Junsok Yang (eds) (1998), *Korea's Economic Reform Measures Under the IMF Programme*, Seoul: Korea Institute for International Economic Policy.

WEF – World Economic Forum (1998), *The 1998 Global Competitiveness Report*.

WEF – World Economic Forum (2002), *The Global Competitiveness Report 2001–2002*, London: Oxford University Press.

Yang, Junsok and Hong-Youl. Kim (2000), *OECD Regulatory Studies: OECD Regulatory Reform and Country Review of Korea: Recommendations and Their Implementation*, Korea Institute of International Economic Policy, Seoul (in Korean).

Yang, Junsok and Hong-Youl Kim (2001), *OECD Regulatory Studies: Regulatory Compliance*, Seoul: Korea Institute for International Economic Policy (in Korean).

# 7. Monetary and Exchange Rate Policies

**Junggun Oh**

## 7.1 INTRODUCTION

In late November 1997 Korea turned to the IMF and other international financial organizations for emergency support funds, to deal with the currency and financial crises that had broken out earlier that month. The government negotiated an extension of the maturities of financial institutions' short-term external debts in January 1998, and issued foreign-currency-denominated government bonds in April that year. In order to restore Korea's international credibility it launched economic stabilization policies, in particular a high interest rate policy, along with a wide-ranging drive for structural reform of the financial, corporate, labour and public sectors, which had a positive effect on the recovery of confidence. Such increased confidence and huge current account surpluses boosted capital inflows.

Along with the recovery of stability in the foreign exchange market, the monetary policy stance could now be turned to the low interest rate policy to encourage the shrunken domestic consumption and investment demand. As a result, a recovery began in the second half of 1998 and gathered momentum in 1999. Such a remarkable V-shaped quick and strong recovery from the crisis was mainly thanks to supportive monetary and fiscal policies and progress in structural reforms.

However, since the second half of 2000, the Korean economy has again begun to show some instability due to the slowdown of growth and the bearish movement of the stock market. Some argue that these mainly resulted from a too-rapid V-shape recovery without sufficient restructuring of the financial and corporate sectors.

This chapter aims at reviewing and assessing the monetary and exchange rate policies implemented to cope with the unprecedented financial crisis in the Korean economy, and their contributions to the rapid and strong recovery. And then, it will be identified what kind of problems lie in the sustaining of the recovery.

## 7.2 FOREIGN EXCHANGE MARKET STABILIZATION

After the crises had broken out, the Bank of Korea at first conducted monetary policy flexibly to assist the government's policy initiatives for economic stabilization and structural reform. It also supported the government's financing of financial restructuring. After the financial markets regained their stability, and the economy began to revive, the Bank placed the focus of its monetary policy on the building of a firm basis for price stability.

When the crises erupted the Bank judged that the most urgent task was to stabilize foreign exchange and financial markets, and its policies were directed toward this goal. To help stabilize the foreign exchange market, the Bank pushed its market intervention rate up dramatically to 35 per cent per annum. This high interest rate policy was seen as the only viable option to engineer a rapid stabilization of the foreign exchange rate and to curb capital outflows. The foreign exchange market settled down rapidly from early in the second quarter of 1998 (see Figure 7.1). This reflected the government's success in negotiating a prolongation of financial institutions' short-term external debts and issuing foreign-currency-denominated government bonds, and the continued monthly surplus on the current account from January 1998.

However, the results of empirical studies on the effects of the high interest rate policy on the stabilization of the foreign exchange market during the crisis in Korea is mixed: Goldfajn and Baig (1998) and Park and Choi (1999) show that an increase in the interest rate did not significantly result in an appreciation of the exchange rate, while according to Cho and West (1999) and Basurto and Ghosh (2000) an increase in the interest rate did significantly result in an appreciation of the exchange rate. Oh (2000c) shows that the positive correlation between the interest rate and the exchange rate, which conflicts with the traditional theory of the interest rate parity condition, is mainly due to the fact that the stock market is more developed and active than the bond market.[1]

On the other hand, there were a number of malign side-effects accompanying the high interest rate policy. It accelerated the slowdown in real economic activities through its contraction of consumption and investment, and it greatly increased the incidence of corporate failure and the accumulation of bad loans by financial institutions.

In response, in order to prevent too deep a contraction of the real economy, from the second quarter of 1998, the Bank shifted its policy focus from stabilizing the foreign exchange market to preventing the economy from contracting too deeply. The Bank steadily lowered its market intervention rate from the second quarter, when foreign exchange market conditions had improved considerably thanks to the sustained current account surplus, the arrival of support funds from the international financial institutions, and renewed inflows of foreign investment capital.

But it cautiously adjusted the scale and pace of the reduction of interest rates, taking into consideration developments in the real economy and the foreign exchange market, since the external environment was still unsettled with international financial markets in turmoil. Call rates consequently dropped to 8.5 per cent by the end of August in 1998 (see Figure 7.1). As the Bank steadily brought down its market intervention rate, the call market rate eased to 6.5 per cent by the end of December. In addition, in September 1998, the bank lowered the interest rate on the 'aggregate credit' it supplies to banks from 5 per cent to 3 per cent, thus inducing them to reduce their lending rates. This effectively brought about a steady decline both in market interest rates and in the lending rates of financial institutions.

During the first half of 1999, the financial and foreign exchange markets attained a fair degree of stability. In contrast, over the second half of the year, financial markets experienced increased uncertainties, and their restabilization became a primary consideration for policy-makers. In particular, the difficulties of the troubled Daewoo group and investment trust companies' overhang of potential beneficiary certificates redemptions led to a renewed focus on financial market stability in the framing of interest rate policy from August onwards. The Bank regarded the stabilization of the financial market as the most pressing issue and thus reduced the call rate step by step, finally bringing it to the level of 4.75 per cent in May 1999 where it was maintained until January 2000.

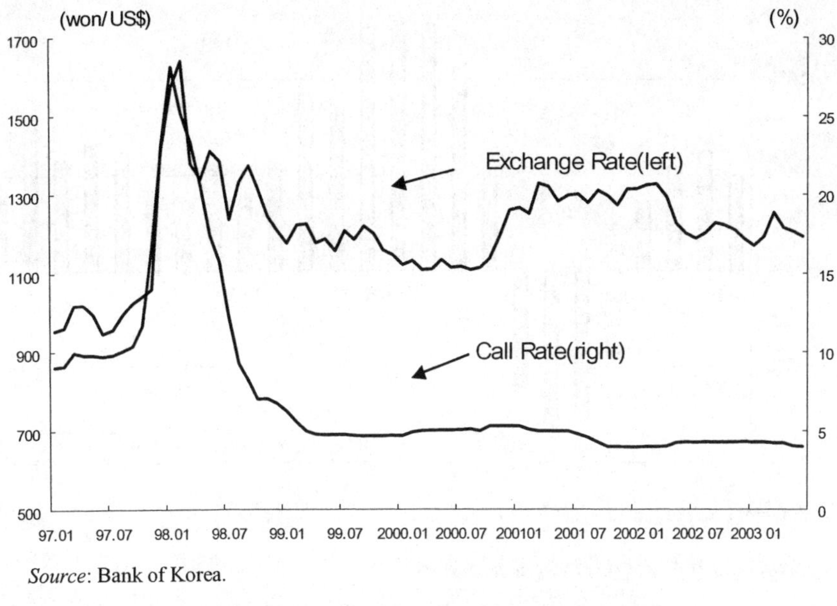


*Source*: Bank of Korea.

*Figure 7.1 Exchange Rate and Interest Rate Movements*

## 7.3 RAPID ECONOMIC RECOVERY AND FINANCIAL MARKET STABILITY

From the fourth quarter of 1998, the economic restructuring efforts began to achieve very gratifying results. Real GDP growth which had registered a deeply negative figure in 1998, bounced back to 10.3 per cent in 1999 led by the revival of domestic demand and by the expansion of exports. The unemployment rate, which had peaked at 8.6 per cent in February 1999, then started to ease and stood at 4.8 per cent in December 1999. The current account meanwhile achieved a sizable surplus of US$24 billion in 1999 following the surplus of US$40 billion in 1998. The rapid recovery of the domestic economy continued until mid-2000, and the current account also remained in surplus by US$10 billion in 2000.

With the assistance of the low interest rate policy the real economy accelerated its upward trend, achieving a GDP growth rate of 10.3 per cent in 1999 (see Figure 7.2). With such a rapid V-shape recovery the economy was estimated to have returned to the potential production level around the beginning of 2000, and to have shown some excess demand during this same year.

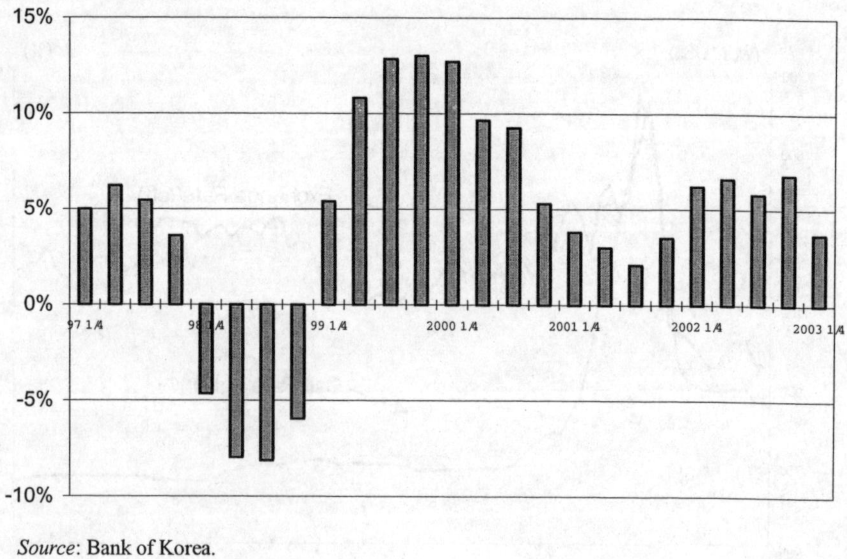


*Source*: Bank of Korea.

*Figure 7.2 GDP Growth Rate*

As a consequence long-term interest rates had been rising in response to the rapid expansion of the real economy and fears of financial market instability, thus widening the spread between long-term and short-term rates. Taking these points into consideration, the Bank of Korea decided to raise its target for the overnight call rate from 4.75 per cent to 5.00 per cent in February 2000.

Inflation pressures had been increasing (see Figure 7.3). Consumer prices had maintained a sharply rising trend since June 2000, mainly due to the surge in international oil prices and rises in public service charges, and in prices of farm, livestock and fisheries products.

On the other hand financial markets showed large fluctuations at one stage due to a combination of factors, including a rapid rise in international oil prices, the drop in semiconductor prices, and the breakdown of the planned deal for the Daewoo Motor Company. Market apprehensions, however, subsided somewhat following the blunting of the surge in international oil prices, and the publication of the plan for corporate and financial restructuring. Taking price movements and the situation of the financial markets into consideration, the Bank of Korea decided to raise its target for the overnight call rate from 5 per cent to 5.25 per cent in October 2000 (see Figure 7.3).

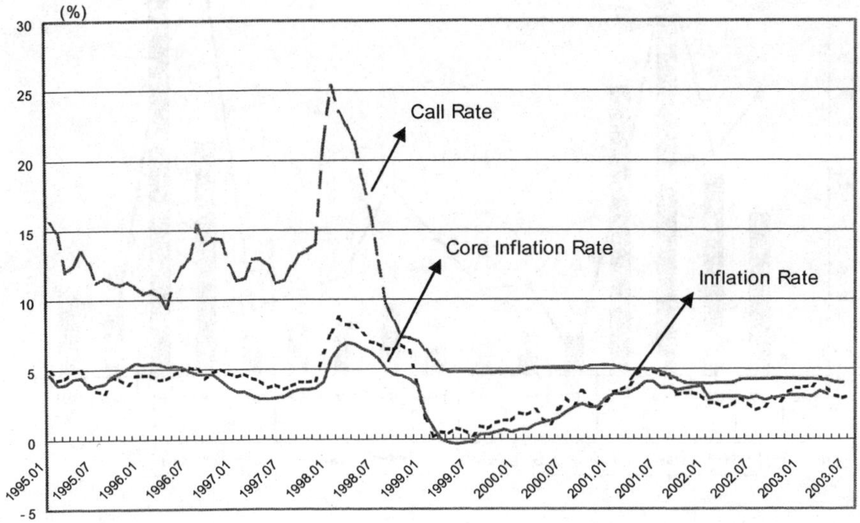


*Source*: Bank of Korea.

*Figure 7.3* *Call Rate and Inflation Rates*

However, after the second half of 2000, the Korean economy again began to show some instability, due to the slowdown of growth and the bearish movement of the stock market. Some argued that this was mainly as a result of a too-rapid V-shaped recovery, without sufficient restructuring of the financial and corporate sectors. In particular, the unveiling of the unhealthy financial structures of some subsidiaries of the Hyundai group in mid-2000 again increased uncertainty in the financial market, which seemed to play a turning point of changing the recovering trend to a further slowdown of the economy. In response to the newly changed situation, the Bank of Korea decreased the call rate from 5.25 per cent to 5 per cent in February 2001.

Stock prices had been exhibiting a sharp increase over a short period, raising apprehensions over an asset price bubble. With the help of a boom in the stock market, stocks of 45 trillion won, equivalent to 31 per cent of total market capitalization at the end of the previous year, were newly issued in 1999. As a result, an excess supply phenomenon began to appear in the stock market. Finally, stock prices began to decline from the second quarter of 2000 (see Figure 7.4).

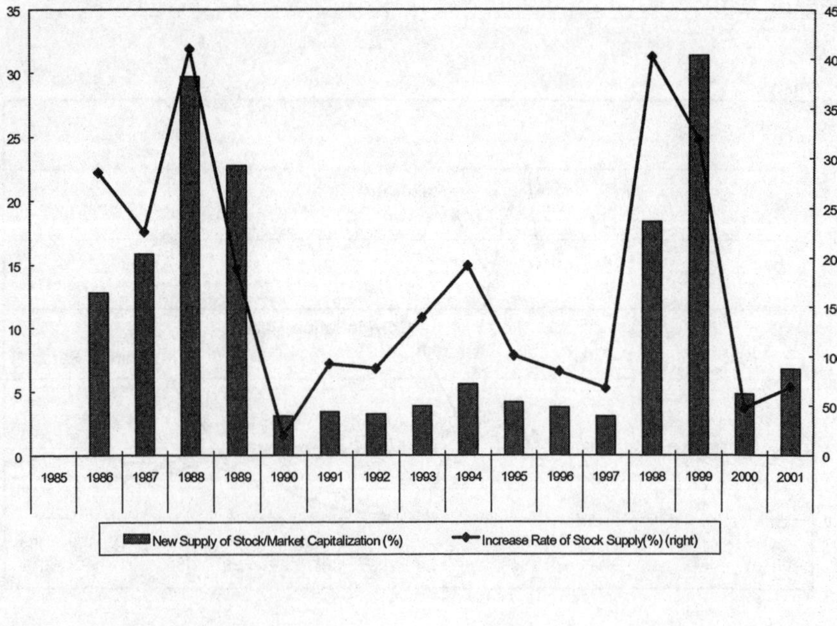


*Source*: Financial Supervisory Service.

*Figure 7.4 Supply of Stocks*

As stock prices began to decline, abundant liquidity supplied to stabilize the financial market began to flow into the real estate market. As a result, real estate prices, in particular the price of apartments in the Seoul area, began to increase from the beginning of the year 2001 when stock prices had almost reached their bottom (see Figure 7.5). In addition, a consumer credit boom, with the help of the low interest rate, further fuelled rising real estate prices. Consumer credit increased 25 per cent, 28 per cent and 27 per cent in 2000, 2001 and 2002 respectively. The increase in household loans that took place centred on two elements: mortgage lending (loans against housing collateral) and credit cards. This consumer credit boom, and increase in real estate prices, accelerated private consumption, enabling the Korean economy to keep up a relatively high economic growth rate even in the midst of the global economic downturn.

However, this situation generated several problems. First, it acted to bring about an increase in banks' non-performing assets and a deterioration of their balance sheets. Second, the management status of credit card companies has become weak and they have been experiencing liquidity difficulties. Third, the activity in the housing market has brought about a rise in real estate prices, which rose 23 per cent in 2002 and in the first four months of the year 2003 by 3 per cent alone.

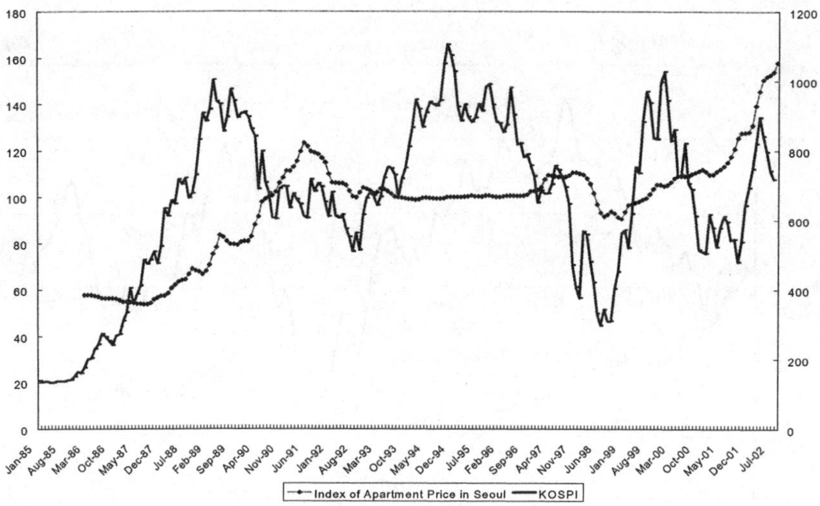


*Source*: Bank of Korea, and Kukmin Bank.

*Figure 7.5 Stock Price and Apartment Price*

The Korean government and financial institutions have taken various steps to counter this situation. First, credit information on individuals has been collected so that it can be managed electronically. Second, financial institutions have taken steps to reduce the loan-to-value ratio on housing loans from its previous 70 per cent level to just 50 per cent. Third, the government has adopted a posture of encouraging credit card companies to break free of their weakened management status and overcome their liquidity crises through their own efforts, for example by raising additional capital. Fourth, to tackle the rise in real estate prices the government has put in place various tax and administrative regulations, including the strengthened taxation of capital gains on transfers of real estate. This gave the Bank of Korea scope to reduce the call interest rate slightly by 25 basis points in May 2003, to stimulate the economy. These policy steps have begun to produce tangible effects. Total household credits saw their rate of growth blunted from the fourth quarter in 2002, and the credit card problem seems to have passed its peak while real estate prices show signs of recovering their stability.

On the other hand a boom in the stock market, encouraged by the low interest rate policy (see Figure 7.6), induced an inflow of capital into the Korean stock market, which led to an appreciation of the Korean won. As a result, the surplus on the current account began to narrow (see Figure 7.7).

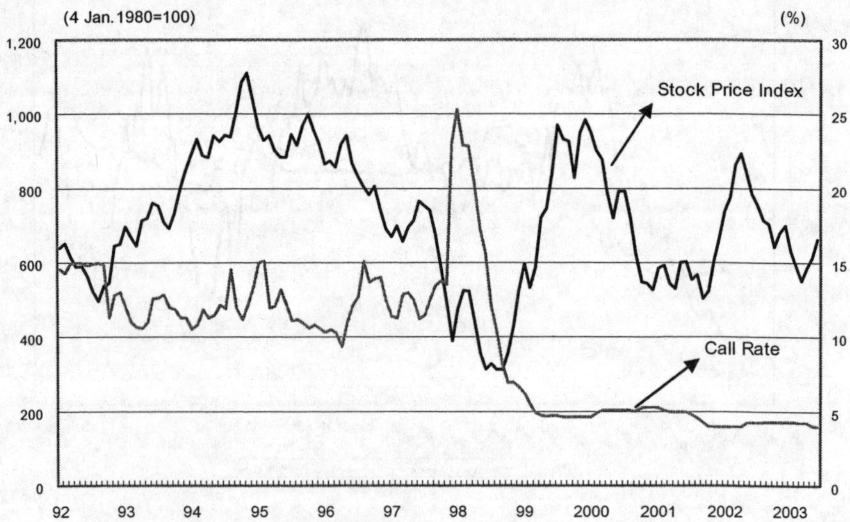


*Source*: Bank of Korea.

*Figure 7.6 Call Rate and the Stock Price Index*

In view of this it seems difficult for a small open economy, such as Korea, to carry out monetary policy focusing only on price stability, and not taking into consideration the current account position and financial market stability even if it adopts inflation targeting. In other words, it may face the problem of 'the impossibility of the holy trinity'.

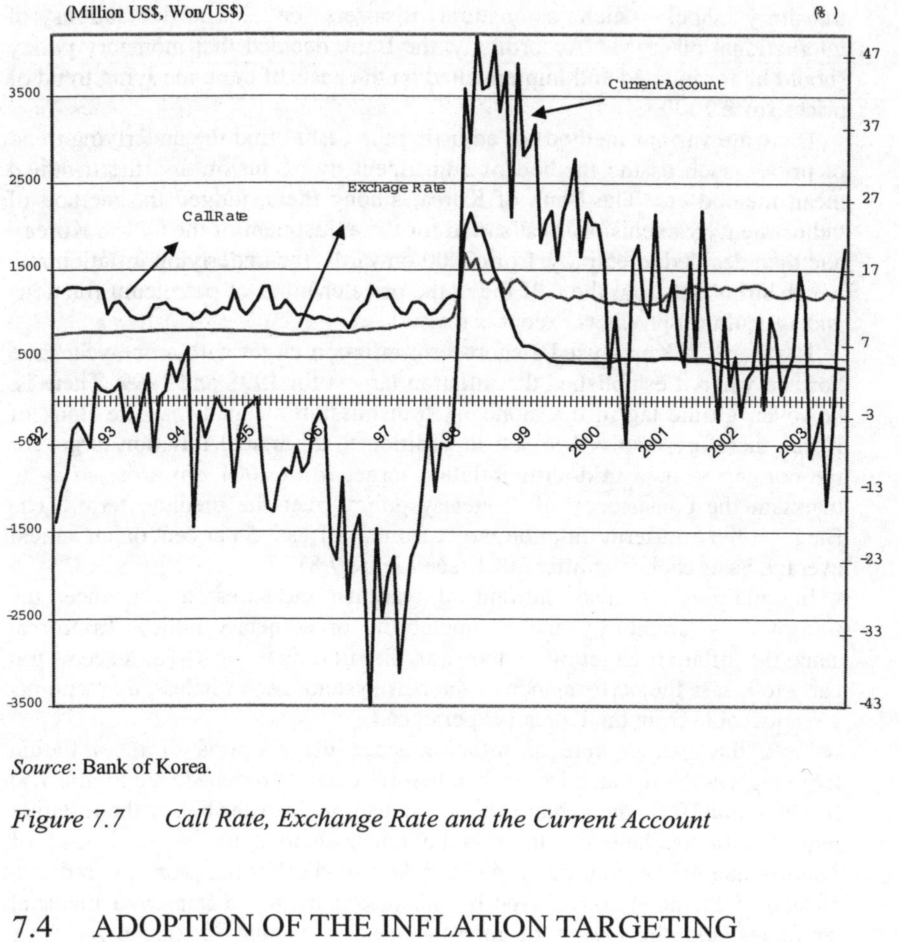


*Source*: Bank of Korea.

*Figure 7.7 Call Rate, Exchange Rate and the Current Account*

## 7.4 ADOPTION OF THE INFLATION TARGETING SYSTEM

The monetary policy framework was also fundamentally changed after the crisis. An inflation targeting system was introduced in Korea under the provisions of the fully-revised Bank of Korea Act of 1997.[2] The Act is concerned with establishing the neutrality and autonomy of monetary policy, with price stability being declared the sole objective of the Bank of Korea. Under its provisions, the Bank of Korea is required to set an inflation target every year and do its best to achieve it. It has set an annual target since 1998, in accordance with the related provisions of the Act.

The Bank of Korea adopted the Consumer Price Index (CPI) in 1998 as its benchmark indicator when the inflation targeting system was first implemented. The CPI is, however, seriously affected by temporary or transitory shocks such as natural disasters or sharp fluctuations of international oil prices. Accordingly, the Bank decided that monetary policy should be formulated and implemented on the basis of the underlying trend of prices since 2000.

There are various methods of adjusting the CPI to find the underlying trend of prices, such as the method of adjustment by exclusion and the trimmed mean method etc. The Bank of Korea, among them, judged the method of 'adjustment by exclusion' best suited for the adjustment of the CPI in Korea,[3] and then decided to employ, from 2000 onwards, the underlying inflation rate which strips out from the CPI index the price changes of petroleum fractions and agricultural products except cereals.

The Bank of Korea used a short-term inflation target with a one-year time horizon when it established the inflation targets for 1998 and 1999. There is, however, a time lag in the monetary transmission mechanism. The Bank of Korea therefore resolved to set, in addition to an annual inflation target for the coming year, a mid-term inflation target from 2001 onwards, so as to maintain the consistency of monetary policy over the medium term.[4] The Bank set the mid-term inflation target from 2001 as 2.5 per cent on an annual average basis each year after 2001 (see Figure 7.8).

In addition, it also introduced various measures to enhance the transparency, credibility and accountability of monetary policy.[5] In Korea, since the inflation targeting system was first introduced in 1998, it seems too early to assess the performance of the new system. Nevertheless, a few points are noticeable from the Korean experience.

First, the average rate of inflation since the adoption of the inflation targeting system is much lower than before it was introduced (see Figure 7.8). In 1998 and 1999, the actual inflation rates remained far below the inflation targets with the help of strong deflationary factors: the reduced costs of imports due to the continuing appreciation of the Korean won; the reduced burden of financial costs borne by businesses owing to improved financial structures and the easing of interest rates; a decline in manpower costs reflecting improved labour productivity and labour market flexibility; and price competition between retailers having become intense in the fight to secure customers in the severe economic depression after the crisis.

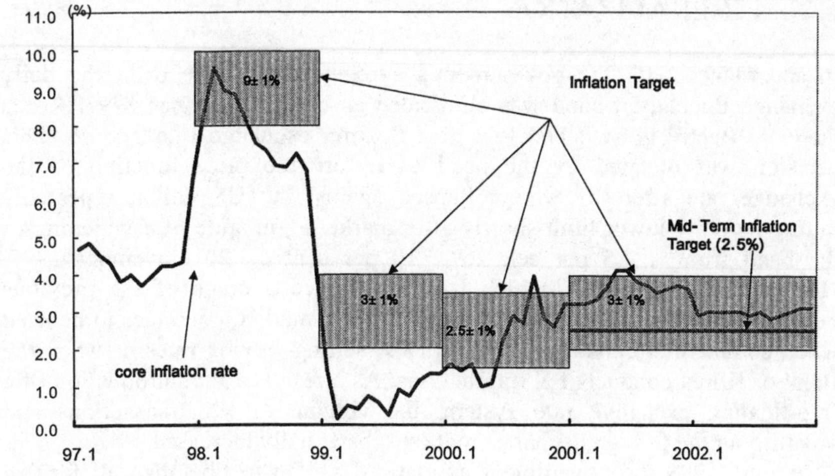


*Source*: Bank of Korea.

*Figure 7.8* *Inflation Targets and Inflation Rates*

In 2000 the economy returned back to a normal situation. In particular, the effects of a sharp rebound of the Korean won after its depreciation during the crisis, which had contributed to making the inflation rates remain below the lower bound of the inflation target in 1998 and 1999, had been almost fully absorbed. Nevertheless, the inflation rate in 2000 remained within the band of the inflation target.

Second, when inflation targeting was adopted in Korea, the country was carrying out financial and corporate restructuring. Accordingly, the Bank of Korea had to take into account financial stability as well as price stability in implementing monetary policies. Upon the outbreak of the currency crisis, the Bank dramatically raised its market intervention rate in consultation with the IMF to 35 per cent in order to engineer a rapid stabilization of the exchange rate. Thus, major market interest rates increased to 30~40 per cent at the end of 1997, and they remained at around the 20 per cent level until March 1998. On the other hand, in 2000, inflationary pressure began to increase, but the Bank increased the call rate step by step, by 0.25 of a percentage point each time, taking into account the ongoing instability of the financial market.

## 7.5 FOREIGN EXCHANGE AND CAPITAL MARKET LIBERALIZATION

In accordance with the government's agreement with the IMF, the daily exchange fluctuation band was eliminated as of 16 December 1997. Korea thereby effectively switched to a free-floating exchange rate system. This decision was dictated by the need to restore the price function of the exchange rate after the won collapsed against the US dollar, repeatedly hitting its daily lower limit shortly after marketing in spite of a widening of the band from ± 2.5 per cent to ± 10 per cent on 20 November 1997. However, the basic rate, which is the weighted average of the previous business day's transactions in the inter-bank FX market, continues to be used when commercial banks set their own FX selling–buying rates or when the Bank of Korea conducts FX transactions. As a result of the introduction of a free-floating exchange rate system, the volume of FX transactions and volatility in the foreign exchange market substantially increased.

In June 1998 the government announced a plan to liberalize all foreign exchange transactions in two stages, for the purpose of establishing a new foreign exchange system under which emphasis is placed on *ex post facto* management through reports and prudential supervision rather than on prior regulation.

The first stage of liberalization, which took effect on 1 April 1999 with the replacement of the old Foreign Exchange Control Act with the new Foreign Exchange Transactions Act, included deregulation of most foreign exchange transactions related to the operations of enterprises and financial institutions. With the exception of a few types of international current account transactions, all current account transactions by business firms and banks, other than individuals, were fully liberalized on 1 April 1999.

In terms of the liberalization of capital account transactions, the legal regulatory framework was changed from a Positive List System to a Negative List System. In order to enhance transparency, all capital account transactions were basically liberalized unless otherwise specifically prohibited on the negative list.

In addition, to reduce inefficiencies stemming from the selective licensing of foreign exchange banks, all financial institutions fulfilling the conditions required to maintain effective *ex - post* transaction management systems were allowed to participate in foreign exchange business.[6]

In the second stage of liberalization, which took effect on 1 January 2001, restrictions on foreign exchange transactions, including current account payments by individuals and domestic deposits by non-residents, were lifted. In regard to FX transactions, the following measures have been implemented: liberalization of residents' FX transactions, such as the elimination of ceilings on overseas travel expenses and foreign currency purchases as well as the abolishment of restrictions on overseas deposits and trusts; liberalization of non-residents' FX transactions, including the elimination of restrictions on non-residents' domestic deposits and trusts with maturities of less than one year; and streamlining the process of securities investment.

Considering the international capital movements and the domestic and international market environment, the government has retained the following restrictions on some capital transactions: limits on Korean won funding by non-residents; and restrictions on overseas short-term borrowings by financially unsound corporations.[7]

Financial liberalization and market opening have been accelerated to induce long-term and stable foreign capital flows and to enhance external credibility. The markets for government and corporate bonds (December 1997), and short-term money market instruments such as Commercial Papers (CPs) (May 1998), were opened up earlier than planned, and ceilings on foreigners' stock market investments (May 1998) have been completely abolished.[8] Hostile takeovers by foreigners were allowed, and the scope of business areas opened to them widened (May 1998). Controls related to foreigners' acquisition of real estate, such as its use, size and other qualifications, were eased or abolished (July 1998).

With the assistance of the widening of market opening, along with the recovery of confidence in the Korean market, foreign portfolio investment substantially increased. Net inflow of foreign portfolio investment was merely US$1 billion in 1997 when the crisis broke out, but since then it considerably increased to US$5 billion in 1998, to US$5.5 billion in 1999, and to US$11.3 billion in 2000 (see Table 7.1).

Accordingly, the ratio of foreign investment outstanding to market capitalization substantially increased. For the Korean Stock Exchange, it increased from 13 per cent in 1996 to 30 per cent in 2000 (see Table 7.2). As a result the movement of foreign portfolio investment considerably influences the Korean stock market. In particular, the co-movement between the Korean market and the US market is substantially increasing (see Figure 7.9).

The other noteworthy aspect increasing in the Korean economy, in line with the widening of market opening, is the negative relationship between the capital account and the current account (see Figure 7.10). An inflow of foreign capital into the Korean stock market leads to an appreciation of the Korean Won. As a result, the current account deteriorates.

## 7.6 TASKS AHEAD

The Bank of Korea's monetary policy paradigm has changed greatly since the currency crisis. A new monetary policy regime of inflation targeting has been introduced to replace the previous monetary targeting. Additionally, in the operation of monetary policy, the central bank's independence has been greatly strengthened. In keeping with the rise in its profile as an independent institution charged with the conduct of monetary policy, the Bank of Korea's responsibility to the public has been heightened and systematic arrangements have been put in place to ensure policy transparency. The monetary policy regime, under which the overnight call rate serves as the policy rate, is taking root. At the same time the Bank makes use of market-friendly methods of conducting monetary policy in the course of employing open market operations as its principal policy tool.

**Table 7.1**
**Foreign Portfolio Investment Trend**

(US$ billion)

| | 1995 | 1996 | 1997 | 1998 | 1999 | 2000 | 2001 | 2002 |
|---|---|---|---|---|---|---|---|---|
| Net Inflow | 2.43 | 4.49 | 0.86 | 4.78 | 5.50 | 11.31 | 7.51 | -1.03 |
| Inflow | 10.18 | 12.46 | 12.65 | 16.48 | 41.74 | 60.15 | 43.98 | 65.17 |
| Outflow | 7.75 | 7.98 | 11.79 | 11.70 | 36.25 | 48.84 | 36.48 | 66.20 |
| Total | 17.93 | 20.44 | 24.44 | 28.18 | 77.99 | 108.99 | 80.46 | 131.37 |

*Source*: Bank of Korea.

**Table 7.2**
**Ratio of Foreign Investment Outstanding to Market Capitalization**

(%)

| | 1996 | 1997 | 1998 | 1999 | 2000 | 2001 | 2002 |
|---|---|---|---|---|---|---|---|
| Korea Stock Exchange | 13.0 | 14.6 | 18.6 | 21.9 | 30.1 | 36.6 | 36.0 |
| KOSDAQ | - | 4.5 | 3.4 | 7.5 | 7.0 | 10.4 | 10.5 |
| Bond Market | 0.04 | 0.09 | 0.3 | 0.3 | 0.2 | 0.1 | 0.1 |

*Notes*: As of the end of the period.

*Source*: Bank of Korea, Financial Supervisory Service.

The additional new monetary policy environment has come about with the complete opening of financial markets and the introduction of a floating exchange rate regime. When there are changes in exchange rates between the currencies of major countries or in the pattern of foreign investors' stock investment under the impact of shocks arising overseas, prices, which are the most important variable for monetary policy, will be affected by changes in the exchange rate of the Korean won.

While the Bank's monetary policy has indeed advanced in terms of its system and practices there are several new challenges and difficulties, and coping with them involves important tasks.

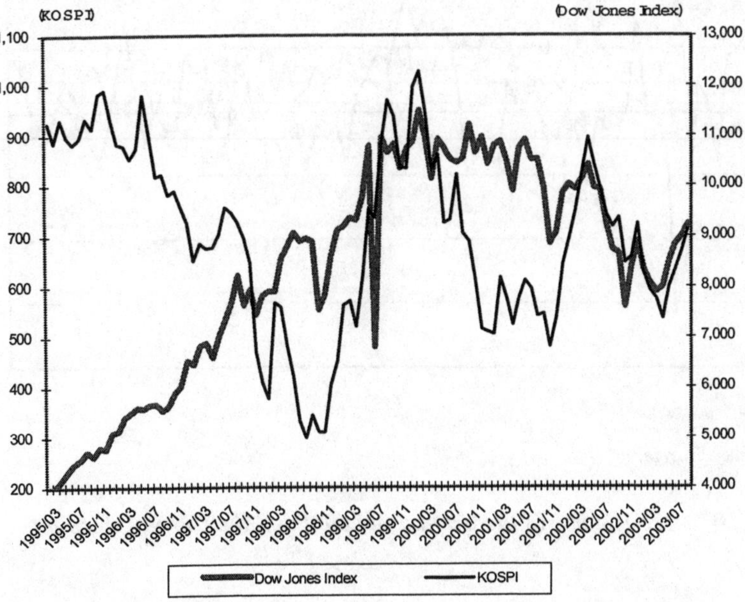


*Note*: As of the end of the period.

*Source*: Bloomberg, http://www.bloonberg.com.

*Figure 7.9 Movements of KOSPI and Dow Jones Indices*

First, it is important now to harmonize different policy objectives in spite of them operating under the inflation targeting regime. Many central banks try to strike a balance between price stability and reducing output volatility. In carrying out policy, however, the Bank of Korea cannot ignore another general policy target: namely, financial market stability. When these three objectives were moving in mutually contradictory directions, such as when it had only the single policy instrument of changes in interest rates at its disposal, the Bank of Korea placed its focus on the objective that it considered most important under the prevailing situation. This is termed employing an eclectic or flexible approach.

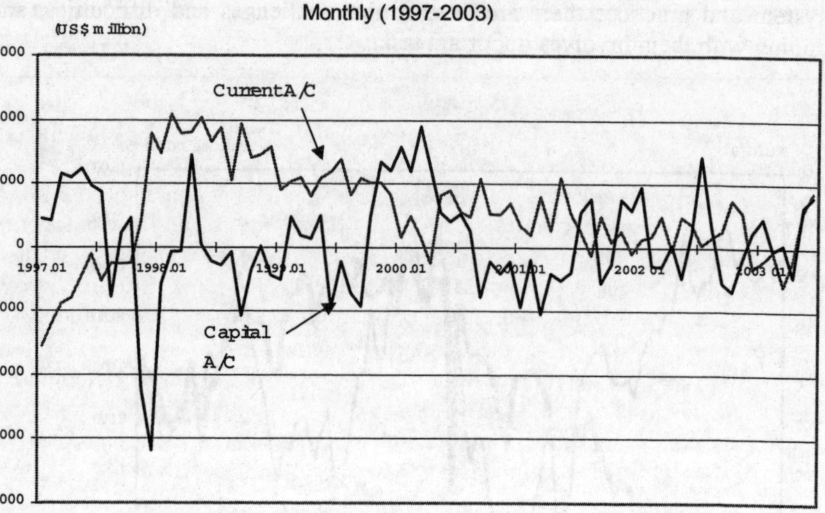


*Source*: Bank of Korea.

*Figure 7.10 Movements of the Capital Account and the Current Account*

Second, it has also been raised as an important issue, to what extent should the exchange rate be taken into account in a small open economy adopting the inflation targeting system, and what kind of an exchange rate system is appropriate to the inflation targeting system. A boom in the stock market encouraged by the low interest rate policy induces an inflow of capital into the Korean stock market, which leads to an appreciation of the Korean won. As a result the current account deteriorates. Accordingly, it seems difficult for a small open economy, such as Korea, to carry out monetary policy focusing only on price stability regardless of its current account situation and financial market stability, even though it adopts the inflation targeting system. In other words the problem of 'the impossibility of the holy trinity' may take place. Countries with an inflation targeting system tend to adopt a freely floating exchange rate regime. The issue is, however, whether the central bank of a small open economy can disregard the short-term volatility of the exchange rate and the long-term misalignment, considering the degree of financial stability and the current account position in that country. Taking into account this issue, Israel adopts a band-crawling exchange rate regime and Canada uses MCI (Monetary Condition Index) as an operating target in spite of inflation targeting.

Thirdly, in order for inflation targeting to be successfully carried out, the effectiveness of the interest rate channel of monetary transmission must be strengthened. Needless to say, monetary policy instruments and financial markets should be developed and government intervention in financial markets should be minimized to strengthen the effectiveness of the interest rate channel. Not only are the financial markets the primary field for the transmission of the effects of monetary policy but they can also be actively utilized as an important source of information for the formation of monetary policy direction, because the many variables that are generated in them provide implications as to the markets' outlook concerning future economic movements. Accordingly, one of the tasks of the central bank is to encourage the development of the financial market.

Finally, the Bank's forecasting capacity on the economy should be enhanced. There is a time lag for the effects of monetary policy. Accordingly, monetary policy must be carried out preemptively, which can only be achieved when it is underpinned by accurate economic forecasting

## NOTES

1 The interest rate parity condition is implicitly based on the bond market, not on the stock market. Therefore, when foreign portfolio investments are mostly concentrated in the stock market, as in the Korean financial market, the theory cannot be effective.

2 Oh (2000b) reviews the Korean inflation targeting system.

3 Oh (1999) estimates two underlying inflation rates using the method of 'adjustment by exclusion' and another using the 'trimmed mean' method. He then examines their stability and usefulness for monetary policy to find which would be the most suitable for inflation targeting in Korea. The results of his empirical analysis show that the underlying inflation rate produced by the method of 'adjustment by exclusion' shows relatively better performance in terms of stability and usefulness for monetary policy.

4 The mid-term inflation target was set at the same level as, or lower than, the short-term inflation target for the year in order to inspire confidence that the Bank would keep inflation low and stable in the long run. The mid-term target was quoted as a point target without a toleration band, because it was judged more important to demonstrate the strong commitment of the central bank to prevent the spread of inflationary expectations among the public than to take economic uncertainties into account.

5 First, the Bank of Korea sets a price stability target for the following year in consultation with the government before the end of each year,

and formulates and promulgates an operation plan for monetary and credit policies including this price stability within 15 days after the setting of the price stability target. Second, every month the Bank of Korea officially announces the monthly direction of monetary policy immediately after the Monetary Policy Committee of the Bank has decided it, and the governor explains its details in a press briefing. Third, the Bank of Korea regularly publishes the minutes of Monetary Policy Committee meetings three months after each meeting. Fourth, the Bank of Korea submits a Monetary and Credit Policy Report to the National Assembly twice a year, normally in March and October, and the governor is required to answer the questions of members of the National Assembly on the report.

6 Along with the above liberalization, some countermeasures were also introduced to avoid unnecessary instability of the foreign exchange market. First, cross-border capital movements have been closely monitored by a newly established comprehensive foreign exchange monitoring network, and individual foreign exchange transactions are being automatically recorded in the computer system in the Foreign Exchange Information Brokerage Centre. Information collected in the centre is shared by the relevant supervisory authorities. Second, the Korea Centre for International Finance (KCIF) was established in April 1999 to collect and analyze information on foreign exchange and international financial market trends. Third, a legal framework was introduced to allow the Korean government to take emergency safeguard measures when necessary. However, the terms and conditions for invoking the measures will be very stringent and conform to international standards, such as the BOP safeguard provisions of the OECD or IMF. Examples of such measures are variable deposit requirements, concentration of foreign exchange, and permission requirement for capital account transactions.

7 Meanwhile, in order to cope with possible capital flight following the deterioration of internal and external economic environments and the increase of illegal transactions such as money laundering and tax evasion, the government has strengthened procedural aspects of its monitoring efforts through such means as the following: strengthening the requirements for reporting some FX transactions to the National Tax Service and to the National Customs Service; maintaining the existing system that requires capital account transactions to be processed through foreign exchange business institutions; introducing a system for reporting large external payments to the Bank of Korea; and introducing a system that requires annually reporting balances of overseas deposits and trust assets exceeding certain amounts to the Bank of Korea.

8 Only for public enterprises, that is Korea Electric Power Corp.;

however, the aggregate foreign ownership ceiling is 30 per cent, while the individual ownership ceiling is 3 per cent.

## REFERENCES


Bank of Korea (2002), *Monetary Policy in Korea*, Seoul.

Basurto and Ghosh (2000), 'The Interest Rate-Exchange Rate Nexus in the Asian Crisis Countries', *IMF Working Paper*, WP/00/19, February.

Cho, Dongchul and Kenneth D. West (1999), 'The Effect of Monetary Policy in Exchange Rate Stabilization in Post-Crisis Korea', presented at the Conference of the Korean Econometric Society, November (in Korean).

Goldfajn, Ilan and Taimur Baig (1998), 'Monetary Policy in the Aftermath of Currency Crisis: The Cases of Asia', *IMF Working Paper,* WP/98/170, December.

Park, D and I. Choi (1999), 'Was High Interest Rate Policy Effective to Stabilize Exchange Rate?', presented at seminar, Bank of Korea, November (in Korean).

Oh, Junggun (2001), 'Governance Reinvented: The Progress, Constraints and Remaining Agenda in Bank and Corporate Restructuring in Korea', in ESCAP (ed.), *Governance Reinvented: The Progress, Constraints and Remaining Agenda in Bank and Corporate Restructuring in East and South East Asia*, Bangkok: United Nations.

Oh, Junggun (2000a), *The Financial Crisis and Financial and Monetary Policies*, Seoul: Dasanbooks (in Korean).

Oh, Junggun (2000b), 'Inflation Targeting: A New Monetary Policy Framework in Korea', in Bank of Thailand (ed.), *Practical Experiences on Inflation Targeting*, Bangkok, October.

Oh, Junggun (2000c), 'Dynamic Correlations between Interest Rates, Stock Prices, the Exchange Rate and the Current Account in an Open Economy in which the Stock Market More Active than the Bond Market', *Working Paper*, No. 104, Bank of Korea, May (in Korean).

Oh, Junggun (1999), 'How Useful Is an Underlying Inflation Rate for Inflation Targeting?', *Economic Papers*, **2**(2), Bank of Korea, December.

Oh, Junggun, J. Kim and B. Bae (2001), *Effectiveness of Economic Policies,* Bank of Korea (in Korean).

# PART III OTHER ISSUES

# 8. A New Economy for Korea

**Dong-pyo Hong, Gae-Iyong Choi and Yongkyu Kim**

## 8.1 INTRODUCTION

Korea has achieved one of the fastest rates of economic development of any country in the world. From a poverty-stricken agricultural economy, with a per capita GDP of US$82 in 1961, Korea has since successfully industrialized its economy and joined the ranks of other OECD countries with a per capita GDP of US$9778 in 2000. Considering its lack of natural resources and small domestic market, this economic achievement has been outstanding.

Korea's growth was based on high capital investments and growth in labour inputs. However, the development based on input-driven growth had begun to reach its limits by the early 1990s. Although its manufactured exports have been expanding rapidly, Korea is squeezed between the developed OECD countries at the higher end and China and other East Asian developing countries at the lower end. Towards the end of 1997, Korea experienced its worst economic crisis since the Korean War. Nonetheless, Korea made a remarkable recovery from the crisis and its economy grew at 10.9 per cent and 9.3 per cent in 1999 and 2000 respectively. However, this performance may not be sustainable because of an input-driven growth structure. Facing a difficult and competitive global environment, the first challenge for Korea is to increase overall productivity.[1] In order to better deal with a difficult and competitive environment and sustain growth, Korea has to pursue a new development strategy. Korea's policy shifted from an input-based to a knowledge-based economy in which knowledge has become the key to competitiveness. The paradigm shift toward a knowledge-based economy has highlighted the significance of IT more than ever.[2]

In the 1990s the IT industry in Korea achieved higher growth than any other major industry, and has been the new engine of growth in the Korean economy. In particular, it helped Korea to recover from the economic crisis in 1997. The IT industry has contributed significantly to sustaining economic growth, reducing inflation, increasing investment, improving the trade surplus and creating jobs. Behind these achievements was the political leadership that provided a clear vision and well-defined policy direction. The government has made consistent efforts to provide the necessary infrastructure and competitive environment through deregulation and liberalization. With its innovative entrepreneurship, the private sector has also made the best use of new business opportunities by increasing investment in IT.

This chapter is organized as follows. In section 2, we provide an overview of the IT industry in Korea. We analyze the structural characteristics of the Korean IT industry and some major products. In section 3, we analyze the contribution of the IT industry to the Korean economy. We especially focus on the IT industry's role in assisting the Korean economy overcome the economic crisis in 1997. In section 4, we examine the IT policies of the Korean government such as informatization promotion, investment in developing IT innovation and building IT skills, financing IT start-ups and regulatory reforms in the telecommunication services sector.

## 8.2 OVERVIEW OF THE IT INDUSTRY

### 8.2.1 IT Industry Structure

The amount of IT production in Korea rose 16.7 per cent in 1998, 30.5 per cent in 1999, and 26.3 per cent in 2000. Production in 2001, however, rose only 3.7 per cent to 150.5 trillion won. The stagnation in sales of IT hardware was the main reason for the industry slowdown in 2001. While telecommunications service and software revenue rose by 18.9 per cent and 17.8 per cent respectively in 2001, production of IT hardware dropped by 1.9 per cent due to the decline in demand on the domestic market and the slowdown in exports. The economic slowdown in Korea coincided with the contraction in the USA, which accounts for about 30 per cent of Korea's exports.

Production of IT industry output, however, is expected to rise by 25.7 per cent in 2002 and reach around 189 trillion won (see Table 8.1). IT exports are showing signs of improvement due to the rise in international prices for major export products such as semiconductors and LCD monitors. Due to the introduction of the IMT-2000 service, expansion of digital broadcasting services and the emergence of new products to support these new services, the growth rate of IT production in Korea is expected to be higher than that of the overall economy by a large margin.

The IT hardware sector is the most significant in terms of production, accounting for more than two-thirds of the industry. Based on the production amount in 2002, IT hardware accounted for 70.6 per cent, telecommunications service 20.0 per cent, and software 9.4 per cent (see Table 8.2). Such a high share of the IT hardware sector can be attributed to the high proportion of IT exports in Korea's IT industry, constituting around 40 per cent of total IT production.[3] The software industry has grown at the highest rate, however its share remains the lowest.

**Table 8.1**
**Production of the Korean IT Industry**

(current trillion won)

| Classification | 1997 | 1998 | 1999 | 2000 | 2001 | 2002 | CAGR (1997–2002) |
|---|---|---|---|---|---|---|---|
| Telecommunications service | 17.0 | 17.9 | 21.6 | 28.5 | 32.9 | 37.9 | 17.4% |
| IT hardware | 55.0 | 65.6 | 86.8 | 105.9 | 102.2 | 133.4 | 19.4% |
| Software | 3.5 | 4.7 | 6.5 | 10.7 | 15.4 | 17.8 | 38.4% |
| Total | 75.5 (33.2%) | 88.1 (16.7%) | 114.9 (30.4%) | 145.2 (26.3%) | 150.5 (3.7%) | 189.1 (25.7%) | 20.2% |

*Note*: Numbers in brackets denote growth rates.

*Source*: Korea Association of Information and Telecommunication (KAIT), 2002.

**Table 8.2**
**Share of Subsectors in the Korean IT Industry**

(%)

| | 1997 | 1998 | 1999 | 2000 | 2001 | 2002 |
|---|---|---|---|---|---|---|
| Telecommunications services | 22.5 | 20.3 | 18.8 | 19.6 | 21.9 | 20.0 |
| IT equipment | 72.8 | 74.5 | 75.5 | 72.9 | 67.9 | 70.6 |
| Software | 4.6 | 5.3 | 5.7 | 7.4 | 10.2 | 9.4 |

*Source*: KAIT (2002).

According to Reed Electronics Research (2002), the Korean IT equipment sector accounts for over 6 per cent of global production, making Korea the third- or fourth-largest producer (see Table 8.3). In 2001, the USA IT recession and global economic uncertainties caused IT equipment production to decline slightly. With China emerging as the production platform for the global IT industry, Korea has dropped to fourth position.

**Table 8.3**
**Rank of Countries by Production Volume**

| | 2000 | | 2001 | | 2002p | |
|---|---|---|---|---|---|---|
| | Country | Total amount ($million) (% of total) | Country | Total amount ($million) (% of total) | Country | Total amount ($million) (% of total) |
| 1 | USA | 313 993 (28.10%) | USA | 244 982 (25.25%) | USA | 247 636 (24.71%) |
| 2 | Japan | 221 623 (19.83%) | Japan | 194 641 (20.06%) | Japan | 196 539 (19.61%) |
| **3** | **Korea** | **69 611 (6.22%)** | China | 70 293 (7.25%) | China | 84 192 (8.40%) |
| 4 | China | 58 620 (5.24%) | **Korea** | **61 559 (6.35%)** | **Korea** | **63 949 (6.38%)** |
| 5 | Taiwan | 48 669 (4.35%) | Taiwan | 41 289 (4.26%) | Taiwan | 42 346 (4.22%) |
| 6 | Singapore | 45 054 (4.03) | UK | 37 367 (3.85%) | UK | 37 938 (3.78%) |
| 7 | UK | 42 370 (3.79%) | Singapore | 36 359 (3.75%) | Singapore | 37 875 (3.79%) |
| 8 | Germany | 37 116 (3.32%) | Germany | 32 740 (3.37%) | Germany | 33 261 (3.32%) |
| 9 | Malaysia | 36 558 (3.27%) | Malaysia | 30 577 (3.15%) | Malaysia | 31 584 (3.15%) |
| 10 | France | 32 874 (2.94%) | France | 29 191 (3.01%) | France | 29 737 (2.97%) |
| Total of 1 to 10 | | 906 488 (81.13%) | | 778 998 (80.29%) | | 805 057 (80.32%) |
| Total Sum | | 1 117 367 (100%) | | 970 167 (100%) | | 1 002 365 (100%) |

*Note*: Data for 2001–2002 are estimates.

*Source*: Reed Electronics Research (2002) rearranged by Korea Information Strategy Development Institute (KISDI).

### 8.2.2 Major Products

**Mobile handsets**

Since 2000, mobile handset production in Korea has become more sensitive to overseas demand rather than domestic demand. With the mobile subscriber base reaching saturation and elimination of the handset purchase subsidy in Korea, production volume has declined 13.3 per cent to only 11.9 trillion won.[4] However, with the explosive growth of handset exports that began in 2000, production rose 32.8 per cent in 2001 to 15.9 trillion won (see Table 8.4). Encouraged by the growth in domestic sales and exports, production in 2002 is expected to grow 10 per cent to 17.5 trillion won. In the future, 13.8 per cent annual export growth and the introduction of the IMT-2000 service should help push production volume of mobile handsets up by 9.2 per cent a year on average.

Exports of Korean mobile handsets in 2001 were US$6.96 billion, a 26.7 per cent increase over 2000. In 2002, exports are forecast to rise 25.5 per cent to US$8.74 billion. This strong growth is due to the proliferation of the CDMA standard throughout the Americas and the strong performance of Korean handsets in current CDMA markets and in European standard GSM markets. Exports are also being fuelled by the expansion of the Chinese CDMA network, and exports of top-end handsets like those with colour screens and attached cameras are increasing profitability. Furthermore, Korean handset makers are putting top priority on international marketing and are aggressively seeking to increase their global exposure in anticipation of market saturation in Korea. Ultimately, the rapid growth of the Asian market, full introduction of the GPRS service, the 2.5G of the European GSM standard, increased exports of high-end handsets such as those with colour screens and cameras should lead to steady growth of exports of handsets overall.

**Table 8.4**
**Production and Trade Balance for Mobile Handsets, 2000–2007**

(won trillion for Production, US$ million for Exports/Balance)

| | 2000 | 2001 | 2002 | 2003 | 2004 | 2005 | 2006 | 2007 | CAGR (2002–07) |
|---|---|---|---|---|---|---|---|---|---|
| Production | 11.9 | 15.9 | 17.5 | 19.0 | 20.7 | 22.6 | 24.7 | 27.1 | 9.2% |
| Exports | 5 499 | 6 967 | 8 740 | 10 025 | 11 386 | 12 936 | 14 687 | 16 713 | 13.8% |
| Balance | 5 447 | 6 929 | 8 647 | 9 924 | 11 275 | 12 815 | 14 556 | 16 571 | 13.9% |

*Note*: Mobile handsets are cellular, PCS and IMT2000. Numbers for 2002 and afterward are forecasted by KISDI.

*Source*: KISDI (2003).

**Semiconductors**

Domestic production of semiconductors in 2001 amounted to 32 trillion won, down 18.0 per cent (see Table 8.5). The decline was especially great in DRAMs, which is the Korean manufacturers' strongest product. In 2002, production volume rose considerably owing to the rebound in prices for DRAMs, thereby increasing the global market share of Korean manufacturers. The overall downturn in the PC and other related industries, increases in inventories, and global economic slowdown resulting from USA economic stagnation, all served to depress the global semiconductor market in 2001. With the USA economy – the major market for semiconductors – reeling from the after effects of the 9/11 terrorist attack and entering recession, investment in semiconductors and corporate IT expenditures were sharply cut back.

Semiconductor exports in the first half of 2002 were expected to be sluggish because of seasonally low demand and low prices, but it seems that actual exports will be higher. In the latter half of 2002, semiconductor exports were expected to gain further momentum due to the need to replace pre-Y2K PCs, increases in PC memory, rising prices, and the shift to 256 MB DRAM. Rising prices for DRAM will be crucial for Korea to reach its 2002 export target, but export growth is forecast to be below earlier expectations because of the war in the Middle East and sluggishness in the telecommunications industry in the USA. Presuming higher demand led by recovery of the USA IT market, increases in memory per PC, and the need to replace older mobile handsets and pre-Y2K PCs, exports are forecast to rise 12.0 per cent to US$16 billion (see Table 8.5).

**Table 8.5**
**Production and Trade Balance for Semiconductors, 2000–2007**
(won trillion for Production, US$ million for Exports/Balance)

| | 1999 | 2000 | 2001 | 2002 | 2003 | 2004 | 2005 | 2006 | 2007 | CAGR (2002–07) |
|---|---|---|---|---|---|---|---|---|---|---|
| Production | 29.0 | 34.2 | 32.2 | 43.7 | 50.3 | 61.3 | 67.1 | 73.9 | 81.2 | 13.2% |
| Exports | 18 852 | 26 015 | 14 310 | 16 027 | 20 355 | 27 682 | 32 111 | 36 286 | 41 003 | 20.7% |
| Balance | 2 722 | 5 977 | -1 373 | -283 | 782 | 2 630 | 2 549 | 2 289 | 1 907 | - |

*Note*: Numbers for 2002 and afterward are forecasted by KISDI.

*Source*: KISDI (2003).

From 2003, higher DRAM prices and rising worldwide demand should push exports up enormously. Exports are expected to rise at an average annual rate of 20.7 per cent until 2007.

Korea's share of the global semiconductor market was 5.7 per cent in 2001, but in DRAM it was 41.5 per cent. Korea's share of the global DRAM market was 46.93 per cent in Q1 and 47.45 per cent in Q2 of 2002. Its Q3 share reached close to 49 per cent, and Korea is poised to exceed 50 per cent for the first time. Production of semiconductors in Korea is expected to rise at a 12.9 per cent average annual rate through 2007. Table 8.6 provides information on the ten largest global DRAM manufacturers.

**Table 8.6**
**Sales of Global DRAM Manufacturers, 2000 and 2001**

(US$ million, %)

| Rank | Company | Sales | | Growth rate (1999–2000) | Market share in 2001 |
|---|---|---|---|---|---|
| | | 2000 | 2001 | | |
| 1 | Samsung | 6645 | 3200 | -51.8 | 27.0 |
| 2 | Micron | 5956 | 2260 | -62.1 | 19.1 |
| 3 | Hynix | 5437 | 1716 | -68.4 | 14.5 |
| 4 | Infineon | 2988 | 1154 | -56.8 | 9.7 |
| 5 | Elpida | 2114 | 1011 | -69.8 | 8.5 |
| 6 | Toshiba | 1947 | 761 | -60.9 | 6.4 |
| 7 | Mitsubishi | 1232 | 303 | -69.1 | 2.6 |
| 8 | Nanya | 982 | 273 | -22.0 | 2.3 |
| 9 | OKI | 885 | 212 | -52.4 | 1.8 |
| 10 | Mosel Vitelic | 588 | 205 | -76.8 | 1.7 |
| | Others | 3091 | 761 | -73.7 | 6.4 |
| | Total | 31865 | 11856 | -62.4 | 100.0 |

*Source*: KISDI (2003).

### Flat panel displays

The performance of flat panel display manufacturers suffered in 2000 due to the accelerating decline in FPD prices. Production volume decreased 1.6 per cent in 2001 to 6.3 trillion won (see Table 8.7). In 2002, the market began to show signs of robust growth as a result of reductions in inventories of TFT-LCD. Flat panel display production is expected to rise sharply by 30.2 per cent. Although the growth of Korean manufacturers is expected to slow in 2003, the mid- to long-term forecast is optimistic. New demand is cropping up from growing needs to replace CRT monitors and rising demand for large-size LCDs for TV and small-size LCDs for handsets and PDAs, while new display markets are being created with FPDs and organic EL.

Exports of flat panel displays in 2001 fell (see Table 8.7) because of a serious sales slump in LCDs and a short-term glut in supply. Despite price fluctuations stemming from the crystal cycle, growth is expected to move steadily upward at an annual rate of 14 per cent until 2007.

**Table 8.7**
**Production and Trade Balance for Flat Panel Displays, 2000~2007**

(won trillion for Production, US$ million for Exports/Balance)

| | 2000 | 2001 | 2002 | 2003 | 2004 | 2005 | 2006 | 2007 | CAGR (2002–07) |
|---|---|---|---|---|---|---|---|---|---|
| Production | 6.5 | 6.3 | 8.3 | 8.5 | 9.8 | 12.2 | 12.9 | 15.4 | 13.3% |
| Exports | 3270 | 2518 | 3625 | 3734 | 4331 | 5458 | 5621 | 6858 | 13.6% |
| Balance | 2693 | 1970 | 2902 | 2909 | 3358 | 4241 | 4259 | 5223 | - |

*Source*: KISDI (2003).

According to DisplaySearch (2002), Samsung Electronics and LG Philips LCD are expected to have the first- and second-largest market shares respectively in large-size TFT-LCDs in the second quarter, indicating that Korean manufacturers maintained their leadership in 2002. Samsung Electronics claimed 16.9 per cent of the market in the first as well as the second quarter to remain the largest maker (see Table 8.8).

**Table 8.8**
**Market Share of TFT LCD Makers, 2000 (based on volume)**

(%)

| | Q2 share | Production growth | Q1 share |
|---|---|---|---|
| Samsung Electronics | 16.9 | 9 | 16.9 |
| LG Philips LCD | 15.4 | 15 | 14.7 |
| AU Optronics | 12.1 | 1 | 13.1 |
| Sharp | 8.8 | 15 | 8.4 |
| CMO/IDT | 7.6 | 8 | 7.8 |
| CPT | 7.0 | 17 | 6.6 |
| Hitachi | 5.6 | 1 | 6.1 |
| TMDisplay | 5.5 | 9 | - |
| Hannstar | 4.4 | 0 | 4.8 |
| Quanta | 3.8 | 41 | 3.0 |
| Hydis | 3.4 | 0 | 3.7 |
| Sanyo | 3.1 | 0 | 3.4 |
| Fujitsu | 2.4 | 66 | 1.6 |
| NEC | 2.1 | 5 | 2.2 |
| ADI | 1.8 | -13 | 2.2 |
| Matsushita | - | - | 0.3 |
| Toshiba | - | - | 5.2 |
| Total | 100.0 | 9.5 | 100.0 |

*Source*: DisplaySearch (2002).

Its sales rose 22 per cent year-on-year. The company's market share in LCDs for notebook PCs rose to 19.5 per cent the previous quarter to 20.9 per cent, and its production of LCDs for monitors declined to 14.0 per cent from the previous quarter to become the second highest. LG Philips LCD was the major producer of LCDs for monitors in the second quarter. Overall, it accounted for 15.4 per cent of the market to rank number two. With Korean makers claiming the first- and third-highest production capacities, and volume expected to further increase in Q3 2002 with the start of fifth-generation production lines, Korean makers are expected to widen their lead over Taiwanese makers and solidify their market dominance. Korea's dominance will become even greater due to lessening inventories of TFT-LCDs in 2003 and delays by Taiwanese makers in establishing their fifth-generation production lines.

**Subscribers of broadband internet services**

Korea emerged as the most advanced country in providing broadband Internet services with an unprecedented rollout of the service in a short period of time. The total number of subscriptions stood at just under 10 million households as of September 2002 (see Table 8.9), which means that almost 70 per cent of households are connected to the broadband network in Korea.[5] Contrary to negative views on the economic viability of this service at the outset, carriers were able to record positive profit during the first half of 2001 with the tariff set as low as US$30 per month. In addition, with economies of scale, the price of ADSL terminal equipment fell from US$700 to less than US$100, making the service more available to more consumers.

**Table 8.9**
**Trend of Broadband Internet Subscribers**

(thousand persons)

| | 2000. 6 | 2000. 12 | 2001. 8 | 2002. 8 |
|---|---|---|---|---|
| ADSL | 678 | 2074 | 3785 | 5264 |
| Cable Modem | 563 | 1386 | 2156 | 3398 |
| Others | 334 | 557 | 819 | 1149 |
| Total | 1575 | 4017 | 6760 | 9812 |

*Source:* Lee (2002).

There are many reasons to explain this rapid penetration. The residential structure, approximately one-third of which is composed of households living in clustered apartment complexes, has made the deployment of the broadband Internet service less expensive. The VoIP service combined with the feature of free call service has served as an extremely attractive application as well. The government's hands-off policy with respect to new services and policies based on the market principle, has made the broadband Internet market more competitive and profitable. In the rapidly changing telecommunications industry, the government has carefully fulfilled its role of providing an environment conducive to innovation and competition. A competitive local exchange carrier, Hanaro, first entered the broadband Internet service market. The success of Hanaro's rapid growth in this market induced Korea Telecom to launch the service as well, which then triggered cutthroat price competition among the service providers.[6]

## 8.3 CONTRIBUTION OF THE IT INDUSTRY TO THE KOREAN ECONOMY

The prodigious vitality of the new economy is grounded in the IT industry – the firms that supply the goods and services supporting IT-related business practices across the economy as well as the Internet and e-commerce.[7] Since the middle of the 1990s, the IT industry has been the new engine of growth in the Korean economy. In particular, it helped Korea to recover from the economic crisis in 1997. Furthermore, the IT industry has contributed significantly to sustaining economic growth, reducing inflation, increasing investment, improving the trade surplus and creating jobs.

### 8.3.1 Contribution to Real Economic Growth and Investment

The rapid upsurge of the IT industry has augmented the wealth of Korea. According to the Bank of Korea, the share of GDP attributable to the IT industry rose steadily to 16.9 per cent in 2002 (see Table 8.10).

**Table 8.10**
**IT Industry's Share of the Economy and Contribution to Real Economic Growth**

(1995 price, %)

| | 1997 | 1998 | 1999 | 2000 | 2001 | 2002 |
|---|---|---|---|---|---|---|
| IT industry share of GDP | 7.7 | 9.9 | 12.2 | 15.1 | 16.0 | 16.9 |
| Growth rate of IT industry | 30.5 | 20.7 | 36.0 | 35.8 | 9.1 | 12.0 |
| Growth rate of GDP | 5.0 | -6.7 | 10.7 | 9.3 | 3.1 | 6.3 |
| Contribution of IT industry to GDP growth | 37.6 | - | 32.8 | 46.8 | 44.3 | 30.4 |
| Growth rate of non-IT industry | 3.3 | -9.0 | 8.1 | 5.7 | 2.0 | 5.3 |

*Source*: Bank of Korea.

A better way to evaluate the importance of the IT industry is to look at its contribution to real growth. In 1998, when the economy suffered from the economic crisis and recorded a negative growth rate, the IT industry grew by 20.7 per cent. Since then the IT industry has grown at much higher rates than the overall economy, accounting for more than one-third of overall economic growth. IT equipment continues to be the largest category of industry spending for all types of capital equipment. In inflation-adjusted terms, IT equipment's share of total investment rose continually to 28.5 per cent in 2002 (see Table 8.11).

**Table 8.11**
**Growth Rates of Investments and IT Share of Total Investment**

(%)

| | 1997 | 1998 | 1999 | 2000 | 2001 | 2002 |
|---|---|---|---|---|---|---|
| Growth rate of total investment | -8.7 | -38.8 | 36.3 | 34.3 | -9.6 | 6.8 |
| Growth rate of investment in IT | 19.4 | -3.0 | 60.7 | 46.5 | -2.8 | -5.2 |
| IT share of total investment | 15.2 | 24.2 | 28.1 | 29.9 | 32.1 | 28.5 |

*Note*: Investment in software is not included in IT investment.

*Source*: Bank of Korea.

### 8.3.2 Price Changes in the IT industry

The prices of goods and services of the IT industry fell due to rapid innovations of IT products such as computers and semiconductors, and from increased competition in the telecommunications service market. The declining prices have contributed to keeping overall inflation in check. Prices fell at an average annual rate of 2.2 per cent for the years 1997 to 2002, whereas overall prices increased at an average annual rate of 3.3 per cent (see Table 8.12).

**Table 8.12**
**Price Changes of IT and Overall Industries**

(%)

| | 1997 | 1998 | 1999 | 2000 | 2001 | 2002 |
|---|---|---|---|---|---|---|
| Overall industry | 3.9 | 12.2 | -2.1 | 2.0 | 1.9 | 1.6 |
| IT industry | -3.7 | 5.2 | -5.7 | -3.2 | -3.8 | -1.9 |

*Source*: Bank of Korea.

### 8.3.3 IT Industry Trade

The IT industry accounted for an increasing share of Korean international trade. Exports by the Korean IT industry increased to US$51.2 billion in 2000 and dropped to US$38.5 billion in 2001 due to the worldwide recession in the IT sector (see Table 8.13). Accordingly, the IT share of Korean exports dropped to 25.4 per cent in 2001 but recovered to 28.3 per cent in 2002. The trade surplus of the IT industry has shown the same trend as IT exports. Major export items of the Korean IT industry include DRAM, mobile telephones, monitors, LCDs, PCs and satellite broadcast receivers, while major import items include non-memory semiconductors, transmission equipment and large-size computers. Major export markets for Korean IT products are the USA, China and Japan.

**Table 8.13**
**Trade of IT Goods in Korea**

(US$ billion)

| | 1997 | 1998 | 1999 | 2000 | 2001 | 2002 |
|---|---|---|---|---|---|---|
| IT Exports | 31.3 | 30.5 | 39.9 | 51.2 | 38.4 | 46.1 |
| IT Trade balance | 9.4 | 12.3 | 13.4 | 15.7 | 10.6 | 15.3 |
| Share of IT exports in total exports (%) | 22.5 | 23.1 | 27.5 | 29.1 | 25.4 | 28.3 |
| Total trade balance | -3.2 | 41.6 | 28.4 | 16.9 | 13.5 | 14.2 |

*Source*: Bank of Korea.

### 8.4.4 IT Workforce Employment

In the IT industry, technology innovation and e-commerce have led to the creation and destruction of jobs. On the one hand, demand for an IT workforce has increased with the growth of the Internet, e-commerce and other IT-related businesses as well as with the growth of IT production. On the other hand, low-skilled labour faces a greater chance of being displaced by IT equipment. Employment growth in the IT industry has outpaced average employment growth. The IT workforce[8] increased rapidly and totalled about 1.7 million workers or 8.0 per cent of all workers in 2001 (see Table 8.14). The demand for IT workers is increasingly focused on highly educated and highly skilled workers such as IT specialists and IT administrators. Among the IT sectors, software has recorded the fastest employment growth.

# 8.4 IT POLICIES IN KOREA

## 8.4.1 Informatization Promotion

The Korean government enacted the Framework Act on Informatization Promotion in 1995, and it set up the first Master Plan for informatization promotion in 1996 and established a committee for planning and implementation of the goals outlined in the Master Plan. In 1999, the government established Cyber Korea 21 as the blueprint for the new information society of the twenty-first century, in order to overcome the financial crisis and to transform the Korean economy into a knowledge-based one.

**Table 8.14**
**Employment of IT Workforce**

(persons)

| | 1998 | 1999 | 2000 | 2001 | 2002[p] | CAGR (1998-01) |
|---|---|---|---|---|---|---|
| Total workers | 19,994 | 20,281 | 21,060 | 21,362 | 21,553 | 2.2% |
| Employment in IT workforce (A+B) | 1,311 (6.6%) | 1,462 (7.2%) | 1,550 (7.4%) | 1,658 (7.8%) | 1,726 (8.0%) | 8.1% |
| Employment in IT occupations (A) | 923 | 1,016 | 1,114 | 1,163 | 1,215 | 8.0% |
| Employment in the IT industry (B) | 388 | 446 | 436 | 495 | 511 | 8.5% |
| IT hardware | 245 | 289 | 281 | 312 | 327 | 8.4% |
| Software | 52 | 66 | 62 | 89 | 89 | 19.6% |
| Telecommunications service | 91 | 91 | 93 | 93 | 95 | 0.7% |

*Note*: Numbers in brackets denote the IT workforce's share in total employment.

*Source*: Korea National Statistical Office, KAIT (2002).

In the 1990s, the Korean government devoted much of its energy to the process of informatization. Both the government and the private sector have concentrated their investments on building a more efficient and faster information infrastructure, which was expected to be in great demand in the future. As a result, a high-speed broadband network was constructed across Korea in all of the 144 call areas. In addition, Internet access was possible for 10 482 elementary, middle and high schools, and 36 689 lines were supplied to the public sector including government offices, local autonomous bodies, research institutions, libraries and museums. According to the plan for the Information Superhighway (KII), which will strengthen the backbone of the subscriber networks, the Korean government has committed itself to the goal of providing high-speed communication services at the 20 Mbps level, on average, to 84 per cent of Korean households by 2005.

Informatization of the overall administrative processes in the government has increased not only administrative efficiency but has also established a solid foundation for e-government (see Table 8.15). The application of IT has spread to major industries such as steel, electronics, shipbuilding, automobiles and textiles in order to reduce costs and to enhance productivity. IT is also extensively utilized in daily activities including financial transactions and health administration.[9] To bridge the digital divide and to enhance the quality of life, the government has wired all elementary, middle and high schools to high-speed Internet services and has also provided e-literacy programmes for the general public.

**Table 8.15**
**Major Indices of Informatization**

| | Pre-Master Plan (End of 1995) | Pre-CK21 (End of 1998) | Post-CK21 (End of 2001) |
|---|---|---|---|
| Proportion on e-approval in the government (%) | - | 21.2 | 80.6 |
| Proportion of e-procurement of the government (%) | - | 19.3 | 87.5 |
| Proportion of e-trade (%) | - | 3.7 | 66.6 |
| Number of internet users (million) | 0.37 | 3.10 | 24.38 |
| Size of e-commerce market (won, trillion) | - | 0.05 | 88.5* |

*Note*: * refers to the period from January to September 2001.

*Source*: Ministry of Information and Communication (2002).

Despite the well-built infrastructure, the benefits from informatization have fallen short of expectations. Due to the lack of information sharing and system networking among government agencies, informatization in the public sector has not been fully realized. The IT utilization by SMEs is low because of weak infrastructure for e-business such as in standardization and logistics. Lack of transparency in transactions is another obstacle to IT utilization. To facilitate IT utilization, the government has provided greater transparency, disclosure of information and accountability for firms as well as for the government. Also the government has established a legal framework to deal with the adverse effects of IT utilization such as hacking and privacy infringement.

### 8.4.2 Investment in Technology Development

The Korean government designated 174 strategic core technologies for technology development projects in 2000, investing 157 billion won in order to gain a technological competitive edge in the world market including next-generation Internet, optical communications, digital broadcasting, wireless communications, and computer software. Accordingly, Korea has made more than 1000 patent applications related to the advancement of core technology within and outside the country. In addition, the Korean government has improved the appraisal system for the selection of research subjects and has helped to establish effective research management methods for efficient R&D management. At the same time, the government is concentrating on the development of innovative technology that will form the basis for securing sustained national competitiveness in the future. Private investments are not readily made in this area since short-term commercialization is generally not feasible.

The Korean government has invested 115.5 billion won in the first half of 2001 to support R&D activities of small venture businesses, to develop information and communications policies, to establish e-libraries and to construct the next-generation Internet platform. The government is continuously searching for leading technologies by appraising their technological and commercial merit, and providing marketing and commercial support in order to create demand. In addition, the government has established a Test Support Centre for Optical Parts and Systems at the Gwangju Optical Industrial Complex to develop a quality control system for optical communication systems.

In order to provide favourable environments for IT usage and to encourage the IT industry to advance into the world market, the Korean government has developed an IT standardization criteria. In addition, to improve the testing and certification systems in the telecommunications sector, the government has improved the operations that regulate technical standards in such a way as to meet the rapid development of IT and the changes in the competitive structures of the telecommunications market. For this reason, the Korean government revised the regulations of the Technical Standards for Telecommunication Facilities in August 2001. Moreover, the government is making improvements to the certification system for telecommunications equipment and promoting mutual recognition among nations in order to overcome technical barriers to trade.[10]

R&D investments in IT have placed little emphasis on basic research. Public IT R&D investment accounted for approximately 10 per cent of total IT R&D investment, and out of this 12.8 per cent is used for basic research. The lack of investment in basic research has resulted in a technology gap in core technologies and royalty payments.

In addition, it is also pointed out that universities do not carry out much scientific research. The distribution of highly-qualified R&D personnel among universities, GRIs (government research institutes), and industries is not in tune with the allocation of R&D expenditure. As Table 8.16 shows, universities retain 76.2 per cent of PhD researchers, but R&D expenditure of universities accounts for only 11.3 per cent of the total expenditure. The share in total R&D expenditure for universities is one of the lowest in OECD countries. Reasons for the low R&D performance point to the sluggish research conditions in universities due to lack of funds and research equipment, and a heavy workload for staff. Increased government funding and greater emphasis on basic research is necessary at universities.

**Table 8.16**
**Allocation of R&D Expenditure and Researchers (2000)**

| | GRIs | Universities | Industries | Total |
|---|---|---|---|---|
| Researchers | 13 913 (8.7%) | 51 727 (32.3%) | 94 333 (59.0%) | 159 973 (100%) |
| Researchers holding PhD | 5 654 (12.3%) | 35 141 (76.2%) | 5 351 (11.6%) | 46 146 (100%) |
| R&D expenditure (in 100 million won) | 2 031 981 (14.6%) | 1 561 865 (11.3%) | 10 254 655 (74%) | 13 848 501 (100%) |
| Government financed R&D expenditure (in 100 million won) | 1 654 373 | 871 562 | 685 308 | 3 211 243 |
| R&D expenditure per researcher (in 1,000 won) | 146 049 | 30 194 | 108 707 | 86 568 |

*Source*: Ministry of Science and Technology (2002).

### 8.4.3 Building IT skills

With the expansion of IT industries and informatization in overall industries, the need for specialist IT workers has increased dramatically. The shortage of IT specialists is estimated to be 99 000 by 2006.[11] In order to build an IT-skilled labour force, the Ministry of Information and Communication has spent more than 1 trillion won since 1997 on building IT skills. Investment to build IT skills can be categorized into 4 programmes: professional IT skills, basic IT skills, industrial IT skills and potential IT literacy skills (see Tables 8.17 and 8.18).

*Basic IT skills programme*: This programme aims to enlarge the enrolment size of IT-related departments. Subsidies are provided to hire instructors in schools and educational institutions specializing in IT. The programme also supports basic research projects in universities.

*Professional IT skills programmes*: This programme aims to produce highly skilled IT workers in domestic and overseas research institutions. The programme supports IT research institutions and overseas scholarship programmes.

*Industrial IT skills programme*: This programme aims to re-train IT workers who are currently employed as well as those who are unemployed. Support is provided to private IT training institutions as well as subsidies for individual educational expenses.

*IT literacy programme*: This programme aims to provide e-literate programmes for the general public including housewives, soldiers, the disabled and low-income families to help resolve the digital divide.

**Table 8.17**
**Expenditure on Building IT Skills by Programmes**

(100 million won)

| | 1997 | 1998 | 1999 | 2000 | 2001 | 2002 | Total |
|---|---|---|---|---|---|---|---|
| Basic IT skill | 184 | 342 | 379 | 350 | 1 908 | 740 | 3 903 |
| Professional IT skills | 300 | 250 | 137 | 201 | 503 | 461 | 1 852 |
| Industrial IT skills | 110 | 514 | 366 | 123 | 591 | 739 | 2 443 |
| Literacy IT skills | - | 54 | 168 | 118 | 1 309 | 616 | 2 265 |
| Total | 594 | 1 160 | 1 050 | 795 | 4 311 | 2 556 | 10 466 |

*Note*: Numbers for 2000 are based on the executed amount while numbers for 2001 and 2002 are budget based.

*Source*: KIPA (Korea IT Industry Promotion Association).

**Table 8.18**
**Outcomes of IT Skills Programmes (2001)**

| | Basic IT skill | Professional IT skills | Industrial IT skills | Potential IT skills | Total |
|---|---|---|---|---|---|
| Beneficiary (persons, A) | 68 009 | 2 236 | 33 809 | 1 303 854 | 1 407 908 |
| Expenditure (billion won, B) | 171.8 | 45.2 | 59.8 | 83.9 | 357.7 |
| B/A (10 thousand won) | 253 | 2 021 | 177 | 6 | 25 |

*Note*: based on the executed investment (357.7 billion won) out of the 2001 budget (431.1 billion won)

*Source*: KIPA (Korea IT Industry Promotion Association).

These programmes have been criticized for an over-emphasis on quantitative reasoning, with a shortage of training in new skills. Actually, it is predicted that higher education for IT, especially in software, is severely in short supply and therefore needs to be expanded (see Table 8.19). The Korean government is to change the policy priority from quantity to quality, and to invest resources to resolve the quality mismatch.

**Table 8.19**
**Expected Shortage of IT Workers**

| Degree | 2002 | 2003 | 2004 | 2005 | 2006 | 2002–2006 |
|---|---|---|---|---|---|---|
| High school or below | -721 | -2 316 | -915 | -352 | -582 | -4 886 |
| Bachelor | -16 972 | -18 586 | -18 389 | -16 544 | -17 668 | -88 158 |
| Master | -854 | -839 | -1 025 | -1 093 | -1 176 | -4 987 |
| PhD | -223 | -249 | -254 | -296 | -275 | -1 297 |
| Total | -18 769 | -21 989 | -20 583 | -18 284 | -19 702 | -99 328 |

*Source*: KISDI (2003).

Educational output has also been pointed out as being inadequately related to the demands of industry. The government encourages educational institutions and industry partnerships to integrate the curriculum to reflect industry demand and include training programmes for new IT skills. To resolve the mismatch between supply and demand, the government is to provide, more efficiently, market information to both sides.

### 8.4.4 Financing IT Start-ups

Small and medium-sized companies and venture enterprises play a particularly important role in the IT industry. With flexible and flat organizations, they can be focused on the specific market and make a fast response to changes in market demand. In Korea they account for 97 per cent of all IT companies, and IT venture enterprises account for more than 45 per cent of the venture enterprises certified by the Small and Medium Business Administration (see Tables 8.20 and 8.21). This shows that the IT industry is the foundation of the new economic paradigm and is a crucible for the creation of dynamic new companies. Though the number of venture enterprises certified has declined, the number of IT companies has increased.

**Table 8.20**
**Small and Medium-Sized Companies in the IT Industry, 1998–2002**

| Classification | 1998 | 1999 | 2000 | 2001* | 2002* (1st half) |
|---|---|---|---|---|---|
| Total number of IT companies | 10 218 | 12 382 | 13 944 | 17 719 | 20 148 |
| Number of small and medium IT venture enterprises | 10 055 | 12 105 | 13 629 | 17 416 | 19 845 |
| Number of new IT venture enterprises | 808 | 2 050 | 1 524 | 3 787 | 2 429 |

*Note*: * Estimates.

*Source*: KISDI (2003).

**Table 8.21**
**Number of IT Venture Enterprises, 2000–2002**

| | 2000 | 2001 | 2002.6 |
|---|---|---|---|
| Total number of Venture Enterprises (A) | 8 798 | 11 392 | 10 182 |
| Number of IT Venture Enterprises (B) | 4 017 | 5 073 | 4 872 |
| Percentage of IT Venture Enterprises (B/A) | 45.7% | 44.5% | 47.8% |

*Source*: KISDI (2003).

Venture capital is an institutional investor that plays an important role in the success of start-ups. The success of high-tech start-ups in the US can be attributed to the existence of the NASDAQ stock market, as well as such regional environments as Silicon Valley that are equipped with various supporting networks enabling a well-developed venture capital industry. In Korea, the venture capital industry was formed by policy initiatives starting in the early 1980s, well before public awareness in start-ups was aroused. In the early stages the venture capital industry served the role of carrying out the government policy of providing funding for small and medium-sized enterprises, and focused more on loans than investments. However, the opening of the KOSDAQ (1 July 1996) gave ample new opportunities for investments when the venture boom, centring around the IT sector, led to a remarkable growth in the venture capital industry. However, the Korean venture capital industry experienced a steep decline after a period of enormous growth. The IT industry is by far the most active sector for venture capital. In recent years, investments in the IT industry have accounted for close to two-thirds of total investments (see Table 8.22).

**Table 8.22**
**Venture Capital Investment in the IT industry (1998–2001)**

| | Investment (won, billion) | % of total investment | Average per deal (won, billion) |
|---|---|---|---|
| IT | 2438.3 | 65.0 | 1.24 |
| Bio | 176.1 | 4.7 | 1.04 |
| Environment | 58.3 | 1.6 | 1.01 |
| Energy | 3.0 | 0.1 | 0.50 |
| Manufacturing | 537.6 | 14.3 | 0.92 |
| Entertainment | 214.0 | 5.7 | 1.75 |
| Others | 322.8 | 8.6 | 0.89 |
| Total | 3750.1 | 100.0 | 1.15 |

*Source*: SMBA.

The government has taken the role of leading investor in newly formed venture investment funds to facilitate the supply of funds, especially during the period of economic recession since the second half of 2000 (see Table 8.23). Currently, government agencies involved in venture investment funds include the Small and Medium Business Administration (SMBA), Ministry of Information and Communication, and numerous other central government ministries and regional government offices. The government encouraged the formation of investment partnership funds by participating and offering seed money. Especially in 2001, when private investors became pessimistic, the government's involvement deepened. In the short run the government helps to stabilize fundraising efforts, but in the longer run the government may displace private efforts.

**Table 8.23**
**Start-up investment funds with government participation**

| | Number | % of total | Amount (won, 100 million) | % of total |
|---|---|---|---|---|
| 1996–98 | 15 | (57.7%) | 949 | (55.5%) |
| 1999 | 16 | (21.6%) | 2077 | (45.6%) |
| 2000 | 77 | (41.2%) | 7384 | (52.2%) |
| 2001 | 68 | (76.4%) | 6600 | (90.3%) |

*Note*: The government typically provides about 30 per cent of total fund commitments.

*Source*: Korea Venture Capital Association (KVCA).

In addition, in 1997, the government established the Act on Special Measures for the Promotion of Venture Businesses and introduced the Venture Certification system.[12] Also, by reducing income and capital gains taxes on their investment through venture capital, the government has encouraged venture investments. In Korea the real history of the venture capital industry is quite short, so accumulated experiences and market reputations are lacking. At the beginning stage, government-supported fundraising directly helped to create a market. But, as the market becomes bigger, government participation should be flexible and cautious so as not to displace private investors. Also, in order to avoid fraud incidents and market manipulation, attempts reported recently to guarantee the long-term viability of the start-up sector, the government has tried to provide a transparent and fair atmosphere and encourage sophisticated covenants and global standard practices.

### 8.5.5 Regulatory Reforms in the Telecommunications Services Sector

As new types of services and technologies became available, the government introduced competition into the market since the monopolistic conditions were far less likely to provide efficient, innovative and inexpensive services to the public. In 1990, the value-added services market was opened for competition, followed by the basic voice telephony market, then the international services market in 1992, the long-distance services market in 1995 and finally the local market in 1997. As a result, there were no longer any legal impediments for market entry of the provision of fixed telecommunications infrastructure and services. As of today, there are 32 facilities-based telecoms service providers (FSPs) that compete fiercely in this competitive market structure.[13]

At the same time, Korea has also placed continuous efforts in privatizing the telecom sector. The government began the process of privatizing Korea Mobile Telecom (KMT) in 1994, and sold off all government shares to complete the privatization process of KT on May 2002. Privatization is expected to eliminate the conflict between ownership objectives and enforcement of impartial regulations, resulting in non-discriminatory decisions.

Furthermore, Korea has taken further steps to open the telecom markets. The multilateral and bilateral negotiation process resulting in the 1997 WTO Basic Telecommunication Agreement has accelerated market opening and, as a direct result of the agreement, Korea has opened the resale market to foreign companies and raised the limits of foreign ownership to a ceiling of 49 per cent for domestic FSPs.

These changes of regulations resulted in market expansion. In 2001, compared to 1991, the subscribers, number of service providers and market size increased by about 73 times, 95 times and 7 times respectively (see Table 8.24).

**Table 8.24**
**Growth of the Telecommunications Service Market in Korea (1991–2001)**

| | 1991 | 2001 | 2001/1991 |
|---|---|---|---|
| Subscribers (1000 persons) | 1 607 | 117 126 | 72.9 |
| Number of service providers | 53 | 5 010 | 94.5 |
| Market size (won, billion) | 4 533 | 29 738 | 6.6 |

*Source*: Park (2002).

After the introduction of competition in the market, the Korea government now pays more attention to regulation reforms for fair competition. It has introduced new regulatory measures such as carrier pre-selection, new interconnection rules, has restructured the licensing framework for entry into the fixed public telecommunications and value-added service markets, and has changed price regulations. These changes have had a positive impact on the opening of the market to competition, the introduction of new services and in price competition. Also, to avoid redundant investment in networks and to facilitate easier entry, Korea enacted a new obligation in December 2000 that outstanding telecoms service providers should provide their unbundled elements to their competitors. Korea also addressed the plan for introducing number portability in fixed-line services in the year 2003, and in wireless services when 3G services are expected to roll out.[14]

Also, facing the technology convergence between telecommunications and broadcasting between wired and wireless, the government has taken reasonable measures to promote converged services by allowing CATV to offer broadband services, and KT and SKT to enter the broadcasting services market. In addition, the government has made a consistent effort in classifying new services based on the Telecommunications Business Act. Further, the Korean government has also addressed new plans on changing the classification system to encompass the new telecommunications environment.[15]

## 8.5 CONCLUSION

With the current paradigm shift toward a knowledge-based economy, the greatest concern for Korea is to enhance its competitiveness and productivity via the promotion of the IT industry and informatization of the society as a whole. Currently, the IT industry stands as the most crucial sector in the Korean economy for its sustained development. We analyzed how the IT industry has contributed significantly to sustaining economic growth, reducing inflation, increasing investment, improving the trade surplus and creating jobs.

Behind these achievements were government efforts to provide the necessary infrastructure and competitive environment through deregulation and liberalization. With its innovative entrepreneurship, the private sector has also made the best use of new business opportunities by increasing investment in IT. In this chapter, we found that the government role calls for the interventionist policies of the past to be changed in Korea. At the early stage, the Korean government actively participated in the market in order to build a firm foundation for the IT sector. However, as technology innovations and globalization evolve rapidly, the market has more information and can allocate resources more efficiently than the government. Government policy has become market friendly as the IT industry has grown into the new leading sector based on an advanced information infrastructure. Now government policies are changing to reinforce market functions and to promote competition and entrepreneurship to facilitate innovation and the utilization of IT.

## NOTES

1 OECD (2000).
2 Hong (2002) provides a detailed explanation of the importance of the IT industry to the Korean economy in the wake of the financial crisis.
3 The Korean industry structure, dominated by large diversified conglomerates such as Samsung, LG Electronics and Hyundai, was well suited to high-volume manufacturing. The *chaebols*' size and diversification gave them the resources for heavy investment in capital-intensive industries such as DRAM and flat-panel displays, and for huge R&D expenditure into IT innovation. Also, their traditional strength in assembling translated into computer monitors. Furthermore, *chaebols*' management style is characterized as the president of a *chaebol* having full authority over the company, and being able to take it into a new risky business without worrying about the threat to stock prices or about achieving consensus among management (Dedrick and Kraemer 1998).
4 The mobile subscriber base was forecast to grow from 29.05 million in 2001 to 31.85 million in 2002, pushing the penetration rate up to 66.8 per cent. However, there is unlikely to be any rapid growth in the subscriber base in the future. The short-term saturation for Korean mobile services is believed to be 75 per cent in consideration of the fact that major European countries had mobile penetration rates of 73.7 per cent as of May 2002.
5 It ranks the highest penetration rate (17.2/100 persons) compared to Canada (8.4/100 persons), Sweden (5.0/100 persons) and the US (4.5/100 persons)
6 For a detailed discussion on the broadband Internet service in Korea, see Lee (2002).
7 US Department of Commerce (2000).
8 The IT workforce covers workers in the IT industry and workers in IT occupations.
9 Informatization of customs services shortened the processing time from more than a day to less than two minutes for exports, and from more than two days to less than 2.5 hours for imports. It also reduced logistics costs by at least 500 billion won. Informatization of government procurement services enhanced the transparency and reduced the process time from more than two days to less than 30 minutes. As of December 2001, 11.3 million customers subscribed to Internet banking services and 66.6 per cent of stock trades are handled on the Internet. About 40 400 health care facilities introduced EDI to handle health insurance matters (Ministry of Information and Communication 2002).

10 Ministry of Information and Communication (2001).

11 The high level of competition and the short product life and development cycles make it tough for companies to train skilled IT workers. Furthermore, companies worry that workers might leave for better jobs after they have received training.

12 A certificate of venture by government is judged by one of the following criteria:
(1) an enterprise with over a prescribed share of equities held by venture capital(s)
(2) an enterprise with over a prescribed proportion of R&D expenses in total sales
(3) an enterprise whose sales or export amount of its product(s) developed by using its own patent/intellectual properties is over a prescribed proportion of total sales. Or an enterprise whose products are manufactured through the new technology business programme carried out by various government agencies occupy over a prescribed proportion of its sales
(4) an enterprise that has received an affirmation of excellence by assessing institutions designated by the government.

13 As discussed earlier, competition among FSPs is a main factor for rapid market expansion in mobile service and high-speed Internet service. The OECD and ITU have officially commended Korea's effort for its successful broadband rollout.

14 To avoid conflicts of interest, the OECD made recommendations to Korea of separating industry promotion and regulation functions and transferring regulatory functions over to the KCC (Korea Communication Commission). Although Korea did not separate the KCC from MIC, Korea has been strengthening its role and function on a sustained basis by securing the tenure of a president for a certain number of years in order for the organization to carry out its duty independently and at its own discretion.

15 For detailed information on regulatory reform in the telecommunications service sector, see Park (2002).

## REFERENCES

Bank of Korea Internet site at http://www.bok.or.kr/statistics.

Dedrick, Jason and Kenneth L. Kraemer (1998), '*Asia's Computer Challenges: Threat or Opportunity for the Unite States and the World*?', New York and Oxford: Oxford University Press.

Display Search (2002), 'Large-Area TFT LCD Shipment Exceed Expectation in Q2, Decline Expected in Q3', (Http://www.displaysearch.com).

Hong, Dong-pyo (2002), 'IT Policies in Korea to Establish a KBE:

Outcomes and Future Directions', the 3rd Korea–OECD Conference, Korea's Road to a Sound and Advanced Economy.

Korea Association of Information and Telecommunication (KAIT) (2002), *Information and Communication Industry Statistics Report.*

Korea Information Society Development Institute (KISDI) (2003), *IT Industry Outlook of Korea 2003.*

Lee, Nae-Chan (2002), 'An Analysis of the Broadband Internet Service Market: Korea's Experience' (in Korean), *Korean Telecommunications White Paper 2001.*

Ministry of Information and Communication (Republic of Korea) (2001), *Information and Communication White Paper 2001.*

Ministry of Information and Communication (Republic of Korea) (2002), *e-Korea Vision 2006.*

Ministry of Science and Technology (2002), '*Report on the Survey of Research and Development in Science and Technology*'.

OECD (2000), *Korea and the Knowledge-based Economy: Making the Transition.*

Park, Chong Hoon (2002), 'Telecommunication Services Sector in Korea', presented at APEC–OECD Cooperative Initiative on Regulatory Reforms', October 17, 2002, Jeju, Korea.

Reed Electronics Research (2002), *Yearbook of World Electronics Data 2002*, Vol. 1–2.

US Department of Commerce (2000), *Digital Economy.*

# 9. Post-Crisis Foreign Trade and Foreign Investment in Korea: Korea's Recovery and Challenges Ahead

**Taekdong Yeo, Young Man Yoon and Kar-yiu Wong**

## 9.1 INTRODUCTION

Since the government adopted aggressive promotion polices in the 1960s, the growth of the Korean economy has been phenomenal. From 1971 to 1990, the economy grew at an annual average rate of 8.1 per cent.[1] Such an impressive growth of the economy, which was frequently compared with that of three other emerging Asian economies – Hong Kong, Singapore and Taiwan – was generally attributed to Korea's trade and the government policies that promoted trade. In the 1990s Korea continued its emphasis on its foreign relations with other countries, and made a considerable effort to further integrate its economy with the rest of the world. Since the early 1990s, Korea has adopted an aggressive liberalization policy within the multilateral trading framework of the GATT/WTO. In 1996, Korea joined the Organization of Economic Cooperation and Development (OECD), an important step that brings Korea closer to the developed countries, making the economy more dependent on the economic situation of the world.

Then, suddenly, things turned for the worse when the Asian crisis broke out in July 1997. Initially, Korea seemed to be immune from the turmoil in the South-East Asian countries such as Thailand and Malaysia. After all, these countries are so far away. Then the crisis spread to other countries like Indonesia, the Philippines and Hong Kong. Korea started to feel the pressure and the pain of speculative attacks and firm failure in its own economy. These events revealed some of the problems of the Korean economy. Finally, at the end of the year, Korea found itself no longer able to fulfill its external debt commitments and to stop the rapid depletion of foreign reserves, which had dropped to an alarming level. Korea had to turn to the International Monetary Fund (IMF) for help.

Korea quickly reached an economic stabilization programme with the IMF. In exchange for the bailout support, Korea was required to implement progressive liberalization and structural reforms. The programme contained macroeconomic remedies and structural adjustment measures, together with trade liberalization, capital account liberalization, labour market reforms and so on. With the progressive liberalization and structural reforms as well as the fiscal stimulus package, Korea successfully accomplished macroeconomic objectives earlier than expected.

Since the onset of the crisis, Korea has been accelerating trade liberalization to support structural adjustments within the framework of its multilateral, plurilateral and bilateral commitments, thus improving the competitiveness of Korean businesses. Furthermore, the Korean government has been conducting intensive reforms of the financial and corporate sectors in order to promote transparency, efficiency and flexibility. These policy objectives were implemented in a WTO-based manner through progressive liberalization and deregulation.

Until recently, Korea had never participated in Free Trade Agreements (FTAs). Nevertheless, in response to the economic crisis and growing regionalism elsewhere, FTAs are now being considered by the Korean authorities as useful means of securing greater market access for Korea's exports. Korea began to show a great interest in establishing FTAs since the 1997 economic crisis. In 1998, Korea announced its plan to proceed with a bilateral FTA negotiation with Chile and also started joint studies with Japan and the United States. The FTA negotiation with Chile was concluded in November 2002. In addition to the FTA with Chile, Korea continues to consider negotiating several bilateral agreements with Japan, Mexico, New Zealand, Thailand, Singapore and even the United States.

Among many factors that have brought about economic growth and structural changes to Korea, the most outstanding was the outward-oriented trade policy. On the other hand, the Korean economy, to which the manufacturing sector contributes a major portion of exports, has benefited from the multilateral trading system. An empirical analysis of the impact of the Uruguay Round Negotiations reveals that the Korean economy gained opportunities for substantially expanding foreign trade and overseas investment. In short, the world trading environment has provided much more economic benefits to the Korean economy than negative effects.

This experience implies that the future of the Korean economy will heavily depend on the following future agendas and Korea's trade policy responses; how efficiently it reacts to new external challenges and how well it creates a favourable business environment for foreign investors as well as domestic firms.

First, the WTO's Doha Development Agenda (DDA) Negotiations will present great challenges as well as opportunities for Korea. It is evident that the growth of the Korean economy depends on trade-oriented development strategies, meaning that the global market is indispensable to Korea's economic growth. In this sense, Korea will be one of the beneficiaries from the more open foreign market expected to result from the conclusion of the WTO's DDA negotiation. However, Korea's agricultural sector, among others to be liberalized at the DDA negotiations, will experience a painful restructuring process in the near future.

Second, Korea needs to actively engage in establishing free trade agreements (FTAs) as regionalism emerges within the world trading system. As of 2001, 155 FTAs had been reported to the GATT/WTO. The number of FTAs rapidly increased after the launch of the WTO in 1995. FTAs not only evade trade barriers but also catalyze the restructuring of trade and industrial structures. For Korea's FTA policy, diverse factors worked together in a complex fashion. Despite having discussions on the FTAs since the early 1990s, Korea was not able to make it materialize largely due to domestic opposition to the opening of market access under FTAs. However, in recent years, the Korean government has been re-evaluating the potential gains of FTAs on a preferential basis, and has decided to pursue establishing bilateral FTAs with some countries. Then the Korean government will make considerable efforts in negotiating bilateral FTAs with Japan, Mexico, New Zealand, Thailand, Singapore and the United states.

Third, there exists an urgent need to substantially eliminate or alleviate domestic barriers such as business practices, government regulations, cultural factors and so on. Since the economic crisis of 1997, the Korean government has carried out extensive deregulation to reduce the operational burden of businesses. Even with the recent intense efforts, many international institutions pointed out that there still exists room for improvement in transparency, accessibility and compliance with international standards. Therefore, the Korean government continues to put its best efforts into creating a favourable business environment for foreign investors as well as domestic firms.

The purpose of this chapter is twofold. First, it reviews the trend of Korea's trade and FDI as well as its policy regime during the period from the mid-1990s through to 2001. The period includes the short sub-period before the financial crisis in 1997, and the sub-period after the crisis where the Korean economy showed a remarkable recovery. Second, this chapter examines three future agendas that the Korean economy faces in the near future and explores Korea's trade policy responses to cope with them.

The layout of this chapter is as follows. In section 2, we present the development of the Korean economy and the government policies that succeeded in transforming the economy from a poor one to a modern one. We also talk about Korea as a member of the GATT/WTO. Section 3 discusses the trade and foreign direct investment of the Korean economy during the financial crisis. Section 4 investigates future agendas of the government and what policy responses the government is likely to choose. Section 5 provides some concluding remarks.

## 9.2 TRANSITION IN KOREA'S TRADE POLICY REGIME

### 9.2.1 Development of Korea's Trade Policy

**Economic development and trade policy**

The aggressive economic development strategies imposed by the Korean government have been credited for the spectacular growth of the Korean economy since the early 1960s. The per capita GDP of the economy unmistakably grew from US$82 in 1961 to US$10 013 in 2002. As a result, Korea was transformed from one of the world's poorest countries into a respected industrialized country.

The economic development strategies adopted by the government led to a number of important structural transformations of the economy. In the early stage of the period, Korea's development strategy focused on unskilled labour and indigenous technology. The government soon changed the course of development, emphasizing the aggressive promotion of export performance, relying on the relatively abundant labour force as well as imported capital and technology. Despite the lack of resources the export-promotion policy, and infant industry protection policy through import substitution, played a crucial role in developing the Korean economy at an early stage.

From 1960 to the early 1970s, Korea established its industrial foundation by exporting labour-intensive light industrial goods and importing general machinery and other capital goods. Because of the lack of resources, and little capital for investment, the Korean government chose to promote exports heavily, which was regarded as a good means for earning foreign exchange for investment and production purposes. Under such a policy, financial resources, domestic or foreign, were favourably allocated to the export sectors. Preferential bank loans were arranged to the exporters at low interest rates and exemption from taxes was provided for exporters. Under the tariff rebate system, import tariffs on raw materials and intermediate inputs were either exempted or returned to foster export-processing sectors. In order to support the export promotion policy, the Korean government conducted an exchange rate policy to maintain appropriate exchange rate levels. Additionally, the world trade environment at that time was quite favourable, so that the Korean economy successfully established a sound industrial foundation for sustained economic growth.

From the third five-year economic development plan (1972–76), the Korean government substantially changed the focus of its industrial structure to heavy and chemical industries such as steel, automotive, machinery, petrochemical, chemicals, electronics and shipbuilding. The policy of promoting heavy and chemical industry in Korea was based on the following rationales. First, in order to set up the industrial structure of an industrialized country, it was believed that it was crucial to develop the heavy and chemical industry. Second, the heavy and chemical industry had huge forward and backward linkage effects on related industries, and thus could generate spillover effects in the rest of the economy. Third, the successful development of these industries was essential for sustained growth of GDP and exports. Last, but not least, according to the so-called national defence argument, the development of these heavy industries was crucial for national self-defence.

Korea successfully transformed its industrial structure from light industries into the heavy and chemical industries from the 1970s to the 1980s. In 1970, the share of heavy and chemical industries was 35.9 per cent in manufacturing but only 14.3 per cent in exports. The share of heavy and chemical industries in manufacturing increased to 40.5 per cent in 1976 and more than 50 per cent in the early 1980s, while that in exports jumped to 41.5 per cent in 1980.[2]

Since the late 1970s, Korea has made efforts to induce foreign direct investment (FDI) from the advanced countries such as the United States and Japan. In order to attract foreign direct investment, the Korean government set up export processing zones[3] in Masan and Iksan (formerly called Yiri).

**Economic liberalization and trade policy**

Since the early 1980s the Korean government began to lower its degree of intervention in economic activities, allowing the economy to become more market oriented. On the external side, the new strategy was reflected in a substantial reduction in its restrictions on the import of foreign goods. From 1986, Korea recorded surpluses in its current account for three years in a row. After consultations with GATT in the late 1980s the Korean government started to liberalize its foreign imports, removing unilaterally many of its restrictions on imports of foreign goods. For example, all agricultural products were scheduled to be liberalized in 2001. Furthermore, the government adopted a unilateral five-year tariff reduction plan first in the 1984–88 period and again in the 1989–94 period. As a result, the average tariff for manufactured goods had been lowered to less than 10 per cent by 1994.

Since its entry to GATT in 1967, Korea has strongly supported the continuous development of the open multilateral trading system. Korea actively participated in the multilateral trade negotiations in the Tokyo and Uruguay Rounds.

The pace of integration of the Korean economy into the world economy continued in the 1990s. In December 1996, Korea joined the OECD. In order to fulfill the conditions of accession, Korea has committed to further liberalizing its economy since the early 1990s. The government undertook further trade liberalization and deregulation programmes and the first stage plan for financial liberalization and opening of the financial sector. The plan envisaged further easing of requirements for foreign exchange transactions, widening the daily won–dollar trading margins, expanding limits on foreign investments in the stock market, and permitting long-term commercial loans.[4]

In the middle of the 1990s, signs that there were troubles in the Korean economy emerged and became more and more obvious. On the external side, the problems were mostly in the form of trade deficits and external debts. The trade deficit reached more than US$10 billion in 1995, and peaked at more than US$20 billion in 1996. While Korea had lowered its import restraints considerably by the mid-1990s, much of the increase in imports in 1995–96 may be attributable to the rapid increase in foreign capital inflows thereby raising the value of the Korean won.

The rapid build-up in private short-term external debt increased the risks of liquidity problems. In 1993, when the Korean government expanded the scope for short-term overseas borrowing by removing controls over banks on such borrowing, it maintained tight restrictions on medium and long-term capital and on direct access to capital markets by Korean corporations. As a result short-term external debt increased drastically, creating a maturity mismatch, as Korean financial institutions borrowed short term overseas to help finance long-term investments. Short-term external debt rose from US$54 billion in 1994 to US$93 billion at the end of 1996, representing 57.1 per cent of total external liabilities (see Table 9.1). Short-term external debt quickly outpaced usable foreign exchange reserves, thus creating the potential for liquidity problems and raising doubts about Korea's external position.

**Table 9.1**
**The Trend of Korean Foreign Debt During 1994–1998**

(US$ million)

| **Year** | **Long-term debt** | | | | **Short-term debt** | | | | **Total debt** | **Net debt** |
|---|---|---|---|---|---|---|---|---|---|---|
| | Total | Public sector | Financial sector | Private sector | Total | Public sector | Financial sector | Private sector | | |
| 1994 | 43 504 | 7 205 | 20 444 | 15 855 | 53 933 | - | 44 641 | 9 292 | 97 437 | - 24 542 |
| 1995 | 55 597 | 6 654 | 30 981 | 17 962 | 71 894 | - | 58 661 | 13 233 | 127 491 | 35 547 |
| 1996 | 70 170 | 6 107 | 43 523 | 20 540 | 93 319 | - | 73 009 | 20 310 | 163 489 | 53 769 |
| 1997 | 95 678 | 22 264 | 47 536 | 25 878 | 63 559 | - | 42 367 | 21 192 | 159 237 | 54 058 |
| 1998 | 118 008 | 36 548 | 52 041 | 29 419 | 30 697 | - | 18 938 | 11 759 | 148 705 | 20 180 |

*Source*: Bank of Korea, *Economic Statistics DB*, available at http://www.bok.or.kr.

Then came the Asian financial crisis in July 1997. Officially, it began with Thailand's abrupt devaluation of its baht and enormous loss of foreign reserves. The crisis spread to other countries such as Singapore, Malaysia and Indonesia. Even Hong Kong was not immune, being hit by waves of speculative currency attacks and a significant drop and fluctuation in stock and real estate prices. The crisis at last came to Korea at the end of 1997. It was the worst economic crisis to affect the economy since the Korean War. It led to massive capital outflow, a sharp depreciation of the won, and severe distress in many industries and the financial sectors. As foreign debt lenders refused to renew the short-term debts of Korean firms and banks, and some of them even withdrew their funds, Korea's foreign exchange reserves were sharply and uncontrollably depleted.

To restore confidence and replenish reserves, Korea received assistance from the IMF. On 2 December 1997, Korea signed a Stand-By Arrangement with the IMF. This arrangement provided to Korea financial loans from the IMF, World Bank and other international financial institutions. In return, Korea imposed an economic stabilization programme.

This programme, designed to stabilize the economy and restore sustainable growth, included macroeconomic remedies and structural adjustment measures, together with trade liberalization, capital account liberalization, improved corporate governance, restructuring and labour market reforms. Furthermore, the Korean government initiated intensive reform of the financial and corporate sectors in order to promote transparency, efficiency and flexibility. As a result of the IMF economic stabilization programme, Korea was made a more open, more competitive and market-oriented economy. The programme also worked to restore much of the confidence of local consumers, domestic producers and foreign investors. As a matter of fact, the programme worked so well that Korea successfully accomplished macroeconomic objectives earlier than expected.

The severe economic downturn in 1997, however, did not dampen significantly the commitments of Korea to liberalization under the WTO agreements. On the contrary, Korea saw that trade liberalization was an effective way to help itself recover from the financial crisis. Since 1998, Korea has accelerated the trade liberalization process including the reduction of tariffs to below the pre-set bounded rates, removal of the import diversification system, elimination of prohibited subsidies, improvement of customs clearance procedures, and enhancement of transparency in trade-related rules. Furthermore, the Korean government has under-taken many measures toward capital market liberalization.

Pursuant to the IMF economic stabilization programme and the Uruguay Round Commitments, effective in January 2001, the Korean government liberalized its quantitative restrictions on beef and dairy products and other agricultural products. Korea's import diversification system, implemented to restrict imports of automobile and machinery from Japan, was completely abolished by July 1999. After the economic crisis, Korea reduced the size and scope of its subsidy programme and rationalized its overall subsidy programme. Under the IMF economic stabilization package, Korea removed some of the prohibited export subsidies, completed in 1998, earlier than the committed date.

Since the WTO's inception in 1995, the Korean government has, in cooperation with its trading partners, concluded agreements on trade in information technology products, financial services, and basic telecommunications services. Since the WTO Doha Development Agenda (DDA) launched in 2001, the Korean government has actively participated in discussions on the comprehensive issues with the belief that an early conclusion of the DDA negotiation is essential to the strengthening of the multilateral trading system.

### 9.2.2 Korea's Trade policy under the Multilateral Trading System

**Uruguay Round and the Korean economy**

On the conclusion of the Uruguay Round (UR) Multilateral Negotiation, Korea made tariff concessions with an average reduction of approximately 55 per cent unilaterally and in accordance with the GATT commitments. Korea also put ceilings on approximately 91.7 per cent of its tariff lines, including all agricultural products, with the exception of rice. As a result, the average tariff levels of Korea were dramatically cut. The average bound level of the tariffs on all products was reduced to 20.1 per cent in 2000, from about 27.6 per cent in 1996. However, the average applied tariff was even lower due to Korea's unilateral tariff reductions. In 2000, the trade-weighted average applied average rate was 6.89 per cent for all commodities, 4.71 per cent for industrial goods, and 41.47 per cent for agricultural products.

The Uruguay Round first made agriculture subject to the GATT rules. However, agriculture was the most contentious area among countries in the UR of trade negotiations. The agreement on agriculture that was signed eventually included three major issues: market access characterized by the principles of tariffication only and minimum market access, the reduction of domestic support, and the reduction of export subsidies. The agreement declares that all products are tariffied and all NTBs replaced by tariffs yielding the equivalent level of protection.

The agreement also covers the reduction of domestic support measures as well as the value and volume of export subsidies. In addition, the agreement reaffirms that the member countries' commitments substantially and progressively reduce the levels of support and protection. Understanding that the market access commitments and the reduction of export subsidies and domestic support contribute to trade liberalization at the global level, the WTO members decided that they will resume addressing these issues in future rounds of multilateral trade negotiations.

In the UR of negotiation, Korea was awarded with the status of a developing country as far as agricultural products were concerned. In terms of the opening of the domestic rice market, Korea received special treatment. Korea was allowed to postpone tariffication until 2004 with the condition of accepting a quantitative guarantee of minimum market access (MMA) in the domestic rice market. In 1995, Korea gave foreign producers 1 per cent minimum market access and will increase it to 4 per cent by 2004. On agricultural products, Korea's average tariff reduction of 34.1 per cent was relatively high compared to the average tariff reduction of 24 per cent for other developing countries. However, Korea was allowed to grant subsidies for structural adjustment.

Multilateral rules on trade in services were first enacted in the Uruguay Round and were described in the General Agreement on Trade in Services (GATS). GATS purports to apply the core WTO principles, including the 'most favoured nations' clause and national treatment, to all internationally traded services.[5] However, different rules for specific sectors are permitted and individual countries can make specific commitments to allow market access to their domestic markets through the negative system. Negotiation on financial services and basic telecommunications continued after the WTO was launched.

Of the total 155 services dealt with in the UR negotiation, Korea has opened 85 services representing approximately 55 per cent of the total. Construction and related engineering services were completely opened. By 1996, when the WTO agreement on financial services was completed, Korea had liberalized financial services with an opening rate of 88 per cent. However, Korea has not made much concession on communications and transport services. So far, Korea has not opened educational services, health-related and social services, and recreational, cultural and sporting services.

It was expected that the WTO accession could bring enough economic benefits to the Korean economy to outweigh the negative impacts. With the reduction of tariffs and non-tariff barriers, Korean exporters could expand their production and their market shares in the developed countries. Simultaneously, the developing countries substantially lowered trade barriers and became the major export markets for Korea. As a result of the UR of negotiations, Korea could expand its export market to the transition economies including the Eastern European countries.

There were other unquantifiable benefits from Korea's accession to the WTO. When Korea faced unilateral trade instruments such as US Section 301, it could raise the complaint before the WTO dispute settlement body. In fact, Korea brought the complaints to the WTO and won in some important cases (US Section 301, anti-dumping actions against televisions, and the Byrd amendment) against the United States. It shows that the WTO system has provided counterfactual benefits for the Korean economy, which has been so dependent on external trade.

However, Korea's WTO membership and trade liberalization do carry costs to the economy. First, some industries, especially those import-competing industries, have substantial pain and costs as a result of import competition. Second, the instruments of industrial and trade policies, including financial and tax supports, must conform to the WTO rules and disciplines. Third, the UR is expected to have negative impacts on the agricultural sector, in terms of both domestic production and income, due to the reduction of subsidies and import competition. Fourth, liberalization of the service sectors would negatively affect domestic industries for some time after the market opening.

These costs are what Korea has to pay as it liberalizes its foreign trade. It is expected, however, that the gains the economy receives in the form of more efficient allocation of resources, higher consumer surpluses, increases in welfare of those exportable sectors, improvement in technology and quality, and rise in competitiveness of Korean products abroad, could outweigh the losses experienced by certain parts of the economy.

It is concluded that, mostly in the manufacturing sector, the Korean economy would acquire major gains due to the dramatic reduction of trade barriers and the reform of anti-dumping and safeguard measures. These outcomes of the UR of negotiation would provide the Korean export sectors easier and wider access to the world markets, and bring in the gains from trade to the Korean economy.

**Korea's trade policy under the WTO regime**

With the launch of the World Trade Organization in 1995, the rule-based multilateral trading system was established to promote freer trade, wider and easier market access, and more transparent and strengthened trade rules. Since then, Korea has faithfully implemented the WTO agreements and Uruguay Round commitments. While keeping its trade regime open and transparent in line with the WTO rules, Korea actively participated in the WTO's initiatives and negotiations, including the liberalization of information technology products, financial services and basic telecommunications services.

Since the WTO's Doha Development Agenda (DDA) launched in 2001 the Korean government has actively participated in negotiations on the comprehensive agenda, and has played its due role in successfully concluding the negotiations. In addition to the implementation of its WTO commitments, Korea undertook a number of additional measures to further open its trade and investment regime. These measures were taken during the process of its accession to the OECD and as part of Korea's overall economic reform and restructuring efforts following the 1997–98 economic crisis.

Korea increased the number of bound tariff lines in accordance with its Uruguay Round commitments. Approximately 91.7 per cent of total tariff lines and 92.6 per cent of industrial goods were bound. In 2001, Korea's average tariff rate was 8.9 per cent. While Korea's tariffs on all agricultural products are bound, tariffs on forestry and fishery products remain unbound. As part of the effort to further promote trade and economic cooperation with developing countries, Korea has extended its duty-free, quota-free treatment to 80 (HS 6-digit) products to the least developed countries since 2000.

Liberalization in the agricultural sector has been continuing in a progressive manner according to Korea's commitments under the WTO Agreement on Agriculture. For the tariff quota items, tariffs were lowered and quota levels increased progressively. Remaining restrictions other than tariffs and tariff quotas were eliminated, except on rice and beef. However, the import of beef was fully liberalized as of January 2001.

Korea has aggressively promoted exports through a variety of policy tools, including export subsidies. It has committed to phasing out export subsidy programmes that fail to conform to the WTO Agreement on Subsidies and Countervailing Measures. Under the IMF bailout package, Korea eliminated four prohibited export subsidies earlier than committed. Korea is continuously rationalizing its overall subsidy programmes and reducing or eliminating the benefits of 68 other subsidy programmes.

Non-tariff trade barriers have also been eliminated or eased significantly. Korea entirely abolished import prohibitions on sensitive products from Japan under the Import Diversification Programme in June 1999. Korea also eliminated all six voluntary export restraints subject to the phase-out under the Agreement on Safeguards. From the perspective of a national economy as a whole, the Korean economy acquires a great deal of benefits from the WTO system because the manufacturing sector constitutes a major portion of GDP and exports.

Technical barriers to trade have also been significantly reduced and unnecessary requirements have been eliminated. The domestic regulatory framework has become more transparent and consistent with international rules and disciplines. Customs procedures have become both more efficient and transparent mainly due to the implementation of an immediate release system and an electronic data interchange (EDI) system for both imports and exports. Changes in customs-related legislation, regulations and guidelines are published and customs-related information is also available on websites in English. Korea joined the WTO Agreement on Government Procurement (GPA) in January 1997. This agreement covers procurement of goods and services over specific thresholds by the Korean central governments, provincial and municipal governments and government-invested corporations. Korea has complied with the GPA by introducing enforcement legislation to regulate the procedures for the international tendering of covered entities.

The Korean government has fully implemented the specific commitments made under the WTO agreement on the trade of services. Korea also actively participated in the extended negotiations, including those on the financial and basic telecommunications services sectors, and consequently provided significantly liberalized commitments in both sectors. As the service sector has been liberalized since the Uruguay Round, Korea's trade in services increased from US$22.8 billion in 1991 to US$61 billion in 2000 and the inflow of FDI in all service sectors increased from US$2.1 billion in 1991–95 to US$8.5 billion in 2000. In particular, FDI into the services sector recorded tremendous hikes, exceeding US$4 billion in 1997. Despite a drop to US$3 billion in 1998, the rising trend continued in 1999–2000.

As a part of the efforts to overcome the economic crisis of 1997, particular emphasis has been placed on restructuring the economy and attracting more FDI. This involves, in part, accelerating the elimination of horizontal and sector-specific restrictions in the service sector beyond the commitments made during the Uruguay Round. For example, restrictions on the foreign acquisition of land and ceilings for foreign portfolio investment in stocks were eliminated.

The financial, distribution, telecommunications and construction service sectors are areas of the domestic economy that have been significantly liberalized. The supply of financial services through commercial presence, including banking, securities, insurance and other services, was liberalized in 1997. As a condition of the IMF bailout package, Korea agreed to bind its OECD commitments on financial services market access in the WTO. Subsequently, Korea revised the schedule of its WTO commitments on financial services in September 1999 to provide more liberal treatment for foreign financial services providers. Moreover, most of the current account transactions of corporations and financial institutions were liberalized through revisions of the regulations related to foreign exchange transactions in 2001.

All distribution sectors, except the wholesaling of meat, were opened by eliminating the economic needs test for department stores and shopping centres from 1998. However, the wholesaling of meat became open to foreign investment of less than 50 per cent in January 2000.

In the telecommunications sector the scope of market access was expanded by raising the ceiling of foreign investment ratios for facility-based service suppliers to 49 per cent. The only exception was Korea Telecom. However, as of June 2002, the Korean government fully divested its holdings in Korea Telecom. Regarding regulatory issues, the Korean government made important progress in 2001 by revising regulations for electro-magnetic compatibility and safety standards.

The construction sector was significantly liberalized. The joint venture requirement for general construction was eliminated in 1994, and the one for special construction in 1996. The establishment of local branches of foreign suppliers for general and special construction was permitted in 1996 and 1998, respectively. Foreign firms may bid on public projects, including the massive infrastructure projects, while they still report some problems such as registration and bonding procedures.

Indeed, the most significant and meaningful liberalization measures since 1996 have been introduced in the service sector. As of 2000 foreign investment in as many as 471 (based on Korean Standard Industry Classification system) service sectors had been liberalized, and only 24 service sectors remained restricted. These sectors mainly consist of those where public interest is of major concern, such as mass-media services. Regulatory reform policies pursued by the Korean government also contributed to the liberalization efforts. Since 1998, a large number of government measures, including those related to the service sector, have been eliminated or relaxed.

The TRIPS Agreement took effect for Korea on 1 January 2000. Korea has taken every possible effort to make the current intellectual property rights protection system in full conformity with the TRIPS Agreement. Korea also provides more extensive protection than required by the agreement, although the United States is still complaining about the weak enforcement of IPR protection by the Korean government and thus including it on the watch list.

Although major amendments of the IPR-related legislation took place in 1995, the Korean government took additional measures to further strengthen IPR protection. Various amendments were made to Korea's IPR-related laws, aimed at improving the protection of copyrights and related rights, trademarks, patents, geographical indications, layout designs of integrated circuits, and undisclosed information, simplifying the application procedure for the registration of patents and industrial designs, and upgrading enforcement. Other amendments were also made, for example, to reflect the provisions of the Trademark Law Treaty (TLT) and the Madrid Protocol Concerning the International Registration of Marks, which Korea joined in 2002.

## 9.3 FOREIGN TRADE AND FDI DURING THE ECONOMIC CRISIS

### 9.3.1 Economic Crisis and the Korean Economy

Korea was hit by a financial crisis at the end of 1997. Many foreign banks and lenders, being nervous about the crisis in South-East Asia, refused to renew the short-term debts of many Korean firms and banks. At the same time, Korea experienced withdrawal of large amounts of investment funds from the country. As a result, Korea's foreign exchange reserves were rapidly being depleted. At the peak of the crisis Korea's usable foreign exchange reserves dropped down to just US$3.9 billion, which was dangerously lower than the US$36 billion recommended by the IMF.[6]

As a result of the unprecedented capital flight, which Korea had not experienced before, the exchange rate of the Korean won skyrocketed from

965.10 won/dollar at the end of October 1997 to 1964.80 at the end of December 1997. To avoid a moratorium Korea asked for an IMF stand-by arrangement, which supplied urgently needed liquidity to its economy.

From the onset of the crisis, and throughout 1998, the Korean economy experienced a serious downturn in all macroeconomic variables. Real GDP fell by 6.7 per cent in 1998. The unemployment rate rose, reaching as high as 8.6 per cent (seasonally adjusted) in early 1999. The crisis affected the manufacturing, construction and service sectors, and caused private consumption to drop to its lowest level. In late 1998 the Korean economy began to recover from the crisis with the efforts of the Korean government under the IMF economic stabilization programme. Statistics show that the Korean economy returned to its pre-crisis levels in 1999. Real GDP rose by 10.7 per cent in 1999, the unemployment rate fell to 4.8 per cent at the end of 1999, and the value of the Korean won recovered, and has remained stable at approximately 1200 won/dollar since 1999. Developments in the exchange rate and the trade balance during the period of the crisis are shown in Figure 9.1.

Despite the negative growth during the economic crisis, the recovery of the Korean economy after the crisis has been spectacular. The GDP and per capita GDP of Korea in 2001 climbed back to close to the corresponding levels before the crisis (Table 9.2). The recovery was even more impressive in terms of foreign trade.

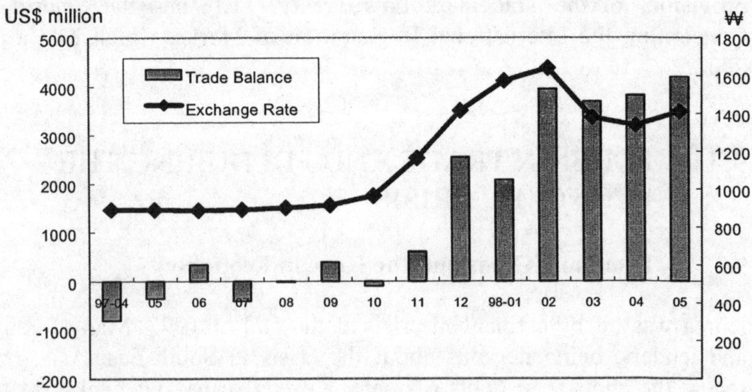


*Source*: National Statistical Office, *KOSIS Data*, at http://www.nso.or.kr.

*Figure 9.1 Trade Balance and Exchange Rate (₩/US$) During the Korean Economic Crisis*

**Table 9.2**
**Structure and Trend of the Korean Economy**

(US$ billion, %)

| | 1970 | 1980 | 1990 | 1995 | 1996 | 1997 | 1998 | 1999 | 2000 | 2001 |
|---|---|---|---|---|---|---|---|---|---|---|
| GDP | 8.0 | 62.2 | 252.5 | 489.4 | 520 | 476.6 | 317.7 | 405.8 | 461.7 | 422.2 |
| Per capita GDP (US$) | 249 | 1 598 | 5 886 | 10 823 | 11 385 | 10 315 | 6 744 | 8 595 | 9 770 | 8 900 |
| Real GDP | 166.7 | 189.1 | 371.9 | 489.4 | 500.5 | 444.6 | 282.1 | 367.9 | 423.2 | 382.1 |
| Real per capita GDP (US$) | 5 188 | 4 857 | 8 669 | 10 823 | 10 958 | 9 622 | 5 989 | 7 792 | 8 955 | 8 054 |
| Trade | 2.8 | 134.9 | 134.9 | 260.2 | 280 | 280.1 | 225.6 | 263.4 | 332.8 | 291.5 |
| Trade dependence ratio (%)* | 34.8 | 53.2 | 53.2 | 57.1 | 53.9 | 58.9 | 71 | 64.9 | 72.7 | 69.0 |
| Exports | 0.8 | 65 | 65 | 125.1 | 129.7 | 136.2 | 132.3 | 143.7 | 172.3 | 150.4 |
| Export dependence ratio (%)* | 10.3 | 25.6 | 25.6 | 27.5 | 24.9 | 28.6 | 41.6 | 35.4 | 37.7 | 35.6 |
| Imports | 2 | 69.8 | 69.8 | 135.1 | 150.3 | 144.6 | 93.3 | 119.8 | 160.5 | 141.1 |
| Import dependence ratio (%)* | 24.5 | 27.5 | 27.5 | 29.7 | 28.9 | 30.3 | 29.4 | 29.5 | 35.1 | 33.4 |

*Note*: 1 The base year is 1995, so that the GDP deflator in 1995 = 100.
2 * The dependence ratio is equal to the ratio of the value of trade, exports or imports, to GDP.

*Source:* The Bank of Korea, *Economic Statistics Yearbook*, at http://www.bok.or.kr.

In 1999, Korean exports and imports recorded a substantial growth of 8.6 per cent and 28.4 per cent, respectively, and resulted in a current account surplus of US$24.5 billion (see Table 9.3). While the surplus became smaller than that of 1998 it marked a positive turn for the economy, because it resulted from increases in both exports and imports.

**Table 9.3**
**Changes in the Balance of Payments, 1995–2001**

(US$ million)

| Year | Current account | | | | | | Capital account | | | Reserve assets |
|---|---|---|---|---|---|---|---|---|---|---|
| | | Goods & service account | | | Income account | Current & transfer account | | Investment account | Other capital account | |
| | | | Goods account | Service account | | | | | | |
| 1995 | −8 508 | −7 423 | −4 444 | −2 979 | −1 303 | 218 | 16 786 | 17 273 | −488 | −7 045 |
| 1996 | −23 005 | −21 144 | −14 965 | −6 179 | −1 815 | −46 | 23 327 | 23 924 | −598 | −1 389 |
| 1997 | −8 167 | −6 379 | 3 179 | −3 200 | −2 454 | 667 | 1 314 | 1 922 | −608 | 11 922 |
| 1998 | 40 365 | 42 651 | 41 627 | 1 024 | −5 638 | 3 352 | −3 197 | −3 368 | 171 | −30 975 |
| 1999 | 24 477 | 27 720 | 28 371 | −651 | −5 159 | 1 916 | 2 040 | 2 430 | −389 | −22 983 |
| 2000 | 12 241 | 13 982 | 16 872 | −2 889 | −2 421 | 680 | 12 110 | 12 725 | −615 | −23 771 |
| 2001 | 8 239 | 9 664 | 13 492 | −3 828 | −1 198 | −227 | −3 275 | −2 544 | −731 | −7 576 |

*Source:* Bank of Korea, *Economic Statistics Yearbook*, at http://www.bok.or.kr.

As a result of increased openness of the Korean economy to international trade, and its integration into the world economy, the ratio to GDP of Korean trade (exports plus imports) in goods increased steadily from 53.2 per cent in 1990 to 57.1 per cent in 1995 and to 69.0 per cent in 2001, despite dropping a little back to 64.9 per cent in 1999, and then picking up to 72.7 per cent in 2000. The fall of the ratio reflected the impact of the economic crisis on trade and particularly the sharp fall in GDP in 1998 and its strong recovery in 1999. The decline of the ratio in 2001 reflected the sharp fall of its exports, influenced by worldwide recession after 2000 (Table 9.2 and Figure 9.2). The outcome was that in 2001 Korea was the world's eighth-largest exporter (counting the EU as one and Hong Kong as an independent territory) and eighth-largest importer of goods, owing to a fast recovery of GDP and trade from the crisis.

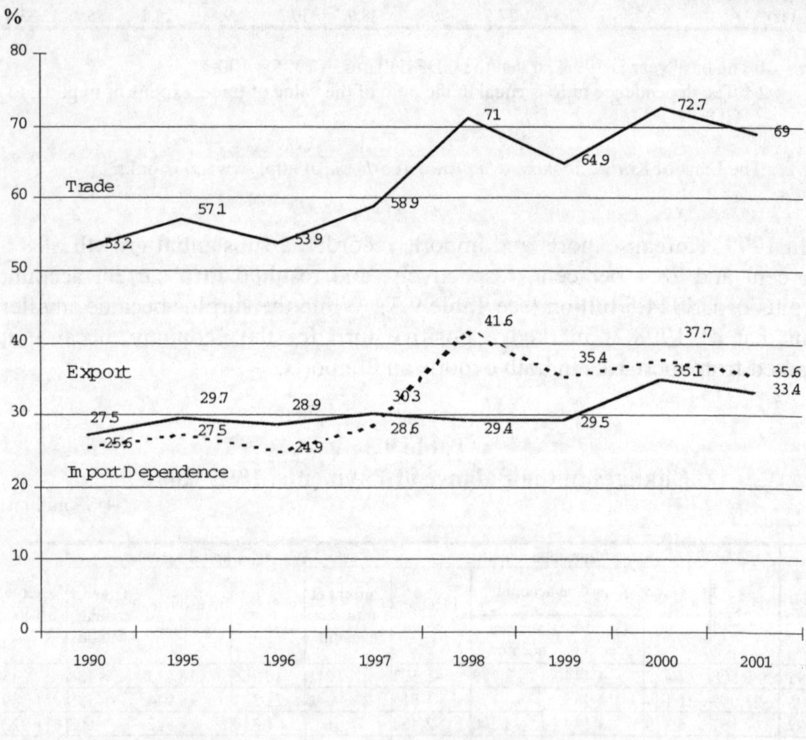


*Source*: National Statistical Office, *KOSIS Data*, at http://www.nso.or.kr.

*Figure 9.2 Trend of Trade Dependence Ratio in Korea, 1990–2001*

### 9.3.2 Developments in Merchandise Trade

**Composition of trade**

Since 1995, Korea's merchandise trade structure has changed slightly. Raw materials and petrolic goods, chemicals, electric and electronic goods, automotive and other transport equipment have increased their shares in total exports (Table 9.4). In the same period, the shares of textiles and clothing, tyres, and food and direct consumer goods in total imports have fallen, as a consequence of a slowdown in overall economic activity and the depreciation of the Korean won.

The composition of Korean imports reflects another important aspect of the Korean economy (see Table 9.4). Korea is poorly endowed with natural resources, and thus relies heavily on foreign sources for such things as fuels and crude oil. As a consequence of sharp increases in oil prices during the late 1990s and early 2000s, the share of crude oil and fuels in Korean imports increased.

**Table 9.4**
**Product Composition of Merchandise Trade, 1995–2001**

(a) Exports

(US$ million)

| | 1995 | 1996 | 1997 | 1998 | 1999 | 2000 | 2001 |
|---|---|---|---|---|---|---|---|
| Food & Direct Consumer Goods | 2 987 | 3 084 | 3 013 | 2 745 | 2 951 | 2 792 | 2 646 |
| Raw Materials & Fuels | 4 609 | 6 121 | 7 713 | 7 385 | 7 847 | 11 572 | 10 000 |
| Petrolic Goods | 2 430 | 3 859 | 5 337 | 4 585 | 5 771 | 9 330 | 7 973 |
| Textiles | 9 203 | 9 330 | 9 580 | 7 850 | 7 998 | 8 523 | 7 012 |
| Clothing | 4 969 | 4 226 | 4 194 | 4 653 | 4 869 | 5 024 | 4 300 |
| Tyres | 1 330 | 1 549 | 1 437 | 1 543 | 1 486 | 1 421 | 1 426 |
| Chemicals | 7 977 | 7 923 | 9 333 | 9 017 | 9 409 | 12 145 | 10 827 |
| Iron & Steel | 9 951 | 8 544 | 9 943 | 11 119 | 10 308 | 11 363 | 10 031 |
| Machinery | 8 682 | 9 428 | 10 189 | 10 064 | 11 594 | 11 997 | 11 640 |
| Electric & Electronic Equip. | 35 017 | 34 021 | 36 745 | 34 284 | 45 807 | 62 043 | 47 360 |
| Transport Equip. | 6 551 | 8 255 | 8 635 | 8 167 | 9 417 | 11 102 | 11 451 |
| Ship | 5 533 | 7 127 | 6 520 | 8 014 | 7 490 | 8 229 | 9 699 |

*Source*: National Statistical Office, *KOSIS Data*, at http://www.nso.or.kr.

(b) Imports

(US$ million)

| | 1995 | 1996 | 1997 | 1998 | 1999 | 2000 | 2001 |
|---|---|---|---|---|---|---|---|
| Agriculture | 2 852 | 3 835 | 3 101 | 2 520 | 2 320 | 2 438 | 2 529 |
| Direct Consumer Goods | 3 577 | 4 095 | 4 155 | 2 373 | 3 656 | 4 647 | 4 787 |
| Non-Durables | 2 125 | 2 914 | 2 745 | 1 091 | 1 623 | 2 549 | 3 091 |
| Durables | 6 941 | 10 369 | 10 900 | 6 644 | 6 397 | 6 424 | 6 217 |
| Fuels | 18 977 | 24 182 | 27 213 | 18 166 | 22 653 | 37 801 | 33 790 |
| Crude Oil | 10 809 | 14 432 | 17 772 | 11 241 | 14 783 | 25 216 | 21 368 |
| Mining | 3 801 | 3 536 | 3 861 | 3 146 | 3 578 | 4 192 | 4 064 |
| Other Raw Materials | 7 026 | 6 433 | 5 699 | 3 732 | 4 185 | 4 845 | 4 409 |
| Chemicals | 11 761 | 11 476 | 11 438 | 7 974 | 9 796 | 11 838 | 11 275 |
| Iron & Steel | 7 120 | 7 188 | 6 256 | 3 319 | 4 750 | 6 007 | 5 030 |
| Non-Steel Metal | 4 796 | 4 319 | 4 664 | 3 347 | 4 016 | 4 845 | 4 222 |
| Machinery | 24 581 | 25 893 | 20 448 | 10 492 | 13 514 | 18 426 | 15 264 |
| Semiconductor | 9 048 | 10 524 | 12 877 | 12 244 | 16 059 | 19 923 | 15 547 |
| Telecom. Equipment | 5 503 | 6 540 | 6 255 | 3 467 | 6 999 | 12 158 | 9 067 |
| Transport Equipment | 6 030 | 6 655 | 3 964 | 2 138 | 2 393 | 2 816 | 2 648 |

*Source*: National Statistical Office, *KOSIS Data*, at http://www.nso.or.kr.

## Table 9.5
## Merchandise Trade by Main Origin and Destination, 1995–2001

(a) Exports

(US$ million)

| | 1995 | 1996 | 1997 | 1998 | 1999 | 2000 | 2001 |
|---|---|---|---|---|---|---|---|
| Total | 125 058 | 129 715 | 136 164 | 132 313 | 143 686 | 172 268 | 150 439 |
| USA | 24 131 | 21 670 | 21 625 | 22 805 | 29 475 | 37 611 | 31 211 |
| China | 9 144 | 11 377 | 13 572 | 11 944 | 13 685 | 18 455 | 18 190 |
| Japan | 17 049 | 15 767 | 14 771 | 12 238 | 15 862 | 20 466 | 16 506 |
| Hong Kong | 10 682 | 11 131 | 11 725 | 9 261 | 9 048 | 10 708 | 9 452 |
| Taiwan | 3 882 | 4 005 | 4 613 | 5 140 | 6 345 | 8 027 | 5 835 |
| Germany | 5 965 | 4 705 | 4 753 | 4 009 | 4 185 | 5 154 | 4 322 |
| Singapore | 6 689 | 6 439 | 5 797 | 4 065 | 4 922 | 5 648 | 4 080 |
| England | 2 874 | 3 222 | 3 984 | 4 179 | 4 776 | 5 380 | 3 490 |
| Indonesia | 2 958 | 3 198 | 3 541 | 1 784 | 2 539 | 3 504 | 3 280 |
| Malaysia | 2 951 | 4 333 | 4 356 | 3 602 | 3 647 | 3 515 | 2 628 |
| Philippines | 1 493 | 1 906 | 2 601 | 2 832 | 3 129 | 3 360 | 2 535 |
| Netherlands | 1 542 | 1 676 | 1 489 | 1 937 | 2 144 | 2 658 | 2 532 |

*Source*: National Statistical Office, *KOSIS Data*, at http://www.nso.or.kr.

(b) Imports

(US$ million)

| | 1995 | 1996 | 1997 | 1998 | 1999 | 2000 | 2001 |
|---|---|---|---|---|---|---|---|
| Total | 135 119 | 150 339 | 144 616 | 93 282 | 119 752 | 160 481 | 141 098 |
| Japan | 32 606 | 31 448 | 27 907 | 16 840 | 24 142 | 31 827 | 26 633 |
| USA | 30 403 | 33 305 | 30 122 | 20 403 | 24 922 | 29 241 | 22 376 |
| China | 7 401 | 8 538 | 10 116 | 6 484 | 8 866 | 12 798 | 13 302 |
| Saudi Arabia | 5 432 | 6 666 | 7 153 | 4 384 | 5 664 | 9 641 | 8 058 |
| Australia | 4 897 | 6 271 | 5 893 | 4 614 | 4 672 | 5 958 | 5 534 |
| UAE | 1 558 | 2 259 | 3 085 | 2 123 | 2 568 | 4 702 | 4 633 |
| Indonesia | 3 325 | 4 013 | 4 107 | 3 057 | 3 986 | 5 286 | 4 473 |
| Germany | 6 583 | 7 239 | 5 824 | 3 345 | 3 826 | 4 624 | 4 473 |
| Taiwan | 2 563 | 2 725 | 2 421 | 1 670 | 2 971 | 4 700 | 4 301 |
| Malaysia | 2 515 | 3 006 | 3 282 | 2 210 | 3 155 | 4 878 | 4 126 |
| Singapore | 2 168 | 2 527 | 2 416 | 1 712 | 2 311 | 3 722 | 3 011 |
| Qatar | 231 | 343 | 722 | 529 | 868 | 2 292 | 2 572 |

*Source*: National Statistical Office, *KOSIS Data*, at http://www.nso.or.kr.

**Directions of trade**

Reflecting the disparity in economic conditions between regions, the share of total exports bound for the United States, Japan and Hong Kong fell, while the share destined for China and European countries increased considerably (Table 9.5). During the crisis the share of goods supplied by Japan and the US sharply decreased, while that supplied by Asia and Oceania increased.

### 9.3.3 Trends and Patterns of FDI

Since the mid-1990s, complying with the Uruguay Round and OECD commitments, Korea has begun to remove its barriers to both incoming and outgoing foreign investment. As a result, Korea's overseas direct investment, as well as foreign investment into Korea, increased gradually throughout the mid-1990s. However, incoming FDI did not increase substantially until the Korean economic crisis, and the resulting drastic liberalization process.

After the economic crisis the Korean government implemented comprehensive policy measures to promote inward foreign investment. The government has accelerated its liberalization schedule, and undertook a liberalization of hostile mergers and acquisitions (M&A) and foreign land ownership in 1998. Since then, Korea has opened most of the business areas previously closed to foreign investment. The financial market, in particular, has been significantly opened. Foreign banks were allowed to establish subsidiaries. Bond markets were also completely liberalized. In the stock market, ceilings on foreigners' stock investments were lifted with the exception of some state-owned enterprises. In addition, most current account transactions related to the operation of financial institutions and corporations have been liberalized. Such liberalization was intended not only to attract foreign capital, but also to introduce market competition and international standards in the Korean economy.

Furthermore, the Korean government has simplified and streamlined the overall investment process to attract more foreign investment. It declared that foreign investment be notified rather than approved. The Korean government has reduced the number of application documents required for the establishment of businesses by foreign investors. In 1998, the Investment Service Centre was established to provide 'one-stop' services to foreign investors. Also, the Office of the Investment Ombudsman was established in 1999 to help foreign investors.

Under these progressive liberalization programmes, FDI into Korea has been steadily growing since the beginning of the 1990s. Especially after the crisis, it sharply grew by 62.5 per cent in 1998 and 90.4 per cent in 1999. By 2002, cumulative FDI inflows (1962–2002) stood at US$78 billion, of which US$53 billion (68 per cent of the total) entered Korea in the period of 1998 to 2002 after the economic crisis. Foreign investment originated largely from the US, Japan, Germany and the Netherlands. Notably, the European Union's FDI into Korea grew by 117 per cent in 1999, making it the largest source of foreign investment in Korea and surpassing the United States. However, FDI into Korea has declined sharply since 2001. Recently, the Korean government has raised great concerns about the fall of FDI. Despite a recent decline, FDI inflows will be growing again if Korea marches on the path of continuous structural reforms.

Table 9.6 shows the trends of FDI inflows to Korea by country. Before the 1997 crisis, FDI from the US and Japan made up a dominant proportion. During the crisis period, Europe's share surged considerably. In particular, FDI from Germany, France and the Netherlands grew tremendously after the 1997 crisis.

Korea's overseas direct investment had been growing before the economic crisis. However, it went through fluctuations after the crisis, as Korean firms reassessed their overseas investment strategies. Korea's overseas direct investment fell by 46.89 per cent from US$4.7 billion in 1998 to US$3.2 billion in 1999 and more than halved during 2001–2002.

Table 9.7 shows the trends of outward FDI by recipient region. The FDI to North America and Asia made up a major proportion.

The investment to the US, Canada and Central America by Korean firms is largely due to their attempts to circumvent US trade barriers. The figure shows that Korea's outward FDI fluctuated in terms of the total size and the target region.

**Table 9.6**
**Inflows of Foreign Direct Investment to Korea, 1995–2002**

(US$ million)

| | 1995 | 1996 | 1997 | 1998 | 1999 | 2000 | 2001 | 2002 |
|---|---|---|---|---|---|---|---|---|
| Total | 1 948 | 3 204 | 6 972 | 8 851 | 15 542 | 15 695 | 11 870 | 1 210 |
| USA | 643 | 875 | 3 190 | 2 971 | 3 739 | 2 922 | 3 889 | 692 |
| Japan | 424 | 255 | 265 | 504 | 1 750 | 2 448 | 772 | 129 |
| Germany | 45 | 95 | 398 | 785 | 960 | 1 599 | 459 | 3 |
| Hong Kong | 58 | 229 | 85 | 38 | 460 | 123 | 746 | 5 |
| Netherlands | 170 | 205 | 831 | 1 323 | 3 322 | 1 768 | 1 245 | 237 |
| Switzerland | 10 | 162 | 103 | 76 | 140 | 25 | 46 | 4 |
| UK | 87 | 79 | 259 | 61 | 479 | 84 | 432 | 0 |
| France | 35 | 90 | 411 | 369 | 750 | 607 | 426 | 10 |
| China | 11 | 6 | 7 | 8 | 27 | 76 | 70 | 8 |
| Others | 465 | 1 208 | 1 423 | 2 716 | 3 915 | 6 043 | 3 785 | 122 |

*Source*: National Statistical Office, *KOSIS Data*, at http://www.nso.or.kr.

**Table 9.7**
**Korea's Overseas Direct Investment, 1995–2002**

(US$ million)

| | 1995 | 1996 | 1997 | 1998 | 1999 | 2000 | 2001 | 2002 |
|---|---|---|---|---|---|---|---|---|
| Total | 3 111 | 4 389 | 3 563 | 4 703 | 3 227 | 4 807 | 4 923 | 2 229 |
| Asia | 1 732 | 1 812 | 1 699 | 2 022 | 1 240 | 1 444 | 1 267 | 1 203 |
| North America | 554 | 1 598 | 889 | 961 | 1 393 | 1 325 | 1 436 | 492 |
| Other America | 122 | 265 | 280 | 243 | 204 | 1 494 | 82 | 131 |
| Europe | 590 | 604 | 384 | 1 226 | 299 | 273 | 2 087 | 309 |
| Middle East | 32 | 26 | 69 | 19 | 1 | 27 | 19 | 19 |
| Africa | 42 | 12 | 113 | 102 | 20 | 156 | 14 | 9 |
| Oceania | 40 | 71 | 129 | 130 | 69 | 89 | 17 | 66 |

*Source*: National Statistical Office, *KOSIS Data,* at http://www.nso.or.kr.

## 9.4 FUTURE AGENDAS AND POLICY RESPONSES

The previous sections indicate that the future of the Korean economy depends heavily upon the following factors: how efficiently Korea undertakes structural adjustments within the WTO multilateral trading system; how actively Korea participates in regional and bilateral trade arrangements; and how well Korea creates a favourable business environment for foreign investors. The present section examines three future agendas that the Korean economy must deal with in the near future, and explores the directions of Korea's trade policy.

### 9.4.1 The WTO DDA Negotiations

Korea strongly supports the continuing development of the open multilateral trading system. Since its accession to the GATT, Korea has been fully committed to complying with multilateral rules and obligations. Also, Korea actively participated in the multilateral trade negotiations of the Tokyo and Uruguay Rounds. After the WTO's inception in 1995, Korea has been faithfully implementing the WTO agreements and Uruguay Round (UR) commitments.

In the fourth WTO ministerial conference in Doha, Qatar in November 2001, a new round of multilateral trade negotiation (called the Doha Development Agenda – DDA) was launched. From the WTO perspective, the launch of the DDA is a turning point in the relations between developed countries and developing countries.

Since the launch of the WTO's DDA, the Korean government has actively participated in negotiations on the comprehensive agenda and has played its due role in successfully concluding the negotiations. For Korea the DDA will present great challenges as well as opportunities, because it will mandate its economy to liberalize all sectors. Even relatively weak sectors, including agriculture and some service sectors, are subject to the liberalization programme. After all, the growth of the Korean economy depends on an outward-oriented trade policy, and it has benefited from the open global market. In this context a freer world trading system, expected to result from the conclusion of the WTO's DDA, could bring considerable potential gains to the Korean economy. According to an empirical analysis conducted by KIEP, the DDA will present substantial benefits to the Korean economy. Although, depending upon the degree of liberalization, negotiation modalities, and model specification, various empirical studies suggest that real GDP and welfare will increase by 2.55–4.21 per cent and 3.06–4.62 per cent, respectively.[7]

However, the WTO's DDA will be considerably painful for some weak sectors of the Korean economy, especially the agricultural sector. This is so because the DDA negotiation deals with the following three issues in agriculture: substantial improvement in market access with the principle of tariffication only, reduction of all forms of export subsidies with the final objective of full phase out, and substantial reductions in trade-distorting domestic subsidies. In particular, the Korean rice market must be opened under the tariffication programme. However, Korea strongly opposes the lifting of its import restrictions on rice.

The WTO's DDA negotiation is to be concluded by the end of 2004. Therefore, the Korean government must prepare well for the strategies in the on-going negotiations, and establish a restructuring programme for domestic industries as early as possible. Most importantly, Korea needs to be well prepared for the DDA negotiations in light of the experience and lessons of the 1993 Uruguay Round. This time, the Korean government must build a national consensus on trade liberalization in agriculture, specifically rice, before the DDA comes to its conclusion.

Through the DDA negotiations on agriculture, the modalities will mandate Korea to substantially reduce tariffs, subsidies and domestic support in agriculture. All of these are unavoidable and will be truly painful for the Korean farmers, specifically for the rice farmers. Therefore, the Korean government must establish a restructuring programme for agricultural products. For rice, the production plan is to be rearranged and an income support package to be continuously substituted for price support. Also, the government must organize a 'friends' group with the non-trade concerns (NTC) countries, such as Japan and Norway, so that the negotiations on agricultural liberalization take the multi-functionality or non-trade concerns of agriculture into consideration. Furthermore, trade liberalization related to fishery and forestry products should take place with full account of their conservation management needs, as Korea proposed.

The DDA negotiations on services are not expected to have much impact on the Korean economy. This is because Korea has already carried out a wide range of liberalization measures since the 1997 economic crisis. However, major trading partners are expected to demand further liberalization and deregulation in some areas of their own interest. In telecommunications, the United States demands that more than 50 per cent foreign ownership be allowed in key industries such as Korea Telecom. In the motion picture and television industry, the screen quota system and quota for TV programmes are to be lowered or eliminated. Liberalization is required in the area of professional services such as legal, medical, accounting and higher education services.

The DDA negotiation would mandate the reduction or elimination of tariffs and non-tariff barriers on industrial goods including high and peak tariffs. Korea must prepare for the negotiations on industrial goods based on various formulas of tariff reduction. Also, the Korean government must prepare the draft of request or offer depending upon the sector-based or item-by-item negotiations. Korea has already expressed the view that the DDA had to conclude as a single undertaking.

Other elements of the Korean position were that commonly agreed rules on competition and trade and investment, as well as a proactive approach in government procurement, were required and that electronic commerce was an important issue. In the light of its recent experience, Korea urged that shortcomings and ambiguities in the WTO Anti-dumping Agreement be corrected. In particular, the DDA negotiation will be an opportunity for tightening existing rules so as to prevent abuse of anti-dumping measures by developed countries, mainly the United States and the European Union.

### 9.4.2 Regional Trade Agreements and Regional Economic Cooperation

Recently, the formation of regional trade agreements (RTAs)[8] has been increasingly prevalent. By 2001, 155 RTAs had been reported to the GATT/WTO. The number of RTAs rapidly increased especially after 1995 when the WTO was established. Notably, this trend was more obvious in the Asia Pacific region. However, North-East Asian countries – China, Japan and Korea – have not participated in any RTAs until recently. Since the economic crisis, these countries began to show a greater interest in establishing RTAs.

Korea has traditionally valued the multilateral trading system, and did not support bilateral or regional free trade agreements. Although its commitment to multilateralism is still firm, Korea has recently altered its position with regard to the role of RTAs in the world trading system. After the economic crisis, Korea has supported the view that RTAs, if properly concluded and managed in accordance with the relevant WTO rules, can supplement the multilateral trading system and contribute to global opening through bilateral and regional acceleration of trade liberalization.

In an effort to avoid the negative effects of being excluded from such agreements, to maintain economic reform and an openness policy, and to actively cope with proliferating regionalism, the Korean government has decided to pursue FTAs with other nations. Forming FTAs will enable Korea to attract foreign investment and establish overseas footholds, as well as allow Korean firms to secure foreign export markets and overcome discriminatory practices under other FTAs.

In a first attempt at forming an FTA, the Korean government formally announced that it would seek an FTA with Chile in November 1998. The main reason for choosing Chile as an FTA partner is that Chile is an APEC partner with a complementary industrial structure and similar trade policy objectives, and represents an entry base to the Latin American market. After several meetings on product concessions, negotiations for an FTA with Chile were concluded in October 2002. While the Korean government explicitly wanted exceptions for agricultural products, the Chilean government did not like any concessions on any products.

This agreement is expected to respond to the expansion of other regional FTAs (that is NAFTA, the EU and ASEAN), to secure export markets in Latin America, to strengthen the competitiveness of domestic firms, and to increase consumer welfare through import liberalization of foreign products.

KIEP estimated that, when implemented, the agreement would increase Korea's exports by US$660 million per year and imports from Chile by US$260 million per year.[9] The main exports to Chile involve cars, machinery, cellular phones, tyres, batteries, textiles, PVC, steel products and other manufactured goods; major imports from Chile include non-ferrous metals and agricultural products. However, rice and some fruits such as apples and pears are excluded and seasonal tariffs are imposed on grapes.

Korea has also been studying the possibility of establishing FTAs with other trading partners – Japan, Mexico, New Zealand, Singapore, Thailand, China and the United States. In this context, Korea and Japan conducted joint research regarding the feasibility of concluding an FTA and exchanged results at an International Joint Symposium in 2001. Currently, the private sectors of the two countries are taking the lead in the bilateral FTA talks through Business Forums. According to the preliminary study, despite many obstacles, a Korea–Japan FTA is strategically significant and offers various economic benefits, by strengthening the strategic alliances among the firms of the two countries. As for a possible Korea–US FTA, no formal bilateral FTA talks have yet been launched but discussions have been ongoing since the late 1990s in academic and business forums. The public view is that a Korea–US FTA and a Korea–Japan FTA seem feasible with greater economic effects. A Korea-Japan FTA is particularly recommendable as it could later be developed into an East Asian FTA through expanding its membership to China and possibly ASEAN countries. Furthermore, active considerations have been taken for other FTAs such as a Korea–Japan–China FTA and an ASEAN+3 FTA (that is ASEAN with Korea, Japan and China) as a way to create regional trading arrangements to counterbalance other major economic blocs such as the EU and NAFTA.

Since Korea lags far behind other countries in establishing FTAs, it should hasten to conclude FTAs with major trading countries. Rather than waiting to complete an FTA with one country before deciding on the next FTA partner, Korea should simultaneously promote FTAs with multiple countries. Finally, in order to build a national consensus, the Korea government should enhance its efforts in improving public awareness of the potential benefits of preferential FTAs.

Korea has been actively engaged in regional cooperation mechanisms, such as the Asia-Pacific Economic Cooperation Forum (APEC), Asia Europe Meeting (ASEM), and ASEAN+3 processes. Korea values the principle of open regionalism. Thus, Korea believes that regional cooperation should not reduce but, rather, promote openness in world trade. Korea also believes that the promotion of market opening in the context of regional cooperation can significantly contribute to worldwide trade liberalization.

Korea is one of the founding members of APEC, which, since 1989, has been promoting trade and investment liberalization and practical economic cooperation in the Asia-Pacific region. Korea has been actively engaged in designing and improving APEC's Individual Action Plans (IAPs) and Collective Action Plans (CAPs) in an effort to promote trade and investment liberalization in the Asia-Pacific region. In 1997, the members of APEC agreed upon an Early Voluntary Sectoral Liberalization (EVSL) initiative. Korea also participated in APEC's efforts to promote trade and investment liberalization at the multilateral level, including sectoral trade liberalization initiatives and the early conclusion of the WTO's DDA negotiation.

In the ASEM process Korea has played an important role in promoting various measures for more trade facilitation and investment promotion between Asia and Europe, such as the Trade Facilitation Action Plan (TFAP) and the Investment Promotion Action Plan (IPAP). Korea has been actively engaged in evaluating TFAP deliverables (1998–2000) and designing TFAP concrete goals (2000–2002).

In addition to APEC and ASEM, Korea has accelerated efforts to promote economic cooperation and freer economic exchange in the East Asian region through the ASEAN+3 meetings. Given the diversity and economic dynamism of the region, Korea regards this process as an important element of its regional cooperation initiatives.

Korea will continue to enthusiastically participate in regional cooperation mechanisms, such as the APEC, ASEM and ASEAN+3 processes. Korea will also seek bilateral free trade agreements with its trading partners. While Korea believes that WTO-centred multilateralism offers the best framework for achieving openness in global trade, it is also of the view that frameworks of properly managed regional cooperation will significantly contribute to creating freer trade worldwide. Korea will continue its best efforts to maintain cooperative and mutually beneficial bilateral trade relationships with its trading partners. Through bilateral consultations Korea will proactively address any trade issues that its partners raise, in accordance with international rules. In this process, Korea will continue to oppose unilateral solutions for trade disputes and will resort to the WTO's dispute settlement mechanism for unresolved bilateral disagreements.

### 9.4.3 Better Business Environments for FDI

The Korean government has made significant progress in the implementation of measures to attract FDI, having initiated several important changes in government policies. These changes include the passage of the Foreign Direct Investment Promotion Act in 1998, the One-Stop Service initiated in 1998, and other regulatory changes in the labour market and relevant tax laws.

Due to her reform-led recovery, Korea is now regarded as one of a few great success stories in terms of the attraction of FDI. Korea, as a matter of fact, has succeeded in recent years in drawing in billions of US dollars in FDI. Opening domestic markets to foreign investors, the permission of hostile M&As, and the liberalization of the real-estate market, have all contributed to the successful attraction of huge amounts of foreign direct investment.

Despite such an optimistic picture of inward foreign direct investment, some problems still exist. It is recognized that, despite the surge in FDI in the couple of years after the 1997 crisis, the inflow of foreign investment has slowed down considerably in recent years. One very plausible reason for such a slowdown was the recession in many parts of the world, but some of the reasons may be found in the Korean economy; for example, Korea may not have provided enough incentives to foreign investors. Some discussion about the situation of the Korean economy is provided as follows.

First, as compared with places like Hong Kong, Singapore and Shanghai, Korea has not provided good tax incentives to foreign firms to bring in their investment. Currently, Korea's income tax rate is 39.6 per cent, which is much higher than Hong Kong's 17 per cent or Singapore's 26 per cent. Korea's corporation tax rate is 29.7 per cent, which is higher than the rates of 16 per cent in Hong Kong and 22 per cent in Singapore. Second, foreign investors in Korea are subject to certain regulations and are apparently discriminated against. According to the IMD report on world competitiveness, Korea is ranked forty-fifth out of 49 nations in the area of foreign company discrimination and thirty-ninth in the area of the overall protection system of foreign investors. Third, many foreign investors have complained about the poor business and living environments in Korea. Compared with other competing nations, Korea has a low level of labour market flexibility and low quality of life. Fourth, in recent years Korea has been experiencing a shortage in big projects to attract foreign investors. It has been argued that the surge in FDI in the two years following the 1997 crisis was due to the sale of Korean companies at bargain prices. As the asset values of Korean companies recovered, instances of fire sale FDI has remarkably diminished.

The policies to attract more FDI should be addressed to cure the above-mentioned problems. They should be geared towards removing and reducing capital market restrictions and distortions, establishing more favourable tax policies for foreign investments (the reduction of corporate tax and so on), installing highly intense one-stop services for foreign investors, and building such infrastructure as highways, foreign schools and hospitals, and so on.

Finally, as recent empirical research shows, both push and pull factors are equally important in terms of overall capital flows and each component of the capital account. In consideration of this, and also the fact that the Korean economy is becoming more integrated into the world economy, the Korean government should improve domestic economic and financial conditions not only to cope with future external shocks but also to attract more stable FDI.

## 9.5 SUMMARY AND CONCLUDING REMARKS

Korea, together with Hong Kong, Singapore, and Taiwan, are called the 'four little dragons' in East and South-East Asia for their impressive growth in the late twentieth century. Although these economies have taken different strategies and paths of development, all of them depend heavily on external trade as a crucial factor of growth of domestic wealth and welfare.

This chapter has examined the policies of the Korean government to promote domestic production and foreign trade. It has described how the government has long been committed to trade liberalization and its promotion, which is believed to have contributed largely to the economy's spectacular growth in the 1970s and 1980s. Among the important policies that played an important role in the economy's development were the government's encouragement of the establishment of large corporations, the use of promotional incentives to encourage export performance of domestic firms, and its decision to join international trade organizations such as the GATT/WTO and the OECD. Such membership reinforces Korea's commitment to trade liberalization. At the same time, the Korean government also viewed its accession to these international trade organizations as an effective way of integrating its economy with the rest of the world and further promoting its growth and welfare.

Before the 1990s, despite its dependence on foreign trade, Korea had not had much emphasis on foreign capital inflow. In the 1990s, things had changed. In order to support domestic capital formation, Korea started to import both direct and financial capital. Partly because of the historically low interest rates in the world financial markets, Korean banks were given more freedom and flexibility to raise foreign loans from abroad. These loans had two main features, which turned out to be significant down the road: most of them were in the form of short-term debt and most of them were unhedged and denominated in foreign currencies. Then in 1997 Korea was hit by a financial crisis, which rocked the domestic economy heavily. While some of the features of the domestic economy and government policies had been used to explain the occurrence of the crisis, the existence of short-term, unhedged debts had made the crisis especially severe.[10]

There is no doubt that Korea recovered quite rapidly from the financial crisis. The recovery can be attributed to the IMF rescue package and the reforms undertaken by the Korean government right after the crisis. However, it is also true that the new policy of the Korean government, emphasizing the liberalization of foreign capital inflows, has directly helped stabilize the local currency and the confidence of domestic investors and consumers.

The financial crisis has not stopped Korea's pace of trade liberalization. Korea added investment liberalization. To further integrate its economy with the rest of the world, Korea not only participates actively in multilateral trade negotiations, it also enthusiastically engages in negotiations about the formation of regional trade blocs, that is free trade areas with countries like Chile, Japan, China and the ASEAN. All these policies taken by the Korean government have been described in detail in this chapter.

What Korea has learned is that its economic growth and welfare are closely linked to the rest of the world through movements of goods and capital. The experience of Korea and other emerging economies demonstrates well the importance of trade and foreign direct investment to the growth of their economies and improvement of the welfare of their consumers. These economies are good examples to support the statement 'trade as the engine of growth'.

## NOTES

1 National Statistical Office, KOSIS Data, available at http://www.nso.or.kr.
2 Korean International Trade Association, *Foreign Trade Statistics*, various issues.
3 It is also called a free trade zone (FTZ).
4 See Kim et al. (2001) for further information on the liberalization of Overseas Portfolio Investment and Trade-related Capital Account Transactions.
5 GATS covers four types of services – cross-border supply, consumption abroad, commercial presence and presence of natural persons.
6 The IMF recommends that the newly industrializing countries keep an amount of foreign exchange reserves that are enough to afford imports for three months. At the end of 1997, Korea should have maintained at least US$36 billion as the normal amount of foreign reserves. Of course, the normal amount of foreign reserves held by a country, as the IMF notes, depends upon the size of short-term debts, country risk and the foreign exchange system of that country.
7 Choi (2002).
8 For details, see WTO Annual Report (2002).
9 Cheong (2002).
10 Wong (2000) argued that the traditional government programmes of interest subsidies had encouraged firms to overinvest, overproduce and overborrow. This directly makes a financial crisis much more severe.

## REFERENCES

Cheong, I.K. (2002), 'Main Issues of Korea–Chile FTA', mimeo, Seoul: Korean Ministry of Foreign Affairs and Trade, and Korea Institute of International Economic Policy.
Choi, N.G. (2002), 'Korea's Trade Policy Regime in the Development Process', mimeo, Korea Institute for International Economic Policy.
IMD, *World Competitiveness Yearbook 2002*, www.imd.ch/wcy.

Kim, S.Y., S.H. Kim and Y.J. Wang (2001), 'Capital Account Liberalization and Macroeconomic Performance: the Case of Korea', mimeo, Korea Institute for International Economic Policy.

Wong, K.Y. (2000), 'Firm Failure and Financial Crisis: the Experience of South Korea', *Journal of the Korean Economy*, **1**(1), 23–51.

World Trade Organization (2000), *Trade Policy Review: The Republic of Korea 2001*, Geneva: World Trade Organization.

World Trade Organization (2002), *Annual Report*, Geneva: World Trade Organization.

# 10. Korea's Embrace of Regionalism and the Economic Effects of its Bilateral FTAs with Chile and Japan

**Inkyo Cheong**

## 10.1 OVERVIEW OF KOREA'S FTA POLICY

Korea has been studying the feasibility of free trade agreements (FTAs) since the 1980s. Although Korea believed that FTAs were necessary for the growth of its exports, it did not join any because of the anticipated difficulties that would arise from such an opening of its markets. From the mid-1990s a special committee was assigned to examine the FTA policy, and in 1997 the then Ministry of Trade and Industry began to examine the FTA policy. In 1998, immediately after the Asian financial crisis, the Office of the Minister for Trade was established. A number of trade expert officials of the then Ministry of Trade and Industry were recruited to the Office of the Minister for Trade, and they began fully examining an FTA on a strategic trade policy level.

The Korean government has come to recognize that FTAs are helpful in attracting foreign direct investment (FDI) and securing overseas footholds for its exports. Expanding the domestic market by entering into an FTA with a major trading partner could trigger new investments from companies deciding to use Korea as a production base. Because the scale of the domestic market and investment system are important factors in attracting foreign investment, Korea hopes to increase the incentive for foreign companies to invest in South Korea by forming FTAs. These investors will benefit from the elimination of tariffs by Korea's trade partners under such agreements. Furthermore, Korean industries will have more secure access to the markets of FTA members.

Though Korea achieved economic growth under the multilateral system of the GATT/WTO, its reaction to a widening spread and deepening of regional trading blocs has been lukewarm due to domestic opposition to market opening under regional trading agreements. However, since the financial crisis began, the Korean government has been re-evaluating the potential gains to be made by removing trade barriers on a preferential basis, and has decided to pursue the establishment of preferential trading blocs.

One major motivation behind Korea's new thinking on regionalism is the trade diversion caused by the growth of regional trading blocs. A WTO (1995) report discussed the causes of the rapidly rising number of regional trading blocs[1] that were created in the early 1990s. The report concluded that the growing trend of regionalism was an insurance policy in the event of failure of the Uruguay Round negotiations. An implication of that conclusion is that regional integration initiatives would be weakened as the multilateral trading system became firmly established. Yet, following the inauguration of the WTO, the trend towards increasing numbers and the deepening scope of regional trading blocs has continued.

Regionalism is one of the most dominant trends in the world economy today. There were only 26 new regional trade agreements (RTAs) reported to GATT prior to 1969. Following a weakening in the pace of regional integration in the 1980s, the number of RTAs exploded in the 1990s. Thirty-five additional regional agreements were signed during the two years of 1995 and 1996, and 17 such agreements were reached in 1997 and 1998. This demonstrates that, rather than simply being a type of insurance policy taken against potential shortcomings of multilateral free trade formation, regionalism has been seen as a viable commercial strategy that complements the multilateral trade agreements.

In line with this increasing trend towards regional integration, Korea has altered its past position opposing regional trade blocs and is now cautiously investigating the establishment of FTAs with major trading countries. Not only was a fear of being left out of the recent trend of growing regionalism a motivating factor for Korea's change, but the outbreak of the Asian financial crisis also played a large role in Korea's decision to pursue the establishment of FTAs. Korea has also opened most of its financial sectors to foreign investors and has implemented unilateral trade liberalization measures.

Korea's new trade policy is aimed at promptly adapting to the changing economic environment, as well as resolving the nation's economic difficulties. Consequently, an ultimate goal of this policy is to transform Korea into an 'open trading country' which makes a meaningful contribution to opening up the world economy at the international level, while at the national level the government remains committed to opening its markets through parallel developments of democracy and a market economy.

In addition, it is recognized that the supplier-oriented trade policy of the past must be changed into a consumer-oriented policy that maximizes the convenience and benefits to the general public. In terms of cost-efficiency, the public's well-being is better served when the majority of consumers can be supplied with low-cost and high-quality goods rather than defending the interests of a minority of producers. Therefore, the government must perform the role of opening up the domestic market, so that its people can enjoy an abundance of low-cost and high-quality goods and services.

For example, the government abolished the import diversification programme (IDP) at the end of June 1999. The IDP, which was introduced in early 1978, was a system of restricting imports from a specific country (targeting Japan) with which Korea was experiencing a serious trade deficit for a list of items. The abolition of the IDP can be regarded as one of the most dramatic liberalization measures.

Most Koreans view this liberalization as having been beneficial, and there is a growing perception that the establishment of FTAs with major trading partners will bring greater welfare gains. Moreover, Korea has recognized the importance of stable export markets; it is thought that the current account deficit that preceded the financial crisis resulted in worsening international confidence in the Korean economy. Another important background factor in the current trend towards regionalism can be found in trade policy-makers' recognition of the necessity of upgrading Korea's economic system to meet international standards.

The Korean government, with its policy goal of building an 'open trading country', is firmly committed to maintaining friendly trade relations with its trading partners, while also promoting strategic alliances in the form of FTAs and bilateral investment treaties (BIT). Through such agreements, Korea seeks to establish alliances with its trading partners in order to secure a forward base in strategic regions and to upgrade its national competitiveness. The Korean government is also actively participating in the process of creating a new free trade framework, such as the WTO New Round, to counter the threat of emerging protectionism.

The pursuit of FTAs is largely based on its view that an expansion of free trade within regional blocs would ultimately complement Korea's trade interests, in the light of today's fast-changing world economic environment. An FTA is a good reminder of how expansion of free trade in the multilateral arena has significantly contributed to Korea's economic growth.

However, Korea's pursuit in forming FTAs with major trading countries does not mean that it is necessarily downplaying the role or significance of the multilateral trade system. Rather, it means that Korea pursues regional economic cooperation within the framework of the WTO, in line with the growing presence of other regional groups including the EU, NAFTA and ASEAN. The Korean government thus plans to sign FTAs with its trade partners, starting with Chile. The presidents of Korea and Chile agreed, during the APEC summit meeting in November 1998, to conduct discussions for the negotiation of a formal free trade agreement between the two countries. By February 2003 a free trade agreement was formally signed.

Though Korea has employed a relatively passive trade policy in the past, in the coming era of unlimited competition the country must be equipped with a more active and assertive trade policy in order to lay the foundation for national prosperity in the twenty-first century. Also, it is important to maintain friendly relations with trading partners, and to secure stable export performance based on the competitiveness of domestic industries. In addition, Korea must attract additional foreign investment, not only for financial purposes but also for acquiring the advanced technology of foreign companies.

## 10.2 ECONOMIC EVALUATION OF THE KOREA–CHILE FTA

### 10.2.1 Overall Effects

Cheong and Lee (1999) analyzed the economic effect of the FTA between Chile and Korea by using a CGE model. The CGE model is a general equilibrium model that has the advantage of determining the reallocation effects of the resources caused by the cross-sectoral reallocation of production factors, which a partial equilibrium approach is not able to deal with.[2]

Since Chile's average applied tariff rates are generally higher than Korea's (9 per cent vs. 6.89 per cent), Korea is expected to gain more benefit from the tariff elimination between the two countries. For example, preferential tariffs imposed by Chile on Canadian and Mexican exports through the FTA between the two countries are now acting as main barriers for Korea's export products such as automobiles and tyres that are highly competitive with those products. In this regard, the conclusion of the Korea–Chile FTA will provide Korean products with price competitiveness, enabling them to better compete with other countries in the Chilean market. This inference can be supported in Mexico's case, which has an industrial structure similar to that of Korea. Taking as an example the Mexico–Chile FTA, Mexican exports to Chile jumped from US$180 million in 1992 to US$930 million dollars in 1996. Korea is also expected to enjoy a similar level of export expansion effect with the establishment of the FTA with Chile.

In examining the effect of tariff elimination, we can assume three basic scenarios. The first scenario is based on the complete tariff elimination of both countries across all sectors. The second assumes zero tariffs in all sectors and 50 per cent tariff reduction for agricultural products. The last scenario is based on complete tariff elimination in general sectors with the exclusion of agricultural products. The results from a general economic effect analysis are as follows.

According to Table 10.1 the three scenarios produce almost the same positive welfare-improving results for Korea of US$960 million. This result, however, does not consider the service trade effect and the market expansion effect. The actual improvement is expected to be even greater if we include these.

Changes in trade flows will be greater, with almost US$660 million and US$260 million dollar increases in Korea's export and import values respectively. The export growth rate will exceed the import growth rate for Korea, resulting in a trade surplus of US$400 million.

Among Korea's export sectors, some competitive sectors with a greater market share in Chile will particularly benefit from the Korea–Chile FTA. They are automobiles (occupying 18 per cent of the Chilean import market), refrigerators (31 per cent), microwave ovens (69 per cent), washing machines (65 per cent), tyres and automobile batteries, textiles, elevators and PVCs.

In the case of automobiles, Japan maintains the most dominant position in the Chilean market. However, with the tariff elimination between Korea and Chile, Korea may emerge as the top exporter to Chile.

Moreover, the formation of the Korea–Chile FTA will greatly improve the export performance of other potential products, including transistors, dry cells and cable, which are now on the way to establishing distribution channels within Chile

**Table 10.1**
**Overall Economic Effect of the Korea–Chile FTA**

(US$ million, %)

| | Korea | | |
|---|---|---|---|
| | Overall tariff liberalization | 50% tariff reduction in agriculture | Without agriculture |
| Welfare | 960 | 960 | 950 |
| Inflation (%) | -0.001 | -0.001 | -0.001 |
| GDP (%) | 0.01 | 0.01 | 0.01 |
| Exports to Chile | 660 | 660 | 660 |
| Imports from Chile | 260 | 250 | 240 |
| Trade balance | 400 | 4.1 | 4.2 |

*Source*: Cheong and Lee (1999).

As for the Korean manufacturing sector the copper processing industry will be most affected by imports of copper and related products from Chile, which will increase with the FTA. This is because Chilean copper leads the world in terms of exploitable reserves, production and export volumes. The mining sector is the most important and competitive sector in the Chilean economy, accounting for more than half of its global exports.

### 10.2.2 Effects on Sensitive Sectors

One of the main reasons why Korea selected Chile as its first FTA partner is that the negative economic effects will not be so great on Korea's agricultural sector. Agricultural imports from Chile were only US$26 million in 1997, US$6 million in 1998 and US$15 million in 1999, accounting for only 0.09 per cent and 0.22 per cent of Korea's total agricultural imports respectively (see Tables 10.2 and 10.3).

**Table 10.2**
**Korea's Imports of Major Agricultural Products**

| | Korea's total agricultural imports (A) | | Agricultural imports from Chile (B) | | A/B (%) | | |
|---|---|---|---|---|---|---|---|
| | 98 | 99 | 98 | 99 | 98 | 99 | Chile was the 19th-largest agricultural exporter to Korea in 1998. |
| Agricultural Products | 6589 | 6931 | 6 | 15 | 0.09 | 0.22 | |
| Fishery | 691 | 1339 | 6 | 12 | 0.87 | 0.90 | |
| Forestry | 1049 | 1481 | 50 | 51 | 4.77 | 3.44 | |
| Total | 8329 | 9751 | 62 | 78 | 0.74 | 0.80 | |

*Note*: Main agricultural exporters to Korea are the US (31 per cent), China (13.2 per cent), Australia (8 per cent), Indonesia (4 per cent), Malaysia and New Zealand.

*Source*: Cheong and Lee (1999).

**Table 10.3**
**Export Structure of Chile**

| | 1996 | | 1997 | | 1998 | |
|---|---|---|---|---|---|---|
| | Amount | Share | Amount | Share | Amount | Share |
| Total Exports | 15 394 649 | 100.0 | 17 016 996 | 100.0 | 14 753 877 | 100.0 |
| Agricultural Products (Total) | 2 996 484 | 19.5 | 3.035 883 | 17.8 | 3 183 436 | 21.6 |
| Fruits | 1491.623 | 9.6 | 1 413 680 | 8.3 | 1 486 886 | 10.1 |
| - Fresh Grapes | 597 540 | 3.9 | 635 629 | 3.7 | 612 492 | 4.2 |
| - Raisin | 34 410 | 0.2 | 41 498 | 0.2 | 37 249 | 0.6 |
| Processed Foods | 1 470 536 | 9.6 | 1 558 029 | 9.2 | 1 618 524 | 10.9 |
| - Wine | 295 666 | 1.9 | 429 060 | 2.5 | 541 173 | 3.7 |
| - Tomato Paste | 88 603 | 0.5 | 72 012 | 0.4 | 86 541 | 0.6 |
| Livestock | 34 325 | 0.2 | 61 174 | 0.4 | 78 025 | 0.5 |
| Fisheries | 1 975 755 | 12.8 | 1 988 148 | 11.7 | 1 823 225 | 12.3 |
| Forestry (Total) | 801 337 | 5.2 | 896 477 | 5.3 | 705 922 | 4.8 |
| - Sown Wood | 245 037 | 1.6 | 303 406 | 1.8 | 249 596 | 1.7 |
| - Plywood | 63 618 | 0.4 | 91 957 | 0/5 | 78 902 | 0.5 |
| Manufacturing Products | 9 621 073 | 62.5 | 11 096 488 | 65.2 | 9 041 294 | 61.3 |

*Note*: The scope of agriculture, fisheries and forestry is based on the definition of the sectors in the Korea–Chile FTA.

*Source*: Cheong and Lee (1999).

In Korea, the main agricultural imports from Chile are confined to some fruits such as fresh grapes, kiwis and tomato paste (see Table 10.4). As for grapes, however, Chile's marketing season is very different from Korea's due to the reverse geographical location (South and North Hemisphere), and Chilean grapes therefore are imported during the March–July period. In addition, as the product quality of Chilean grapes also differs greatly from Korean grapes, they do not appear to be directly competitive with Korean grapes.

**Table 10.4**
**Chile's Major Agricultural Exports and Korea's Agricultural Imports**

(US$ million)

| Item | Chile's total exports (97) | Korea's tariff rate (%) | Korea's total imports 97 | Korea's total imports 98/9 | Imports from Chile (98/9) | Imports by country (98/9) |
|---|---|---|---|---|---|---|
| Avocado | 32 | 30.0 | 0.2 | 0.09 | 0.0 | US (0.09) |
| Grapes (fresh) | 628 | 47.0 | 18.9 | 2.1 | 2.0 | US (0.09) |
| Apples (fresh) | 211 | 48.0 | 0.0 | 0.0 | 0.0 | |
| Poke | 102 | 50.0 | 0.08 | 0.0 | 0.0 | US (0.2) |
| Cherry | 15 | 33.6 | 0.7 | 0.2 | 0.0 | |
| Peach | 29 | 50.0 | 0.0 | 0.0 | 0.0 | New Zealand (4) |
| Plums | 72 | 48.0 | 0.0 | 0.0 | 0.0 | |
| Kiwi | 78 | 48.0 | 14.5 | 4.3 | 0.4 | |
| Frozen fruit | 27 | 30.0 | 0.1 | 0.006 | 0.0 | |
| Grapes (dried) | 42 | 29.4 | 4.2 | 2.4 | 0.0 | US (1.9) |
| Prunes (dried) | 20 | 25.3 | 0.005 | 0.005 | 0.0 | US (1.90 |
| Vegetable seed | 21 | 0.0 | 25.6 | 17.8 | 0.4 | Japan (7.2) |

*Source*: Cheong and Lee (1999).

Other agricultural products imported from Chile are wood products used as raw material, and some fruit such as apples and pomes in which Korea is already sufficiently competitive in the world market.

The Korean government needed, as a matter of course, to take a deliberate stance against the potential industrial damage to sensitive sectors by carefully examining the economic effect of the Korea–Chile FTA. To minimize severe restructuring costs, Korea also needed to consider partial exclusion of the most affected sectors from the FTA or demand the provision of a transition period for the sensitive sectors.

In spite of imports of grapes from Chile, Korean domestic production of grapes has been increasing (see Table 10.5). This is partly due to the increase in domestic consumption of grapes. The different marketing periods of

Chilean and Korean grapes also prevented Chilean imports from discouraging domestic production. The marketing period of Chilean grapes in the Korean market is from March to June. After June, however, Chilean grapes are likely to lose their competitiveness due to the problem of maintenance of freshness and the full-scale marketing of alternative fruit such as watermelons and melons. Therefore, we can expect that there will be no overlapping of marketing periods of Chilean and domestic grapes.

On the other hand, as Korean greenhouse-grown grapes, which account for 2.5 per cent of the total area of grape cultivation, come onto the domestic market in May, they will have to compete with Chilean grapes. However, they will not be severely affected by the Chilean grape imports, as the product quality of the two grapes is quite different.

**Table 10.5**
**Korea's Production and Import of Grapes**

(tons)

| | 93 | 94 | 95 | 96 | 97 | 98 | 99 |
|---|---|---|---|---|---|---|---|
| Domestic Production (A) | 163 780 | 211 930 | 316 443 | 357 274 | 393 195 | 397 784 | 470 124 |
| Area of Cultivation (ha) | 16 991 | 19 773 | 26 030 | 27 196 | 28 290 | 29 871 | 30 537 |
| Imports from Chile (B) | - | - | - | 2 403 | 8 897 | 1 140 | 6 062 |
| B/A | | | | 0.67% | 2.26% | 0.29% | 1.29% |

*Source*: Eur, et al. (1999).

In terms of price competitiveness the elimination of tariffs on grapes will not bring severe harm to Korean grape producers, as the transport, storing and bidding cost, as well as importers' profits, are estimated to raise the wholesale price of Chilean grapes in the Korean market at least by more than twice the CIF price.

## 10.3 ECONOMIC EFFECTS OF A KOREA–JAPAN FTA[3]

Most FTAs pursue complete trade liberalization within a timeframe of ten years, with some exceptions for highly sensitive items.[4] This satisfies the requirements for regional trading blocs, specified in Article XXIV of the GATT/WTO. Since an FTA between Korea and Japan would most likely follow this requirement, with minor modifications, this chapter assumes complete bilateral trade liberalization. In order to estimate the dynamic impacts, it is assumed that Korea will experience an annual total factor productivity (TFP) growth of 1 per cent for ten years (10 per cent for ten years) under an FTA between the two countries.[5, 6] As the productivity gap between Korean and Japanese companies is expected to narrow by 10 per cent over the ten years that follow the implementation of the agreement, we assume that only Korea's TFP will grow in the simulation using the CGE model. As it seems rather arbitrary to presume that productivity will increase by 1 per cent under a Korea–Japan FTA, two more assumptions, of 0.5 per cent and 1.5 per cent, will be employed to implement a sensitivity test about the stability of the estimates.

The results of the analysis of the economic effects of a Korea–Japan FTA, by using a CGE model, will be categorized as follows: effects by industry, effects on the balance of trade, and changes in real GDP and welfare levels. Each of these categories will be discussed respectively.

### 10.3.1 Effects on Production Activity by Industrial Sector

Table 10.6 summarizes the effects of a Korea–Japan FTA on production activities by industrial sector in Korea. It indicates that the dynamic effects would surpass the static effects for the major Korean export industries, such as transport equipment, electronic goods and appliances, implying that these industrial sectors will expand their scales of production. Observation of the static effects of tariff elimination reveals that there would be little impact on the production of the industrial sectors, other than for apparel and leather goods.

When the two countries eliminate their tariffs, 12 out of 20 industries classified in this research will exhibit a contraction in production activities. However, the rates of production are expected to decrease by 2 per cent, or less, annually with the exception of the beverage and tobacco industries.[7] Major Korean export industries are expected to experience production declines. They are the chemicals, steel and metal goods, electronic goods and appliances, machinery, and other manufacturing industries. The industries whose levels of production are expected to grow are the primary industries and the textile, apparel, leather goods and automobile industries. It is anticipated that the apparel and leather processing industries will record the highest production increases, at 8.75 per cent and 9.56 per cent, respectively. This implies that these industries will be the biggest beneficiaries of trade liberalization under the Korea–Japan FTA.

This is due to the particularity of Korean–Japanese economic relations. In other words, Korea has followed the Japanese model for its own economic development. As a result, Korea has been competing with Japan in its major exporting industries while lagging behind Japan in the world market. It is natural that opening up markets will consequently lead to a reduction of the production activities of these industries in Korea. In addition, Korea's tariff rates for these industries have been higher than those of Japan, which indicates that Japanese firms will benefit from a bilateral elimination of tariffs due to improving price competitiveness. In contrast, the Korean industries will be in a relatively disadvantageous position. The Korean tariff rates applied to steel, automobiles, machinery and chemicals are 7 to 8 per cent (trade-weighted average tariff rates) while Japan applies much lower tariffs of only 0 to 2 per cent.

**Table 10.6**
**Effects of a Korea–Japan FTA on Production by Industry**

(% changes)

| | Static effects | Dynamic effects | Total |
|---|---|---|---|
| Agriculture | 0.15 | -0.21 | -0.06 |
| Food processing | 1.05 | 0.19 | 1.24 |
| Forestry | 0.02 | 0.15 | 0.17 |
| Fisheries | 0.24 | -0.01 | 0.23 |
| Mineral resources | -0.30 | -0.34 | -0.64 |
| Non-ferrous metals | -0.93 | 0.67 | -0.26 |
| Beverages & tobacco | -2.38 | 0.91 | -1.47 |
| Textiles | 0.69 | -3.26 | -2.57 |
| Apparel | 8.75 | -4.16 | 4.59 |
| Leather goods | 9.56 | -7.20 | 2.36 |
| Wood & pulp | -0.30 | 0.71 | 0.41 |
| Paper & printing | -0.49 | 0.13 | -0.36 |
| Chemical industry | -0.79 | 2.68 | 1.89 |
| Steel industry | -1.80 | 6.91 | 5.11 |
| Metal goods | -1.14 | 4.99 | 3.85 |
| Automobiles | 0.68 | 6.63 | 7.31 |
| Other transport equipment | -1.31 | 14.67 | 13.36 |
| Electric & electr. industry | -0.65 | 6.90 | 6.25 |
| Other equipment | -1.65 | 8.23 | 6.58 |
| Other manufacturing | -1.86 | -3.98 | -5.84 |

*Note*: Estimates are changes of quantity.

*Source*: Cheong (2001).

However, the dynamic analysis, based on the assumption of a productivity increase, leads to results contrary to those presented in the static analysis. For instance, the apparel and leather processing industries, whose production is assumed to increase according to the static analysis, are now projected to undergo a contraction of their production activities. Furthermore, it also suggests that Korea's major exporting industries, including the transport equipment, electric and electronic, and machinery industries, will experience greatly expanded levels of production.

The total effects of the FTA are calculated by totalling the static and dynamic impacts. It can be summarized that an FTA between the two countries will result in expanding production for Korea's major industries and a contraction of production for Korea's primary industries. Korea will gain most significantly in the transport equipment, machinery, electric and electronic, and steel industries with annual growth rates of 5 to 13 per cent. According to the static analysis, production levels for the primary industries are presumed to contract. The negative effects of the FTA, however, will be minimal with only a slight increase of 0.2 per cent for both forestry and fisheries production and a small decline in agricultural production.

### 10.3.2 Effects on Korea's Trade with Japan

As was the case with the analysis of the effects on Korea's production by industries, the effects on Korea's exports to Japan and the balance of trade will be divided into a static and dynamic analysis (see Table 10.7).

According to the static analysis, tariff elimination under a Korea–Japan FTA will boost Korea's exports of most items to Japan. The apparel industry will experience the biggest export growth (US$1 billion annually) followed by food processing (US$0.86 billion) and the leather goods industry (US$0.73 billion), all of which were expected to expand production on a massive scale. Meanwhile, other industries will record medium levels (less than US$0.1 billion) of export growth.

However, Japan's exports to Korea will see notable gains in all sectors. The net increase in Japan's exports to Korea will be as high as US$8.4 billion, thereby exacerbating Korea's trade deficit with Japan by US$5.4 billion. Imports of Japanese machinery, on which Korea has already been highly dependent, will grow substantially and will account for half of the estimated import growth from Japan of US$8.4 billion. In the meantime, Korea will see an improvement in its trade balance with the rest of the world of US$3.9 billion. All told, Korea's balance of trade with the world will worsen by US$1.5 billion.

There exist few, if any, similarities between the effects on the pattern of exports to Japan generated by productivity improvement in Korea's major industries, and those by tariff elimination. First of all, the share of the heavy and chemical industries in Korea's total exports to Japan will grow notably, although those of the other industries will shrink. Contrary to the estimated effects of the tariff elimination there will be a drop in exports for the apparel and leather processing industries, which were expected to account for half of the total exports to Japan.

Furthermore, productivity improvement does not seem to result in any remarkable increase in Korean exports to Japan when compared with tariff elimination. In fact, the elimination of tariffs will contribute significantly to the escalation of Korean exports to Japan by nearly US$3.1 billion. On the other hand, the export of Korean goods to Japan will grow by only US$0.2 billion when productivity improvement is preconditioned. However, Korea's trade balances with other trading partners will be augmented by US$3.4

billion (US$5.4 billion due to an increase in exports with a subsequent import growth of US$2.0 billion) when anticipating the improvement of productivity. Consequently, it can be said that most of the dynamic effects on Korean exports will be through export growth to other countries rather than to Japan. Although Korea's trade balance with Japan would deteriorate by US$0.4 billion, the US$3.4 billion increase in exports to other regions will explain the US$3 billion augmentation of Korea's trade balance in total.

**Table 10.7**
**Effects of a Korea–Japan FTA on Exports to Japan and the Balance of Trade**

(changes in US$ million)

| Industry | Static effects | | | Dynamic effects | | | Effects on overall TB |
|---|---|---|---|---|---|---|---|
| | Exports to Japan | Balance of trade (TB) with Japan | TB with the world (1) | Exports to Japan | TB with Japan | TB with the world (2) | (1+2) |
| Agriculture | 62.41 | 49.07 | -137.39 | -33.70 | -34.98 | -228.05 | -365.44 |
| Food processing | 854.61 | 764.78 | 624.62 | -96.90 | -98.21 | -207.00 | 417.62 |
| Forestry | -0.02 | -0.14 | -0.45 | -0.04 | -0.07 | -16.10 | -16.55 |
| Fishery | 30.18 | 19.02 | 7.67 | -8.03 | -8.92 | -36.51 | -28.84 |
| Mineral resources | -0.20 | -5.82 | 88.89 | -0.99 | -1.50 | -361.05 | -272.16 |
| Non-ferrous metal | 8.82 | -228.70 | -104.53 | -35.55 | -102.26 | -432.89 | -537.42 |
| Beverage/Tobacco | 53.11 | -389.29 | -232.57 | -4.35 | -13.53 | -47.33 | -279.90 |
| Textile | 73.66 | -193.25 | -359.15 | -26.62 | -18.83 | -495.24 | -854.39 |
| Apparel | 1006.95 | 961.63 | 940.03 | -170.91 | -173.93 | -536.43 | 403.60 |
| Leather goods | 732.88 | 695.41 | 535.62 | -84.37 | -84.20 | -420.55 | 115.07 |
| Wood·Pulp | -2.71 | -28.30 | -29.61 | -10.49 | -12.49 | -99.32 | -128.93 |
| Paper·printing | 0.03 | -50.15 | -62.57 | -4.93 | -13.55 | -196.87 | -259.44 |
| Chemical industry | 91.15 | -1047.62 | -469.98 | 78.86 | 39.27 | 424.36 | -45.61 |
| Steel industry | 166.49 | -880.79 | -221.01 | 136.15 | 30.29 | 60.45 | -160.57 |
| Metal goods | 0.66 | -173.18 | -125.48 | 40.19 | 38.30 | 263.99 | 138.51 |
| Automobile | 11.89 | -524.73 | -11.93 | 8.83 | 11.53 | 1093.38 | 1081.46 |
| Other transportation | 8.74 | -235.81 | -178.06 | 17.74 | 26.45 | 1267.23 | 1089.17 |
| Electric/Electronic | 48.76 | -481.66 | -307.66 | 108.96 | 100.13 | 1365.60 | 1057.94 |
| Machinery | 82.89 | -4845.12 | -1180.98 | 389.18 | -49.85 | 2055.98 | 875.00 |
| Other Manufacturing | 1.20 | -231.11 | -235.11 | -59.55 | -73.45 | -439.77 | -674.89 |
| Total | 3125.07 | -5354.34 | -1459.64 | 243.46 | -439.70 | 3013.88 | 1554.23 |

*Note*: Estimates are based on quantity changes.

*Source*: Cheong and Lee (1999).

The heavy and chemical industries are the main contributors to the improvement of the trade balance. Machinery, whose trade balance with Japan was assumed to deteriorate the most, will account for a US$2.1 billion improvement in the trade balance, as a result of the expected increase in productivity. In addition, it can be anticipated that the trade balance will be improved by more than US$1 billion in the automobile, other transport equipment, and the electric and electronic industries.

Even though the elimination of tariffs worsens Korea's trade balance with the world, the amelioration of the trade balance by the productivity improvements assumed under an FTA will surpass the deterioration of the trade balance resulting from the adverse effects of tariff elimination. As a consequence, it turns out to be beneficial for the trade balance as a whole. The right-hand column in Table 10.7 provides the impacts of a Korea–Japan FTA on Korea's overall trade balance, which is expected to grow annually by approximately US$1.6 billion.

### 10.3.3 Effects on Welfare and Real GDP

After Korea and Japan eliminate their tariff barriers, the real GDP and welfare level would decline by 0.07 per cent and 0.19 per cent respectively (see Table 10.8). Generally speaking, the elimination of tariffs raises the level of welfare by redistributing the factors of production in a more efficient way. Thus the predicted decline in the Korean welfare level can be seen as being quite exceptional.

**Table 10.8**
**Effects of a Korea–Japan FTA on Real GDP and the Level of Welfare**

| | Static effects | Dynamic effects | Total effects |
|---|---|---|---|
| Welfare level (%) | -0.19 | 11.43 | 11.24 |
| Equiv. variation (US$ billion) | -0.77 | 46.27 | 45.50 |
| Real GDP (%) | -0.07 | 2.88 | 2.81 |

*Note*: Equivalent variations are changes in the GDP equivalent to the changes of the level of welfare.

This is intimately related to the above-mentioned effects on the production levels, by industries, that tariff elimination causes. When Korea's tariff rates are higher than those of Japan, tariff elimination has the effect of diverting its factors of production from the major export industries to the primary and light industries of low value-added[8] as well as deteriorating the terms of trade, real GDP and the level of welfare.[9, 10]

However, according to the dynamic effects, Korea's welfare level and real GDP will be elevated to a large degree. This is because the advancement of productivity in the heavy and chemical industries will improve international competitiveness under an FTA between the two countries, thereby enlarging the scale of production. As a result, unlike in the tariff reduction case, Korea's factors of production will exhibit higher productivity as a whole, resulting in an increase in real GDP and an improvement in the level of welfare. If the tariffs of the two countries are completely eliminated and the productivity of Korea's major export industries is enhanced, Korea can expect a growth in real GDP of 2.81 per cent and an annual welfare growth of US$45.5 billion.

## 10.4 CONCLUSION

There was considerable progress made in the Korea–Chile FTA after the leaders of Korea and Chile declared the official launch of the negotiation for an FTA at the Auckland APEC leaders' meeting in September 1999. The two economies finished the sixth round of negotiations, and concluded the bilateral FTA in October 2002. Korea and Chile formally signed the FTA in February 2003 and, in the case of Korea, efforts now need to be taken to firmly establish a domestic FTA policy.

Korea chose Chile as its first FTA partner because its trade structure is highly complementary and it has plentiful experience in regional trading agreements. Chile chose Korea because it highly valued Korea's close linkage with neighbouring Asian countries (Chile can take advantage of Korea's trade linkages for widening its market access to other Asian countries), as well as Korea's growth potential through performing strong reforms in several sectors including the financial sector.

The Korean government is currently pursuing the establishment of FTAs with smaller strategic countries as a precursor to establishing trade agreements with its larger trade partners. This has been in response to the continued trend towards regional blocs, and the fact that the recent financial crisis has opened Korea's eyes to the necessity of opening its economy.

In addition to the Korea–Chile FTA, Korea looked into the economic feasibility of an FTA with Japan in 1999 and came up with a positive prognosis. Korea's FTA with Japan is expected to yield substantial benefits from strengthening strategic alliances between firms in the two countries. A strategic alliance with Japan is especially critical, not only because of Japan's vast potential for providing investment capital but also because the combination of Japan's advanced technology with Korea's production capability will substantially enhance the competitiveness of domestic businesses. Moreover, an effective Korea–Japan partnership will mitigate Korea's trade imbalance with Japan.

Recently, Korea has been undertaking joint studies with New Zealand, Thailand and Singapore to look into the viability and feasibility of pursuing individual FTAs with each of these economies. These studies will provide the basis for an expansion of Korea's policy towards FTAs.

## NOTES

1 Preferential trading blocs that must report their arrangements to GATT/WTO under GATT XXIV, GATS V, and the Enabling Clause.

2 This model, however, is not able to reflect the effects of economies of scale as it is based on constant returns to scale. Moreover, it has the limitation of disregarding most of the dynamic effects such as the effect of productivity enhancement due to the intensified competition as well as the effects of investment expansion and labour growth

3 Some of this section is taken from Cheong (2001).

4 For example, NAFTA classified most products into four categories for trade liberalization, whose tariffs were supposed to be eliminated completely. Though extremely sensitive items were allowed to be liberalized within 15 years, most of them were agricultural products such as dairy products, poultry and sugar, and the share of these items out of the total number of products is less than 1 per cent.

5 The annual growth rate of 1 per cent consists of a 0.85 per cent growth in productivity, produced by enlarged investment, and an additional 0.15 per cent of growth caused by the promotion of competition. Under most FTAs, preferential rules of origin are established in order to apply preferential treatment to originating goods, thereby inducing an increase in intra-regional investment. Considering the costs of labour, rental costs for land and so on, it is likely that Japanese investment in Korea will dominate the foreign direct investment between the two countries. As there exists no previous study on the effects of competition promotion, this research presumes the rate of 0.15 per cent for the sake of convenience. A sensitivity test will be performed in order to test the stability of estimates, using different assumptions of productivity growth. Refer to KIEP (2000) for the estimates of Korea's TFP growth under a Korea–Japan FTA.

6. Although TFP will increase in most industries, this research presumes that the productivity improvement is limited to the heavy and chemical industries, including chemicals, steel, automobiles, other transport equipment, and the electric and electronic industries, whose productivities have increased most significantly over the last few decades.

7. The base year applied for these estimates is the time when trade liberalization is implemented fully and the internal reorganization of institutions for the FTA is completed. It is proper to think that the base

year suggested in this research is ten years after the agreement comes into force, since trade liberalization for most items is generally accomplished within ten years with the exception of highly sensitive items. This base year is applied to all the estimates provided in this chapter.

8. Korean economists studied the variations of factor productivity based on the outputs by sector, indicating that the heavy and chemical industries showed noticeable growth in the productivity of production factors while lower marks were recorded for resource (non-ferrous metal) and labour intensive industries (light industries embracing beverages, textiles, apparel, leather processing, wood and wood products, and other manufacturing). For example, Nam's study (1999) (using production data between 1971 and 1996) came up with similar results, suggesting low capital and labour efficiency in the agriculture, food and beverages, textiles, apparel, leather processing, wood and furniture industries, and a high rate of efficiency for the metals, transport equipment, and electric and electronic industries.

**Korea's Trend in the Productivity of Capital, Labour and TFP in the Manufacturing Sectors (1971–96)**

(% changes)

| Sector | K-productivity growth rates | L-productivity growth rates | Total factor productivity growth rates |
|---|---|---|---|
| Food, beverage and tobacco | -0.48 | 9.69 | -0.64 |
| Textiles and apparel | 2.28 | 10.72 | 2.45 |
| Wood and furniture | -2.04 | 7.29 | -1.09 |
| Paper and its products | 0.33 | 10.77 | 2.58 |
| Chemicals and plastics | 0.25 | 10.64 | 1.21 |
| Basic metals | 2.91 | 13.51 | 3.23 |
| Metal products and machinery | 5.75 | 16.09 | 5.18 |
| Electronic and electric products | 7.76 | 19.21 | 7.24 |
| Transportation equipment | 6.04 | 16.12 | 5.02 |

*Source*: Nam (1999).

9. Apart from the deterioration in the terms of trade and the degraded efficiency of production factors, the level of welfare is affected by the loss of governmental revenue due to the elimination of tariffs.

10. The terms of trade deteriorate because Korean tariff rates are higher than those of Japan, and Korea shows a preference for Japanese goods.

## REFERENCES

Cha, Dong-Se, Kwang-Suk. Kim and Dwight H. Perkins (1997), *The Korean Economy 1945–1995:Performance and Vision for the 21st Century*, Seoul: Korea Development Institute (in Korean).

Cheong, Inkyo (1995), *The Economic Effects of Asia–Pacific Economic Cooperation (APEC) and Asia-Based Free Trade Area (AF-11): A Computational General Equilibrium Approach*, PhD dissertation. Michigan State University.

Cheong, Inkyo (2001), *Economic Effects of a Korea-Japan FTA and Policy Implications*, Korea Institute for International Economic Policy (KIEP) Policy Analysis, Seoul: KIEP.

Cheong, Inkyo and Kyunghee Lee (1999), *Economic Effects of a Korea–Chile FTA and Policy Implications.* KIEP Policy Analysis. Seoul: KIEP.

Eur, Myunggeun, Jaeok Lee and Yunkook Choe (1999), *Korea–Chile FTA and Policy for Agriculture*, Internal Report, Seoul: Korea Rural Economic Institute (in Korean).

IMF (1997), *Direction of Trade Statistics Yearbook.* IMF Statistics Department, Washington DC

KIEP (2000) 'Toward a Korea–Japan FTA: Assessment and Prospects', Presented at an international seminar *Towards Closer Korea-Japan Economic Relations: Proposal for Formulating a 21th Century Partnership*, Seoul.

Kim, Wonho (1996), *New Economic Order in Latin America and Korea's Policy orientation for Economic Cooperation,* Seoul: KIEP (in Korean).

Korea's National Statistical Office (1999), *Quarterly Bulletin of International Statistics*, Seoul (in Korean).

Nam, SangYul (1999), 'Total Factor Productivity Growth in Korean Industry and Its Relationship with Export Growth', *KIEP Working Paper*.

OECD (1999) *Financial Market Trends*, Paris.

WTO (1995) *Regionalism and the World Trading System*, Geneva.

# 11. A Development Strategy for the North Korean Economy

**Dongho Jo**

## 11.1 INTRODUCTION

North Korea has made bold changes in its economic policies since the latter half of 2002. As of 1 July 2002, North Korea introduced new measures to improve economic management such as several tenfold increases in price and wage levels, devaluation of the North Korean won, and a reduction of government subsidies.[1] Later, in October, North Korea designated Sinuiju, a north-western border city close to China, as a Special Administrative Region in a scheme to attract foreign investment. The law on the Sinuiju Special Administrative Region pertains to more independent legislative, administrative and judicial rights than that of previous special economic zones at Rajin and Sonbong. Again, in November, North Korea established economic and tourist zones in Kaesong and the Mt Kumkang area, respectively. Between late October and early November, an 18-member North Korean economic delegation, headed by the chairman of the State Planning Commission, visited the South for an inspection tour of South Korean major industrial sites, and displayed great interest in learning about South Korea's economic development strategy in the past.

Such unexpected changes have caused serious disputes on whether the North's new economic measures reflect a market-oriented transition or are merely an attempt to normalize its currently paralyzed planned economic system. Some experts even argue that the North has already stepped into the early stage of Chinese-style economic reform and opening.

It is no doubt crucial to understand properly North Korea's underlying intention for its recent economic changes, because it provides a basis for guiding North Korean policy in the right direction. At this moment, however, the most important issue is whether the North Korean economy can revive by introducing such economic policies. In fact, transformation of the economic system itself is probably of trivial interest for the North Korean leaders. Rather, their current focus is on how to resolve economic difficulties and to make an underdeveloped economy a developing one.

Not only is North Korea's economic development important for the North, but it also has significant implications for the South in order to improve inter-Korean economic relations and to secure peace on the Korean peninsula. North Korea's political stability cannot be expected without economic development, and the effect of an unstable North Korean regime will ripple to the entire Korean peninsula and indeed to all of North-East Asia. The economic development of North Korea is also a precondition for expanding inter-Korean economic cooperation. Due to its economic difficulties the North lacks the financial ability to buy more goods from the South, and the South can only purchase limited items from the North. This holds for investment as well. The economic difficulties hinder North Korea from allocating enough resources to improve its industrial infrastructure, hence leaving the investment environment extremely poor. As a natural result, South Korean firms have little interest in the North.

Thus, revitalization of the North Korean economy becomes a prerequisite for survival of the North Korean regime, improvement of inter-Korean economic relations, and stability in the North-East Asian region. This leads to two key questions: are the new economic measures being pursued by North Korea likely to succeed in boosting its economy, and, if not, what would be the best strategy to revitalize the North Korean economy?

This chapter intends to answer such questions. Section 2 briefly reviews the current state of the North Korean economy. Section 3 evaluates the new economic measures being implemented in North Korea, while focusing on the likelihood of their success. Based on the discussion in section 3, section 4 suggests a development strategy for the North Korean economy.

## 11.2 CURRENT ECONOMIC SITUATION

### 11.2.1 The Macroeconomic Situation

North Korea experienced a serious economic crisis in the 1990s. People suffered from a great shortage of food and daily necessities, and the operation rates of most factories plunged below 30 per cent due to the lack of electricity and raw materials.[2] As the central distribution system was nearly paralyzed, unofficial economic activities spread widely. According to a recent study, 27.1 per cent of the North Korean GDP is comprised of a market economy.[3]

After having shown negative growth for nine consecutive years since 1990, however, the North Korean economy shifted to positive growth. The Bank of Korea estimates that North Korea achieved economic growth of 6.2 per cent, 1.3 per cent and 3.7 per cent in 1999, 2000 and 2001, respectively (see Table 11.1).[4]

However, economic difficulties still continue. For example, the size of the

North Korean GDP in 2001 is estimated to remain at only 78 per cent of that of 1989. There is a wide gap in economic power between North and South Korea, and this has been on an increasing trend. In 2001, North Korea's GNI and per capita GNI were only 3.7 per cent and 7.9 per cent of those of South Korea, respectively. Although North Korea's foreign trade had shown signs of recovery in recent years, the trade volume in 2001 had not reached even half the level of that in 1990 (see Table 11.1).

Furthermore, recent economic recovery is evaluated to be fragile since it has resulted from external factors, not from internal factors such as an increase in inputs or production efficiency. In fact, foreign aid and favourable weather conditions basically contributed to the positive economic growth in recent years, so that the North Korean economy has yet to provide a momentum for economic growth.

The international community, as well as South Korea, has provided a considerable amount of humanitarian aid to North Korea since the mid-1990s. As shown in Table 11.2, the amount of foreign aid in 1999 was about US$400 million, which was equivalent to 78.2 per cent of North Korea's total export volume. Although foreign aid in 2000 decreased by about US$100 million it increased sharply again in 2001, reaching about US$500 million. Taking into account that the net gain from exports is just a small fraction of total export volume, because various inputs are required in the production process, we can easily see how much supportive foreign aid there has been for the North Korean economy. However, foreign aid cannot continue indefinitely, and North Korea's nuclear weapons development programme may lead to a sharp retrenchment in the amount of foreign aid.[5]

**Table 11.1**
**Major Economic Indicators of North Korea**

| Year | Nominal GNI (US$ billion) | Per Capita GNI (US$) | GDP Growth Rate (%) | Exports (US$ billion) | Imports (US$ billion) |
|---|---|---|---|---|---|
| 1990 | 23.1 | 1142 | -3.7 | 1.96 | 2.76 |
| 1991 | 22.9 | 1115 | -3.5 | 1.01 | 1.71 |
| 1992 | 21.1 | 1013 | -6.0 | 1.03 | 1.64 |
| 1993 | 20.5 | 969 | -4.2 | 1.02 | 1.62 |
| 1994 | 21.2 | 992 | -2.1 | 0.84 | 1.27 |
| 1995 | 22.3 | 1034 | -4.1 | 0.74 | 1.31 |
| 1996 | 21.4 | 989 | -3.6 | 0.73 | 1.25 |
| 1997 | 17.7 | 811 | -6.3 | 0.91 | 1.27 |
| 1998 | 12.6 | 573 | -1.1 | 0.56 | 0.88 |
| 1999 | 15.8 | 714 | 6.2 | 0.52 | 0.96 |
| 2000 | 16.8 | 757 | 1.3 | 0.56 | 1.41 |
| 2001 | 15.7 | 706 | 3.7 | 0.65 | 1.62 |

*Source*: Bank of Korea (2002).

Increased agricultural production also contributed greatly to the economic upturn, especially in 1999 and 2001, realizing growth rates of 9.2 per cent and 6.8 per cent, respectively. Table 11.3 implies that agriculture has been the most important sector for the recent positive growth. The growth rates of the service sector, which ranks highest in North Korea's industrial structure, have always been lower than the overall economic growth rates. Even though the construction sector had shown the largest growth rates its impact on economic growth was limited, due to its small share in the industrial structure. A similar argument can be applied to the mining sector. Thus, we can conclude that the agricultural sector, the second-largest but only a little smaller than the service sector, has been the main contributor to recovery in recent years.

**Table 11.2**
**Foreign Aid and Its Significance to the North Korean Economy**

(US$ million, %)

| Year | South Korea | | | International | Total | NK's | Ratio |
|---|---|---|---|---|---|---|---|
| | Gov't | Private | Total (A) | (B) | (A+B=C) | Exports (D) | (C/D) |
| 1999 | 28.25 | 18.63 | 46.88 | 359.88 | 406.76 | 520 | 78.2 |
| 2000 | 78.63 | 35.13 | 113.76 | 181.77 | 295.53 | 560 | 52.8 |
| 2001 | 70.45 | 64.94 | 135.39 | 357.25 | 492.64 | 650 | 75.8 |

*Source*: Ministry of Unification (2003).

**Table 11.3**
**Growth Rates by Industrial Sector in North Korea**

(%)

| | | 1999 | 2000 | 2001 |
|---|---|---|---|---|
| Agriculture | Growth rate | 9.2 | -1.9 | 6.8 |
| | Share | 31.4 | 30.4 | 30.4 |
| Mining | Growth rate | 14.1 | 5.8 | 4.8 |
| | Share | 7.3 | 7.7 | 8.0 |
| Manufacturing | Growth rate | 8.5 | 0.9 | 3.5 |
| | Share | 18.3 | 17.7 | 18.1 |
| Electricity, Gas, Water | Growth rate | 6.8 | 3.0 | 3.6 |
| | Share | 4.5 | 4.8 | 4.8 |
| Construction | Growth rate | 24.3 | 13.6 | 7.0 |
| | Share | 6.1 | 6.9 | 7.0 |
| Services | Growth rate | -1.9 | 1.2 | -0.3 |
| | Share | 32.4 | 32.5 | 31.8 |
| Economic growth rate | | 6.2 | 1.3 | 3.7 |

*Source*: Bank of Korea (2002).

However, the recent increase in agricultural production has been mostly bolstered by favourable weather conditions during the ripening season. Thus, the country cannot rely on growth in the agricultural sector to be the locomotive of economic growth in the future.

### 11.2.2 Causes of the stagnation of the North Korean economy

**Direct cause: the breakdown of economic relations with 'comrade' countries and natural disasters**

The economic crisis of North Korea began with the breakdown of external economic relations, especially with the former USSR and China. The shares of these two countries in North Korea's export and import volumes in 1990 were 64 per cent and 71 per cent, respectively.[6] Moreover, they charged so-called 'comrade prices' on their exports to North Korea, which were much lower than international prices. In the case of crude oil imports, for instance, China charged US$58 per ton in 1990. However, it increased to US$126 per ton in 1991 as China demanded international prices.[7]

The sudden collapse of the former USSR and the transition to a market economy by China, with the need for hard currencies for trade, caused a sharp reduction in imports of raw materials and energy that are indispensable for industrial production. This resulted in a contraction of overall economic activity. In addition, the reduction of export markets decreased the acquisition of foreign exchange necessary to import necessary materials, thus aggravating economic difficulties. The collapse of the former USSR was especially critical to the North Korean economy. The former USSR took 56.4 per cent of North Korea's exports in 1990, and provided 57.1 per cent of its imports. However, the trade with the former USSR in 1991 decreased by nearly 90 per cent from 1990.

The North Korean economy seemed to escape from the shock caused by the collapse of external economic relations since 1993. Unfortunately, however, natural disasters such as floods and drought hit the North Korean economy. Most importantly, summer floods in 1995 and 1996 crashed the efforts for revitalization, and plunged the North Korean economy into deep stagnation.

**Fundamental cause: the delay of economic reform**

The fundamental cause for the current economic crisis of North Korea stems from the structural problems of the socialist planned economic system. A comparison of the economic growth of North Korea with that of the former socialist countries in Eastern Europe makes this point clear. The economic growth rates of North Korea and those countries display similar patterns (see Figure 11.1).

Socialist countries, including North Korea, adopted an extensive economic growth strategy, which strives for economic growth by mobilizing all available resources within the economy. Since there are many untapped resources when the economy is underdeveloped, an extensive economic growth strategy can be effective during the initial stages of economic development. As the economy reaches a state of full employment, however, the strategy begins to reveal its limitations. Furthermore, the accumulation of structural problems in the planned economic system becomes an obstacle to continue further economic growth. The centrally determined economic plan limits the scope of free decision-making of economic agents. The resource distribution is distorted due to non-existent market prices. The lack of an incentive system decreases the willingness to work hard or improve productivity. Therefore, the economic growth rates began to decline in the 1970s in all of the socialist countries, and North Korea was no exception.

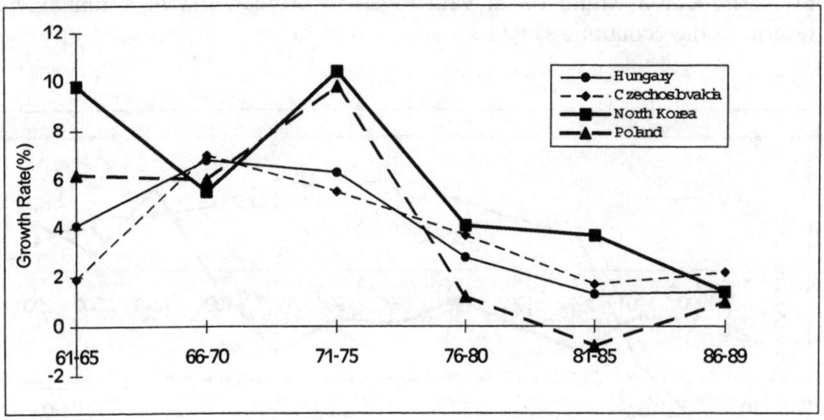


*Figure 11.1 Economic Growth Rates of North Korea and the Former Socialist Countries in Eastern Europe (before 1990)*

Around 1990, the Eastern European countries launched a programme for a transition of their economic systems. Although the speed and details of the programme differed, depending on the political and economic situation of each country, the core of the economic transition was to reform the economic system toward a market-based one. By its nature, economic reform brings about a great shock to the economy. As a result, the Eastern European countries experienced a serious depression in the early years of transition, as was seen by the sharp reduction in production and increase in unemployment. Such a transitional shock was overcome after 3–4 years, and the positive effects of economic reform began to be realized. As a result, economic growth rates changed from negative to positive from 1993 to 1994 (see

Figure 11.2). If there had not been economic reform, these economies might have avoided serious depression in the short run. However, the eventual collapse of the economy would be inevitable in the long run, since the socialist planned economic system would only deepen the structural problems.

The same logic can be applied to North Korea. In fact, the need for economic reform is greater in North Korea, since the structural problems of the planned economic system were compounded by certain characteristics peculiar to the North Korean economy. For example, the North Korean economy has been in a much worse condition than other socialist countries, by maintaining a closed economic management system based on a principle of self-reliance, emphasizing ideology and loyalty without introducing a material incentive system, and spending an excessive amount on military expenditure. Thus, any efforts made to overcome the current economic crisis of North Korea would be in vain unless coordinated with a fundamental reform of the economic system.

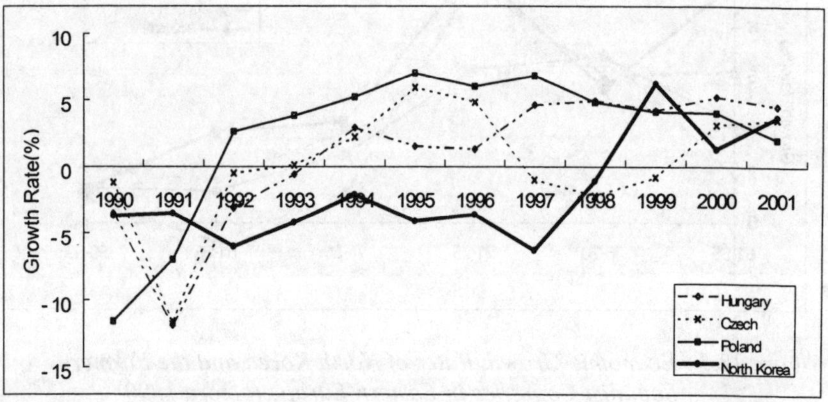


*Figure 11.2 Economic Growth Rates of North Korea and the Former Socialist Countries in Eastern Europe (after 1990)*

## 11.3 THE POLICY REACTION OF NORTH KOREA

### 11.3.1 The Policy Reaction Before 2000

The basic principle of North Korea's national economic management is to build an absolutely self-reliant economy. As stated by Kim Il Sung, in one of his many national addresses, 'North Korea will succeed in rehabilitation by our efforts and establishment of a self-reliant national economy.' [8] According to the North Korean authorities, the goal of the country's economic policy is to supply the necessary industrial and technical means to satisfy domestic demand for material goods.[9] In the eyes of the ruling elites, this can only be done by building a self-reliant autarchic economy.

Even in the New Constitution of North Korea announced on 6 September 1998, the basic idea remains the same. Article 19, which is the first article of the economic section, declares that North Korea is based on a self-reliant national economic system. Thus, the North Korean government has attempted to restrict international trade to those goods and materials it produces insufficiently or cannot produce at all. As a result, the ratio of North Korea's international trade volume to its GNP in 2001 was only 14.4 per cent in contrast to 69.2 per cent for South Korea. The economic advantages of an international division of labour have been disregarded by the North Korean government. Indeed, pursuit of a self-reliant economy, and closed economic management, has continued to seriously impede economic growth and technological progress.

In the early 1980s North Korea began to recognize the limitations of its closed economy, which merely mobilizes domestic resources for economic growth. Therefore, North Korea started to introduce new policy measures to expand international trade and cooperation. In fact, North Korea set the expansion of international trade as one of its major policy goals in the 1980s, and introduced the Joint Venture Law in 1984 to attract severely needed foreign capital. The success of the Joint Venture Law, however, was limited because it was not based on a solid and clear determination for opening and reforming the economy. In addition, the poor economic environment such as political inflexibility, lack of a viable financial system, underdeveloped infrastructure and lack of skilled workers, made foreign businessmen shy away from North Korea.[10]

In the 1990s, North Korea once again intensified its efforts to expand trade and foreign direct investment. With the collapse of North Korea's foreign economic relations caused by the demise of the former USSR and the transition to a market economy by China, the country could not help but look for new economic partners among Western countries. In 1992, North Korea reorganized institutions for external economic relations and introduced the 'New Trade System' in order to promote trade.[11] In December 1993, North Korea also declared that the policy of giving top priority to trade would be pursued for the following three years. However, with similar reasons to the failure in the 1980s, such efforts could not produce any successful results.[12]

In order to induce foreign direct investment, North Korea established the Rajin-Sonbong Free Economic and Trade Zone in December 1991.[13] The establishment of the zone surprised foreign observers since it was the first attempt to introduce a market-oriented economic system into North Korea, even though it was limited only to the zone. The efforts of the North Korean government to vitalize the zone were enormous. North Korea had sent several delegations to Western countries, including the United States, in order to carry on its propaganda on a large scale. In June 1997, North Korea introduced an independent cost accounting system and a floating exchange rate system in the zone, and entry visas were not required for foreign investors.

In spite of such efforts it was destined to fail, basically due to the same reasons discussed above. Though figures which show the volume of investment attracted have not been published since 1999, the total value of investment contracts in the Rajin-Sonbong Economic and Trade Zone was known to be only US$520 million as of July 2000.[14] According to data provided by the UNDP Tumen Secretariat, however, the value of investment that had actually been implemented was much less, and was reported to be only US$88 million by the end of 2001. This result was far from North Korea's original expectation and, as shown in Table 11.4, was extremely disappointing compared to the relative success of competing areas to North Korea such as Yanbian of China and Primorsky of Russia.

### 11.3.2 The Recent Policy Reaction: New Economic Measures in July 2002

North Korea's economic difficulties were exacerbated in the 1990s. Even official North Korean documents name the 1990s a period of 'Parade of Ordeal,' and most North Koreans recall 'the living standard in the 1980s were better than that in the 1990s, and the 1970s than the 1980s.'[15] Under these circumstances, the North Korean government could not help but approve tacit expansion of unofficial, and even illegal, economic activities. It was nearly impossible to prepare any long-term economic plans after 1994, in North Korea's 'planned' economy.

**Table 11.4**
**Foreign Direct Investment Attracted to the Tumen River Area (actually implemented investment)**

(US$ million)

| | 1985–93 | 1994 | 1995 | 1996 | 1997 | 1998 | 1999 | 2000 | 2001 | Total |
|---|---|---|---|---|---|---|---|---|---|---|
| Rajin-Sonbong | 1 | 1 | 4 | 31 | 26 | 25 | - | - | - | 88 |
| Yanbian | 42 | 61 | 78 | 134 | 95 | 47 | 33 | 29 | 32 | 551 |
| Primorsky | 141 | 2 | 53 | 97 | 95 | 56 | 54 | 78 | 66 | 642 |

*Source*: UNDP Tumen Secretariat.

With signals of economic recovery, to some extent, the North Korean government had begun to normalize economic management. Otherwise, unofficial economic activities that run by their nature on the principle of the market system would prevail over the entire economy, which may lead to collapse of the socialist planned economic system and eventually of the North Korean regime itself.

**Contents**

North Korea introduced new economic measures as of 1 July 2002. The new economic measures include increasing price and wage levels, adjusting the exchange rate to more reasonable levels, extending freedom of decision-making by production units and providing higher work incentives. The information on these measures is limited and some are even contradictory, since the North Korean government has yet to officially announce their new policy measures. The following is a brief summary of the economic adjustments reported by the media:[16]

- Commodity prices:
  Rice: 0.08 North Korean won/kg → 44 North Korean won/kg
  Subway fare: 0.1 North Korean won/person → 2 North Korean won/person
- Wages:
  110 North Korean won/worker in manufacturing → 2000 North Korean won/worker in manufacturing
- Exchange rate adjustment:
  2.15 North Korean won/US$ → 150 North Korean won/US$
- Increase in managerial autonomy and work incentives
- Workers' wages may change according to the profit gain of factories or farms.

Although wages have increased around twentyfold, consumer prices seem to have surged even more. Additionally, the exchange rate has adjusted upward to near black market levels. Managerial autonomy from the central authority has been improved in factories and other enterprises. Also, work incentives have increased by adjusting the allotted share according to the production results of factories, enterprises and workers. However, though some commodities may have been removed from the rationing list, the basic framework of the public distribution system appears to remain the same.

**Background**

The top priority of the North Korean government is to maintain firmly its communist regime. In order to achieve this goal, stability in all sectors of the country is a fundamental condition. North Korea asserts that, since it has already established political and social stability, it only needs to secure economic stability to maintain its regime. Therefore, North Korea must now seek out methods that can secure economic stability and prepare a basis for sustainable growth. Economic stability can be gained from economic growth, which cannot be obtained without an increase in production factors such as capital, labour and technological progress. This basic principle holds for all economies, regardless of its system (be it a centrally planned or a free market economy).

Capital is the most urgent and fundamental factor required to boost North Korea's economic growth. Capital is an essential element for modernizing North Korea's deteriorated production facilities, and providing energy and adequate raw materials to promote economic growth. Unfortunately, due to the serious economic conditions, North Korea cannot self-supply massive amounts of capital. It can only seek out foreign capital. Normalization of relations with the United States, Japan and South Korea is a prerequisite to induce foreign capital, for the absence of a pacific relationship will make any large-scale investment from the outside world into North Korea hard to anticipate. However, normalization of relations with those countries cannot be expected in the near future.

The situation is similar for labour. Since all available manpower has already been put into the workplace, scope for recruiting a new labour force is extremely limited. Furthermore, even if the labour force were to be increased, it would be unlikely to enhance economic activity due to an insufficient capital supply.

Under these circumstances technological progress has been the sole method for North Korea to self-generate economic growth, because it can create more output even with the same amount of capital and labour. This explains why North Korea has continuously emphasized technological progress in recent years (for example 'new thinking'). However, efforts to increase production efficiency through technological progress alone have not displayed satisfactory results for economic growth under the current North Korean economy. For instance, even if a new production idea is generated through 'new thinking', there are clear limitations in improving production efficiency in their decaying factories without the modernization of production facilities.

**Purpose**

Based on the assessment above we conclude that North Korea is now at a stage to efficiently mobilize all available capital and labour within the economy, while simultaneously continuing to promote technological progress and welcome foreign investment. The difficult economic situation in the North has resulted in the development of an unofficial market that coexists with the official one. Recently, this unofficial sector has been expanding significantly. In order for the North Korean economy to recover, capital and labour that has moved into the unofficial sector must be absorbed back into the official channel.

Thus, the basic purpose of the new economic measures is to escape from the economic difficulties, and to seek economic growth by mobilizing more capital and labour resources circulating in the unofficial sector to the official one. The increased commodity prices and exchange rate will help absorb capital and labour scattered in the unofficial sector. Since official commodity prices have been adjusted similarly to unofficial commodity prices, there will be less of an incentive for these resources to stay in the unofficial market. Price increases will also lead to increased tax revenues, and thus contribute to the government's budget to pay higher wages for workers.

In the past, low wages reduced workers' incentives to produce for the official market and, rather, steered them to participate in the unofficial market. Therefore new upwardly adjusted wages for workers can provide higher work incentives. In addition, workers will no longer be evaluated by how long they have worked, but by how much they have produced. Also, wages will be allocated according to the profit of the factory or enterprise. This will boost work incentives of the workers by increasing their work efficiency, which will consequently increase production supply and normalize the official sector. Thus, this is another form of the labour mobilization movement in the sense that it is designed to extract maximum effort from workers within the same amount of working hours, while the past labour mobilization movement mainly focused on expanding working hours.

In analyzing the new economic measures it is clear that the ultimate intention of such efforts is to normalize the planned economic system, which has been considerably paralyzed by allowing the unofficial sector to expand tremendously. The new economic adjustments have been implemented to mobilize capital and labour resources from the unofficial sector to the official one. The new economic measures are a price realization, not price liberalization. Price and quantity are still controlled by the government, not by the law of supply and demand. Thus, it is still too early to conclude that these measures are a great step toward a market-oriented economic system, for they are only 'improvements within the centrally planned system.'

**Future prospects**

Whether the new economic measures can completely rescue the plunging North Korean economy is still questionable, even if there is still a faint possibility of development to some extent in the short - run since the measures will contribute to some economic progress by stimulating the official sector, hence further increasing production.

However, due to the limitations on the size of capital stock that can be mobilized within the economy, the new economic measures are evaluated as insufficient for preparing a firm basis for sustainable growth. In recognition of this, North Korea is likely to reallocate its capital from inefficient sectors to more efficient ones in order to have the same effect as obtaining new capital. Capital reallocation is expected to be conducted in the form of priority changes in resource allocation, and in the merging and acquisition of factories and enterprises. Nevertheless it should only have a limited effect on the economy.

Without comprehensive reform history teaches North Korea's planned economic system will inevitably collapse in the long run due to unsustainable economic development, as it has been proven to be the case in other socialist countries. This implies that the North Korean economy will be required to undertake comprehensive reform sooner or later in order to survive.

Thus we can conclude that the North Korean economy cannot pursue economic growth without a massive inflow of capital from abroad. Furthermore, economic reform toward a market-oriented system should be a prerequisite for further considerable and sustainable growth.

## 11.4 A DEVELOPMENT STRATEGY FOR THE NORTH KOREAN ECONOMY

As discussed above the North Korean economy is in acute need of foreign capital, and in fact North Korea has made efforts to attract foreign investment. So far, however, the results have been disappointing, because of limited economic exposure and a poor investment environment to attract foreign capital and investors. In addition, comprehensive economic reform has not yet begun, although the reform is a prerequisite for inviting foreign capital and efficiently utilizing capital invested in North Korea.

In this sense, many observers have suggested that North Korea should commence nationwide economic opening and active economic reform, as in China and Vietnam. However, we do not believe that the North Korean leaders are ignorant of the need for economic opening and reform. Rather, it is very likely that they clearly understand this point and know the required factors to develop their economy. However, this suggestion is simply not viable because of fears of being absorbed by the South Korean economy as an outcome of economic opening and reform.

Here exists a fundamental difference between the case of North Korea and the cases of China and Vietnam. Economic opening and reform are inevitably followed by some negative effects on the traditional political system, and the worst scenario could be a collapse of the regime. For example, Vietnam would still exist, since there is not another Vietnam even in the worst scenario. This holds for the Chinese case as well. Considering the size of economic power and population, it is unimaginable for China to be absorbed by Taiwan. Unfortunately, however, North Korea's southern counterpart pertains much stronger power, both economically and politically. This explains why North Korea has been so reluctant to actively launch any economic opening and reform policies.

Therefore we need to make policy suggestions that reflect the current political situation and are realistically plausible for North Korea to accept. In other words, the suggestions should be acceptable to the leaders of North

Korea. Thus the approach must not be 'normative' (that is, 'should do in this way'), but 'positive' (that is, 'is effective given a situation') from a third-party perspective. A summary of the development strategy is contained in Table 11.5.

### 11.4.1 The Vision

The vision of the development strategy is to build 'an economically powerful nation'. This is consistent with the national slogan of Chairman Kim Jong Il's era of focus on economic development: 'Building a Powerful Socialist Nation'. This slogan is based on the recognition that North Korea can maintain its regime if it is able to secure economic stability, because North Korean leaders believe political and social stability is already ensured. In fact, solving economic difficulties is the most urgent task for North Korea. Thus the vision proposed is considered as viable.

**Table 11.5**
**The Development Strategy of the North Korean Economy**

| | |
|---|---|
| The vision | To build an economically powerful nation |
| The goals | To improve the people's living condition<br>To establish a foundation for growth<br>- to sustain an annual growth rate of 7 percent and<br>- to reach a per capita income of US$1000 |
| The strategy | New Planned Economy for the 21st century<br>- to allow a market economy in the islands and<br>- to uphold the plan mechanism in the mainland |
| The preconditions | Improved foreign relations<br>Efficient and reliable leadership |
| The six major tasks | Increase in food supply<br>Security of consumer products supply<br>Improvement of human capital<br>Enhancement of production technology<br>Enlargement of infrastructure<br>Fortification of the strategic industries |

*Source*: Author

### 11.4.2 The Goals

To realize this vision, the goals are set to 'improve people's living conditions, and establish a foundation for growth' Considering the devastating current living conditions, the improvement of such conditions should be given the highest priority. In addition, considerable support and active participation of the people can be obtained only when living conditions in their daily lives are enhanced. Also, and equally important for sustainable growth, is the establishment of a solid foundation for growth. During the 1990s the production foundation had crumbled remarkably. Thus, without provision of a firm foundation for growth the North Korean economy cannot achieve economic progress, and the economy is very likely to return to stagnation, even from trivial shocks, even though it is able to realize growth in the short run.

More specifically, the goals are to sustain an annual growth rate of 7.0 per cent and to reach a per capita income of US$1,000 within five years. Considering the cases of South Korea as well as China and Vietnam, these goals are not implausible. During the first and the second five-year economic plans in South Korea, back in the 1960s and 1970s, annual growth rates were set at 7.1 per cent and 7.0 per cent, respectively. Similarly, in the early periods of the economic reform in China and Vietnam, from 1979 to 1983 and from 1987 to 1991, respectively, the annual growth rates were 7.6 per cent for China and 5.3 per cent for Vietnam.

### 11.4.3 The Strategy

In order to successfully achieve these goals, we propose a strategy called the 'New Planned Economy for the Twenty-First Century' as a model for North Korean economic development. The main tool for this development strategy is to allow a market economy to flourish in a few special economic zones ('islands'), while simultaneously upholding the planning mechanism in the remaining areas ('mainland'). The islands will serve as a window to the outside world and attract foreign direct investment. This method, in principle, is different from the case of China where a market-based economic system has been gradually expanded from a few special economic zones to the entire economy. Therefore, the development strategy proposed here is not to encourage the collapse of North Korea's socialist planned economy but rather to fortify it, though in the process North Korea may need to apply several elements of a market economy in segregated special economic zones. Considering the small size of the North Korean economy, such a moderate change could bring significant changes.

**Basic direction**

A substantial amount of capital is needed to pursue the goals, but the North Korean economy is not capable of mobilizing such an amount of capital internally. Thus preparing an environment to attract foreign capital is the very core of the development strategy. However, North Korea is in a situation in which it cannot open the entire economy to the world due to political reasons, and it lacks the ability to handle such a wide opening. Furthermore, foreign investors are not currently interested in investing in North Korea, even if North Korea fully opened its economy.

Thus it is desirable to establish a few special economic zones to invite in foreign direct investment, while disconnecting these islands from the mainland. In the past North Korea put up a 'mosquito net' on the special economic zones, in order to allow in only capital, while blocking out all information about the outside capitalist world. However, such a policy cannot succeed in attracting foreign capital. Hence North Korea must now put up a 'mosquito net' between the islands and the mainland, not on the islands, and introduce a full-scale market economy into the islands. The islands must be utilized not only as a window to attract foreign capital, but also as a place to learn advanced technologies and management skills from the developed countries.

On the other hand the planned economic system is maintained in the mainland, while increasing managerial autonomy and work incentives as introduced by the new economic measures in July 2002. The mainland must be able to acquire the urgently needed foreign exchange by promoting exports, since it will take some time to vitalize foreign direct investment in the islands. The mainland functions also as a base for production that supports the islands by supplying raw materials and consumption goods. Several footholds for exports should be built eventually in the mainland based upon the capital and technologies acquired in the islands.

**The development strategies for the islands**

Without the bold introduction of a market economy, the islands are hardly expected to succeed as proven in the case of Rajin-Sonbong Economic and Trade Zone. Thus, North Korea should allow direct employment[17] and free dismissal, independent rights of determining and adjusting wage levels according to the quality of workers, free remittance, substantial reduction and exemption of taxes, adoption of foreign civilization and so on. In other words, the islands must become 'totally capitalist' with great attractiveness. In particular, North Korea should recognize, since it holds a comparative advantage in labour, low enough wage levels can induce foreign direct investment.

It is desirable to synthetically determine the location of each island by three factors: the geo-economic condition, the distance from its major target country, and the ease with which it is possible to block capitalistic influences on the mainland. It is better to limit the islands to as small a number as possible, though it should be enough to induce foreign direct investment as much as necessary. Also, each island should be specialized according to its own economic and geographic characteristics in order to guarantee international competitiveness. For instance, the Sinuiju Special Administrative Region cannot be successful if North Korea sticks to the current proposal that plans to make the region a centre for international finance, trade, manufacturing, commerce, information and technology, entertainment, and a tourist resort. Such a multi-functional zone can hardly be expected to produce any fruitful results. Thus, Sinuiju should be developed as a manufacturing and export base, focusing on light industry and establishing a very close connection with Dandong in China.

**The development strategies for the mainland**

In the mainland it is necessary to foster export industries to support the 'New Planned Economy for the Twenty-First Century', and to promote a decentralized planned economy at the same time. Efforts should be made to promote the export of current export items in the short run, and to build export bases for the long run. Central government must play the role of securing social cohesion by sharing the visions and strategies with various economic agents and providing guidelines, while expanding the autonomy of subordinate units in the process of decision-making. For this goal, it is necessary to accelerate decentralization and gradually relieve price control.

First of all, efforts must be made to increase exports in order to acquire sufficient capital required for economic development, because exports are the primary source of foreign exchange in the short run. It should be said, however, that the North Korean economy does not satisfy the preconditions for substantially expanding exports in the long run. Due to outdated facilities, low technology and insufficient design and marketing capabilities, only a small number of primary products, such as agricultural, fishery and mining products, are competitive in the world market. In addition, processing on commission is limited to items with low value-added, and are not competitive enough in terms of commission level. Therefore it is recommended to improve the competitiveness of the export items by depreciation, which could increase exports and processing on commission substantially. In particular, if the export prices decrease so as to compensate high transportation costs, it is possible to expand processing on commission with South Korea considerably in a short period. In the long run, export bases should be built in the mainland, which makes it possible to minimize the financial need for building infrastructures and to take advantage of the synergy effect through the agglomeration of firms and industries. Considering the market conditions, the best candidates for export bases are Nampo, Wonsan and Chungjin, respectively targeting the markets of South Korea, Japan and South Korea, and Japan and Russia.

It is also recommended to gradually reduce direct orders from the central planning authorities, with the exception of a few strategic industries. Specifically, it is necessary to expand the autonomy of factories, firms and farms, while improving the central government's managerial skill to accomplish industry-wide goals, thereby combining the coordinating capacity of the central planning authorities and the creativity of the subordinate units. It is important as well that in the long run the central government supplies only public goods such as electricity and water, and that the transactions of other goods and materials are carried out in the 'socialistic markets'. The establishment of various state-run banks in addition to the central bank should also be considered: for example, to establish a Business Bank for corporate credits in order to support industrial policy and an Export and Import Bank to support export industries. In addition, it is also essential to attract individuals' hoarded capital into the banking system and utilize it for capital accumulation. The improvement of the management system is required so that the role of the factory committee of the Labour Party is confined to political projects, to expand the autonomy of the managers, and to strengthen the incentive system.

The price control system should be curtailed gradually. Considering the fact that rapidly relieving price control could lead to hyperinflation, a gradual method according to consecutive stages of growth is recommended in order to attain stable economic growth. In the first stage it is desirable to keep the current statutory price system, since it is not easy to secure a stable supply of goods in a short period. It is important however that the signals of the markets are properly reflected in the statutory prices. In the second stage, efforts must be made to establish a decentralized planned economy by reducing the range of statutory prices.

### 11.4.4 The Preconditions

**Improved foreign relations**

It is impossible to achieve rapid economic growth through the 'New Planned Economy for the Twenty-first Century' without the cooperation of three countries – South Korea, the United States and Japan – since only these three countries have the capability and the willingness to help North Korea's economic growth. Economic aid from China only aims at maintaining a strategic buffer, while Russia, although interested in economic cooperation with North Korea, lacks the financial capability. Though relations with the EU countries have improved, this has not yet led to active economic cooperation.

Improving relations with the United States must be given the top priority, since North Korea's economic growth will always be limited as long as the United States considers North Korea part of the 'axis of evil'. High tariff rates limit access to the huge United States market, and the hostile relations hinder the acquisition of advanced technologies and the accession to international financial institutions. Furthermore, to expect substantially improved relations with South Korea and Japan are nearly impossible without improvement in the North Korea–US relationship.

It is most critical to perceive the importance of South Korea as the source of economic benefits. The South Korean government is willing to support North Korea's economic growth, based on such factors as ethnic identity, war prevention, reduced unification costs and the need to proceed to the Chinese market. South Korean firms are also highly interested in doing business in

North Korea. North Korea can also benefit by improving relations with Japan, thereby utilizing capital inflows from Japan in the process of economic recovery.

Easing military tension is a critical factor to build good relations with these three countries. It would be impossible to attract foreign capital and foster export industries as long as there exists military tension in the international community, regarding such issues as nuclear weapons, missiles and terrorism. In order to improve relations with Japan, it is necessary to resolve the issues of kidnapping, nuclear weapons and missiles. Therefore in this respect it is desirable to approach military issues and economic cooperation simultaneously. Full-scale economic cooperation with South Korea also requires the alleviation of military tension at the Truce Line.

It is essential to note that military expansion and economic growth cannot be achieved at the same time, since satisfactory economic growth requires the reduction of military expenditure. It is impossible to build - up military forces while simultaneously improving the national economy. North Korea must choose one over the other.

**Efficient and reliable leadership**

An efficient and reliable leadership is an essential factor in pursuing economic development strategies, in particular for the 'New Planned Economy for the Twenty-First Century experiment in North Korea. First of all the leadership must provide clear policy directions to which all the economic agents can adjust their economic activities, thereby enhancing its efficiency. In addition, efforts must be made to provide consistent policy directions based on a long-term vision, so as to reduce any confusion that the agents may perceive. This will reduce the uncertainty of the North Korean economy and thus will substantially contribute to attracting foreign capital.

It is essential for the leadership to persistently pay full attention to economic performance, and to adjust policy directions and measures accordingly. The Economic Trend Meeting and the Export Promotion Meeting of South Korea, supervised by the president, are good examples.

Efforts must also be made to enhance the leadership of the mid-level managers, considering their role in policy enforcement in the field. Domestic cooperation also depends on the efficiency and reliability of the mid-level managers. It is critical to note the importance of reliability not only to the leader but also to the outside world. For example, it was not a desirable decision to appoint Yang Bin as the minister of Sinuiju Special Administrative Region. Even if a capable foreigner had been appointed, however, the existence of capable mid-level managers is still questionable.

A desirable strategy for efficient policy enforcement is to 'practice and adjust'. That is to enforce suggested policy tools in a small number of provinces or firms, monitor the performance and make proper adjustments, and then expand the range, which will minimize the adverse effects caused by the new policies.

### 11.4.5 Six Major Tasks

North Korea is required to concentrate its resources on a set of six tasks: (1) increased food supply, (2) security of consumer products supply, (3) improvement of human capital, (4) enhancement of production technology, (5) expansion of infrastructure, and (6) fortification of strategic industries.

A brief description of the major points in each of the six tasks is as follows. First, North Korea should alter its self-sufficiency food strategy by allocating less resources to food production, and instead substituting domestic shortages with imports. Then it will be possible to reallocate what is not invested in food production to other more urgent sectors. Second, to secure the supply of consumer products, North Korea should promote light industry in local areas and also improve the distribution system of consumer products. Third, human capital should be emphasized through better technical training and higher education provision. Fourth, it is important to imitate technology from more-developed nations to enhance production technology. Fifth, infrastructure facilities can be improved through more effective logistics by balancing development among railways, highways, waterways and ports. Finally, the energy industry should be developed prior to other metal and machine industries.

## NOTES

1 For more details, see Section 3.
2 For a review of the economic difficulties faced by this sector, see Harvie and Lee (2003), pp. 183–86.
3 Nam and Moon (2000).
4 Bank of Korea (2002).
5 Foreign aid fell from US$492.6 million in 2001 to US$392.2 million in 2002. Ministry of Unification (2003), p. 176.
6 The Research Institute of National Unification (1992), pp. 345–7
7 Chun and Kim (1997), p. 4.
8 North Korean Scientific Encyclopedia Press (1983), p. 160.
9 North Korean Workers' Party (1963), p. 2.
10 For discussion of the early history of North Korea's economic opening, see Yeon (1995).
11 The major objective of the 'New Trade System' is to decentralize the authority on trade. For more detailed information and assessment, see Chun and Kim (1997).
12 For example, a paper representing the official view of North Korea says that the 'New Trade System' does not imply trade liberalization or decentralization to rural authorities, but reinforcement of a planned

guideline for trade of the central authority. Lee (1992), p. 31.

13 In the late 1990s, North Korea deleted 'free' in the name of the zone. For comparative studies of the zone with the cases of other countries, see, for instance, Namkoong (1995).

14 Lee (2003), p. 58. He also reports that 130 companies were operating in the Zone in July 2002, 90 per cent of which were Chinese.

15 Interview with North Korean refugees.

16 For more detailed information on the new economic measures, see Jo et al. (2002), pp. 253–68.

17 According to current North Korean laws on foreign investment, foreign firms must go through the North Korean labour authority to employ North Korean workers. Since the authority has the right to choose workers, foreign firms are unable to judge their employees in advance.

## REFERENCES

Bank of Korea (2002), 'The Estimation Results of the North Korean GDP in 2001', 14 May (in Korean).

Chun H.T. and S.G. Kim (1997), *The Current Situation of the North Korean Economy and the Prospects for Reform*, Policy Study Series 97-02, Korea Development Institute (in Korean).

Harvie C. and H.H. Lee (2003), *Korea's Economic Miracle: Fading or Reviving?*, Basingstoke: Palgrave Macmillan.

Jo, D. (2002), *A Study on Strategies to Develop the North Korean Economy*, Research Monograph 2002-09, Korea Development Institute (in Korean).

Lee, C.H. (2003), 'Ten Years of Tumen River Area Development: Evaluation and Issues', *ERINA booklet*, 2, February, Economic Research Institute for Northeast Asia.

Lee, S.H. (1992), 'The Fundamental Characteristic of New Trade System and Its Superiority', *Economic Study*, April (in Korean).

Ministry of Unification (2003), *Monthly Report: Intra-Korean Interchanges and Cooperation and Humanitarian Projects*, No. 138 (in Korean).

Nam, S.W. and S.M. Moon (2000), 'A Study on Estimating the Size of Market Economy in North Korea', *North Korean Studies Review*, **3**(1), 149–216 (in Korean).

Namkoong, Y. (1995), *A Study of Investment Environment of North Korea's Economic Special Zone: A Comparison with China and Vietnam*, Research Institute for National Unification (in Korean).

North Korean Scientific Encyclopedia Press (1983), *Complete Encyclopedia*, (in Korean).

North Korean Workers' Party (1963), *Our Party's Policy to Develop a Self-*

*Reliant Economy* (in Korean).
Research Institute of National Unification (1992), *A Comparative Study of Trend of National Powers of South and North Korea* (in Korean).
Yeon, H.C. (1995), 'Inter-Korean Economic relations', in L.J. Cho and Y.H. Kim (eds), *Economic Systems in South and North Korea: The Agenda for Economic Integration*, Korea Development Institute (in Korean).

# PART IV PROSPECTS

# 12. A New Paradigm for the Korean Economy: Advanced State Development (ASD) Model Approach

**Jong Won Lee**

## 12.1 INTRODUCTION

Korea has drawn worldwide attention for its unprecedented economic growth and recent financial crisis. A unique Korean-style 'developmental state model' approach has often been cited as a root cause for both the success and failure of the Korean economy. This chapter shares similar views with it in principle. It has been analyzed that the government-led economic operations functioned efficiently in the early stages of economic development, but created low - efficiency and a high-cost economic structure during the later stages. For this reason, even before the outbreak of the crisis, the neoclassical principle has been suggested to replace the traditional development model approach. The IMF policy recommendations were also based on the neoclassical doctrine. The main argument of this chapter is, however, that extreme neoclassical strategies cannot be a successful substitute for the statist model approach in Korea. The so-called 'advanced state model' approach is suggested instead as an alternative.

It was a big surprise to witness the Korean economy suddenly experiencing a dramatic financial crisis, in spite of its impressive experience as one of the most rapidly growing economies in the world over the previous four decades. At the onset of the financial crisis, Korea went through a painful output decline (6.8 per cent in 1998) and a sharp increase in the level of unemployment that had not been experienced during the years of its economic miracle from the early 1960s. Major restructuring of the economy was carried out through reforms in the financial and corporate sectors, labour market and public sectors. A remarkable economic recovery was achieved during 1999 and 2000. Economic growth has, however, slowed down again in subsequent years.

The financial and economic crisis of the late 1990s has resulted in a reappraisal of the Korean and the Asian development model.[1] Many commentators are now suggesting different development models. Among them the neoclassical model is the leading one. It is time to assess whether the neoclassical principles can be an appropriate paradigm for the future development of the Korean economy. If not, are there any alternatives?

## 12.2 LIMITATION OF THE TRADITIONAL DEVELOPMENT MODELS

Less-developed countries (LDCs) have studied the economic development processes of advanced countries in order to learn about their economic development, and the establishment of capitalistic civil societies as well. However, most of these studies and economic development theories have concentrated on the economic growth aspects of already established capitalist countries. They have neglected the development process of capitalism, especially in the transition from the pre-capitalistic or feudal society. It is obvious that the simple plantation of advanced economic systems cannot successfully settle down in LDCs, whose economic conditions are not yet fully matured enough to absorb Western-style fully-fledged capitalism. Many traditional approaches are misleading in this respect. Thus, we need a model that can complement the drawbacks of such analyses, and interpret LDCs' development problems more properly. With this notion in mind, let us briefly review leading development models such as the economic development stage model, neoclassical model, structural model, neo-Marxian model, and so on.

### 12.2.1 Economic Development Stage Model

The traditional development stage model of the nineteenth century connected societies of different development stages in historical order by differentiating them according to their characteristics. In fact, they did not offer any explanation on the cause of transition between neighbouring societies. In addition, their version of societal characteristics was in general oversimplified, and thus could not provide a proper explanation for diverse areas and societies.

In the twentieth century, modern stage models were presented by W. Rostow, P. Kuznets and C. Clark, which have been evaluated as an improvement over old development stage models. For example, Meier (1995) saw Rostow's work in particular as a provocative application of a stage approach to the course of development, by pointing out that his model was a dynamic theory of production which emphasized the composition of investment and the growth of particular sectors in the economy. In fact, Rostow argued that the growth of certain leading sectors would be instrumental in propelling the economy forward.

Nevertheless, the basic feature of any stage theory of long-term economic change still assumes that the sequence of stages succeeds in such a way that, first, distinct time segments of a historical order are characterized by different sources and patterns of economic changes; second, these segments succeed specifically so that 'b' cannot occur before 'a', etc; third, succession of these segments is the process of development and growth rather than of devaluation and shrinkage and the process of a unidirectional rather than cyclic view of history.

In short, stage models implicitly assume that all economies pass through the same individual stages in order as they develop. In addition, since they prescribe a sequence of stages as an inescapable law of economic development, even in the process of decline, the return to a previously experienced stage level or recurrence of an earlier stage cannot be viewed. It is highly improbable that such a simple design can be a sufficient summary description or a plausible analytic classification of the vast and diverse field of historical change.

To summarize, stage models in general do not provide any logic of causal relations to explain the succession of stages. Furthermore, they cannot provide any description of a society that could succeed in the future, no matter how they define a modern society. On the other hand, although W. Rostow and A. Gerschenkron may avoid some of the general criticisms of traditional stage models, their models simply concentrate on the transition toward an industrialized society from traditional and underdeveloped ones. They simply described the degree of economic backwardness based on the characteristics of stages, and presented prerequisites of industrial development. Further, their models can hardly avoid the criticism that they neglect the details of pre-modern societies unlike the old traditional stage approach. From all the considerations made above, we can conclude that the stage model approach in general cannot provide sufficient and specific guidance for the successful economic development of LDCs.

### 12.2.2 Neo-classical Approach

The neoclassical tradition recognizes economic development as the increase in real income per capita, and sees that GNP rises as the result of the long-term effects of capital formation, labour expansion and technological change, which are assumed to take place under conditions of competitive equilibrium.

Coupled with the influence of Keynesian economics, the formation of capital began to be considered as the single most important factor for economic growth. In consequence, in the Harrod-Domar model, which occupied centre stage in the late 1940s and early 1950s, a strict link between the growth of the capital stock and the consequent growth of potential output was assumed, which was its dominant characteristic as well as its ultimate flaw. It was an assumption that was imaginable only when a market price system could work smoothly; this was definitely unrealistic in LDCs.

Nevertheless, this extreme vision that physical capital accumulation was the only ultimate source of economic growth under the assumption of correct market conditions, was able to gain worldwide acceptance for some period of time due to the notion that the marginal product of labour was almost zero due to extreme labour surpluses in the LDCs.

It was discovered, however, that the above logic could not be backed up by sufficient empirical support. When factor earnings were used as measures of the contributions of productive factors to the process of economic growth, a substantial amount of growth remained unexplained. Efforts were made to find out these contributing factors to the unexplained part of output growth. The most reasonable initial guess was that technological progress might be responsible for that part. It was, however, quickly recognized to be a composite of effects from many different factors such as (1) improvement in the quality of labour through education, experience and on-the-job training, (2) reallocation of resources from low-productivity to higher-productivity uses, and (3) realization of economies of scale, and so on.

Consequently, development economists went beyond their (neo) classical predecessors and suggested central planning for efficient capital formation with a distrust of markets and a belief in the pervasiveness of market failure. Further, coupled with pessimism regarding the external conditions of development of primary-product exporting LDCs, unbalanced growth strategy, suggested by A. O. Hirschman, began to be in full swing in the development literature, putting neoclassical tradition aside. Such a tendency brought about a structuralist approach to development problems later on.

### 12.2.3 Structural Analysis

The structural approach has not been successful in presenting the same rigorous formulation as the traditional general equilibrium theory, although it has provided a basis for empirical analysis. The essence of this line of structural analysis can be summarized as follows:

1. Structural analysis may be more suitable for the development of LDCs, since disequilibrium phenomena are more significant in LDCs than in developed countries (DCs).
2. Thus, it can establish the importance of moving resources from less-productive sectors to more-productive ones, for example from agriculture to industry. These shifts are considered as more important sources of growth in LDCs than the mere increments to input factors.
3. In addition to neoclassical sources of growth and resource reallocation to higher-productivity sectors, the structural approach also suggests the reduction of internal and external supply bottlenecks, and the

exploitation of economies of scale as efficient ways to provide a potential for accelerating growth.
4 Learning by doing or the importation of more productive technology available from advanced countries, is also considered as another channel of productivity improvement and consequent economic growth.

On the basis of such an analysis, many empirical studies have been conducted emphasizing the effects of disequilibrium on economic growth and the economic consequences arising from a reallocation of labour and capital, growth of exports and capital inflows, and so on. In short, while neoclassical models emphasize increments to production inputs, investment in human capital and technological progress, structural approaches concentrate more on supply bottleneck problems (to cure market failure), infrastructure build-ups (to generate spillover effects), export-oriented industrialization, and a shift of resources to more-productive sectors. Active government intervention in the economy has been suggested, not only to correct market failures but also to restore the role of market prices.

### 12.2.4 Neo-Marxian Approach

Based on the fact that LDCs were inserted into the international capitalist system through colonization, and that exterior economic conditions for them were disadvantageous and making it difficult to achieve economic development, critical views on neoclassical approaches to development, such as dependency theories of underdevelopment, have arisen in Latin America. The dependency school argues that there exist asymmetrical power relationships between the centre (the US, Western Europe, and so on), previously the imperial powers, and the periphery, previously the colonies, and that the major source of underdevelopment is dependency of the periphery on the centre. Thus, underdevelopment of the periphery has been considered as the Siamese twin of development of the centre. Further, dependency economists argue that even though LDCs can achieve some level of industrialization, they are still dependent on the superior power of the advanced countries. Thus they (the periphery) are still exploited by the world's real power (the centre)-by biasing the production structure toward the supplying of raw materials, by aggravating the terms of trade and balance – of - payments, and by thwarting autonomous national development. By characterizing centre–periphery trade as 'unequal exchange' dependency theorists even contended that capitalistic development of presently advanced countries has been achieved at the expense of others, that is the underdevelopment of the dependent periphery.

Whether policy inferences of Marxist approaches are extreme or not, they are lacking in specifics and thus cannot serve as a substitute for the traditional approaches. In addition, most of their policy suggestions could not bring about favourable consequences in reality either. Furthermore, they came to lose their ideological ground as the socialist economies had collapsed by the turn of 1990. The historical experiment of socialism turned out to be a failure although it contributed to human history in many ways, especially in terms of discussions on equity problems.

## 12.3 NEW ANALYTIC MODEL OF ECONOMIC DEVELOPMENT

By reviewing neoclassical, structural and alternative approaches to economic development, we have found that even extended versions of these perspectives still have some limitations in one way or another to serve as a proper reference for LDCs. For example, stage-making approaches are misleading due to their linear conception of history, which is postulated to be based on distinctive segments of succeeding societies in a specific order. They cannot avoid criticism at the same time that no logical interpretation for a causal relationship is provided to explain succession between neighbouring societies. Neoclassical approaches turn out to be much more systematic and logical than stage models, but depend on unrealistic assumptions, especially for LDCs, such as perfect markets, flexible prices, and so on. The shortcomings of neoclassical models have thus often been overcome by considering structuralist perspectives as a complement. On the other hand, neo-Marxist perspectives, suggested as an alternative approach in the form of dependency models in areas like Latin America, failed to provide successful policy inferences for LDCs due to their inherent drawbacks in logic.

More sophisticated development models have been suggested recently to make up for some of the shortcomings of these previous models. Some improvements have been made in this endeavour: Rostow's model over traditional stage models, a new endogenous growth model over neoclassical perspectives, and so on. On the other hand, much literature has been developed on issues such as modernization strategies, late-comers effect, flying-geese pattern of growth (or catch-up theory) and limits to growth in LDCs at the same time. In spite of these efforts, we still need to establish a new analytical model in order to properly analyze developing national economies.

It may not be easy to build a model which is based on proper causality-oriented logic to explain the development of human history but we may be able to minimize the shortcomings of existing models and properly consider socio-economic characteristics of LDCs, while still providing a systematic and realistic analysis as well as policy implications. Elsewhere, the author has developed a new model by incorporating Marxist perspectives and Max Weber's methodology in part, in addition to staging model logic. In other words, the model, though based on the stage model approach in principle, was built in such a way as to provide causality-oriented logic based on the Marxist and Weberian views.

Since the main objective of this chapter is not to discuss development models, the details of a new approach will not be introduced here. Instead, only a brief summary of the main features and conclusive ideas of the model is presented as follows.[2]

First, evaluation of economic development should be made on the basis of the degree of welfare improvement, rather than the contents of simple environmental or institutional change.[3]

Second, the root cause, or motive, of the development of human history originates from the ownership and control structure of key production means, and the consequently resulting mode of production which will determine the level of economic efficiency and equity attainable. In other words, economic development basically depends on who owns the key production inputs, and how production is carried out under the prevailing principal ownership system.

Third, the decentralization process of ownership has contributed to the enhancement of both economic efficiency and equity, since a greater number of owners will have more opportunities and incentives to exploit and to share consequent benefits.

Fourth, key production means that have played a major role in transforming societies have appeared in the order of natural resources, land and physical capital and are now moving toward human capital.

Fifth, it is difficult to provide proper explanations for development patterns at different times and areas, since economic development is to be realized in diverse forms and orders depending on the characteristics of cultural values that are formed, based on some economic environments, institutional habitats and customs.

Sixth, a new system emerges with leading production modes that can lead a new period with improved efficiency, where the basis of existing systems is relatively poor.[4]

Seventh, once any successfully established economic system emerges, it will influence other remaining systems and areas with pressure for change. In spite of the pressure for change from the leading economic system, there are many areas that are not capable of incorporating a new paradigm into their systems. Some areas may skip some of the usual development stages or may experience others totally different from the leading ones. In any case, those areas that cannot adopt a leading economic system have to remain as relatively underdeveloped areas.

Figure 12.1 shows the economic development process that moves from society $A$ to $B_k$ ($k$ = 1,2,…$K$), where human welfare of society $B_k$ is superior to that of society $A$.

This process prescribes that the transition process can take various different paths and result in different forms of societies ($B_k$).

Basically, there are three main sources for succession of neighbouring societies. First of all, transition may occur as new production input owners begin to take over a leading role in production from the existing ones (for example from land to capital). Second, system change may result as ownership patterns start to change in such a way that economic efficiency and welfare are improved (for example through decentralization of ownership). Third, a new paradigm can be created when a nation can incorporate pressures for change that come from neighbouring nations, which have already accomplished a paradigm shift with either one of the two sources stated above.

Different nations or regions have their own unique cultural ethics, which are termed 'Ideal Typus' by Max Weber. Consequently, even faced with the same pressures for change, they may go through different paths of transition. The Ideal Typus that individual nations or regions have formed will function as a filter in determining the probability and direction of change.

Assume that $C_{ij}$ ($I$ = 1,2,...$M$, and, $j$ = 1,2,...,$N$) represents different characteristics of different regions in such a way that a region of lower $i$ has a stronger basis for the existing system, and a region of higher $j$ has greater absorptive capacity for change. Then, $C_{11}$ will be the region that has the least chance for change, while $C_{MN}$ will have the best chance for change since it represents the region where the basis of the existing system is relatively poor but has a mature environment to incorporate a new paradigm. It is the region that has the best chance to settle in a new paradigm. An individual region, ranging between $C_{11}$ and $C_{MN}$, will experience different paths and establish different societies in terms of the welfare level to prevail. $B_k$ will promise the highest level of welfare improvement, while $B_l$ will promise only the lowest level. The region that accomplishes $B_k$ will play a leading role in the new era.

With all the ideas developed in the new model, which is a revised version of the development stage model, we can provide a logical interpretation for causal relationships to explain the succession between neighbouring societies. In addition, it can provide proper explanations not only for the development processes foregone, but also those to be realized in the future. The new analytic model could successfully explain both the occidental and oriental economic development process. Details are not introduced here, since that is not the main objective of this chapter.[5] What can be said here is that the new model recognizes capitalistic society as the one that contributed to the enhancement of human welfare and freedom (compared to the preceding feudal society), and the establishment of modern civil society. Further, capitalistic society was a physical capital-oriented society, but capital ownership has been decentralized as more people and organizations have become shareholders in its development process.

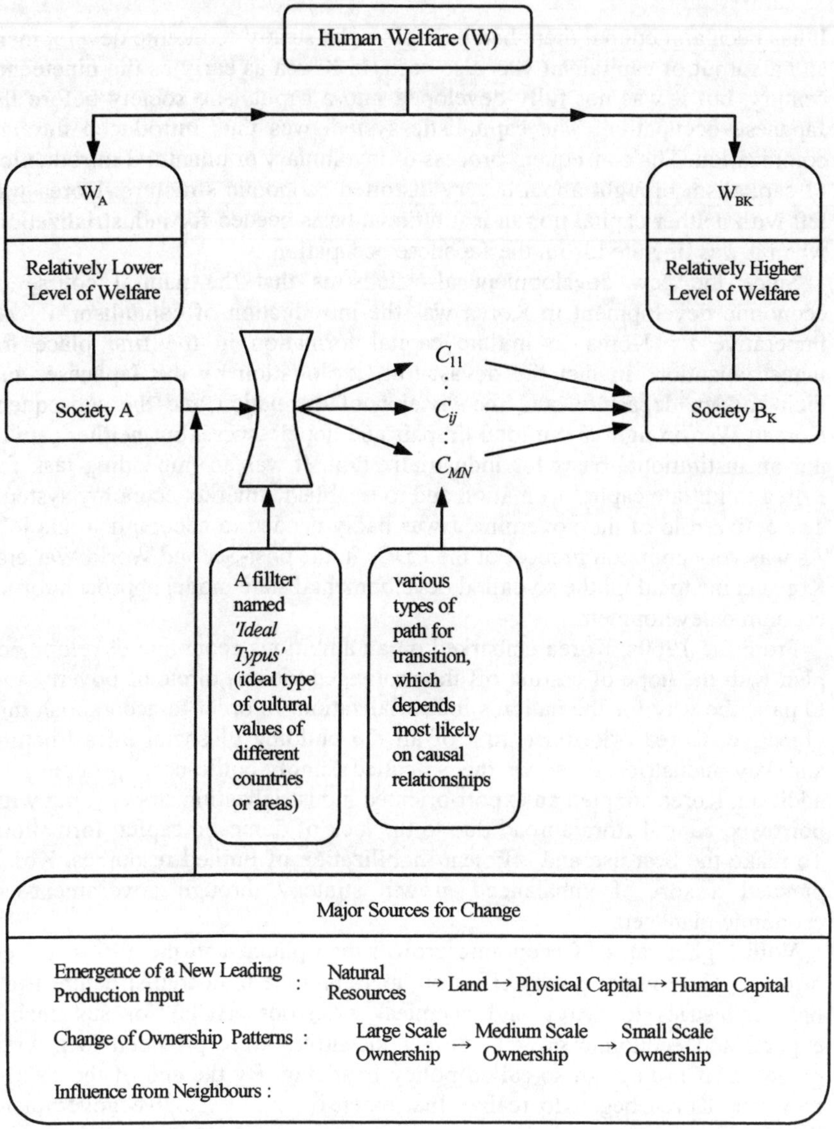


*Figure 12.1 Economic Development Process*

## 12.4 ASSESSMENT OF THE KOREAN ECONOMIC DEVELOPMENT PROCESS

It has been argued that there had been slow but steady economic development, and a sprout of capitalism was also seen, in Korea as early as the nineteenth century, but it was not fully developed into a capitalistic society before the Japanese occupation. The capitalistic system was thus introduced through colonization. The consequent process of involuntary or unnatural introduction of capitalism brought about a very distorted economic structure. Korea was left with neither capital nor an institutional basis needed for industrialization, when it was liberated from the Japanese occupation.

Since the new development also tells us that the natural course of economic development in Korea was the introduction of capitalism, it was imperative for Korea to initiate capital formation in the first place for industrialization. In fact the devastating exploitation by the Japanese, and their sudden departure, and the division of the nation and the subsequent Korean War brought about total despair and hopelessness, but neither capital nor an institutional basis for industrialization. It was an impending task for Korea to initiate capital formation and to establish a market economy system. The active role of the government was badly needed to accomplish this job. As was very common in most of the LDCs in the post-Second World War era, Korea came to adopt the so-called developmental state model approach for its economic development.

From the 1960s, Korea embarked on an ambitious economic development plan with the hope of cutting off the prolonged vicious circle of poverty and to pave the way for the nation's industrialization. In order to accomplish this objective, Korea prioritized first of all the building of social infrastructure and key industries to solve the so-called supply-bottle-neck problem. In addition, Korea adopted an export-oriented industrialization strategy, but with borrowed capital from abroad due to the lack of domestic capital formation. To make the best use and efficient mobilization of limited resources, Korea pursued a sort of unbalanced growth strategy through government-led economic management.

With higher rates of economic growth than planned in the 1960s, Korea began to place major policy effort on upgrading the industrial structure from light industries to heavy and chemical industries (HCIs) for sustainable exports and economic growth. Strong incentives were provided to a wide range of HCIs through so-called policy financing. By the end of the 1970s, however, Korea began to realize that extensive and excessive government intervention in resource allocation could be counter-productive due to its inefficient nature and consequent economic complications. Thus, major policy priorities were given to anti-inflationary economic stabilization, economic liberalization and partly to decentralization in the 1980s. Industrial incentives were reformed, while regulations on the financial sector were relaxed. In addition, the competitive market was emphasized and promoted with reduced restrictions and regulations, and with decreased international trade barriers.

The Korean economy began to face new challenges in the late 1980s. In the course of rapid economic growth, there was a growing perception among people that distributive equity had been aggravated and the basic needs of people were not adequately met. In addition, investment in social infrastructure also turned out to be inadequate to support continuous economic growth, since production costs, especially the cost of logistics, began to rise significantly as a consequence. Furthermore, as the competitiveness of Korean exports began to lose ground, due in substantial degree to a rapid increase in wages and the appreciation of the won, industrial restructuring became an urgent task.

In the 1990s the rapid development of information and communications technology, and the birth of the WTO, brought about unlimited global competition and deepening integration of the world economy. In order to survive and prosper in this environment, Korea had to step up its self-motivated globalization efforts with deregulation geared to promoting competition and harmonizing domestic institutions with international rules and regulations as well as the acceleration of industrial restructuring. The government however failed to introduce appropriate measures in time in spite of the emerging symptoms and evidence of the crisis.

Now, the problem is how to interpret such a development process in Korea. In the view of this author it can be interpreted as the establishment, development and waning process of the CME (Centralized Management Economy) system, which represents the Korean-style government-led economic operating system.

The terminology, Centralized Management Economic System, is employed in this chapter to describe characteristics of the Korean economic development process. Using this term, emphasis is placed on the role of the government (or political power group) and its bureaucrats who have played a leading role in establishing economic development plans and executing policy. Emphasis is also given to the fact that the managerial power of the government and its bureaucrats played a larger role in the Korean economy than its artificial or legal ownership. In other words, business firms were privately owned but were managed by both government and private owners. Some authors (Kim and Kim 1997) even say that the government had a superior position over private owners, since the government controlled all the financing channels.

Since the 1960s, economic development plans have been carried out with strong leadership from the government. It led the process of creating, managing and accumulating capital, and then achieved economic development based on that.

At any rate, due to the above features, from the very start the development plan became a sort of enforcement plan, unlike the indicative plans adopted by most other LDCs. Since the success of the enforcement plan depends on whether the major objectives or goals of the plan are successfully fulfilled or not, it necessitates strong control by the government. In fact, the military government specifically defined the system they wanted to build up as 'guided capitalism'. This means that all the important decisions on economic planning and policy implementation were made by the superstructure, the central government. It also implied that the government actively intervened in the private sector economy whenever necessary.

Economic development policies and strategies are, in general, implemented, depending both on international and external conditions. The degree of modern institutional establishments, the degree of the current stage of development, and the international economic environment are the major items to be considered. The model that Korea and many other LDCs chose was the so-called 'development state model' approach, in which a strong state is essential for economic growth. The model that Korea built assumed one of the strongest governments by establishing the CME system.

Rodrick (1995) emphasized the fact that the government played the crucial coordinating role in Korea to encourage private (and public) investment in sectors where market allocation of resources would have failed. He also pointed out that this government-led model of development was rather successful in mobilizing and allocating resources until the 1970s. Over the years the effectiveness of this structure waned progressively, however, in the rapidly changing market and economic environment of the 1980s and 1990s.

In fact, the shift towards a more market-oriented economic system had been under discussion in Korea during the 1990s. Some reforms were implemented and Korea was also forced from the outside world to begin opening its domestic market to international competition. However, the implementation of reforms was slow and its impact on the economic system was marginal. When the 1997 financial crisis hit the country it resulted in a tremendous ordeal for the Korean people, but at the same time an opportunity for real change in the Korean economy and society as well.

## 12.5 RATIONALE AND LIMITATIONS OF THE STATIST MODEL

Since the early twentieth century the government is believed to have played a proper role as a corrector of market failures, such as that arising from inequality and depression. The importance of the government role was, however, emphasized more strongly in LDCs, which came to adopt the market economy system through the colonization process by the world powers. Since the market economy system was established when its natural development was not foreseen, and yet an escape from the absolute poverty, and an engagement of the economic development through industrialization were an urgent agenda, the leading role of government was seen as indispensable.

The elimination of supply bottlenecks was needed in the initial stage of development to break through the vicious circle of poverty. Only the government could accomplish this by expanding public expenditures extensively on social overhead capital (SOC) (roads, ports, railways, and so on) and key industries (electric power, fertilizer, cement and construction industries). It was also improbable for the private sector to raise enough funds for industrialization from domestic sources, and thus government intervention appeared inevitable.

Under these circumstances Korea aimed at economic development through export-oriented industrialization, with borrowed foreign capital to be invested in specific sectors (a disequilibrium growth approach) and under strong-government-directed economic development plans, that is the so-called CME (Centralized Management Economy) system. It was natural for the government to take a leading role in establishing consistent and systematic economic development plans, when an autonomous establishment of the market economy system was improbable and yet the need for modern industrialization was imminent. This situation was similar in most of the LDCs. The NICs were the most successful countries to accomplish fast economic growth with this line of policy. For this reason, aggressive intervention by the government in the market has been singled out as a leading contributing factor to economic success in this region. Following the financial crisis, however, doubts were cast on the government-led economic development strategies. Consequently, Korea began to move away from the old principle in its pursuit of economic reforms. The question is whether the government-led economic policy doctrine has become an old norm to be sublimated.

A strong supporter of the strong developmental state model approach, Chalmers Johnson (1994), emphasized the existence of a small group of elite decision-makers, especially elite economic bureaucrats, to play the role of a pilot agency. As a matter of fact, they functioned as a think tank to initiate economic development in Korea. In this process, they constantly made decisions on which industries to maintain or to relieve in order to maintain international competitiveness. Johnson termed this 'soft authoritarian societal cooperatism'.

Robert Wade (1990) was one of the strong supporters for the government-led economic development doctrines. He proposed a governed market theory and provided both theoretical and empirical evidence, and in doing so advocated the governed market theory over the free market theory.

Amsden (1989) was another major supporter of the strong interventionist state. In her book, *Asia's Next Giant: Evaluating the Paradigm of Late*

*Industrialization*, she proposed a successful development model of strong government intervention, by taking Korea as an example. To be specific, she pointed out three major contributing factors: (1) successful breakthrough of the vicious circle of poverty through concentrated public investment in SOCs and key industries in the early stage of economic development, (2) efficient allocation of resources with priority given to growth-led sectors, and (3) upgrading industrial structure to build up a high value-added oriented industrial restructuring process. The World Bank report, *The Asian Miracle* (1993), basically stood for a similar logic. Their views had to face, however, a big challenge following the recent financial crisis in Korea and South-Eastern Asia. Flynn (1999) and Henke and Boxill (2000) have drawn attention in this regard.

Both parties, however, provided convincing logic regarding the consequences of development policies at different times and areas. We can condone Johnson and Wade's argument in the sense that the developmental state model can contribute to the early stage development plans, when internal and external conditions are able to work favourably. Flynn, Henke and Boxill provided evidence on what government intervention could bring about when the principle was held too long in spite of the advancement of development. Besides, it seems that LDCs can no longer imitate the old Korean development strategies, since neither government subsidies nor import restrictions are allowed in the new international economic order under the WTO system.

Faced with the realization of limitation and problems involved in the developmental state model in the late 1970s, the neoclassical doctrine began to resurge. It began to draw attention to excessive government-led economic operations fostering bureaucratic corruption, and deteriorated resource allocation. Reduction of the government role together with activation of the market began to gain popular support. Such a movement was strengthened by the setbacks of Keynesian economics, experienced through oil shocks and consequent stagflation. The logic was built in such a way that market-oriented economic operations and trade liberalization can create a more competitive economic structure.

In fact, following the financial crisis, or even before the crisis, economic reform policies had been based largely on neo-classical doctrines. Competition, instead of government intervention and regulation, and trade and capital liberalization, instead of import restrictions and protection, have been suggested and pursued to promote economic efficiency through elevated competition. The liberalized and competition-based market economic system has been advised to replace the traditional development strategies of the developmental state model approach.

The argument that unconditional liberalization is more beneficial to economic development, however, can hardly be supported empirically either. Supporting evidence has seldom been found even in newly industrialized countries, which accomplished economic development to some degree. The time has come to establish a new paradigm to replace the old with regard to the government's role. The successful one still remains to be seen.

**Factors in the Success and Failure of the Korean Economy**

It was proved elsewhere (Lee 2002) that Korean economic development was achieved not merely through more input (physical capital and labour force) but through human capital and technological development as well, contrary to the arguments of Krugman (1994).

It was also found that accumulation of human capital and technological change were accelerated by the expansion of international trade. This result, in part, proved the efficiency of the export-led growth strategy in LDCs.

Lee also conducted a comparative cross-country study on major sources for rapid economic growth. Both the 1994 Barro-Lee data and the 1991 Summers and Heston data utilized in the study, and 12 development model countries, were compared in ten categories. Most importantly, Korea turned out to be superior in its human capital investment and technology improvement to comparable LDCs

The most striking evidence found by Lee, however, was that the strong role of government was proved to have had a positive influence on economic growth only in the early stage of development, but a negative influence in the later stage.

This finding in part supports the main argument of this chapter: that Korea should replace the traditional 'developmental state model' (DSM) with the new 'advanced state development model' (ASDM) as an economic development paradigm.

## 12.6 CAN THE NEOCLASSICAL REMEDY BE AN APPROPRIATE ALTERNATIVE?

The sudden collapse of the Asian economies raised two important issues. One is whether the system of a 'strong state' can any longer usefully serve the objective of economic development of the LDCs. The other is whether the neoclassical orthodoxy, manifested in the forms of liberalization and deregulation, is appropriate for the Asian economies.

Based on the critiques that the authoritarian regimes could deliver rapid growth with insufficient diversity and ineffective management, a more accountable, responsive and transparent form of governance was suggested as the key policy measures for the Asian crisis countries. Market principles were emphasized, while the government was advised only to play a complementary role in the private sector by providing an environment conducive to the development of the private sector.

Chowdhury and Islam (2001), however, argue that the 'Washington

Consensus' could neither satisfactorily explain growth in pre-crisis Asia, nor the outbreak of the crisis. After all, Asian economies were paragons of the neo-classical principles in recent years. The Washington Consensus, which reflected the intellectual influence of Washington-based institutions such as the US Treasury, the IMF and the World Bank, advocated free markets, and free flow of trade and capital across the globe. Stiglitz has led the way in criticizing conventional liberalism as a development policy, and also pointed out that it was misguided in the context of the East Asian crisis.

Chowdhury and Islam even argue that the follies of the Washington Consensus, which represents a significant departure from the conventional Asian development model, partially contributed to the Asian crisis, and aggravated it by severely constraining the macroeconomic policy mix.[6] They saw that the progressive withdrawal of governments from regulating both the real and financial sector of the economy since the mid-1980s, in line with the Washington Consensus, drove Asian nations into a status of hostages to international financial markets. The only thing that the government could do was simply to keep foreign capital inflows to maintain economic growth.

On the other hand, the government had to give up its investments in SOCs, education and so on, which in turn damaged economic efficiency and productivity. Capital began to be utilized inefficiently, and people began to direct their savings to speculative investment as a consequence.

Others like Hutson and Kearney (2001) pointed out the fact that there is a growing consensus that the international financial market and the world financial system have exhibited an increasing degree of fragility. As a matter of fact, during the 1980s and 1990s, we have witnessed four financial crises of varying degrees of seriousness. The Asian crisis has been the most serious one among them. The amount of capital that fled out of the region is estimated to be as high as 11 per cent of the affected countries' combined GDP. What is worse, the crisis even threatened the stability of the international financial system, notwithstanding the catastrophic damage inflicted on the affected countries.

What scared the countries directly involved in the crisis, was that the IMF forced them to adopt its policy advice against the interests of the troubled economies. There has been a growing concern that the IMF operation has been moving away from the international community, in favour of the USA. It is believed by many that international financial market failures, such as from information asymmetries and moral hazard, aggravated the crisis, albeit that it may have basically resulted from fundamental weaknesses in the Asian economies, such as often-cited crony capitalism, poor corporate governance, inadequate financial supervision and inappropriate exchange rate policies.

In any case, at the very least, the IMF cannot avoid extensive criticism that it forced the afflicted countries to accept its loan conditions, which were in fact against traditional macroeconomic requirements. Somehow, the IMF should have made an effort to reduce the size of its bailouts. Furthermore it should have assisted the rescheduling of debt repayments, instead of bailing out lenders alone. Unfortunately, the final decision was to ask the Asian nations in crisis to adopt high interest rates and tightened government budget principles, which contributed to aggravation of the depression.

It is obvious that neoclassical principles may contribute to enhancing the efficiency of the international market system, but we should remember that they will also widen the gap between the rich and the poor countries since they will bring about an unfavourable atmosphere to LDCs in world trading most of the time.

In a nation, poor people can be protected by national policies in the form of a social safety net, health care, a pension system and so on. There are no comparable policies or systems that can work for the poor countries. It is quite predictable that the world economy will turn toward a more unstable position than now, unless some countervailing measures are prepared.

One more important note to make is that extreme liberalization and deregulation, at the national and international levels, will make weak and poor small nations helpless in implementing proper domestic stabilization policies.

## 12.7 THE ADVANCED STATE MODEL APPROACH: A NEW ALTERNATIVE

By establishing the CME system Korea was able to achieve unprecedented economic growth, but came to experience an economic crisis as well just before the turn of the twentieth century due to its inherent structural shortcomings. The government-led economic operations, that functioned efficiently in the early stages of economic development, created low - efficiency and resulted in a high-cost economic structure at a later stage.

Excessive government intervention, for example, deteriorated the creative and responsive power of the market system. Even decisions on R&D investments were being made by the government, making the private sector even more dependent on government decisions. This in turn brought about bureaucratic corruption. The government-led economic operations are, by their nature, inappropriate as industrialization reaches a certain level. Excessive and overlapping investments, which stemmed from preferential government support, brought about not only business but also national bankruptcy. The cause of the crisis is believed to have stemmed from the government's failure in institutional operations.

Disaster from the crisis was able to work as an opportunity for Korea to make a real change in its economic structure. In fact, Korea executed four major reform programmes that it would have been improbable to see realized in the past, and assisted its economy bounce back quite strongly.

As witnessed, however, in the mishap of neoclassical policy

recommendations before and after the crisis, the role of the government in developing countries should not be given up although some modifications may be needed.

If the neoclassical principle cannot successfully substitute for the conventional development state model, what then can replace the traditional approach? An alternative, to be presented here, is termed the 'advanced state model' approach (see Table 12.1).

The capitalistic system, or the market economy, is basically an efficiency-oriented system. Survival of the fittest is the name of the game. Inequality is a natural consequence. The weak or handicapped must devise their own protective measures such as the infant-industry protection doctrine. Government intervention is another way of making up for their structural weakness and backwardness. The developmental state model, or the statist model, has played a leading role in this regard, especially in the East Asian countries during the latter half of the twentieth century.

Korea and other neighbouring East Asian countries still have considerable structural and institutional backwardness, and are thirsting for sustainable economic growth to catch up with the advanced countries. Only compressed growth can make developing countries achieve further advancement in their economies. For faster growth under a less favourable economic structure, the East Asian nations still need to identify an appropriate role for government intervention in the years to come.

Based upon the foregoing discussions, a new development model, which we may call 'the advanced state model', is suggested. This emphasizes the role of the government but in different aspects. The paradigm will simply be shifted from the old to the new, in such a way that it will suffice the new role of government for further advancement of the economy in Korea and the (Asian) NICs. The basic idea behind this model can be summarized as follows.

First of all the new paradigm will concentrate on sustainable and qualitative growth to reach an advanced state of economic development, replacing the early-stage economic development strategies for fast and quantitative growth.

Second, the economic operating mechanism of the government should move from the centralized management system to a decentralized one through democratization, privatization and liberalization in such a way as to improve both economic efficiency and equity.

In fact, Korea embarked on the so-called economic democracy movement from the late 1980s, albeit not robustly enough to accomplish needed economic structural adjustments. Economic democracy can safely be defined as a concept that incorporates the economic efficiency of capitalism and the democratic ideology of equity. In other words, economic democracy can be understood as a system that can improve both economic democracy and equity. The basic idea behind economic democracy paves the way for the 'advanced state development model' approach.

The various roles of government suggested to move in the direction of a new paradigm of economic democracy, are shown in Figure 12.2.

**Table 12.1**
**Economic Development Paradigms**

| Models / Issues | Developmental state model (for early stage economic development) | Advanced state model (for later stage economic development) |
|---|---|---|
| Internal and external surroundings | · Pursuit of free trade<br>· Favourable attitudes toward economic support for the LDC's | · Globalization and unlimited competition<br>· Developed countries' interest-oriented international economic order |
| Development strategies | · Government-led economic development planning<br>· CME system<br>· Physical capital-oriented quantitative growth<br>· Growth-first principle<br>· Unbalanced growth through export-led industrialization | · Decentralization and privatization<br>· Decentralized and liberal economic operations<br>· Human capital-oriented qualitative growth<br>· Stable growth with equity and welfare improvement<br>· Upgrading of industrial structure and correction of industrial disequilibrium |
| Role of government | · Removal of supply bottleneck problems<br>· Minor interest in correcting market failures<br>· Neglect of equity and welfare improvement | · SOC expansion and productivity improvement<br>· Major interest in correcting market failures<br>· Equity and welfare improvement |
| Miscellaneous | · Capitalism is an efficiency-oriented system.<br>· Proper role of government is needed to alleviate inherent drawbacks of the system and to pursue economic development.<br>· Active and appropriate role of government is necessary for LDCs to advance their economies | |

Third, equity and welfare-oriented development principles should replace the growth-first principle. Various unhealthy consequences and disequilibria caused by past development strategies need to be corrected.

Fourth, future development should be directed toward the establishment of a human capital-oriented, and knowledge-and information-oriented society, which will definitely improve both economic efficiency and equity at the same time.[7] Fifth, in order to accomplish the above objectives, the government should return private sector businesses to business firms and financial institutions, and concentrate on its original role of supplying public goods (investment in SOCs and education, for example), correcting market failure and an embodiment of the welfare state.

Finally, the role of the government needs adjustment depending on the development stages of a nation, but should not be given up. An active role of the government is indispensable for developing countries to move toward becoming an advanced state.

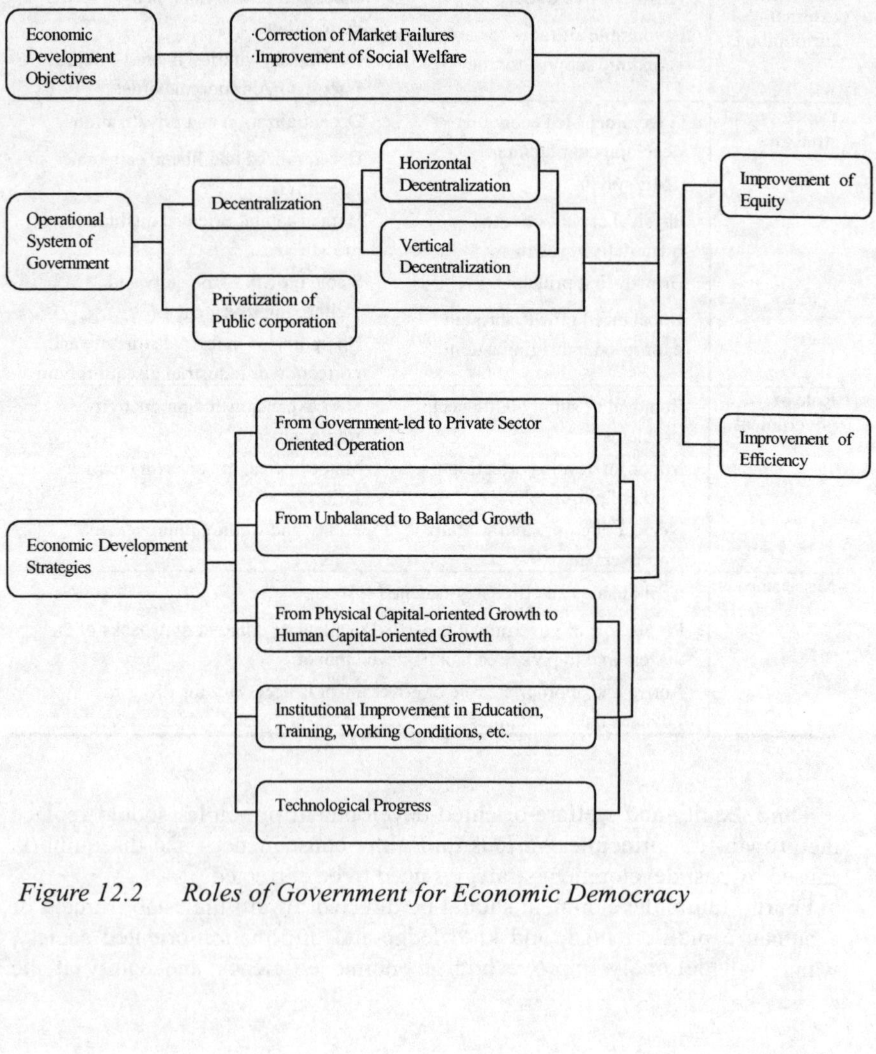


*Figure 12.2 Roles of Government for Economic Democracy*

A knowledge and information society is one in which the status of human capital owners is elevated, and capital ownership is dispersed to many small owners. Human capital owners have an improved position over physical capital owners. Subordinate capital–labour relationships and extreme conflicts between them will fade away gradually, since cooperation between them is essential to promote efficient production in the human capital-oriented society. Capital and labour will pursue a positive sum game through cooperation.

The essence of the knowledge and information society lies at the development of human capital through investments in education, training and R&D. In particular, expansion and improvement of public education will increase the portion distributed to labourers, and thus improve social equity. In the end, a knowledge and information society will create a win-win society and thereby enhance equity and efficiency through improving the position of labourers. This society can be the leading paradigm for the future and thus serve as a target for the future development policy agenda of the government.

## NOTES

1 Debates on 'Asian values' have drawn a lot of attention recently in relation to the Asian economic development model. 'Asian value' is not well-defined economic terminology, and had not grabbed much attention until the 1997 East Asian economic crisis. Revival of disputes on this issue was initiated by the fact the 'Asian dragons', symbolic countries of successful economic development in the 1970s and 1980s, came to experience a sudden collapse. Asian values have often been emphasized by the former prime minister of Singapore, Kwan Yiu Lee and the former prime minister of Malaysia, Mahatir. The essence of the argument is that there is a strong causal relationship between rapid economic growth and traditional Asian ethics of Confucianism such as enthusiasm toward education, diligence, self-sacrificing and cooperative spirit. Asian values have been cited as a major cause, at the same time, for the recent Asian economic crisis by others. Excessive government intervention, blood- or religion-(and school-) related sectorism in politics, economic corruption, lack of inventive spirit caused by a strict seniority rule, and excessive emphasis on interpersonal relationships, which have originated from Asian cultural values in large part, are believed to be responsible for the economic crisis in East Asia. There are many other development economists, however, who consider policy factors as the prime cause for the crisis rather than cultural factors. The debate on this issue will continue for some time to come.

2 See Lee (1993, 2002) for details.

3 As mentioned at the outset of this chapter, human history has recorded continuous development and thereby improved human welfare. Again, here, development means improvement of living conditions, human rights and so on. Consequently we need to approach economic development problems from the human welfare aspects.

4 Note that a new economic system emerged beside areas of the existing one, not at the centre of it. For example, the feudal system was initiated at the edges of the fallen ancient slavery society, capitalism, outside of the feudal strongholds, and socialism, as the way out of the capitalistic countries. Also we need to know that the Western economic system could settle down easily in Japan, which belonged to side areas of the main Oriental civilization.

5 See Lee (2002) for details.

6 To be specific, Chowdhury and Islam put forward the following arguments. In the wake of the East Asian crisis, governments were forced by the IMF to give up policy independence, to depart from their fixed exchange rate regimes but maintaining open capital accounts. In other words, governments forfeited the ability to fight an incipient recession through expansionary demand management policies. On the basis of the Washington-led international community, Asian governments were directed to win the 'confidence game' at all cost. Thus, interest rates were raised and budgets were tightened. The Keynesian compact was broken, albeit temporarily, but its inexorable logic prevailed. A prospective recession became an inescapable reality. Specifically, they say: 'Thus the answer to the puzzles pertaining to the sudden demise of the miracle economies of Asia now seems to lie in an undue faith in the virtues of globalization that made macroeconomic policy subservient to the interests of international money markets. In fact, prominent economists (for example, Corden, 1999; Krugman, 1998a, 1999; Sachs, 1998; Stiglitz, 1998b) have concluded that the very IMF adjustment package aggravated the crisis.'

7 For details, see Lee (1999).

## REFERENCES

Amsden, Alice H. (1989), *Asia's Next Giant: South Korea and Late Industrialization*, New York: Oxford University Press.

Chowdhury, Anis and Iyanatul Islam (2001), 'Introduction: Responding to the Challenges of the Post-crisis Era', in Anis Chowdhury and Iyanatul Islam (eds), *Beyond the Asian Crisis*, Cheltenham: Edward Elgar Publishing.

Flynn, Norman (1999), *Miracle to Meltdown in Asia: Business, Government and Society*, Oxford: Oxford University Press.

Henke, Holger and Ian Boxill (eds) (2000), *The End of the 'Asian Model'?*, Amsterdam: John Benjamins Publishing Company.

Hoa, Tran Van (2001), 'The Asia Recovery and Sustainable Development and Growth: an Overview', in Tran Van Hoa (ed.), *The Asia Recovery*, Cheltenham: Edward Elgar Publishing.

Hutson, Elaine and Colm Kearney (2001), 'The IMF and the New International Financial Architecture', in Anis Chowdhury and Iyanatul Islam (eds), *Beyond the Asian Crisis*, Cheltenham: Edward Elgar Publishing.

Johnson, Chalmers (1994), 'What is the Best System of National Economic Management for Korea', in L.J. Cho and Y.H. Kim (eds), *Korea's Political Economy: Institutional Perspective*, San Francisco: Westview Press.

Kim, Kwang Suk and Joon-Kyung Kim (1997), 'Korean Economic Development: An Overview', in D. Cha, K.S. Kim and D. Perkins (eds), *The Korean Economy 1945–95: Performance and Vision for the 21st Century*, Seoul: Korea Development Institute.

Krugman, Paul R. (1994), 'The Myth of Asia's Miracle', *Foreign Affairs*, **73**(6), 62–78.

Lee, Jong Won (1993), 'A Study on the Economic Development Process in Korea', *Kyong Je Hak Yon Gu*, **41**(2), 335–71 (in Korean).

Lee, Jong Won(1999), 'How Can We Interpret the Knowledge and Information Society: An Economic Developmental Model Approach', *Korean Economic Review*, **26**, 1–16

Lee,. Jong Won (2002), *The Korean Economy*, Seoul: Haenam, (in Korean).

Meier, Gerald M. (1995), *Leading Issues in Economic Development*, 6th ed, New York: Oxford University Press.

Rodrick, D. (1995), 'Growth Policy: Getting Interventions Right: How South Korea and Taiwan Grew Rich', *Economic Policy*, **20**, 1995, 55–107.

Wade, R. (1990), *Governing the Market: Economic Theory and the Role of Government in East Asian Industrialization*, Princeton: Princeton University Press.

World Bank (1993), *The Asian Miracle*, Oxford: Oxford University Press.

# 13. Towards a New Economic Development Model for Korea*

**Charles Harvie and Hyun-Hoon Lee**

## 13.1 INTRODUCTION

After the devastation of the Korean War and the partitioning of the country, South Korea was one of the poorest countries in the world. Economic recovery during the period 1953 to 1961 was characterized as being very slow, heavily dependent upon US financial assistance, and was focused upon an import substitution development policy. By the early 1960s the import substitution policy was recognized as having failed and, by 1962, a 'switching point' was reached whereby emphasis instead was to be placed on the development of export-oriented industries. The country's starting point for its export-led industrialization was however inauspicious with a per capita GDP at only US$87 in current prices in 1962, much lower than that of most of its regional neighbours.

The introduction of the country's First Five-Year Plan (1962–66) proved to be a catalyst for the remarkable transformation of the economy, enabling it to achieve by 1970 the status of a Newly Industrializing Country (NIC). Korea continued its rapid growth during the 1970s despite the two oil crises, and by the late 1970s had even overtaken Malaysia, on a per capita income basis, which was then the second most advanced ASEAN nation. By the mid-1980s Korea overtook countries such as Mexico, Argentina, Brazil, Portugal, Poland, Yugoslavia and Hungary. By 1989 Korea joined the highest income developing countries group, consisting of Israel, Hong Kong, Singapore and Taiwan. Over the period 1962–89, characterized by rapid and sustained economic and trade growth, per capita income increased from US$87 in 1962

*This work was supported in part by a 2003 Research Grant of Kangwon National University. This work was presented at a joint conference of RCIE, AKES and KDI on 'Korea and the World Economy II,' Seattle, 1–2 August 2003. The authors would like to thank Helena Guimaraes and other participants for their helpful comments and suggestions.

to US$ 5199 by 1989, the economy's GDP expanded from US$2.3 billion in 1962 to US$220.7 billion in 1989, and exports increased from US$55 million in 1962 to US$61.4 billion in 1989.

From the mid-1980s the economy entered a new phase with the onset of the so-called 'three lows' – low oil prices, a lower US dollar and low interest rates. For the first time in the economic history of Korea domestic savings began to consistently exceed investment, with the saving rate rising to over 30 per cent of GDP, and the country's balance of payments turned from a chronic deficit position to a surplus. As a result Korea was able to rapidly reduce its foreign debt, which had peaked at US$46.7 billion in 1985. It was no longer necessary for Korea to worry about foreign debt and rely on advanced countries for economic assistance. By the late 1980s Korea appeared to have achieved its goal of realizing economic independence. An economic 'miracle on the River Han' appeared to have been achieved.

Few countries in history have attained so rapidly such a high level of development. In a single generation this poor nation, consisting primarily of subsistence farmers in the 1950s and early 1960s, had become by the mid-1990s the world's largest producer of home appliances, the second-largest producer of semiconductor chips, the second-largest ship builder, the fifth-largest car maker, the eleventh-largest economy, and the twelfth largest trading nation. Rapid economic growth and development with low unemployment, driven by high savings and investment and export growth, became the norm for the country. By 1996, per capita income surpassed US$ 10 000 and remained relatively equally distributed, while living standards for ordinary Koreans increased dramatically. The country's attainment of OECD membership in December 1996 signified the culmination of 35 years of extraordinary growth and the economy's coming of age. For many developing countries, Korea's economic development model appeared to offer a viable framework with which to replicate such rapid development. Without doubt, the Korean economy was hailed as a model of achievement for other emerging economies to emulate.[1]

But the financial crisis of 1997 and economic crisis of 1998 revealed that the Korean development model, which had been adequate throughout most of the period of high growth until the late 1980s (or the early 1990s at the most), was no longer adequate in the face of a new international environment and for the country's stage of economic development. Therefore, the Korean growth and development model required an overhaul. This chapter examines the 'old' growth and economic development model of Korea, and then constructs a 'new' model that will give the Korean economy a new dynamism that will enable it to return to its earlier strong and sustained growth path.

In section 2, we first examine the 'old' economic development model of Korea. That is, we construct a systemic framework that can explain the major factors behind Korea's success over the period from the early 1960s to the late 1980s. Then, in section 3, we suggest a coherent explanation of why the financial crisis of 1997 occurred. In section 4, we construct a new development model of Korea. Section 5 provides some concluding remarks.

## 13.2 THE 'OLD' KOREAN DEVELOPMENT MODEL[2]

Before suggesting a new development model for Korea, we start with a summary of the main elements of the 'old' development model. There have been numerous attempts to explain the so-called 'miracle' performance of Korea.[3] Table 13.1 summarizes the major determinants of the performance of the Korean economy. As seen in the table we attempt to divide the framework into initial conditions, external environment, policy factors, and interim and final outcomes.

**Table 13.1**
**The 'Old' Development Model – Key Ingredients**

| | |
|---|---|
| Initial conditions | Backward economy<br>Sound work ethic and low labour costs<br>High spirit of education and good primary education system<br>Legacies from the period of Japanese rule<br>Division of the country into North and South |
| External environment | Trade liberalization under the GATT<br>Free trade approach by the US<br>Flying geese pattern pioneered by Japan<br>Global capital flows/international capital markets |
| Policy factors | Primarily market-based mechanisms of competitive discipline<br>Tailored government intervention<br>Outward orientation<br>Stable macroeconomic management<br>Emphasis on education |
| Interim outcome | High savings<br>High investment<br>Increasing human capital<br>Rapid growth of exports<br>Rapid catching-up of technology |
| Final outcome | Rapid industrialization<br>Rapid and sustained economic growth<br>Reduced poverty<br>Improving social indicators |

*Source*: Authors

### 13.2.1 Initial Conditions[4]

First, and similar to that for most other East Asian countries, Korea's rapid development took place from an initial position of 'economic backwardness', characterized by a low level of national income and income per capita. The historical record strongly suggests that really rapid growth of real income per capita is confined to cases where countries, that initially lag behind the leaders in terms of income and productivity levels, go through a phase of rapid catching up (Crafts 1998). But catching up is not automatic. In his famous discussion of the opportunities and difficulties of 'economic backwardness', Gerschenkron (1962) suggested that economically backward countries could achieve a take-off into very rapid growth only if they take radical measures to promote development through institutional innovations and controlled capital markets. The development strategies of Korea, and most of the East Asian countries, to achieve rapid catch-up growth bear strong resemblance to Gerschenkron's recipe (Crafts 1998).

Economic backwardness has another dimension, not central to Gerschenkron's account 'As economies develop, they typically undergo a demographic transition in which birth and death rates both fall to a much lower level but during which there is an acceleration of population which tends initially to reduce and then significantly to increase the proportion of working age' (Crafts 1998, p. 11). Korea underwent a similar demographic transition. This change in age structure may have offered a substantial growth bonus in Korea.

Second, the sound work ethic of the Korean people was another asset. Koreans were diligent, as proven by their long working hours and high savings rates. Such diligence, in combination with low costs of labour employment, made the products of Korea competitive in terms of both quality and price. A high pool of available savings, mainly from the mid-1970s, provided the necessary funds for high rates of domestic investment (see Table 13.1). A number of factors have been advanced to explain the high level of domestic saving in the economies of East Asia including Korea (see, for example, World Bank 1993). First, the rapid economic growth experienced by these countries. Studies suggest that savings are an outcome of high growth (see for example Carroll et al. 1993) although this does vary by country. Second, the rapid demographic transitions experienced by these countries. The size, age distribution, and ratio of working to non-working population can exert an influence on aggregate saving (see for example Modigliani and Ando 1963 and Modigliani 1970). Third, sound policy fundamentals. Low fiscal budget deficits, and surpluses, focusing upon restraining government spending, enabled public savings to complement private savings including that from the private corporate sector. Fourth, specific policy measures to encourage saving were adopted including the establishment of financial systems (for example postal savings institutions);

effective protection of deposits at financial institutions; tax incentives; restrictions on consumer credit and spending; and forced savings through mandatory pension schemes.

Third, in Korea people were well educated due to the strong Confucian emphasis on education, focusing upon the development of a good primary education system. In the 1960s the illiteracy rate was already well below 10 per cent. The strong desire for education provided a high-quality labour force and modern management ability as the stages of industrialization unfolded (see for example Tae 1972, p. 56). Total expenditure, both public and private, on education regularly exceeded 10 per cent of GDP, the highest level among all the developing countries.

Fourth, Japan formally colonized Korea from 1910–45, but even before this time it had already introduced a series of measures into traditional Korea that initiated the transformation of the country both economically and socially (see Amsden 1989). Although the growth rate of the Korean economy during the whole colonial period was nearly 4 per cent per annum, in absolute terms the well-being of ordinary Koreans worsened. With liberation from the Japanese in 1945 the Koreans were therefore left in dire poverty. The deterioration of the Korean people's economic welfare during the colonial period can be traced to a number of factors (see Song 1990). (1) Korea was regarded by the Japanese as a source of cheap rice. (2) The country's other resources, such as timber, fishing and mining, were exploited for the benefit of the Japanese economy and not the Korean economy. (3) Korea was used to settle Japan's surplus population, who were given the best jobs in Korea. (4) The Japanese used cheap workers from Korea for the development of Japanese mining and manufacturing industries. Skilled workers were also transferred to work in Japan. (5) Japan used Korea as a base for military training, and forcibly drafted young Koreans into the Japanese army. (6) Koreans were generally restricted to no more than a primary education. (7) Koreans were discriminated against and used in lower organizational positions and consequently had few opportunities to accumulate experience as leaders, managers or negotiators. Hence Korea had a severe lack of competent politicians, bureaucrats, scholars, entrepreneurs and technocrats. (8) Finally, the period of colonialism resulted in Koreans being largely isolated from experience in the international arena.

For all the negative features of Japanese colonialism there were some positive impacts as well, such as education, infrastructure (finance, transportation and commerce), and management experience in modern organizations (Amsden 1989, p. 32). Japan also dismantled 1000 year-old dynastic institutions that had held back the advancement of the country. Koreans learned the Japanese way of doing business and managing the economy, and remain the Asians who understand Japan best. Because of the colonial experience Koreans were in a position to make selective use of various Japanese institutions. Not surprisingly, Korea's experience of rapid development is often compared with that of Japan's.

Fifth, another historical legacy was the division of the country after the liberalization from the Japanese rule in 1945 and the Korean War in 1950–53. Despite the devastation of the physical infrastructure in both the North and the South, the North was in a better position to rehabilitate its economy. It had the best mines and most advanced heavy industries. The South's legacy was less auspicious, being primarily agricultural, having been developed by the Japanese as a supplier of cheap foodstuffs for Japan's industrial workforce. The country's capital city, Seoul, had been severely damaged during the period of the war,[5] with over 80 per cent of industrial and infrastructure facilities and over half its dwellings destroyed. In addition, after the war the South experienced a flood of refugees from the North, resulting in it being left with two-thirds of the entire Korean population. As stated by Song (1990), p.42, 'The South began its national reconstruction with too many people on too little land'. In addition, the maintenance of its borders required considerable military expenditure. The urgent need to catch up with, and outperform, the North necessitated the maximum possible growth, or growth at any cost, and became the basic cause of the forced expansion of exports and investment.

### 13.2.2 External Environment

Korea's fast growth occurred in favourable international circumstances, at least until the late 1980s. First, the international movement towards freer trade under the GATT enabled Korea, which became a member in 1967, to effectively pursue an export-oriented growth strategy. Following a number of multilateral trade talks, under the auspices of the GATT, the developed countries moved toward the opening of their domestic markets, yet Korea, as a developing country, was allowed to keep its domestic markets effectively closed until the end of the 1980s.

Second, the free trade approach on the part of the US, which provided the largest market for Korea's exports, assisted the export-oriented industrialization strategy. Also, Korea received a considerable amount of explicit and implicit economic assistance from the United States during the Cold War era, and this provided seed money at the initial stage of economic development.

Third, like flocks of geese flying in a 'V' formation to make their flying easier, Korea (and the other East Asian countries) followed the export-oriented development model of Japan – the lead goose. Japan successfully developed globally competitive high-technology products that it was able to export successfully, while its domestic market remained almost effectively closed to foreign competition. After the Plaza Accord in 1985, however, the yen began to increase in value relative to the US dollar. The strong yen encouraged many Japanese companies, particularly in the automotive and electronics industries, to establish overseas plants in order to maintain their international competitiveness (Sato and Rizzo 1986). The stronger yen also increased the cost of employing labour, relative to that of its regional competitors such as Korea, and resulted in many of Japan's labour-intensive industries moving offshore to production units in the lower labour cost countries of East Asia.[6] Instead of Japan exporting these products to East Asia, these countries now started to export to Japan. In the process Japan, through its FDI, had passed on its production technologies to the East Asian nations. Specifically, Korea and Taiwan followed Japan with a certain time lag, and later, as their labour costs increased, the economies of South-East Asia followed during the period of the 1980s, and increasingly so into the 1990s, as they adopted a more export oriented policy and increasingly opened their financial sectors to further inflows of short- and long-term capital flows.

Fourth, it is also important to bear in mind that the Korean economy, particularly from the period after the breakdown of the Bretton Woods agreement, began to benefit from the rapid development of international financial markets and the globalization of capital flows. This assisted Korea in foreign borrowing, the accumulation of FDI and the expansion of regional growth of output and exports. However, such flows of capital increased dramatically, enabling Korea to sustain very high rates of investment, but also contributing to problems on current account and in the accumulation of foreign debt.

### 13.2.3 Policy Factors

First, the Korean economy operated within an environment of primarily market-based mechanisms of competitive discipline. This contributed to the development of competitive enterprises subject to hard budget constraints, and, by limiting price distortions, the system contributed to a more efficient and productive allocation of scarce resources.

Second, there was a strong leadership role by the government in creating and developing the 'markets', and their credible commitment to its long-run development. This is a somewhat controversial argument, as there is plenty of evidence that Korea's industrial policies did not contribute to the growth of industries' productivity.[7] However, at least until the early 1980s a strong government leadership was rather necessary and desirable, because the domestic markets were incomplete or missing and the structure of domestic industry was rather simple. Even if the net benefits of government intervention policies are still controversial, they clearly allowed some Korean firms to establish themselves in industries such as steel, chemical engineering, shipbuilding, electronics and automobiles, where the costs of entry were high.

Third, an outward-looking development strategy, particularly a dynamic export sector, has been a crucial ingredient of the miracle. There were several reasons for the Korean government pursuing this strategy (see Harvie and

Lee 2003b). (1) The Korean economy started from a very low level of national income and income per capita. Consequently, domestic producers faced a very limited domestic market, suggesting that developing an industrial base through import substitution had severe limitations. (2) Korea's natural resource endowment was so poor that a development strategy based on domestic resource utilization was inconceivable. (3) US assistance, which financed most of the post-war Korean reconstruction, peaked in 1957 and was gradually but continually declining in the early 1960s. Faced with this reduction in foreign aid, Korean policy-makers had to consider how best to expand domestic saving and generate an alternative source of foreign exchange to finance projects and meet balance of payments requirements. (4) The availability of an abundant, cohesive and well-motivated labour force with a high educational level, and relatively low wages, provided the country with an initial comparative advantage in exporting light manufactured labour intensive consumer goods whose capital and technology requirement was minimal. This was ideal given the country's shortage of capital. (5) There was the determination of the military leadership to attain a high rate of growth, and a virtual lack of constraints on its ability to make decisions and to carry them out.[8] The only way forward was an export-oriented industrialization growth and development policy, requiring the development of globally competitive enterprises.

Many export industries, and indeed the economy as a whole during the early stages of its development, were subject to extensive involvement by the government, and the country's initial export expansion was effectively 'forced' by the actions of the government (Song 1990, p. 58). The Korean government set firm- and industry-specific export targets and developed export-marketing institutions. They also made selective use of tariff protection, export incentives ranging from moral suasion to subsidies, and provided industry with financing at lower cost. The outward-oriented development forced domestic firms to become more efficient and absorb foreign technology and managerial know-how in order to compete in world markets. It also promoted growth by providing access to larger markets and generating increasing returns to scale in production. The export-oriented development was a means of achieving viable external balances, generating foreign exchange to purchase essential technology and imported inputs, and generating the demand needed to accelerate GDP growth.

Fourth was the adherence to stable macroeconomic management. This was seen as being essential to: encourage the development of the private sector; encourage domestic saving; contribute to vigorous accumulation of investment; encourage efficient resource allocation through the market by reducing inflation and distortions in relative prices; and to maintain international competitiveness through a competitive real exchange rate, and this required the attainment of stable prices. However, during much of the period of the 1960s and 1970s Korea experienced relatively high and volatile rates of inflation. From the early 1980s the need to reduce this became a key policy objective, and considerable success was achieved in this regard from 1982 onward.

As can be seen from Table 13.2 the saving rate increased rapidly from 1973 but was still insufficient to meet domestic investment requirements, resulting in the need to borrow from overseas and a consequential rapid accumulation of foreign debt. However by 1986, for the first time during the period of rapid growth, domestic saving exceeded domestic investment requirements, and the level of foreign debt began to decline. The country was now able to finance most of its investment requirements from its own domestic resources. Reflecting this development exports exceeded imports for the first time also in 1986, and the trade balance moved into surplus.

Fifth, education policies that focused on primary and secondary schools generated rapid increases in labour force skills, and enhanced the productivity and employability of the workforce. The Korean government successfully addressed the market failures of missing information and positive externalities in the educational field, by focusing spending on universal primary and secondary education. The share of expenditure allocated to tertiary education tended to be low, and this was more focused upon the acquisition of technical skills, vocational training and technically sophisticated disciplines. The percentage of high school graduates advancing to colleges or university during the period of the 1980s was the second-highest in the world after the US. This investment in education enabled Korean growth to be accompanied by a high level of income equality that remained relatively unchanged during the course of development. In fact, Rodrik (1994) showed that countries that were poorer, but that had good primary education systems and less inequality of income and land distribution around 1960, grew faster during subsequent periods.

Advocates of free markets saw the triumph of the Korean economy (and the East Asian economies) as being in its small government, the market mechanism and unfettered private initiative. On the other hand interventionists saw the Korean economic miracle as being the triumph of selective interventionist policies by the Korean government. Trade economists viewed it as a miracle based on outward orientation, labour economists stressed the early emphasis on education, and macroeconomists pointed to the region's fiscal conservatism. But the truth is in between: to varying degrees, all of these policy factors contributed to the fast growth performance of Korea.

### 13.2.4 Interim Outcome

The Korean development model produced impressive results by any standard. These included high levels of domestic financial savings and private domestic

## Table 13.2
## Major Indicators of Korean Economic Growth 1960–89

| | GDP per capita (US$)* | GDP (US$ billion) | Real GDP growth rate (%) | CPI (%) | Savings ratio (%) | Invest. ratio (%) | Trade balance (US$ mill) | Exports (US$ mill) | Foreign debt (US$ mill) | Unem. Rate (%) | Exch. rate (won/US $) |
|---|---|---|---|---|---|---|---|---|---|---|---|
| 1960 | 79 | 2 | 1.2 | na | 0.8 | 10.9 | -273 | 33 | - | 11.7 | 65.0 |
| 1961 | 82 | 2.1 | 5.9 | na | 2.8 | 13.2 | -242 | 41 | - | 12.7 | 130.0 |
| 1962 | 87 | 2.3 | 2.1 | na | 3.3 | 12.8 | -335 | 55 | - | 9.8 | 130.0 |
| 1963 | 100 | 2.7 | 9.1 | na | 8.7 | 18.1 | -410 | 87 | 157 | 8.2 | 130.0 |
| 1964 | 103 | 2.9 | 9.7 | na | 8.7 | 14.0 | -245 | 120 | 177 | 7.7 | 256.0 |
| 1965 | 105 | 3.0 | 5.7 | na | 7.4 | 15.0 | -241 | 175 | 206 | 7.4 | 272.1 |
| 1966 | 125 | 3.6 | 12.2 | 12.0 | 11.8 | 21.6 | -430 | 250 | 392 | 7.1 | 271.5 |
| 1967 | 142 | 4.2 | 5.9 | 10.7 | 11.4 | 21.9 | -574 | 335 | 645 | 6.2 | 274.6 |
| 1968 | 169 | 5.2 | 11.3 | 11.3 | 15.1 | 25.9 | -836 | 486 | 1 199 | 5.1 | 281.5 |
| 1969 | 210 | 6.5 | 13.8 | 11.6 | 18.8 | 28.8 | -992 | 658 | 1 800 | 4.8 | 304.5 |
| 1970 | 248 | 8.0 | 8.8 | 16.9 | 16.2 | 24.6 | -992 | 882 | 2 245 | 4.5 | 316.7 |
| 1971 | 286 | 9.4 | 8.6 | 12.2 | 14.5 | 25.1 | -1 044 | 1 133 | 2 922 | 4.5 | 373.2 |
| 1972 | 316 | 10.6 | 4.9 | 11.9 | 15.7 | 20.9 | -574 | 1 676 | 3 589 | 4.5 | 398.9 |
| 1973 | 396 | 13.5 | 12.3 | 3.5 | 21.4 | 24.7 | -566 | 3 284 | 4 260 | 4.0 | 397.5 |
| 1974 | 542 | 18.8 | 7.4 | 24.8 | 19.3 | 31.8 | -1 938 | 4 516 | 5 937 | 4.1 | 484.0 |
| 1975 | 598 | 21.1 | 6.5 | 24.7 | 16.9 | 27.5 | -1 671 | 5 003 | 8 456 | 4.1 | 484.0 |
| 1976 | 806 | 28.9 | 11.2 | 15.4 | 22.2 | 25.7 | -590 | 7 814 | 10 533 | 3.9 | 484.0 |
| 1977 | 1 019 | 37.1 | 10.0 | 10.0 | 25.4 | 27.7 | -477 | 10 046 | 12 648 | 3.8 | 484.0 |
| 1978 | 1 407 | 52.0 | 9.0 | 14.7 | 27.3 | 31.9 | -1 780 | 12 711 | 14 871 | 3.2 | 484.0 |
| 1979 | 1 649 | 61.9 | 7.1 | 18.5 | 26.5 | 36.0 | -4 395 | 14 705 | 20 287 | 3.8 | 484.0 |
| 1980 | 1 632 | 62.2 | -2.1 | 28.7 | 20.8 | 32.1 | -4 384 | 17 214 | 27 170 | 5.2 | 659.9 |
| 1981 | 1 797 | 69.6 | 6.5 | 21.3 | 20.5 | 30.3 | -3 849 | 20 747 | 32 433 | 4.5 | 700.5 |
| 1982 | 1 892 | 74.4 | 7.2 | 7.1 | 20.9 | 28.6 | -2 827 | 20 934 | 37 083 | 4.4 | 748.8 |
| 1983 | 2 062 | 82.3 | 10.7 | 3.4 | 25.3 | 29.9 | -1 849 | 23 272 | 40 378 | 4.1 | 795.5 |
| 1984 | 2 242 | 90.6 | 8.2 | 2.2 | 27.9 | 31.9 | -1 089 | 26 486 | 43 053 | 3.8 | 827.4 |
| 1985 | 2 289 | 93.4 | 6.5 | 2.3 | 28.6 | 31.1 | -19 | 26 442 | 46 729 | 4.0 | 890.2 |
| 1986 | 2 611 | 107.6 | 11.0 | 2.8 | 32.8 | 30.2 | 4 299 | 34 128 | 44 500 | 3.8 | 861.4 |
| 1987 | 3 248 | 135.2 | 11.0 | 3.1 | 36.8 | 37.7 | 7 529 | 46 560 | 35 600 | 3.1 | 792.3 |
| 1988 | 4 302 | 180.8 | 10.5 | 7.1 | 38.6 | 39.1 | 11 283 | 59 973 | 31 500 | 2.5 | 684.1 |
| 1989 | 5 199 | 220.7 | 6.1 | 5.7 | 35.4 | 35.9 | 4 597 | 61 408 | - | 2.6 | 680.0 |

*Notes*: GNP and GNP per capita are in current prices. The rate of inflation is based on the GNP deflator. The rate of interest is the bank interest rate on time deposits for the period of one or more years.
* GNP per capita before 1970.

*Source*: Song (1990), pp. 60–61, Bank of Korea, http://www.bok.or.kr, National Statistical Office http://www.nso.go.kr.

investment; rapidly growing human capital; rapid growth of exports; and rapid catching-up of foreign technologies (see Table 13.2). These we describe here as being major interim outcomes which became the principal engines of growth.

The Korean government encouraged private investment with a wide array of mechanisms such as low capital goods prices, subsidized interest rates for corporate investment and limited risk for private investors. Where investment could not be provided by the private sector alone, particularly during the early stages of economic development, the government used its own investment resources for the construction of key industries and for the formation of social overhead capital. A stable business environment with relatively low inflation also encouraged investment in long-gestation fixed assets. High rates of investment were financed by domestic saving, as well as through increasing flows of foreign debt and investment. High human capital, rapid growth of exports and rapid technological change further laid the foundations of rapid growth and development.

### 13.2.5 Final Outcome

The interim outcomes contributed to rapid industrialization, rapid and sustained economic growth and considerably improved social indicators. Poverty declined significantly and other social indicators, such as equality of income, life expectancy and fertility rates, compared favourably with other countries at a similar level of income before and during the period of rapid growth (Park and Kim 1998). Table 13.3 indicates for example that the Korean economy compares very favourably with the economies of East Asia and Pacific, Sub-Saharan Africa, the Middle East, and Latin America and the Caribbean in terms of GDP per capita, adult literacy, primary, secondary and tertiary education gross enrolment, the UNDP Human Development Index, life expectancy, infant mortality rate, total fertility rate and income inequality. While the gini coefficient improved only slightly in East Asia during the period of the 1990s in comparison to that of the 1980s, Korea's income inequality performance continued to improve. While East Asia compared very favourably against economies in South Asia, Sub-Saharan Africa, the Middle Eastern economies and Latin America in terms of life expectancy, infant mortality, and particularly well in terms of fertility rates throughout its period of rapid economic development and growth, Korea's performance can certainly be regarded as outstanding within the context of this overall regional performance. Given the less than auspicious circumstances at the beginning of its growth and development from the early 1960s, characterized by a very low GDP per capita (Table 13.2), the outcomes from Korea's development model produced tangible social improvements for its citizens.

### 13.2.6 Adverse Consequences[9]

Of course there were also adverse consequences from the 'old' model. First, the country experienced high but volatile economic growth (see Table 13.2). From the 1960s, because of the growth-first development policy, the economy experienced more year-to-year fluctuations. Since the scale of the Korean economy was relatively small, well into the 1970s, the growth rate was also susceptible to large fluctuations caused by construction phases in large investment projects. The economy's outward orientation also exposed it to fluctuations from oil price hikes and other external influences. The inexperience of policy-makers, especially during the 1960s, also contributed to economic fluctuations.

Second, as the expansion of industrial capacity tended to be excessive, the amount of domestic investment generally exceeded the amount of domestic savings (see Table 13.2). In addition, much of this domestic saving was diverted into real estate as a hedge against high inflation. Hence the level of available domestic saving in Korea was lower than that required to meet the productive investment needs of the country. This gap had to be filled through foreign borrowing, and this, along with the need to import oil and many other industrial raw materials, explains why Korea's foreign debt continued to rise until 1985 (see Table 13.2). Also, the debt-to-equity ratio of large Korean firms, forced to overexpand their production and export capacity, tended to be higher than that of other Asian NICs. Korean growth was, therefore, characterized by domestic investment exceeding domestic savings, a high debt–equity ratio for most firms, and a large foreign debt.

Third, the expansion of industrial capacity in Korea was achieved through an expansion of existing firms rather than through the creation of new firms. This pattern persisted for over two decades and resulted in the growth of a small number of very large firms and business conglomerates (*chaebols*), causing a large gap between large and small firms. The market concentration ratio in Korea was much higher than in either of its regional neighbours, Japan or Taiwan. In Japan, growth was based on a significant number of very large firms as well as a large number of small firms, while in Taiwan emphasis was placed on the development of small firms. Hence the Korean economy may be called a large-firm economy, in contrast to the small-firm economy of Taiwan or the bi-polar economy of Japan. The structural imbalance between large and small enterprises remained unchanged, even though the government attempted to restrain market concentration during the period of the 1980s.

Fourth, Korean growth was accompanied by trade and balance of payments deficits until 1985 (see Table 13.2). This was caused to some extent by Korea's resource poverty, but was principally due to the policy of allowing exporting companies to import raw materials, parts and machinery required

## Table 13.3
## Social Indicators : An International Regional Comparison

| | GDP per capita (PPP US$) | Adult literacy rate (%) age 15 and above | Combined, primary, secondary and tertiary gross enrolment ratio (%) | Human Development Index (HDI) value | Life expectancy (Years) | Infant mortality rate per 1000 live births | | | Total fertility rate, births per woman | | Income inequality – Average Gini coefficient | |
|---|---|---|---|---|---|---|---|---|---|---|---|---|
| | 2000 | 2000 | 1999 | 2000 | 1970–75 | 1995–2000 | 1970 | 2000 | 1970–75 | 1995–2000 | 1980s | 1990s |
| Korea | 17 380 | 97.8 | 90 | 0.882 | 62.6 | 74.3 | 43 | 5 | 4.3 | 1.5 | 33.6[1] | 31.6[2] |
| East Asia and Pacific | 4 290 | 85.9 | 71 | 0.726 | 60.4 | 68.8 | 87 | 33 | 5.0 | 2.1 | 38.7 | 38.1 |
| South Asia | 2 404 | 55.6 | 53 | 0.570 | 49.9 | 61.9 | 128 | 68 | 5.6 | 3.6 | 35.0 | 31.9 |
| Sub Saharan Africa | 1 690 | 61.5 | 42 | 0.471 | 45.3 | 48.8 | 135 | 107 | 6.8 | 5.8 | 43.7 | 47.0 |
| Central & Eastern Europe and CIS | 6 930 | 99.3 | 77 | 0.783 | 69.2 | 68.4 | 34 | 20 | 2.5 | 1.5 | 25.0 | 28.9 |
| Arab States | 4 793 | 62.0 | 62 | 0.653 | 51.9 | 65.9 | 132 | 46 | 6.5 | 4.1 | 40.5 | 38.0 |
| Latin America and the Caribbean | 7 234 | 88.3 | 74 | 0.767 | 61.1 | 69.4 | 86 | 30 | 5.1 | 2.7 | 49.8 | 49.3 |
| OECD | 23 569 | - | 87 | 0.905 | 70.4 | 76.4 | 40 | 12 | 2.5 | 1.8 | - | - |
| High income OECD | 27 848 | - | 94 | 0.932 | 72.1 | 77.8 | 20 | 6 | 2.1 | 1.7 | 33.2 | 33.8 |

*Note*: 1 Figure for 1988.
2 Figure for 1993, source UNDP.

*Sources*: UNDP, *Human Development Report*, 2002, World Bank, *World Development Reports* (various), World Bank, *World Development Indicators* (various), Deininger and Squire (1996).

for the production of export goods on a large scale. This has been called a negative import substitution policy because exporting firms tried to import as much as possible. From 1986, however, the trade and international balance of payments turned positive and Korea changed from a young debtor nation to a mature debtor nation.

Fifth, during its period of rapid economic development Korea experienced sharply fluctuating wholesale and consumer prices (see Table 13.2). Indeed from the early 1960s until 1981 Korea had the highest inflation rate among the Asian NICs. This was especially true when the economy was hit by oil price hikes, poor harvests, changes in government and high levels of investment and capacity-building. This high inflation was mainly due to an excessive expansion of demand associated with a rapid expansion of industrial capacity and the abnormal, compulsory, expansion of exports. The aggressive export promotion and growth policy necessitated that the economy had to consistently perform far beyond normal capacity, resulting in the forced expansion of investment and output. This was particularly prevalent during the heavy and chemical industries (HCI) drive of the 1970s (see Harvie and Lee 2003b). Overly ambitious investment plans caused the inflationary financing of investment. Excessive investment demand was, therefore, one of the links between the forced export growth strategy and the high inflation that persisted until 1982.

Finally, government-driven industrialization resulted in an excessive concentration of industries and population in large cities, especially in Seoul and the Seoul region. The level of urbanization in Korea was generally higher than the norm observed in other countries. As a result, such urban problems as housing shortages, lack of educational facilities and poor public services began to emerge as serious domestic issues, in particular, after the 1970s.

## 13.3 THE FINANCIAL CRISIS

Korea, one of the highest-performing economies in the world, suffered an abrupt financial crisis in 1997. The crisis started with an unprecedented number of business insolvencies (including eight of the 30 largest *chaebols*), and the devaluation of the Thai baht, the effect of which quickly spread to other regional currencies. Between October and December 1997 this new OECD member, and the world's eleventh-largest economy, was reduced to an economy surviving on overnight loans from the international money markets. Assistance from the IMF was sought in November 1997.

The events of 1997 induced academics, policy-makers and journalists alike to re-evaluate the Korean development model (and more generally the East Asian development model), and to identify whether this required a fundamentally different economic growth paradigm, or model, or whether the old model was still applicable but just required some fine-tuning. Different views on the Korean development model (and the East Asian development model more generally) stemmed from different explanations for the causes of the crisis. While a number of explanations have been offered for Korea's financial crisis, they can be broadly divided into five groups.

### 13.3.1 Exogenous Shock

The first argument is that the crisis was nothing but an accident owing to an exogenous shock. For example Kim In-Ho, the then chief economic advisor to the Korean President, was quoted as arguing later in an interview with a newspaper that:[10]

> The foreign exchange crisis came all of a sudden in the last few days like a thunderstorm … Up until the end of October, the situation was not that serious … The situation became aggravated all of a sudden in November.

Kim In-Ho seems to be trying to avoid his responsibility for the unfortunate financial crisis, which had occurred during his stay in office. But this kind of argument had been raised not only by the then government officials, but also by some well-known economists. Jeffrey Sachs is the most prominent advocate of this kind of argument:[11]

> The Asian crisis was akin to a bank run … The weaknesses in the Asian economies were real, but far from fatal … But as often happens in financial markets, euphoria turned to panic without missing a beat. Suddenly, Asia's leaders could do no right. The money fled.

Unlike Kim, however, he uses a theoretically supporting framework called a 'self-fulfilling expectations model' to explain the herding phenomenon of investors, leading to a sudden financial crisis. According to this model there are multiple equilibria in the financial markets, and a financial panic is an adverse equilibrium outcome in which short-term creditors suddenly withdraw their loans from a solvent borrower. This happens because it is rational for each creditor to withdraw its credits if the other creditors are fleeing from the borrower, even though each creditor would also be willing to lend if the other creditors were to do the same (see also Radelet and Sachs 1998).

Joseph Stiglitz, senior vice-president of the World Bank, also agrees that the financial crisis of the Asian countries was more like an accident.[12]

> Small open economies are like rowing boats on an open sea. One cannot predict when they might capsize; bad steering increases the chances of disaster and a leaky boat makes it inevitable. But their chances of being broadsided by a wave are significant no matter how well they are steered

and no matter how seaworthy they are.

In fact in July 1997, when the financial crisis was at its climax in Thailand, most of the Korean economic research institutes and the Bank of Korea publicized their optimistic predictions for the second half of 1997 for the Korean economy:[13]

> In their newly adjusted economic forecasts, the national and private economic research institutes have recently anticipated that the Korean economy will perform even better this year than their previous anticipations. The Korea Development Institute (KDI), Bank of Korea and some private institutes increased their expected economic growth rate from their previous 5 per cent to over 6 per cent and expected that the Korean economy would be going upward in the second half of 1997.

Thus, the financial crisis was not predicted by most of (maybe all of) the Korean economists, policy-makers, research institutes and the like. Even the IMF's annual report, which was published just a few months before the crisis, praised Korea for its impressive macroeconomic performance and the government for its enviable fiscal record. Having done a cross-country probit analysis, Park and Rhee (1998) agreed that it was hard to predict the Korean crisis at least up until the first half of 1997. Thus it seems undeniable that the crisis came as a surprise to the Korean public and to economists. This implies that no matter what the causes were, the crisis came as a sudden shock to the Korean economy.

### 13.3.2 Policy Mistakes

The second argument is that when the contagion from South-East Asia was imminent and the foreign investors were gradually turning their backs on Korea, inappropriate and belated policy responses caused the crisis to actually occur and make the situation even worse. That is, had the Korean government swiftly and decisively responded to the herd-like panic among foreign investors in the months preceding the eruption of the crisis, Korea would not have suffered as much as it actually did. This argument seems to have been more supported by politicians than by academics.

For instance, the parliamentary hearing in early 1999 on the causes of the financial crisis was mainly focused on the policy mistakes made by the then president and government officials. The then finance economy minister and some other key government officials were later charged with neglect of duty. The prosecutors charged that the then government should have installed a very good lightning rod when thunder and lightning was striking. The following is a newspaper report on the charges:[14]

> The prosecutors rejected the argument made by the then vice-prime minister Kang Kyong-Shik and the then chief economic advisor Kim In-Ho that 'they couldn't help it because the financial crisis erupted without an a priori symptom'. The prosecutors claimed that they should have prepared for the financial crisis in the same way as we prepare for lightning and thunder.

In diagnosing the causes the IMF also focused on the policy mistakes made by the Korean government. But the IMF also pointed out that the major policy mistakes were made well before the actual crisis, mainly related to inadequate financial sector supervision. The following is part of an official document by the IMF on the Asian crisis, and is available at the IMF's Internet homepage:[15]

> The crisis unfolded against the backdrop of several decades of outstanding economic performance in Asia, and the difficulties that the Asian countries face are not primarily the result of macroeconomic imbalances. Rather, they stemmed from weaknesses in financial systems and, to a lesser extent, governance. A combination of inadequate financial sector supervision, poor assessment and management of financial risk, and the maintenance of relatively fixed exchange rates led banks and corporations to borrow large amounts of international capital, much of it short-term, denominated in foreign currency, and unhedged.

### 13.3.3 Fundamental Weaknesses

According to this argument, the financial crisis was like a volcanic eruption. That is, structural shortcomings and weaknesses that had accumulated in Korea and other Asian countries, finally erupted when they reached their maximum level.

Interestingly, however, those who point out the fundamental weaknesses of Korea, and other Asian crisis countries, are divided into two groups, depending upon the sector they blame most: some blame the public sector, while others blame the private sector.

**Structural weaknesses in the public sector**

This kind of argument is well summarized as the moral hazard model of financial crises. According to the model, implicit and/or explicit government bailout guarantees, which were common practice in Korea and other Asian crisis countries, led to moral hazard among borrowers and lenders which resulted in overborrowing and overlending in the financial sector.[16] According to Paul Krugman, a prominent exponent of this viewpoint:[17]

The story I believe does not deny that there is a strong element of panic in the Asian crisis – but argues that the preconditions for that panic were created by bad policies in the years running up to the crisis. The crisis, in short, was a punishment for Asian sins, even if the punishment was disproportionate to the crime. What were these Asian sins?... The specific sin that pushed Asia to the brink was the problem of moral hazard in lending – mainly domestic lending.

Some of those in this group take the argument further, seeing the financial crisis of the Asian countries as a victory for the American model of free market capitalism over the Asian model of state-led capitalism. For instance, Jeffrey Frankel, a member of the Council of Economic Advisors in the United States, claims that:[18]

> One lesson now widely drawn from the crisis – and I believe correctly so – is that the Anglo-American Style financial structure apparently works better after all, as compared to the Japanese-Asian model.

Charles Wolf, a senior economic advisor of RAND, comes to a similar conclusion. The crisis finally broke out because of the accumulated shortcomings of the Asian development model of too much government control:[19]

> What we are now seeing in Asia's financial turbulence are the (Asian development) model's accumulated shortcomings ... Lacking the corrective, mediating responses that market mechanisms and intensives provide, the shortcomings accumulate until a systemic breakdown occurs.

**Structural weaknesses in the private sector**

This group also points out that internal structural weaknesses were the main causes of the crisis. However, unlike those who see the crisis as the failure of government-led capitalism, this group argues that structural weaknesses are not rooted in the public sector, but in the private sector. Joseph Stiglitz, senior vice-president of the World Bank, is one of the proponents of this viewpoint. According to him:[20]

> Many of the problems these countries face today arise not because governments did too much, but because they did too little – and because they themselves had deviated from the policies that had proved so successful over preceding decades.

Janet Yellen, chair of the Council of Economic Advisors in the US, also agrees that the crisis was rooted mainly in the fragile financial system of the private sector. She refutes the argument that the crisis revealed the failure of the Asian development model:[21]

> One irony of this interpretation is that the extensive press coverage of the crisis, and the view commonly expressed in the press that the crisis revealed the failure of an Asian or Japanese model of capitalism, may actually have substantially accelerated and exacerbated the failure of that model. Again, the point is that a transparent financial system in which investors can judge the soundness of banks and corporations on the basis of objective and reliable data would have been much less vulnerable to such contagion.

Stephen Marvin, who was considered a prominent critic of the Korean economy even before the crisis, claimed that the crisis erupted mainly because of huge over-investment by the family-controlled conglomerates (*chaebols*):[22]

> The seeds of this destruction, however, were sown long before by senior *chaebol* management. From the 2nd half of 1993 to the first half of 1997, Korean companies indulged in an orgy of investment. Driving this spending was the monomaniacal pursuit of market share and empire expansion; it was carried out in total disregard of market dynamics and return of investment …. The beginning of the end came in the 2nd quarter of 1995, when export unit prices started to sag. As a result, cash flow came under pressure, and corporate balance sheets showed the initial signs of serious deterioration. Export volume growth, however, remained buoyant, and the reckless spending – and borrowing – continued for another 18 months. In the 3rd quarter of 1997, currency turmoil in Southeast Asia abruptly braked export volume growth, cutting deeply into cash flow. The investment spree finally lurched to a halt in the 4th quarter of 1997.

### 13.3.4 Hostile Environment

According to this argument, an unfriendly international environment in the years before the crisis contributed to the crisis. Some argue that there had been drastic shifts in external market conditions before the crisis erupted. For example, Korea's competitiveness dropped dramatically when the Chinese yuan was devalued by 50 per cent in January 1994, and after the Japanese yen depreciated significantly against the US dollar from June 1995 until 1997. Furthermore, the price of semiconductors, which had accounted for about 20 per cent of Korea's total exports by value in 1995, fell as much as 80 per cent in 1996. As a result, Korea's current account recorded deficits for several years, resulting in a huge build-up of external debt.

Some advocates of Asian values, such as former Malaysian prime minister, Mahatir Mohammad, claimed that the West could not accept the fact that

Asia was becoming the centre of world power, and the Asian financial crisis was the result of hegemonic conflict between the East and the West.

### 13.3.5 The Stroke Hypothesis Explanation of the Causes of the Crisis

As reviewed above, each group suggests its own explanation for Korea's (and East Asia's) financial crisis. Blaming only one factor for the crisis, however, does not seem to be appealing. For example, attributing it exclusively to irrational (or rational) speculative attacks and contagion does not seem to make sense, because the contagion varied widely across the East Asian countries. Blaming it solely on an economic system once praised as a successful model for development is also inconsistent. There is likely to be some truth in each of these explanations. That is, had at least one of these four factors been different from what they actually were, then the financial crisis would not have occurred, or it would not have been as destructive as it actually was. In other words, Korea's financial crisis, and perhaps most other Asian countries' crises as well, occurred not due to one single reason but due to elements from all of the four explanatory categories. Using the 'stroke' hypothesis Lee (2003)[23] synthesizes most of the appealing explanations and theories of the financial crisis, and shows how the numerous factors were coherently intertwined in causing the financial crisis in Korea in 1997.[24]

The financial system of an economy is analogous to the human circulatory system in terms of its structure and functions. A financial crisis normally starts with a sudden liquidity crunch in the financial system. This is also analogous to the human stroke, which happens with the sudden blockage of an artery in the brain. These two are also very similar in that a financial crisis can result in the real sector's paralysis while a stroke can limit the body's normal functions such as thinking, movement, speech and the other senses.

Therefore, it may be very useful to understand the nature of a stroke in order to understand the nature of a financial crisis. To most people, a stroke normally seems to occur all of a sudden in a person who has been living his or her life quite normally. As a matter of fact, however, it does not strike a really healthy person. The chance of having a stroke is dependent upon the person's physical constitution, how well the person responds to the warning signs of a stroke and how friendly the person's surroundings are.

Korea's financial crisis underwent a very similar process to that of a typical stroke. To most people it appeared to have erupted all of a sudden when the panicked foreign investors turned their backs on Korea. Like a stroke, however, it erupted after several early symptoms. Fundamental weaknesses, policy mistakes, unfriendly international circumstances and exogenous shocks all contributed to the crisis. The four factors played a role and intertwined with each other systematically, resulting in the financial crisis. That is, since the late 1980s the fundamental weaknesses have accumulated, and hence the international competitiveness of Korean corporations has weakened. On the other hand, the international environment, which used to be friendly towards Korea's export-oriented growth strategy, has rapidly become hostile. This also exerted adverse pressure on Korea's competitiveness, and made the Korean economy even more vulnerable to sudden changes in the world economy. However, the Korean government overlooked the signs of weakening competitiveness and the possibility of financial crisis, and instead aggravated the situation by making consecutive policy mistakes. Finally, a sudden exogenous shock (that is a drastic increase in corporate insolvencies and the financial crisis in South-East Asia) in early 1997 triggered the financial crisis to erupt (see Lee 2003 and Harvie and Lee 2003a for more detailed explanations.)

## 13.4 TOWARDS A NEW DEVELOPMENT MODEL[25]

The events of 1997–98 induced academics, policy-makers and journalists alike to re-evaluate the Korean development model (and more generally the East Asian development model). The stroke hypothesis, our preferred explanation for the cause of the crisis, explains systematically that the financial crisis occurred as a result of a combination of fundamental weaknesses of the Korean economy that were aggravated by policy mistakes on the eve of the crisis and an increasingly hostile international environment. The financial crisis revealed the old Korean development model, which was adequate throughout most of the period of high growth until the late 1980s (or the early 1990s at the most), to be no longer adequate in the face of the new international environment, and for the country's stage of economic development. If this is true, the old Korean development model will need to be overhauled in order to give the Korean economy a new dynamism that will enable it to return to its earlier strong growth path. Even if the main cause of the recent crisis was largely due to volatile international financial markets, the crisis exposed several structural problems that require urgent attention if Korea is to return to sustained rapid growth. In any case, the financial crisis has irrevocably altered the economic landscape of Korea.

In this section we construct a new development model, the core ingredients of which are summarized in Table 13.4. As in Table 13.1 we begin with reviewing the initial conditions and external international environment, and attempt to suggest plausible policy factors and desired, or targeted, outcomes.

### 13.4.1 Initial Conditions

It is worth noting that Korea can no longer be described in early 1997 as a less-developed, but more accurately as a maturing, economy. However, there still remains a good deal of scope for rapid catch-up growth before diminishing returns to heavy capital accumulation bite severely (Crafts,

1998). But the growth bonus due to change in age structure in Korea, which was inherently temporary, is now over. This implies that the fast growth rates the Korean economy enjoyed before are no longer attainable. Korea still possesses a sound work ethic amongst its people, which still remains as a valuable asset. But as the Korean economy matures further, its workers will increasingly expect to be compensated in terms of higher wages and by improved social safety net coverage. Hence its traditional advantage in labour-intensive production will be steadily eroded.

A high spirit of education also remains valid, and, as Korea develops into an advanced economy and with the technology and skill-intensive demands of the 'new economy', it will increasingly require a highly skilled and creative labour force. But deficiencies in the current education system in Korea means an inadequate provision of the kind of labour force needed most.

In the first year of the new millennium President Kim Dae Jung of South Korea and Chairman Kim Jong Il of North Korea held an inter-Korean summit, marking a historic turning point in inter-Korean relations. The summit produced the South–North Joint Declaration, an agreement that aims to promote peace, reconciliation and cooperation between the two Koreas. North Korea, consisting of 22 million people, is the other half of the divided Korean peninsula, and has been effectively isolated from South Korea and the rest of the Western world since the end of the Korean War in 1953. How the South copes with the newly shaping North Korea, will determine whether the country can find new ways to revive its own economy which presently stands at a crossroads.

### 13.4.2 External Environment

The global economic environment continues to change at a rapid pace, and those economies best able to adapt to these changes will be the big winners in the new millennium. First, with the conclusion of the Uruguay Round, and the establishment of the World Trade Organization (WTO), the Korean economy will face a more rapid opening of its domestic markets to both trade and investment flows. Korea is no longer considered as a developing economy by the WTO, and hence cannot expect to be able to have access to global markets without at the same time opening its own markets to foreign competition.

Second, unlike in the earlier period of rapid growth, the Korean economy is now facing a proliferation of regionalism in both Europe and the Americas, making the task of further expanding exports to these key markets increasingly difficult. Hence, maintaining an export growth momentum in these markets appears to be increasingly unlikely. In recent years a new regionalism has begun to emerge in East Asia that represents a clear break from the region's strong history of multilateralism. The countries of East Asia have been giving more attention to ways of expanding intra-regional trade that include the establishment of regional trade agreements (RTAs) such as ASEAN+3; plans to establish a free trade area involving the economies of ASEAN and China; and moves towards bilateral trade agreements (BTAs).

Third, within East Asia the next wave of rapidly developing economies is coming through – in particular China, the economies of Indo-China and, more specifically, Vietnam. This will further intensify competition in both regional and global markets. China's recent accession to the WTO will represent a major threat to Korea and other East Asian economies that compete in labour-intensive and low value-added products (Lee and Koo 2000).

**Table 13.4**
**New Development Model Paradigm**

| | |
|---|---|
| Initial conditions | Maturing economies<br>Sound work ethic<br>High spirit of education, and good primary and intermediary education system<br>New relationship with North Korea |
| External environment | WTO, trade and investment liberalization (Globalization)<br>Proliferation of global regionalism<br>Intensification of domestic and foreign market competition (including China, and Indo-China)<br>Fair trade approach by the US<br>No more flying geese pattern, due to Japan's loss of economic momentum<br>Rapid growth of international financial markets<br>Worldwide knowledge revolution |
| Policy factors | Primarily market based mechanisms of competitive discipline<br>Improved Governance (corporate, banking and public sectors)<br>Encouragement of small and medium enterprises<br>Trade and domestic economy orientation (balanced growth)<br>Stable macroeconomic management<br>Emphasis on high quality education<br>Stronger cooperation within East Asia in both trade and finance<br>Economic integration with North Korea |
| 'Targeted' interim outcome | High savings<br>High investment with prudence<br>Increasing human capital<br>Rapid growth of trade<br>Rapid catching-up and pioneering technology in some areas |
| 'Targeted final outcome | Rapid growth of the 'new' economy and in the service sector<br>Rapid and sustained economic growth<br>Reduced poverty<br>Improving social indicators |

Fourth, the US market, the single biggest market for Korean products, that previously emphasized a free trade approach, has changed its attitude toward a fair trade approach. Export-oriented industrial development has increasingly been constrained by protectionist policies in the US and other industrial countries.

Fifth, the foundation of the flying geese process, whereby countries at different levels of industrialization and development move together on the basis of a progressive upgrading of their industries, has recently been shaken by the economic difficulties faced by Japan. Japan, which had invested nearly US$50 billion in developing East Asia from the mid-1980s onward, lost its bearings in the early 1990s. Japan's foreign direct investment, which totalled 35.3 trillion yen at the end of 1997, dropped to 31.2 trillion yen at the end of 1998 and to 25.5 trillion yen at the end of 1999. No new lead goose has come forward to replace Japan.

Sixth, there has been a phenomenal growth of international financial markets and a rapid opening of domestic financial markets in Korea during the period of the 1990s. The crisis of 1997–98 was triggered by a rapid withdrawal of short-term capital from Korea and other crisis-afflicted economies in East Asia. The rapid growth of short-term capital flows has the potential to result in greater financial market volatility, and indeed to wreak havoc if there is a rapid reversal of such flows.

Finally, the world is today experiencing a knowledge revolution. In other words the world is currently experiencing a major transition from an industrial society to a new economic paradigm, where information and knowledge are the principal drivers of competitiveness. The driving force behind this has been the rapid advance in information and communications technology (ICT). Rapid advances in ICT have brought fundamental changes to the economic transaction modes of business, government and lifestyles. Indeed, access to ICT-related tools and skills are becoming crucial components in economic development worldwide (see Chapter 8 of this book).

### 13.4.3 Policy Factors

Given the changed economic circumstances in the wake of the financial crisis, as well as developments in the external environment previously identified, a reappraisal of the conduct of certain aspects of policy becomes essential. First, the primarily market-based mechanisms of competitive discipline will remain and intensify. It is no longer possible to protect certain sectors of the economy behind trade and non-trade barriers. Consequently, the development of domestic enterprises capable of competing domestically and internationally will be essential (see Chapter 4 of this book).

Second, the Korean government needs to play a new role in the economy that focuses upon establishing the necessary institutional framework that supports competitive and open markets, and contributes towards capacity building. Key to this will be policies that focus upon good governance in both the private and public sectors. In the private sector, the development of stock markets and financial institutions, with the capacity to monitor the performance of private sector enterprises, will be essential to ensure a more efficient and productive usage of financial resources (see Chapter 3 of this book).

Third, more policy emphasis also needs to be devoted to the development of small and medium-sized enterprises (SMEs). In the wake of the crisis a reappraisal of the role of SMEs has taken place. Korea has traditionally emphasized the role and importance of large enterprises, the *chaebols*, and suffered severely during the period of the crisis, while Taiwan, dominated by SMEs, came through the crisis relatively unscathed (see for example Harvie and B.C. Lee 2002). The development of the SME sector has the potential to expand growth, employment, exports, reduce poverty, enhance regional development, empower groups such as women, and contribute to a more crisis-resilient economy (Harvie and B.C. Lee 2002). The issue of whether industry policy should give more focus to the development of large or small enterprises remains a contentious issue in the literature, see for example Hallberg (2000); however the contribution of SMEs to the future development of the region remains of paramount importance and particularly so for the developing economies (Gregory et al. 2002).

Fourth, the Korean government should continue to pursue an outward-looking development strategy as the relationship between openness and growth appears to be fairly robust. But in the new framework trade should be promoted through not only exports but also imports. This is not just because of the increasing pressure from the industrialized and industrializing countries elsewhere in the world, but also because, by embodying technologies of the country of origin and other countries contributing to the product, imports are an effective vehicle for assimilating new technology (Bayoumi et tal. 1996). In addition, higher priority should be given to greater integration between the domestic and external sectors of the economy, as well as giving more emphasis to the development of sectors that primarily serve the domestic market. The former, in particular, implies the need to increasingly incorporate domestic enterprises in the supply chain of multinational enterprises located domestically, and also those located overseas. Hence, an important change of emphasis would be to move towards a more balanced approach to growth of the economy, in which domestic and foreign market oriented enterprises are given a more equal treatment.

Fifth, stable macroeconomic management should continue to be maintained. In the wake of the crisis of 1997–98, Korea built up a considerable amount of government debt to finance the restructuring of its financial institutions and corporations. Therefore special efforts to maintain stable macroeconomic policies are required, which will entail the maintenance of low budget deficits, or surpluses, and the reduction of public debt to a sustainable level; monetary policy aimed at price stability; ensuring that the real exchange rate remains competitive; ensuring a reduction of foreign debt, particularly short-term debt; and encourage the rapid repayment of any international loans arising from assistance given during the period of the financial and economic crisis of 1997–98. This, in collaboration with reform of the financial and corporate sectors, will be essential for the establishment of a platform for the long-term sustainable recovery of Korea, and the regional economies more generally.

Sixth, Korea will need to improve its current education system so as to provide the economy with a high-skilled and creative labour force, which is needed as it advances towards the stage of being a developed economy. In addition, as noted previously, the world is moving towards a stage where knowledge and information are key to economic growth. But the current education system has not adequately provided the economy with the kind of labour force that is increasingly being required. Therefore, developing an appropriate education system to produce a creative, skilled and adaptable workforce will be fundamental for Korea to embrace the new economy for the twenty-first century. The Korean education system needs to embrace the new economy, and to encourage its businesses, individuals and government to create, acquire, transmit and use knowledge and information effectively for greater economic and social development (Harvie and Lee 2003a).

Seventh, stronger cooperation with other East Asian economies in both trade and finance is desperately needed. As discussed in Lloyd and Lee (2001) and Harvie and H.H. Lee (2002), there has been an increasing trend towards regionalism in East Asia. The driving forces behind this have been, the slowing liberalization process under the WTO, proliferation of regionalism elsewhere in the world, and the 1997–98 financial crisis which demonstrated the risk of contagion and investors' perception of the region as a 'single market'. If the world is a free market as a whole at the multilateral level, or keeps moving towards it, the policies of free trade on the part of Korea and other East Asian countries may be superior to one that relies on regionalism. However, more efforts to build regional cooperative frameworks within East Asia can be justified with the current worldwide trend towards regionalism. This suggests that the East Asian countries should pursue an outward-looking development strategy that relies on both worldwide globalization and Asian-wide 'regionalization' by forming FTAs among themselves (see Chapter 10 of this book).

Finally, as Harvie and Lee (2003a) and Chapter 11 note, the events of the year 2000, including the historic inter-Korean summit, herald a fundamental strategic reorientation on the part of North Korea, and it is now taking preparatory steps to introduce greater openness and carry out major reform to revive its moribund economy. South Korea will need to continue its efforts of engaging North Korea, especially in the form of economic exchanges and cooperation, and this will contribute to a reduction of tensions and ultimately lead to the attainment of reconciliation and unification. Of course, economic cooperation alone cannot ensure reconciliation and peace as long as military conflicts remain. But economic cooperation will increase mutual trust and lead to an institutionalized peaceful coexistence. In particular, a gradual economic integration between the two Koreas will pave the way to the ultimate peaceful reunification of the peninsula. One can imagine a series of progressively deeper steps of cooperation and integration that the two Koreas could undertake. Specifically, it is highly plausible that inter-Korean economic integration would take the simplest form such as a free trade area in the initial stage, and later move towards more complicated forms such as a customs union and so forth.[26] In the process the two Koreas will gain many different kinds of benefits, including enhancing the efficiency of resource allocation in both economies (see Harvie and Lee, 2003a).

### 13.4.4 'Targeted' Interim and Final Outcomes

It is essential that the fundamentals for achieving high and sustainable growth are put in place. Targeted interim outcomes must aim at the maintenance of high rates of domestic saving to reduce the reliance on foreign funds, foreign borrowing in particular, as much as possible. A second objective, and a key lesson from the crisis, is the need for such funds to be put to productive usage with prudence. Excessive investment in non-productive assets, such as real estate and property development, resulted in excessive borrowing for this purpose from both domestic and external sources. Third, attaining a high level of human capital to meet the demands of the new economy for a technologically literate and skilled workforce. Fourth, maintaining export growth while ensuring the development of domestic market opportunities. The expansion of export growth is likely to increasingly focus upon intra-regional trade in East Asia. Finally, in order to maintain its international competitiveness, it will be essential for Korea to continue the process of technological catch-up in key sectors, as well as to engage in pioneering technology development of its own.

If these key building blocks can be put in place, then Korea, in this new global environment of intensive competition, improved information and communications technology, and openness of markets, can flourish. It can be at the forefront of the rapid growth of the new economy as well as of the service sector, return to relatively high and sustainable growth rates, achieve further major progress in alleviating poverty, despite the setbacks arising from the recent crisis, and once again be at the forefront of developing economies in terms of improving social indicators.

## 13.5 CONCLUDING REMARKS

The World Bank (1993) study provided support for the high productivity growth thesis relating to the East Asian economies. High estimates were obtained for productivity growth, and higher contributions of TFP to output growth, in Korea, Taiwan, Thailand, Hong Kong and Japan. The study concluded that this resulted from their superior success in allocating capital to high-yielding investments, to their catching-up technologically to the industrialized economies, and their pursuit of export-oriented growth strategies. The World Bank claimed that, compared with other economies, `the East Asian economies stand out sharply with high absolute levels of total factor productivity' (World Bank, 1993, p. 55). The study by Osaka (1997) also found significant growth in productivity in South Korea over the period 1989–93.

The contrasting view, epitomised by the 'Krugman thesis', questions the existence of the so-called 'East Asian miracle' (Krugman 1994). Krugman argued that capital accumulation rather than productivity growth was responsible for the rapid economic growth experienced by the East Asian developing economies. Krugman argued that economies that relied on the accumulation of factors of production as mechanisms for growth would eventually experience a slowdown in their growth performance, as diminishing returns to factors of production take their effect. Empirical support for the view that the growth of the East Asian developing economies can largely be explained by the accumulation of factors of production is provided in the works of Young (1992, 1994b, 1995), Kim and Lau (1994) and Collins and Bosworth (1996). They all estimated productivity growth to be low in most East Asian developing economies except for Young's estimate for Hong Kong in the 1994 study and Taiwan in the 1995 study. Kim and Lau recorded zero growth for Korea, Taiwan, Hong Kong and Singapore.

The current state of the debate over the sources of growth for the East Asian developing economies therefore appears to have reached a stalemate (Cook and Uchida 2002). One thing for sure is that during the 1990s the contribution of factor inputs to growth has been slowing. A further deceleration in the contribution by factor inputs to growth is likely during the first decade of the new millennium as labour inputs are expected to slow sharply for demographic reasons (OECD 2001). In addition, capital accumulation may make a smaller contribution than before as firms scale back investment arising from greater awareness of the risks of borrowing. On the other hand, the contribution of productivity growth will tend to fall as the technology gap between Korea and the leading industrial nations narrows. Therefore, whether Korea will be able to revive and sustain its economic miracle in the long term will depend on how it tackles the problem of these diminishing sources of economic growth.

Harvie and Lee (2003a) identified three areas that need to be dealt with successfully, in order to tackle the problems and overarching challenges facing Korea's future development. First of all, successful restructuring is important to increase the efficiency of the overall economy, including that of factor markets for labour and land, and particularly that of the 'old' economy. Second, successfully implementing ICT and Internet innovation, and transforming the Korean economy into the new economy, will be crucial because ICT and Internet innovation assists in the accumulation of 'knowledge', the most important production input, enabling an increase in the productivity of the overall economy. Third, expanding Korea's new economic territory, by successfully pursuing economic integration with North Korea, is another key to the revival of the Korean economic miracle. The gradual development of economic integration between the two Koreas will enable North Korea to become a new market for South Korean exports, a new investment opportunity for South Korean firms, and a new source of labour.

This chapter has reviewed Korea's old economic development paradigm. The original development model has now run its course, but in the process has produced remarkable social and economic outcomes. The Korean economy is now matured and faces a different global trade and financial environment. This chapter has developed a new growth and development paradigm. The new development paradigm calls for: (1) intensifying the market-based mechanisms of competitive discipline; (2) a new role for government in the economy that focuses upon establishing the necessary institutional framework that supports competitive and open markets; (3) more emphasis on the development of SMEs; (4) continuing an outward-looking development strategy which promotes not only exports but also imports; (5) continuing stable macroeconomic management; (6) developing an appropriate education system to produce a creative, skilled and adaptable workforce that will enable Korea to embrace the new economy; (7) stronger cooperation with other East Asian economies in both trade and finance; and (8) a gradual economic integration between the two Koreas.

If these key policy measures are tackled adequately, and positive preconditions are met, then Korea, in this new global environment, can flourish again and will move toward further relatively high and sustainable growth in the twenty-first century.

## NOTES

1 Korea was not alone. Japan, Hong Kong, Singapore, Taiwan, Indonesia, Malaysia and Thailand were also high-performing Asian economies (HPAEs). This remarkable achievement of the East Asian economies was once described by the World Bank (1993) as an 'East Asian economic miracle'.

2 This section draws upon, and develops further, Harvie and H.H. Lee

(2002).

3 See Harvie and Lee (2003a, 2003b) for a more detailed discussion of the economic performance of the Korean economy up until the late 1980s.

4 Korea's period of rapid economic growth was profoundly shaped by a number of social and historical developments. See Song (1990), Amsden (1989), and Harvie and Lee (2003b) for a more detailed discussion.

5 The city changed hands four times during the period of the war.

6 Resulting in the so-called hollowing out of Japan's manufacturing industries.

7 For instance, Lee (1996) finds that industrial policies in Korea were not directed towards the higher-growth industries.

8 In a military coup on 16 May 1961, General Park Chung Hee ascended to power.

9 This draws on Harvie and Lee (2003b).

10 Interview with Kim In-Ho, the ex-chief economic advisor for the President, *Chosun Ilbo*, 23 February 1998. (Translated by the author.)

11 Sachs, (1997).

12 Stiglitz, (1998b).

13 *Korea Economic Newspaper*, 10 July 1997. (Translated by the author.)

14 *Chosun Ilbo*, 6 June 1998. (Translated by the author.)

15 IMF, (1999).

16 Authors who have stressed the role of moral hazard in the Asian crisis are, among others, Krugman (1998a) and Corsetti et al., (1998).

17 Krugman, (1998b).

18 Frankel, (1998).

19 Wolf, (1998).

20 Stiglitz, (1998a).

21 Yellen, (1998).

22 Marvin, (1998).

23 This paper first appeared as a University of Melbourne Department of Economics Research Paper, 696, June 1999. Harvie and Lee (2003a) also discuss the stroke hypothesis.

24 The same approach could be applied to the crisis elsewhere in East Asia.

25 This section draws upon, and develops further, the ideas presented in Harvie and H.H. Lee (2002).

26 Noland (2000) shares a similar view with this.

## REFERENCES

Amsden, A.H. (1989), *Asia's Next Giant: South Korea and Late Industrialization*, Oxford: Oxford University Press.

Bayoumi, T., D.T. Coe and E. Helpman (1996), 'R&D Spillovers and Global Growth, *National Bureau of Economic Research*, No. 5628.

Carroll, C., D. Weil and L.H. Summers (1993), 'Savings and Growth: A Reinterpretation', Paper presented at the Carnegie-Rochester Public Policy Conference, Bradley Policy Research Centre, 23–24 April.

Cook, P. and Y. Uchida (2002), 'Productivity Growth in East Asia: A Reappraisal', *Applied Economics*, **34**, 1195-1208.

Collins, S. and B. Bosworth (1996), 'Economic Growth in East Asia: Accumulation versus Assimilation', *Brookings Papers on Economic Activity*, **2**, 135-203.

Corsetti, G., P. Pesenti and N. Roubini (1998), 'What Caused the Asian Currency and Financial Crisis?, Part 1: A Macroeconomic Overview', mimeo, September.

Crafts, N. (1998), 'East Asian Growth Before and After the Crisis', *IMF Working Paper*, WP/98/37.

Deininger, K. and S. Squire (1996), 'A New Data Set Measuring Income Inequality', *World Bank Economic Review*, **10**(3), 565–91.

Frankel, J.A. (1998), 'The Asian Model, the Miracle, the Crisis and the Fund', dlivered at the US International Trade Commission, 16 April.

Gerschenkron, A. (1962), *Economic Backwardness in Historical Perspective*, Cambridge: Belknap Press.

Gregory, G., Harvie, C. and H.-H. Lee (2002), 'Korean SMEs in the 21th entury: Strategies, Constraints and Performance in a Global Economy', *Economic Papers*, **21**(3), 64–79.

Hallberg, K. (2000), 'A Market Oriented Strategy for Small and Medium Enterprises', *IFC Discussion Paper*, 40, Washington, DC.

Harvie, C. and B.C. Lee (2002), *The Role of SMEs in National Economies in East Asia*, Cheltenham: Edward Elgar Publishing.

Harvie, C. and H.-H. Lee (2002), 'New Regionalism in East Asia: How Does it Relate to the East Asian Economic Development Model?', *ASEAN Economic Bulletin*, **19**(2), 123–40.

Harvie, C. and H.-H. Lee (2003a), *Korea's Economic Miracle: Fading or Reviving?*, Basingstoke: Palgrave Macmillan .

Harvie, C. and H.-H. Lee (2003b), 'Export Led Industrialization and Growth: Korea's Economic Miracle 1962–89', *Australian Economic History Review*, **43**(3), 256–86.

IMF (1999), 'The IMF's Response to the Asian Crisis', 17 January, http://www.imf.org/External/np/exr/facts/asia.HTM.

Kim, J. and L. Lau (1994), 'The Sources of Growth of the East Asian Newly Industrialized Countries', *Journal of the Japanese and International*

*Economies*, **8**, 235-71.

Krugman, P. (1994),'Myth of Asia's Miracle', *Foreign Affairs*, **73**, 62-64.

Krugman, P. (1998a), 'What Happened to Asia', mimeo, http://web.mit.edu/krugman/www/disinter.html.

Krugman, P. (1998b), 'Will Asia Bounce Back?', speech for Credit Suisse First Boston, Hong Kong, March.

Lee, H.-H. (2003), 'A Stroke Hypothesis of Korea's 1997 Financial Crisis', in M.J. Tcha and C.S. Suh (eds), *The Economic Crisis and the Korean Economy at the Crossroads*, London: Routledge.

Lee, H.-H. and C.M. Koo (2000), 'China, the World Trade Organization and Regional Economic Cooperation', in Tran Van Hoa (ed.), *China's Trade and Investment and Economics Globalization*, Cheltenham: Edward Elgar Publishing.

Lee, J.W. (1996), 'Government Interventions and Productivity Growth', *Journal of Economic Growth*, **1**(3), 391–414.

Lloyd, P.J. and H.-H. Lee (2001), 'Subregionalism in East Asia and Its Relation with APEC', *Journal of the Korean Economy*, **2**(2), 211–27.

Marvin, S. (1998), 'Death Throes', mimeo, 2 June.

Modigliani, F. (1970), 'The Life Cycle Hypothesis of Savings and Intercountry Differences in the Savings Ratio', in W.A. Eltis, M.Fg. Scott and J.N. Wolfe (eds), *Induction Growth and Trade: Essays in Honour of Sir Roy Harrod*, Oxford: Clarendon Press.

Modigliani F. and A. Ando (1963), 'The Life Cycle Hypothesis of Savings: Aggregate Implications and Tests', *American Economic Review*, **53**(1), 55-84.

Noland, M. (2000), *Avoiding the Apocalypse: the Future of the Two Koreas*, Washington DC: Institute for International Economics.

OECD (2001), *Economic Surveys – Korea*, Paris: OECD.

Osaka, H. (1997), 'Productivity Growth Analysis for Selected Asian Countries', *Asia-Pacific Development Journal*, **4**, 93-110.

Park, C. and M. Kim (1998), *Current Poverty Issues and Counter Policies in Korea*, Seoul: Korea Institute for Health and Social Affairs.

Park, D. and C. Rhee (1998), 'Currency Crisis in Korea: Could It Have Been Avoided?', mimeo, April.

Radelet, S. and J. Sachs (1998), 'The East Asian Financial Crisis: Diagnosis, Remedies, Prospects', *Brookings Papers on Economic Activity*, **1**, 1–74.

Rodrik, D. (1994), 'King Kong Meets Godzilla: The World Bank and the East Asian Miracle', in A. Fishlow, C. Gwin, S. Haggard, D. Rodrik, and R. Wade (eds), *Miracle or Design? Lessons from the Past Experience*, Washington DC: Overseas Development Council.

Rodrik, D. (1999), 'East Asian Mysteries: Past and Present', NBER Reporter Online, Spring, http://www.nber.org/reporter/archive.html.

Sachs, J.D. (1997), 'The Wrong Medicine for Asia', *New York Times*, 3

November.

Sato, R. and J.A. Rizzo (1986), 'The Other Side of the Trade Imbalance: What will Japan Do?', *NBER Working paper*, No. 2111, Cambridge: NBER.

Song, B.N. (1990), *The Rise of the Korean Economy*, Hong Kong: Oxford University Press.

Stiglitz, J. (1998a), 'Bad Private-Sector Decisions', *Wall Street Journal*, 4 February.

Stiglitz, J. (1998b), 'Boats, Planes and Capital Flows', *Financial Times*, 25 March.

Tae, W.S. (1972), *Development of the Korean Economy: Past, Present and Future*, Seoul, Korea: Samwha Publishing Co.

Wolf, C., Jr. (1998), 'Too Much Government Control', *Wall Street Journal*, 4 February.

World Bank (1993), *The East Asian Miracle: Economic Growth and Public Policy*, New York: Oxford University Press.

Yellen, J. (1998), 'Lessons from the Asian Crisis', remarks to the Council of Foreign Relations, 15 April.

Young, A. (1992), 'A Tale of Two Cities: Factor Accumulation and Technical Change in Hong Kong and Singapore', in O. Blanchard and S. Fisher (eds), *NBER Macroeconomics Annual*, Cambridge: MIT Press.

Young, A. (1994a), 'Accumulation, Exports and Growth in the High Performing Asian Economies: A Comment', *Carnegie-Rochester Conferences Series on Public Policy*, **40**, 237-50.

Young, A. (1994b), 'Lessons from the East Asian NICs: A Contrarian View', *European Economic Review*, **38**, 964-73.

Young, A. (1995), 'The Tyranny of Numbers: Confronting the Statistical Realities of the East Asian Growh Experience', *Quarterly Journal of Economics*, **110**, 641-80.

# Index


Agency, 26
theories, 65
Agriculture, 100, 106, 135, 198, 201, 212, 225, 230, 232, 236, 241, 266
Agricultural, 291
production, 231, 241-2
product(s), 152, 195, 197-9, 201, 212, 213-15, 224, 226-7, 235
sector, 193, 200-201, 212, 226, 241-2
APEC, 214-16, 223-4, 234
ASEAN, 215, 219, 223, 286, 308
ASEAN+3, 4, 215-16, 308
Asian economic development model, 264, 283, 303
Asian financial crisis, 9, 38, 120, 197, 221-2, 305
Bad
debts, 7
loans, 5, 32-3, 144
Banking
industry, 5, 33
sector, 2, 3, 15, 17, 38, 43
system, 39, 254
Bankruptcy(ies), 6, 28, 40, 43-6, 48, 53, 56, 64, 71, 279
rate, 52
Bank of Korea, 8, 29, 84, 144, 147-8, 150-60, 174, 239, 301
Bank(s), 6, 8, 12, 15-16, 25, 27-31, 33, 39-43, 51-3, 58-9, 71-2, 83, 129, 145, 149, 154, 156, 196-7, 203, 210, 218, 255, 300, 304
loans, 34, 194
Basel Accord ratio, 33
Big
deals, 6, 18, 50-51, 58, 71
five, 6, 48, 53, 71
four, 6, 54, 71
Bilateral trade agreements (BTAs), 308
Broadband internet, 173-4
Capacity-building, 299, 310
Capital, 5, 12-14, 18, 30, 143-4, 150, 155, 158,160,185,188,194, 219, 234, 236, 248-50, 252-5, 265, 267, 269-70, 272-3, 277-8, 283, 292-3, 296, 302, 313
accumulation, 18, 254, 266, 307, 313
adequacy, 33
adequacy ratio, 17
flight, 203
flows, 288, 292
formation, 265-6
inflow(s), 19, 218, 267
intensive, 42
investments, 8, 165
market(s), 5, 7, 19, 25-6, 44, 67, 196-7, 217, 289
outflows, 197
structure, 31, 48, 72-3
system, 46
Capitalization, 19, 155
Chaebol(s), 6, 12, 15, 18, 25-6, 38-46, 48, 50, 53-8, 60-61, 63-5, 71-3, 127, 188, 297, 299, 304, 310
Chile, 9, 192, 214-15, 219, 221, 223-7, 234
China, 4, 165, 167, 176, 209, 214-15, 219, 238, 242, 245-6, 250-53, 255, 308
Chun Doo-Hwan, 127
Competition, 65, 68-9, 71-2, 98-9, 129, 134, 185-6, 189, 210, 213, 223, 273, 276, 281, 291, 307-8, 312
Competitiveness, 5, 16, 26-7, 41, 47, 50, 66, 165, 179, 187, 192, 200,

214, 223-4, 228, 230, 234, 254, 273, 275, 292-3, 304-6, 312
Construction, 199, 204, 241
sector, 202, 241
Contagion, 38, 120, 301, 305
Control pyramid system, 46
Corporate, 143
debt, 38
debt restructuring, 39, 73
governance, 5-6, 17, 38-9, 46-7, 53-4, 58-61, 65, 71-2, 197, 278
governance system, 25
reforms, 53
restructuring, 6, 8, 27, 31, 38-9, 48,-9, 52, 57, 65-6, 69, 72-3
Restructuring Vehicles (CRVs), 52
sector(s), 3-4, 7-8, 12, 16-8, 20, 25-6, 32, 38-42, 44, 46-8, 58-9, 65-6, 71, 148, 192, 197, 263, 311
sector reform(s), 47, 58, 120
sector restructuring, 6, 17, 34, 38, 47
Corporate Restructuring Accord, 51
Corporate Restructuring Promotion Act, 31-2
Crony-capitalism, 41
Cross-debt guarantees, 42-3, 50, 56, 61
Daewoo Group, 31, 48, 50, 53, 56-7, 73, 145
Debt(s), 15, 17, 31, 38, 40, 46, 50-52, 54, 56, 58, 64-5, 71-3, 191, 279, 310-11
equity-ratio(s), 17, 31, 40, 46, 50, 53-4, 56-8, 72-3, 297
equity swaps, 52, 71
guarantee(s), 43-5, 47, 64
rating, 6
ratio(s), 44, 45
resolution, 47
restructuring, 4, 16
workouts, 19
Decentralization, 269, 270, 272, 280, 282
Deregulation, 7-8, 29, 120, 133-4, 136, 138, 140, 154, 166, 187, 192-3, 196, 213, 273, 277, 279
Digital divide, 178
DRAM(s), 169-71, 176, 188
East Asian development model, 299, 300, 306
E-commerce, 174, 176, 214
Economic
crisis, 3, 8, 10, 38-9, 86, 165-6, 192-3, 198, 200, 202-4, 206, 209-10, 213-14, 239, 242, 263, 283, 287, 311
reform, 3, 275-6
Economies of scale, 39, 235, 266-7
Efficiency, 32, 89, 98, 100, 121, 123-4, 126-8, 132, 136, 138, 192, 197, 222, 236, 240, 248-9, 256, 263, 269-70, 276, 278-9, 280-81, 312, 314
Employment Insurance System (EIS), 96-8, 102-4, 108-9, 112-13, 116
Entrepreneurship, 8-9, 166, 187
European Union (EU), 95, 206, 210, 215, 223, 255
Exchange rate(s), 16, 19
policies, 7
Export(s), 3, 9-10, 16, 19, 25, 66, 146, 165-71, 176, 188-9, 192, 194-5, 198, 201, 205-7, 209, 212, 214, 218, 221, 223-7, 229, 231-2, 234, 240, 242, 253-6, 267, 272, 275, 277, 286-8, 291-6, 299, 304, 306-7, 309-10
growth, 16, 312
sector, 4
subsidies, 198
External debt(s), 196, 304
Fair Trade Commission, 42, 58, 61, 63
Federation of Korean Trade Unions (FKTU), 80-82, 85, 114
Financial, 3, 143, 311
crisis, 5-7, 9-11, 16, 19-20, 25-7, 38-9, 46, 49, 56, 66, 68, 78, 105, 107, 110, 120-21, 124-9, 133, 137-8, 143, 177, 188, 193, 197, 203, 218, 221, 223, 234, 263, 274-6, 278, 287-8, 299-303, 305-6, 309, 311
liberalization, 19, 26, 154
market(s), 5, 8, 309
restructuring, 5, 8, 16, 26-8, 32, 35

sector(s), 3-5, 8, 12, 16, 19-20, 25-6, 32, 36, 38, 40-43, 46-7, 58, 71, 133, 148, 192, 196-7, 202, 222, 263, 273, 278, 292
sector reforms, 120
sector restructuring, 5, 17, 32
sector supervision, 302
supervision, 278
system, 5, 12, 19, 21, 26-7, 32, 40, 46, 303
Financial Supervisory Agency, 139
Financial Supervisory Commission, 17, 30, 59, 73, 122, 139
Financial Supervisory Service, 30, 122, 125, 139
Fixed exchange rate (s), 5, 284, 302
Floating exchange rate, 8, 246
Foreign,
aid, 293
capital, 38, 248, 250, 252-3, 256, 275, 278
debt(s), 38, 50, 72, 197, 287, 292, 294-6, 297, 311
direct investment (FDI), 6, 9, 66-70, 72, 88, 133, 140, 193, 195, 202-3, 209-11, 216, 219, 221, 235, 245-6, 252-3, 292, 309
exchange, 7, 219, 242
exchange reserves, 4, 14, 19, 38, 191, 196-7, 203
investment, 35, 60, 120, 129, 155, 191, 202-3, 210, 214, 224, 248, 250, 258
Free Trade Agreement (FTA), 9, 192-3, 214-16, 221, 223-5, 227-35, 311
Free trade area, 218, 308, 312
GATT, 9, 191, 193, 195, 198, 212, 214, 218, 221-2, 228, 235, 288, 291
General Agreement on Trade in Services (GATS), 199, 219, 235
Germany, 18, 82, 98, 114, 210
GDP, 13-14, 120, 174, 195, 201, 204-6, 212, 225, 229, 233-4, 239-40, 278, 286-7, 290, 295
growth, 13, 16, 20, 78, 174, 293
growth rate, 146, 240
per capita, 78, 165, 194, 204-5, 295-6, 298
Globalization, 19, 187, 280, 284, 292, 311
GNP, 245, 265
Governance, 277, 302, 310
corporate, 308
Heavy and chemical industries (HCIs), 25, 39, 41
drive, 40-41, 43
Heavy and Chemical Industry Promotion Plan (HCIP), 39
Hong Kong, 191, 197, 206, 209, 217, 286, 313-4
Human capital, 17, 257, 267, 269, 271, 277, 281-3, 288, 296, 308, 312
IMF, 10, 11, 13, 16-17, 19, 47, 61, 78, 133, 143, 153-4, 160, 191-2, 197-8, 201-4, 218-19, 263, 278, 284, 299, 301-2
programme, 4
Import(s), 10, 188, 195-6, 201, 205, 207, 219, 223, 225-8, 231-2, 240, 242, 257, 294, 297, 310
competing, 200
competition, 200
substitution, 194, 286, 293, 299
Indonesia, 16, 314
Industrial policies, 315
Industrialization, 3, 267, 272, 275, 279, 286, 288, 290-91, 296, 309
growth, 293
Infant industry, 194, 280
Inflation, 8, 11, 13, 16, 40, 147, 152, 166, 174-5, 187, 225, 293-4, 296-7
rate(s), 153, 159, 299
target, 152-3
targeting, 8, 151, 155, 157, 159
targeting regime, 8
targeting system, 7, 152, 158-9
Information and communications technology (ICT), 309, 312, 314
Information technology, 56, 112, 198, 200
Informatization, 166, 177-8, 180, 187-8
Infrastructure, 8-9, 132, 166, 178, 186-7, 217, 239, 245, 251, 254, 257,

267, 272-3, 290-91
projects, 202
Innovation(s), 9, 174, 176, 187-9, 314
Interest coverage ratio(s)(ICR), 56, 59, 71
Interest rate(s), 7-8
International Labour Organization (ILO), 79, 80-83, 85-7, 115
Internet, 126, 134, 137, 174-9, 183-4 187-8, 314
Investment(s), 8, 11, 18, 25-6, 44, 46, 52, 65-6, 68-9, 89, 99, 133, 143-4, 155, 166, 174-5, 177, 179, 181, 184-6, 192, 194, 196, 200, 203, 210, 213, 215, 217-18, 221, 234-5, 246, 250, 264, 267, 274, 278-9, 283, 287-9, 291, 292-7, 299, 304, 307-8, 312-14
liberalization, 308
IT Industry, 165-7, 174-6, 179, 183-4, 187-8
sector, 9, 184
Japan, 4, 18, 46, 72, 81, 95, 98, 100, 114, 176, 192-3, 195, 197, 201, 209-10, 213-15, 218, 221, 223, 225, 228-34, 236, 248, 254-6, 284, 288, 290-2, 297, 308-9, 313-14
Japanese, 272, 288
Joint venture, 68-9
KCTU, 80-2, 85, 87, 114
Kim Dae Jung, 7, 48, 88, 121, 125, 129, 133-4, 136-9, 307
Kim Jong Pil, 139
Kim Jong 11's, 251, 307
Kim Young-Sam, 121, 128, 133
Kim 11 Sung, 244
Korea Asset Management Corporation (KAMCO), 52
Korea(n) stock
exchange, 73, 155-6
market, 158
KOSDAQ, 53, 73, 156-7, 184
KOSPI, 46
Labour, 143
market, 3, 6-7, 98-100, 102, 104-5, 107-13, 116, 152, 216-17, 263
market reforms, 120, 192, 197
standards, 7
Liberalization, 6-8, 12, 38-9, 65-8, 154, 160, 166, 187, 191-2, 195-7, 200-201, 203, 209-10, 212-16, 218-19, 222-3, 228, 249, 272, 276-7, 279-80, 291, 311
London Approach, 50, 73
Malaysia, 191, 283, 286, 314
Management transparency, 32
Manufacturing, 204, 241, 253
industries, 229, 290
sector, 66, 192, 200, 201, 225, 236
market failure(s), 266-7, 274, 281-2, 294
Mergers and acquisitions (M&As), 6, 39, 42-3, 46, 53, 59, 67-70, 72, 85, 115, 209, 216
Ministry of Planning and Budget, 7
Moral hazard, 25-6, 38, 40-41, 43, 116, 278, 302-3, 315
Multinational enterprises, 310
Multilateralism, 307
NAFTA, 214, 223, 235
Non-performing, 30
assets, 6, 26, 28, 33, 149
loan(s) (NPLs), 32-3, 36, 38, 45-6, 52
New Zealand, 215, 234
Newly industrializing countries (NICs), 275, 286, 297, 299
OECD, 12, 67, 78-9, 81-4, 86-7, 89, 92, 94, 98-100, 102-4, 106, 108, 111-14, 136, 160, 165, 180, 189, 191, 195, 200, 202, 209, 218, 287, 298-9
Park Chung Hee, 127
Portfolio investment, 8, 13, 155, 159, 202
Poverty, 78, 107-8, 165, 272, 275-6, 288, 290, 296-7, 308, 310, 312
line, 112
Private sector, 274-5, 277, 279, 282, 293, 296, 303, 310
Privatization, 6-7, 35, 39, 68, 70, 127-32, 137-8, 140, 186, 280-82
Productive welfare, 7

Productivity, 7, 29, 88-9, 99-100, 113, 152, 165, 178, 187, 229-36, 243, 266-7, 278, 281, 289, 292, 294, 313
growth, 89, 92, 98, 313
Profitability, 5-6, 12, 18-19, 25, 29, 32-3, 46, 56, 58, 71, 169
Prudential
regulation(s), 19, 25, 27, 30, 36, 46
supervision, 46, 133, 154
Public sector(s), 3, 143, 263, 303, 310
reform(s), 7, 120, 132, 137, 138-9
Recapitalization, 26, 28-9, 33, 50
Reform(s), 210, 216, 218, 234, 242, 244, 250, 252, 279
Regional trade agreement (RTAs), 214, 222, 308
Regional
trading blocs, 218, 221-2, 228, 234
Regionalism, 192-3, 214-15, 221-3, 307, 311
Regulation(s), 12, 41-3, 135-6, 154, 201-2
Regulatory Reform Commission, 7
Restructuring(s), 3, 6-7, 16, 26, 39, 44, 47-8, 50, 53-4, 58-9, 68, 71, 86, 122-7, 129, 137, 143-4, 146-8, 153, 193, 202, 227, 263, 273, 276, 310, 314
efforts, 200
programme, 213
Roh Moo Hyun, 88, 129-30, 137-8, 140
Roh Tae Woo, 127-8
Russia, 246, 254-5
R&D, 179, 188-9, 279, 283
investments, 180
Saving(s), 11-12, 18, 278, 287-8, 290, 293-5, 297, 308
rate(s), 289, 294, 312
Service sector(s), 203-4, 212, 241, 308, 312
Short-term
capital, 4, 309
capital inflows, 15
debt(s), 16, 203, 218-19, 311
Singapore, 191-3, 197, 215, 217, 234, 283, 286, 314
Small and medium-sized enterprises (SMEs), 10, 41-3, 48, 52-3, 85-6,
96, 110, 114, 122, 178, 183-4, 308, 310, 314
Social overhead capital (SOC), 275-6, 278, 281-2, 296
Social safety net, 7, 79, 88, 91, 94, 99, 102, 107, 113, 307
Special economic zones, 253
Spillover effects, 267
Stabilization, 144, 153, 192, 204, 279
package, 198
programme, 197
State owned enterprises (SOEs), 120, 127-32, 133, 137, 138, 210
reform(s), 7, 127
Stock market(s), 310
Structural reform, 16, 192
Supervision, 19, 30, 36
Supply chain, 310
Taiwan, 191, 218, 250, 286, 292, 297, 310, 313-4
Technological progress, 282
Technologies, 66, 185, 253, 255, 292, 296, 310
Technology, 4, 18, 176, 179, 180, 187, 189, 194, 200, 224, 234, 251, 253-4, 257, 267, 273, 277, 288, 291, 293, 307-8, 312
Telecommunications, 213
sector, 202
Thailand, 16, 191, 193, 197, 215, 234, 301, 313-14
Tokyo, 212
Total factor productivity (TFP), 229, 235-6, 313
Trade
diversion, 222
liberalization, 214, 218, 229, 235, 257, 276, 288
Transparency, 5-6, 8, 12, 17, 47, 50, 53, 60-61, 73, 126, 132, 135-7, 152, 154, 156, 178, 179, 188, 192-3, 197
TRIPS, 203
Tripartite Agreement, 83-4, 88
Tripartite Commission, 80-84, 86, 88,

114
Unemployment, 3
rate, 13
Uruguay Round(s)(UR), 192, 195, 197, 199-200, 202, 209, 212-13, 222, 307
USA(United States, US), 18, 46, 72, 95, 135, 140, 166, 170, 176, 184, 192-3, 195, 199, 203, 209-10, 213-15, 246, 248, 255, 267, 278, 286, 288, 291, 293, 303, 308-9
USSR, 242, 245
Venture capital, 184-5, 189
Vietnam, 250, 252, 308
Washington Consensus, 278
Workout(s), 53
programme(s), 31, 48, 50, 52, 57-8, 72
World Bank, 276, 278, 300, 313
World Economic Forum (WEF), 127, 135, 141
World Trade Organization (WTO), 9, 186, 191-3, 197-202, 212-14, 216, 218, 221-3, 228, 235, 273, 276, 307-8, 311